ZomBie PaReNtS

and Other Hopes For a More Perfect World

Also By Jerry Scott and Jim Borgman

Zits: Sketchbook 1
Growth Spurt: Zits Sketchbook 2
Don't Roll Your Eyes at Me, Young Man!: Zits Sketchbook 3
Are We an "Us"?: Zits Sketchbook 4
Zits Unzipped: Zits Sketchbook 5
Busted!: Zits Sketchbook 6
Road Trip: Zits Sketchbook 7
Teenage Tales: Zits Sketchbook 8
Thrashed: Zits Sketchbook 9
Pimp My Lunch: Zits Sketchbook 10
Are We Out of the Driveway Yet?: Zits Sketchbook 11
Rude, Crude, and Tattooed: Zits Sketchbook 12
Jeremy and Mom
Pierced
Lust and Other Uses for Spare Hormones
Jeremy & Dad
You're Making That Face Again: Zits Sketchbook 13
Drive!: Zits Sketchbook 14

Treasuries

Humongous Zits
Big Honkin' Zits
Zits: Supersized
Random Zits
Crack of Noon
Alternative Zits
My Bad
Sunday Brunch

Gift Book

A Zits Guide to Living with Your Teenager

Zombie PaReNts

and Other Hopes For a More Perfect World

Zits
Sketchbook
15

by JERRY SCOTT and JIM BORGMAN™

Andrews McMeel
Publishing, LLC
Kansas City • Sydney • London

Andrews McMeel Publishing, LLC
an Andrews McMeel Universal company
1130 Walnut Street, Kansas City, Missouri 64106

www.andrewsmcmeel.com

12 13 14 15 16 RR2 10 9 8 7 6 5 4 3 2 1

ISBN: 978-1-4494-0973-9

Library of Congress Control Number: 2011932648

─── **ATTENTION: SCHOOLS AND BUSINESSES** ───

Andrews McMeel books are available at quantity discounts with bulk purchase for educational, business, or sales promotional use. For information, please e-mail the Andrews McMeel Publishing Special Sales Department:
specialsales@amuniversal.com

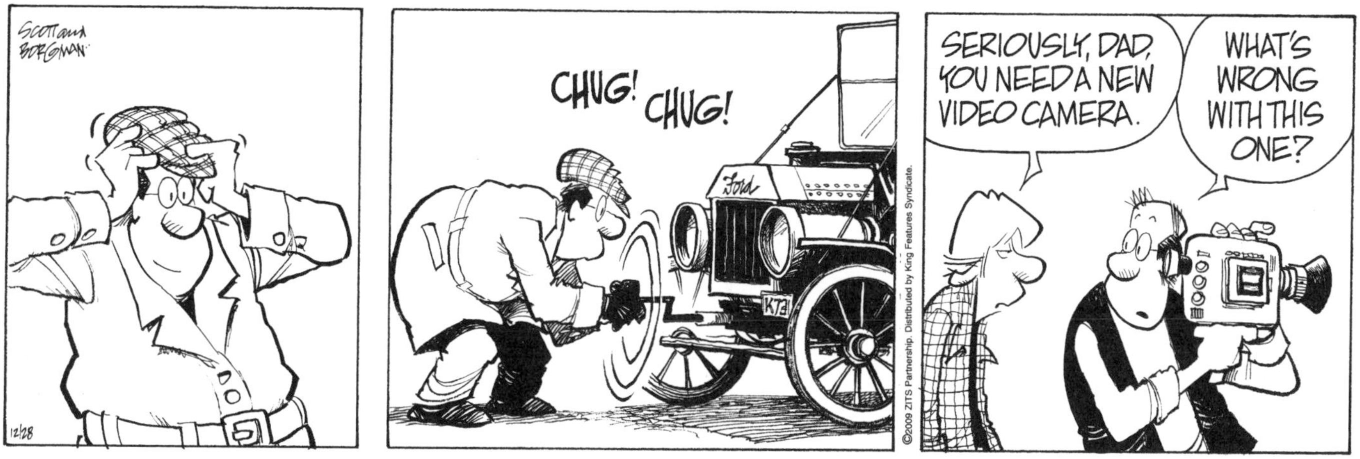
SCOTT and BORGMAN
12/28
CHUG! CHUG!
©2009 ZITS Partnership. Distributed by King Features Syndicate.
SERIOUSLY, DAD, YOU NEED A NEW VIDEO CAMERA.
WHAT'S WRONG WITH THIS ONE?

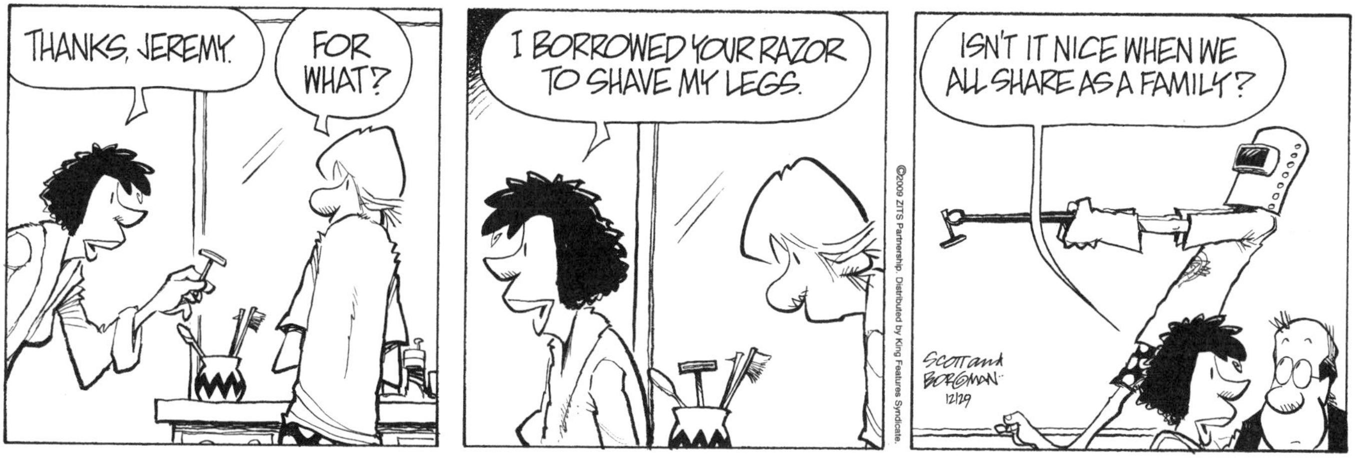
THANKS, JEREMY.
FOR WHAT?
I BORROWED YOUR RAZOR TO SHAVE MY LEGS.
©2009 ZITS Partnership. Distributed by King Features Syndicate.
ISN'T IT NICE WHEN WE ALL SHARE AS A FAMILY?
SCOTT and BORGMAN
12/29

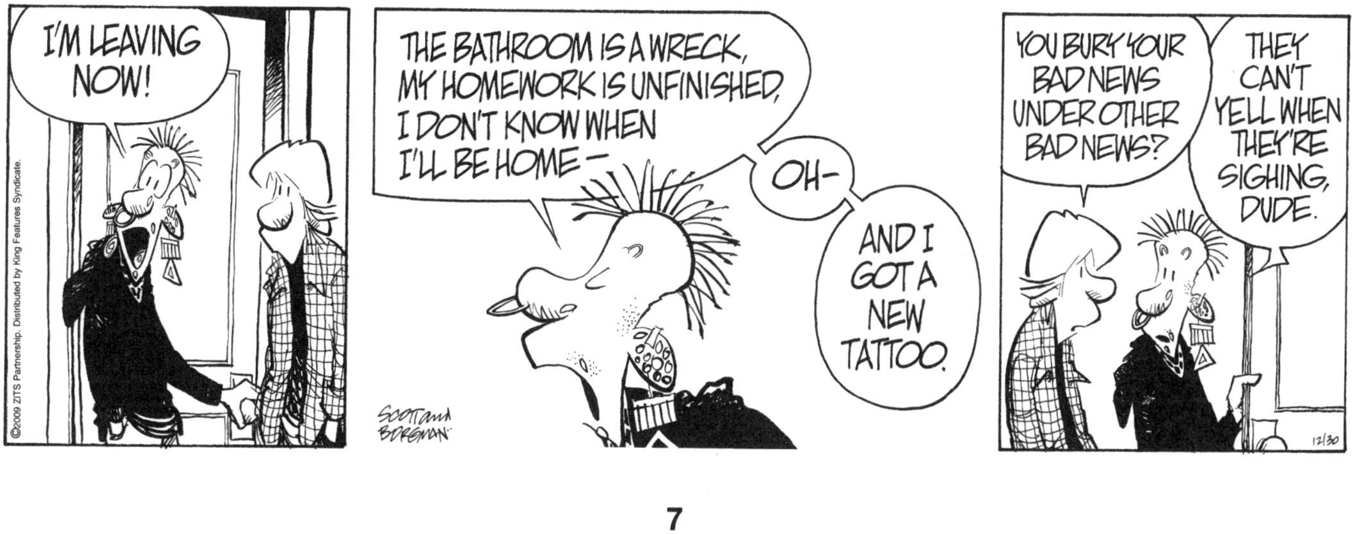
I'M LEAVING NOW!
©2009 ZITS Partnership. Distributed by King Features Syndicate.
THE BATHROOM IS A WRECK, MY HOMEWORK IS UNFINISHED, I DON'T KNOW WHEN I'LL BE HOME –
OH-
AND I GOT A NEW TATTOO.
SCOTT and BORGMAN
YOU BURY YOUR BAD NEWS UNDER OTHER BAD NEWS?
THEY CAN'T YELL WHEN THEY'RE SIGHING, DUDE.
12/30

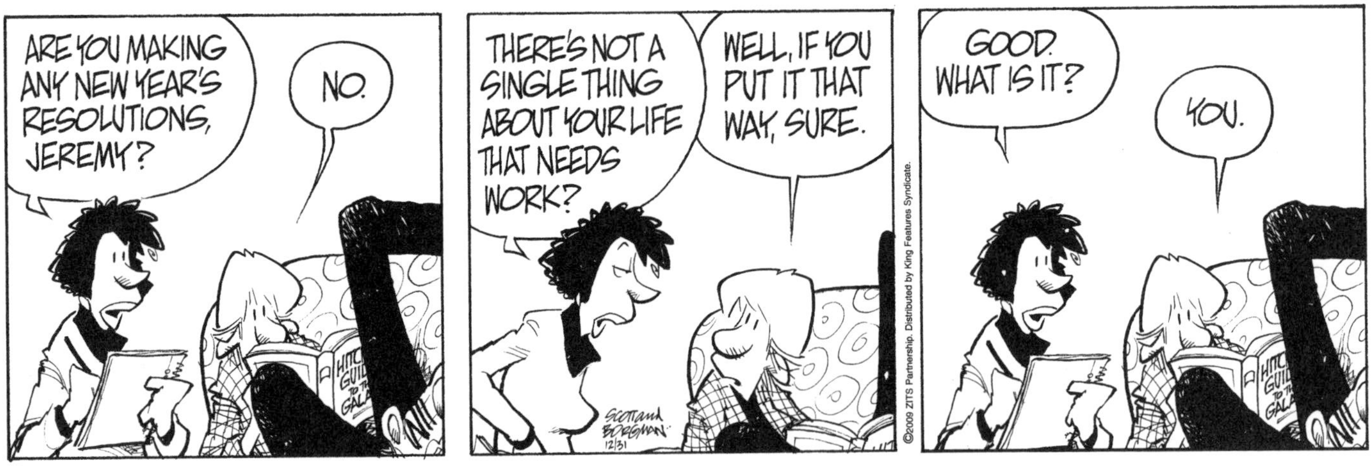
ARE YOU MAKING ANY NEW YEAR'S RESOLUTIONS, JEREMY?
NO.
THERE'S NOT A SINGLE THING ABOUT YOUR LIFE THAT NEEDS WORK?
WELL, IF YOU PUT IT THAT WAY, SURE.
GOOD. WHAT IS IT?
YOU.
SCOTT and BORGMAN 12/31
©2009 ZITS Partnership. Distributed by King Features Syndicate.

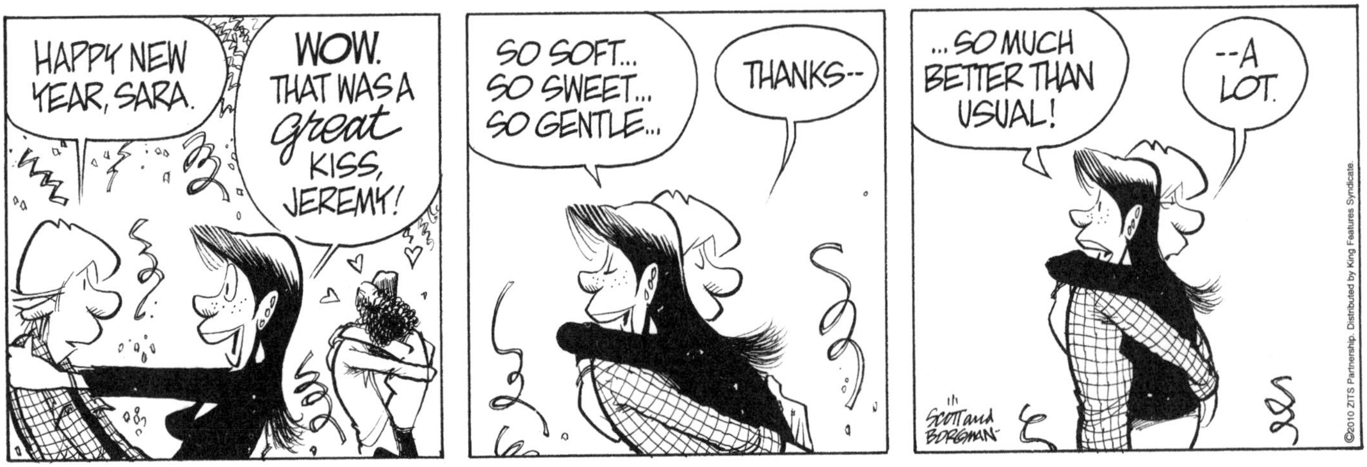
HAPPY NEW YEAR, SARA.
WOW. THAT WAS A *great* KISS, JEREMY!
SO SOFT... SO SWEET... SO GENTLE...
THANKS--
...SO MUCH BETTER THAN USUAL!
--A LOT.
1/1 SCOTT and BORGMAN
©2010 ZITS Partnership. Distributed by King Features Syndicate.

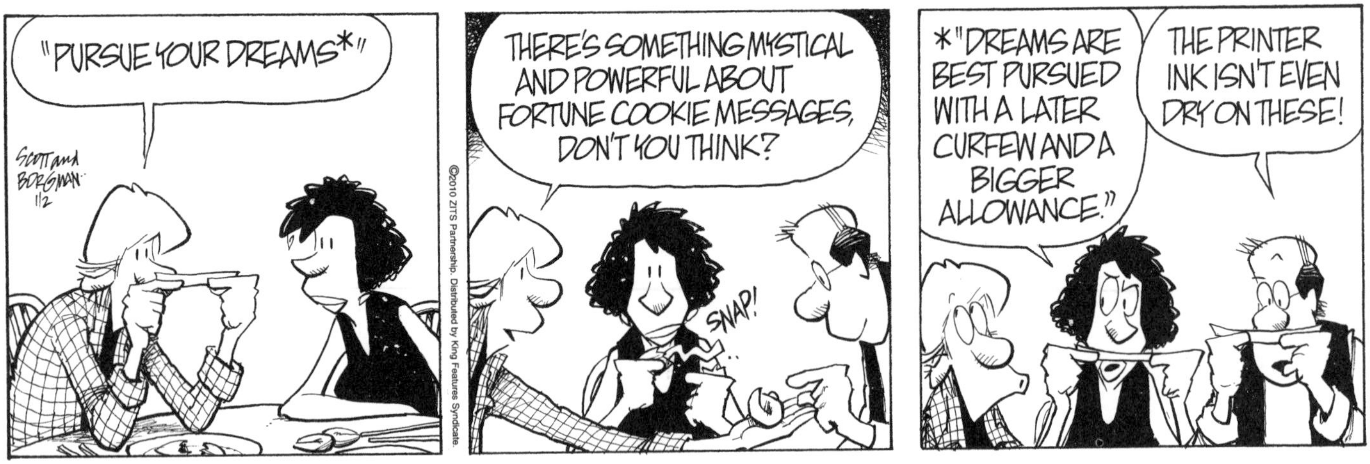
"PURSUE YOUR DREAMS*"
SCOTT and BORGMAN 1/2
©2010 ZITS Partnership. Distributed by King Features Syndicate.
THERE'S SOMETHING MYSTICAL AND POWERFUL ABOUT FORTUNE COOKIE MESSAGES, DON'T YOU THINK?
SNAP!
*"DREAMS ARE BEST PURSUED WITH A LATER CURFEW AND A BIGGER ALLOWANCE."
THE PRINTER INK ISN'T EVEN DRY ON THESE!

Zits
by
JERRY SCOTT and
JIM BORGMAN

JEREMY?
YEAH?
WHAT ARE YOU DOING IN THERE?
STUDYING.
IN YOUR VAN?
IT'S NICE IN HERE.
I HAVE MY MUSIC... COMFORTABLE SEAT... SOME SNACKS...
... A HEAT SOURCE...
FLATTERER.
SCOTT and BORGMAN
©2010 ZITS Partnership. Distributed by King Features Syndicate.

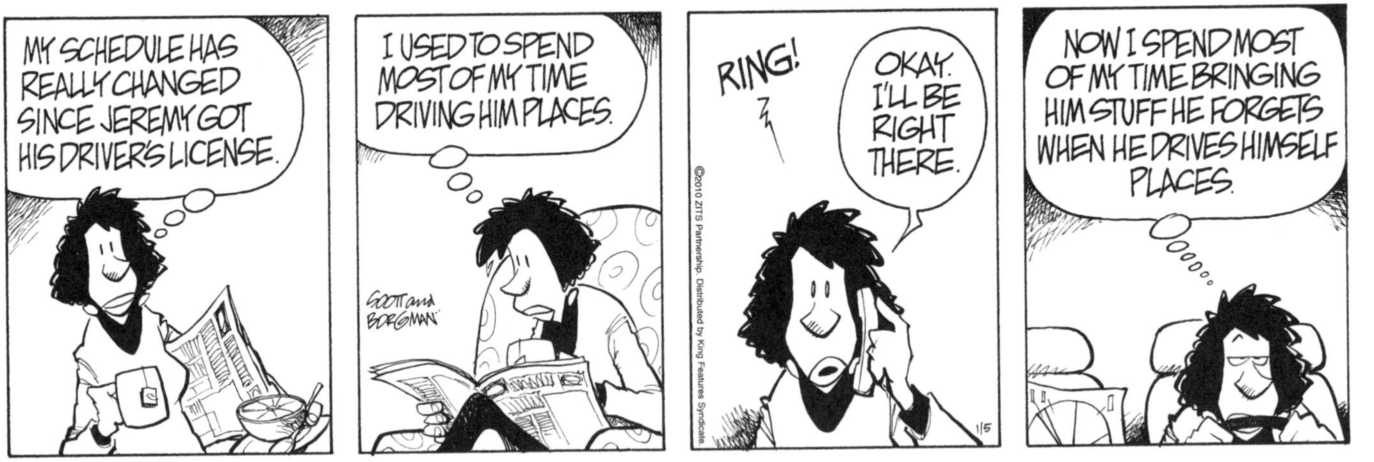
MY SCHEDULE HAS REALLY CHANGED SINCE JEREMY GOT HIS DRIVER'S LICENSE.
I USED TO SPEND MOST OF MY TIME DRIVING HIM PLACES.
SCOTT and BORGMAN
RING!
OKAY. I'LL BE RIGHT THERE.
©2010 ZITS Partnership. Distributed by King Features Syndicate.
NOW I SPEND MOST OF MY TIME BRINGING HIM STUFF HE FORGETS WHEN HE DRIVES HIMSELF PLACES.

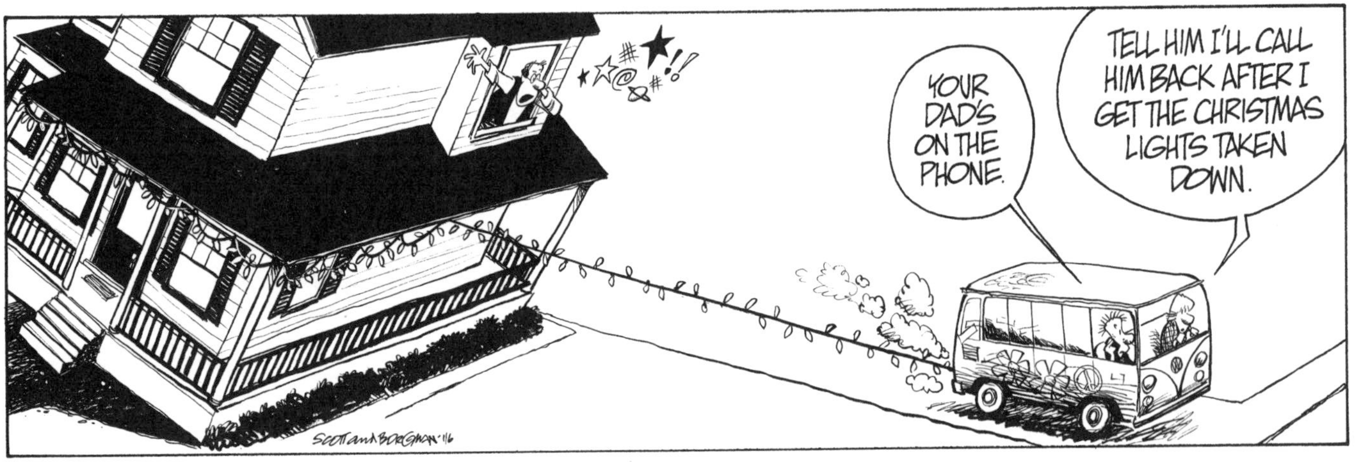
YOUR DAD'S ON THE PHONE.
TELL HIM I'LL CALL HIM BACK AFTER I GET THE CHRISTMAS LIGHTS TAKEN DOWN.
SCOTT and BORGMAN

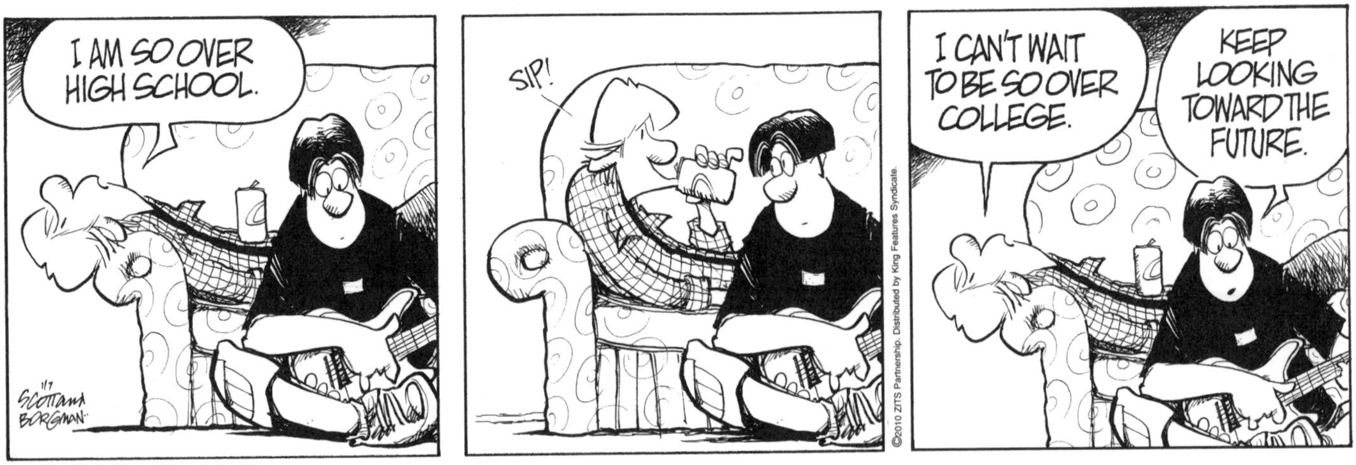
I AM SO OVER HIGH SCHOOL.
SCOTT and BORGMAN
SIP!
©2010 ZITS Partnership. Distributed by King Features Syndicate.
I CAN'T WAIT TO BE SO OVER COLLEGE.
KEEP LOOKING TOWARD THE FUTURE.

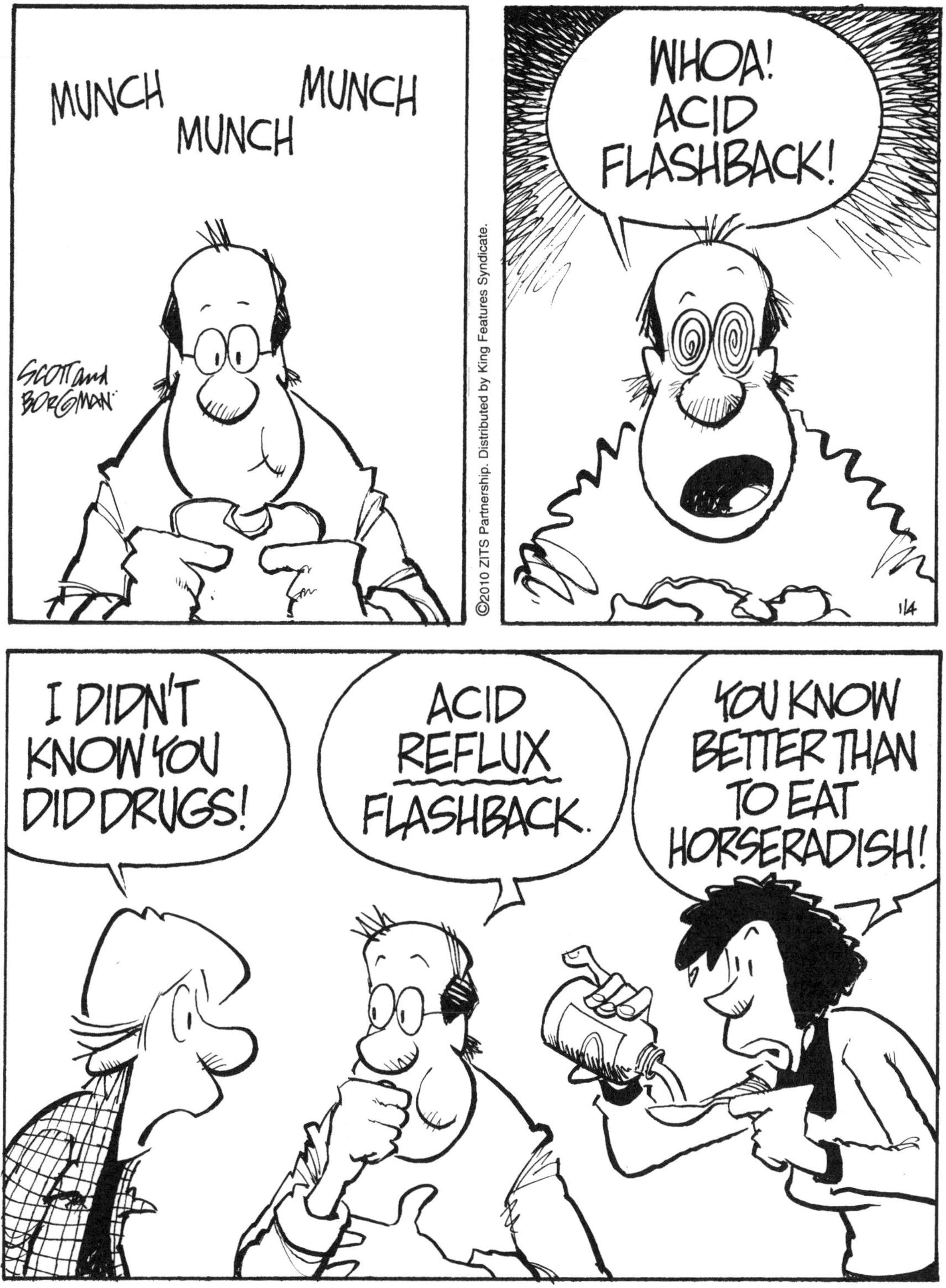
MUNCH
MUNCH
MUNCH
SCOTT and BORGMAN
WHOA! ACID FLASHBACK!
1/4
I DIDN'T KNOW YOU DID DRUGS!
ACID REFLUX FLASHBACK.
YOU KNOW BETTER THAN TO EAT HORSERADISH!

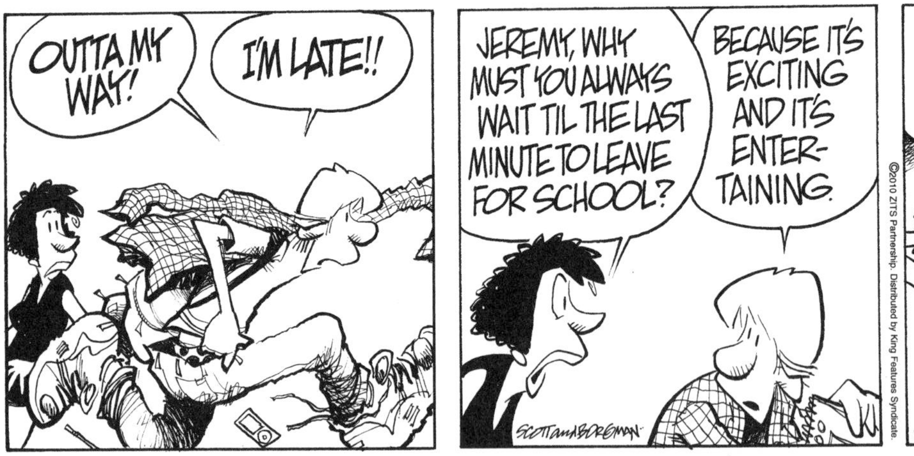
OUTTA MY WAY!
I'M LATE!!
JEREMY, WHY MUST YOU ALWAYS WAIT TIL THE LAST MINUTE TO LEAVE FOR SCHOOL?
BECAUSE IT'S EXCITING AND IT'S ENTER-TAINING.
BUT IT DRIVES ME INSANE!
THAT'S THE ENTERTAINING PART.
©2010 ZITS Partnership. Distributed by King Features Syndicate.

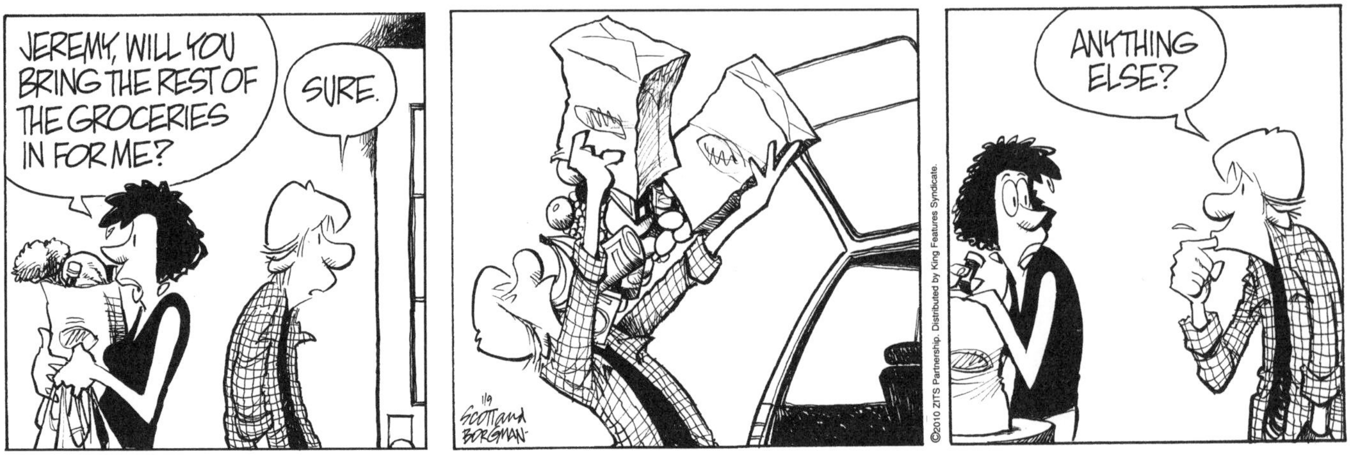
JEREMY, WILL YOU BRING THE REST OF THE GROCERIES IN FOR ME?
SURE.
ANYTHING ELSE?
©2010 ZITS Partnership. Distributed by King Features Syndicate.

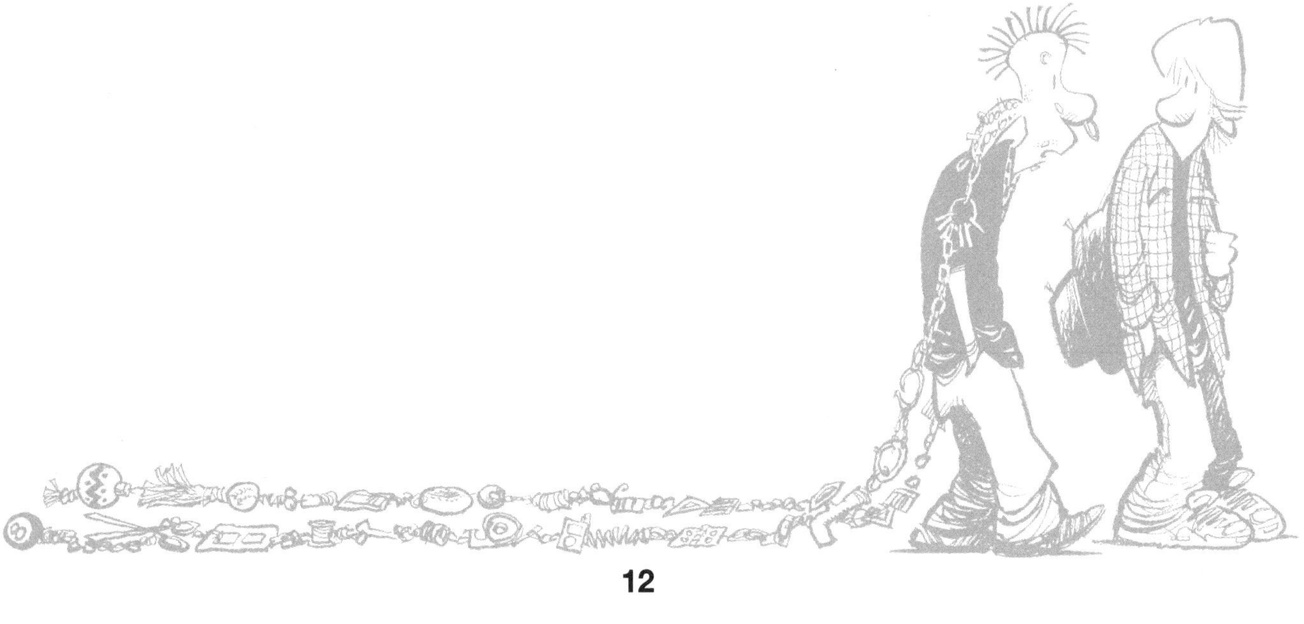

Zits
by
JERRY SCOTT and
JIM BORGMAN

WHAT ARE YOU DOING?
I JUST CAME DOWN TO GET A PENCIL.
©2010 ZITS Partnership. Distributed by King Features Syndicate.
1/10
SCOTT and BORGMAN

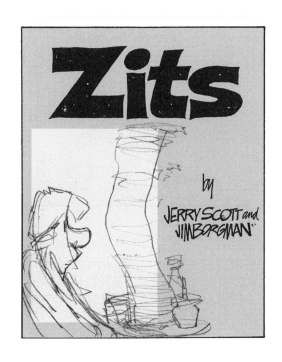

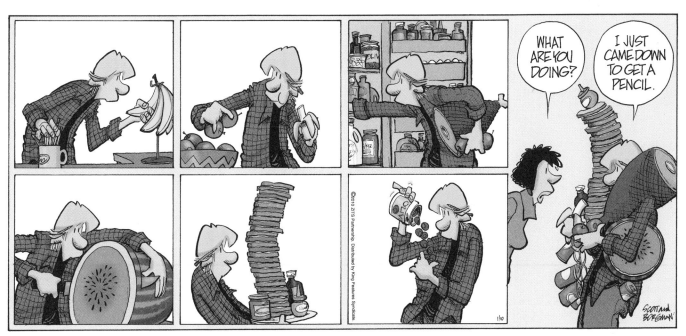

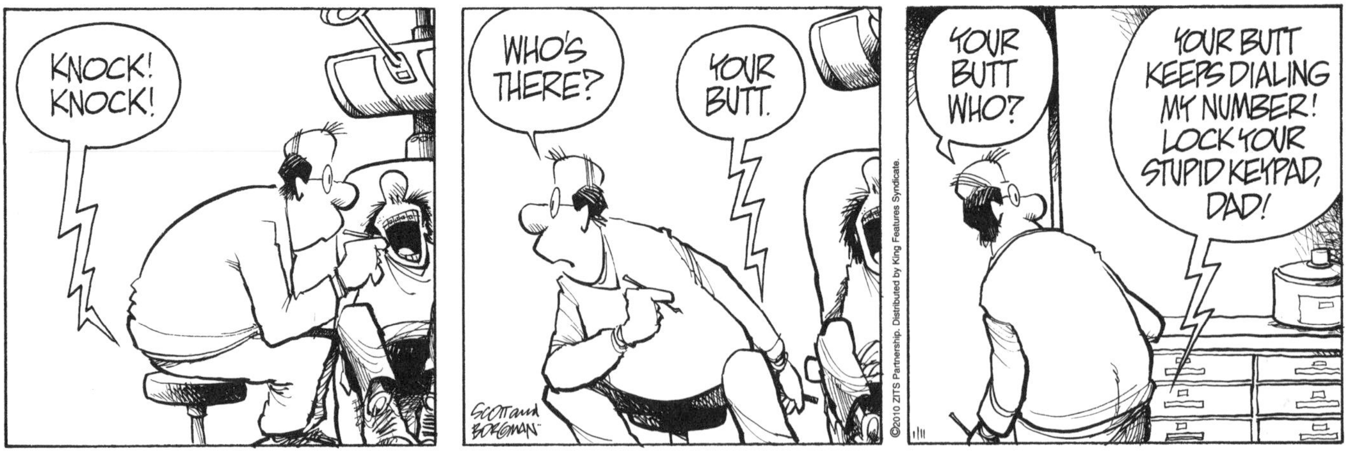
KNOCK! KNOCK!
WHO'S THERE?
YOUR BUTT.
SCOTT and BORGMAN
©2010 ZITS Partnership. Distributed by King Features Syndicate.
YOUR BUTT WHO?
YOUR BUTT KEEPS DIALING MY NUMBER! LOCK YOUR STUPID KEYPAD, DAD!
1/11

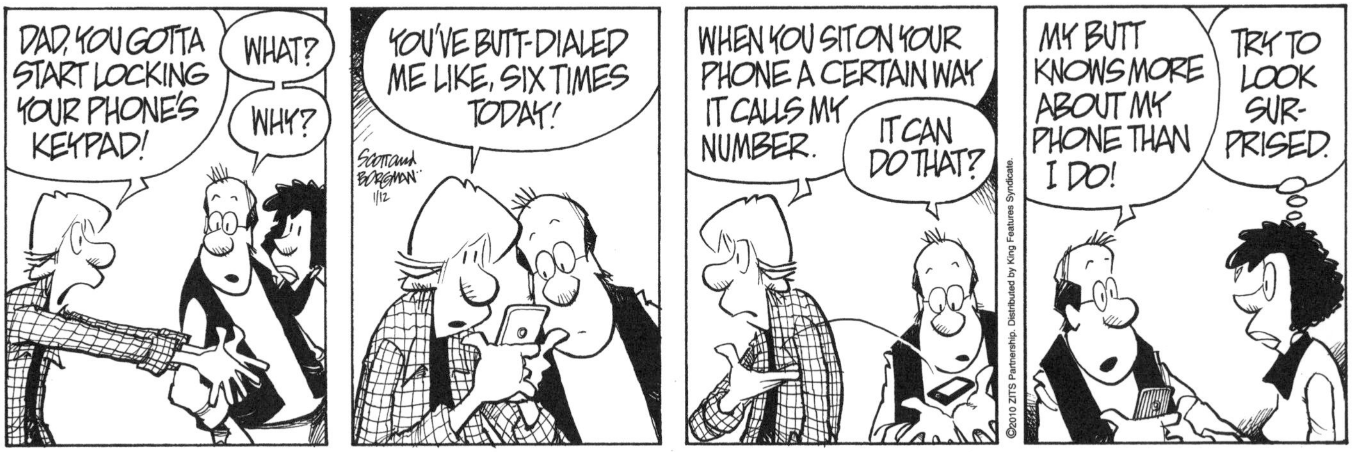
DAD, YOU GOTTA START LOCKING YOUR PHONE'S KEYPAD!
WHAT?
WHY?
YOU'VE BUTT-DIALED ME LIKE, SIX TIMES TODAY!
SCOTT and BORGMAN
1/12
WHEN YOU SIT ON YOUR PHONE A CERTAIN WAY IT CALLS MY NUMBER.
IT CAN DO THAT?
©2010 ZITS Partnership. Distributed by King Features Syndicate.
MY BUTT KNOWS MORE ABOUT MY PHONE THAN I DO!
TRY TO LOOK SUR-PRISED.

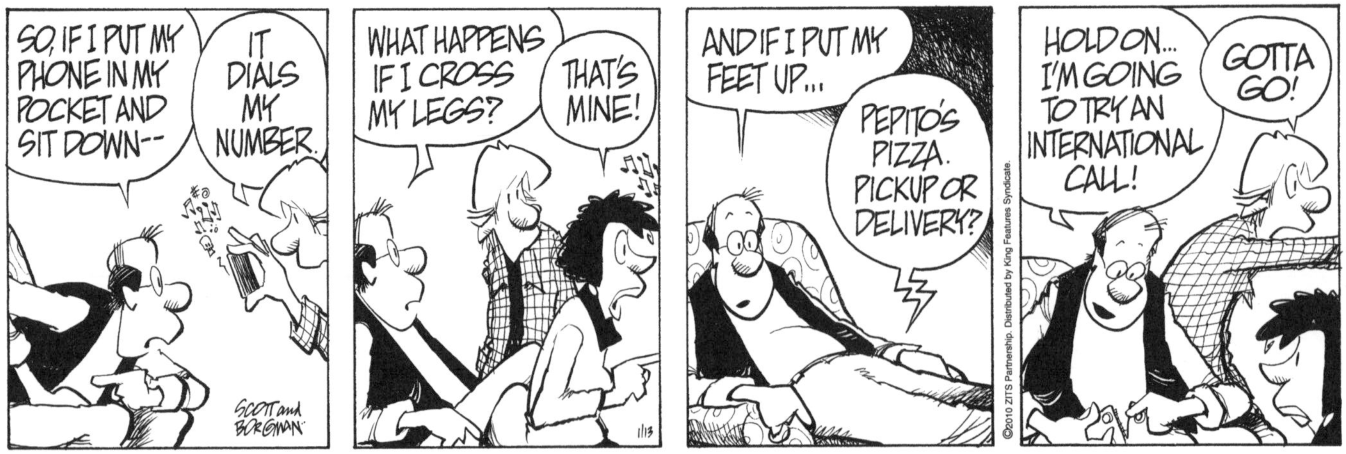
SO, IF I PUT MY PHONE IN MY POCKET AND SIT DOWN--
IT DIALS MY NUMBER.
SCOTT and BORGMAN
WHAT HAPPENS IF I CROSS MY LEGS?
THAT'S MINE!
1/13
AND IF I PUT MY FEET UP...
PEPITO'S PIZZA. PICKUP OR DELIVERY?
©2010 ZITS Partnership. Distributed by King Features Syndicate.
HOLD ON... I'M GOING TO TRY AN INTERNATIONAL CALL!
GOTTA GO!

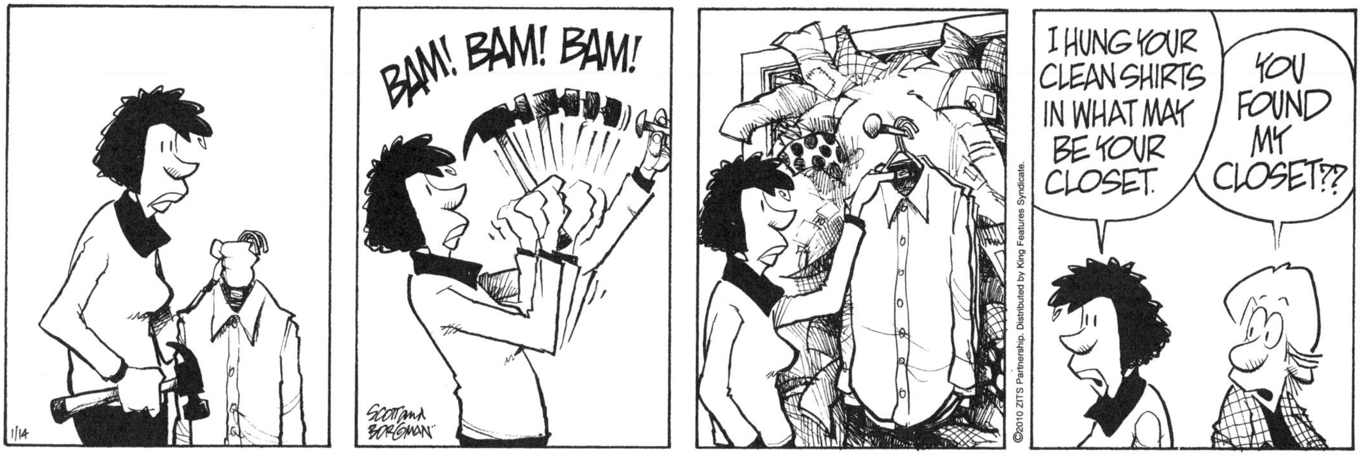
1/14
BAM! BAM! BAM!
SCOTT AND BORGMAN
I HUNG YOUR CLEAN SHIRTS IN WHAT MAY BE YOUR CLOSET.
YOU FOUND MY CLOSET??
©2010 ZITS Partnership. Distributed by King Features Syndicate.

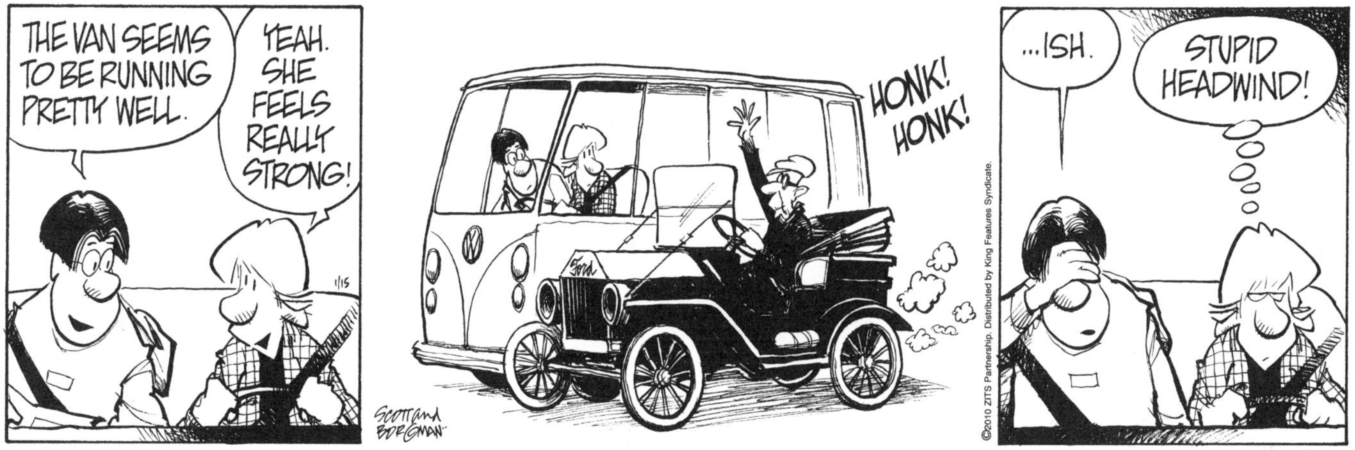
THE VAN SEEMS TO BE RUNNING PRETTY WELL.
YEAH. SHE FEELS REALLY STRONG!
1/15
HONK! HONK!
SCOTT AND BORGMAN
...ISH.
STUPID HEADWIND!
©2010 ZITS Partnership. Distributed by King Features Syndicate.

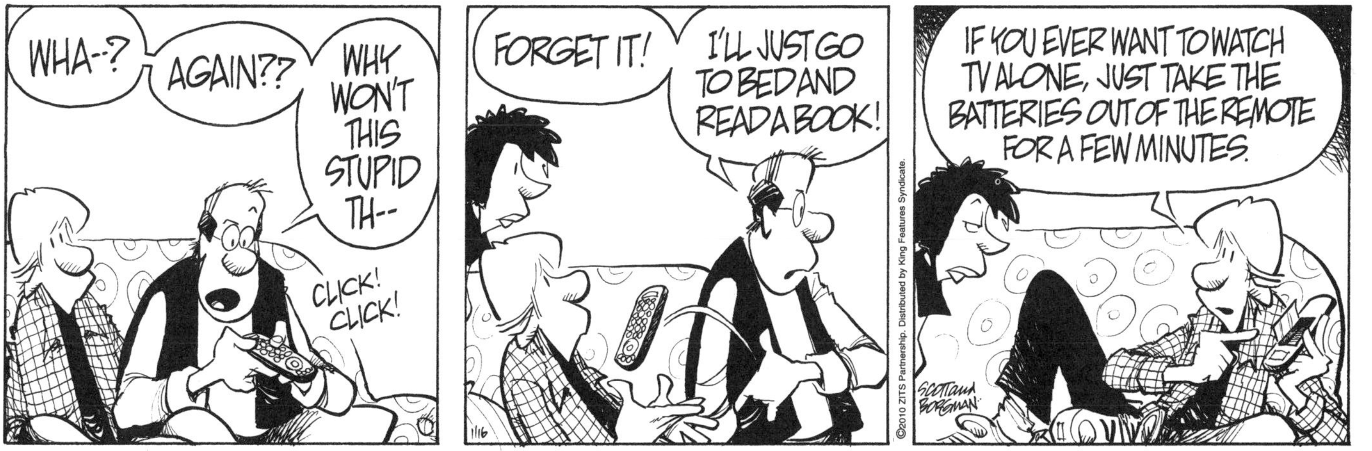
WHA-?
AGAIN??
WHY WON'T THIS STUPID TH--
CLICK! CLICK!
FORGET IT!
I'LL JUST GO TO BED AND READ A BOOK!
1/16
©2010 ZITS Partnership. Distributed by King Features Syndicate.
IF YOU EVER WANT TO WATCH TV ALONE, JUST TAKE THE BATTERIES OUT OF THE REMOTE FOR A FEW MINUTES.
SCOTT AND BORGMAN

Zits
by JERRY SCOTT and JIM BORGMAN

WHAT DID YOU THINK?
WHOA!
FAN-TASTIC!
JEREMY, YOUR TEACHER IS GOING TO BE THRILLED!
HOW MUCH TIME DID YOU SPEND CREATING SUCH A SPECTACULAR PRESENTATION?
ALL TOGETHER?
ABOUT TWENTY MINUTES.
STOP THE INTERNET. I WANT TO GET OFF.
I FELL OFF A WHILE BACK.
©2010 ZITS Partnership. Distributed by King Features Syndicate.

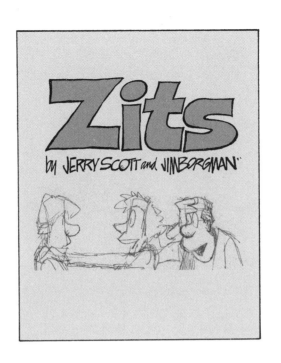

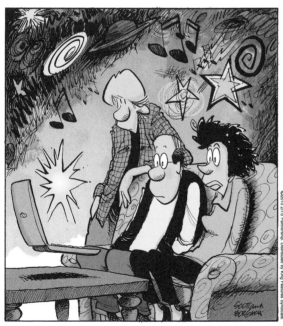

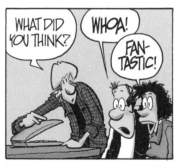

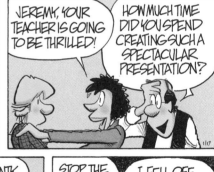

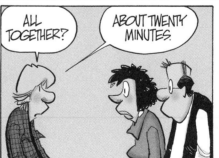

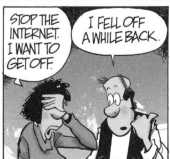

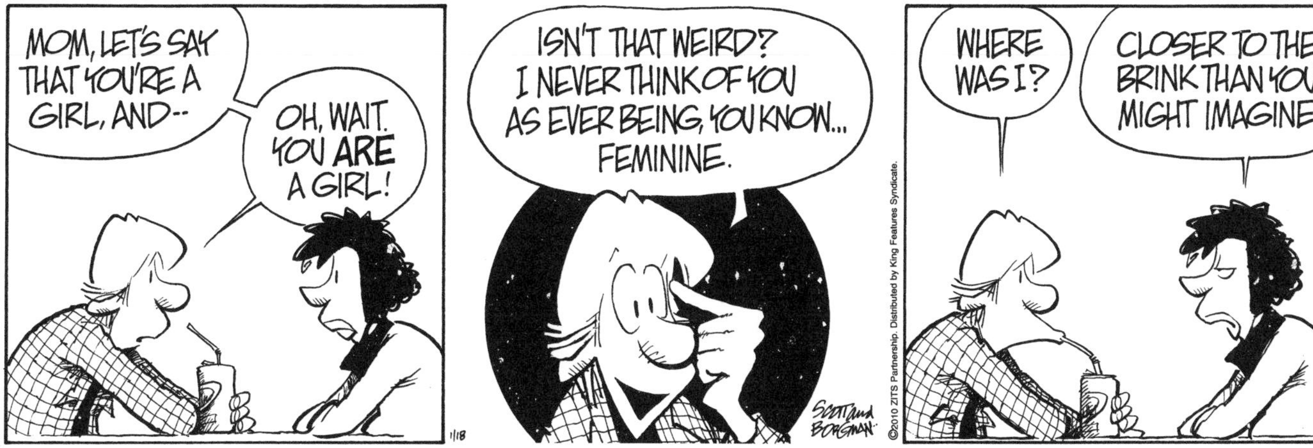
MOM, LET'S SAY THAT YOU'RE A GIRL, AND--
OH, WAIT. YOU **ARE** A GIRL!
ISN'T THAT WEIRD? I NEVER THINK OF YOU AS EVER BEING, YOU KNOW... FEMININE.
WHERE WAS I?
CLOSER TO THE BRINK THAN YOU MIGHT IMAGINE.
©2010 ZITS Partnership. Distributed by King Features Syndicate.

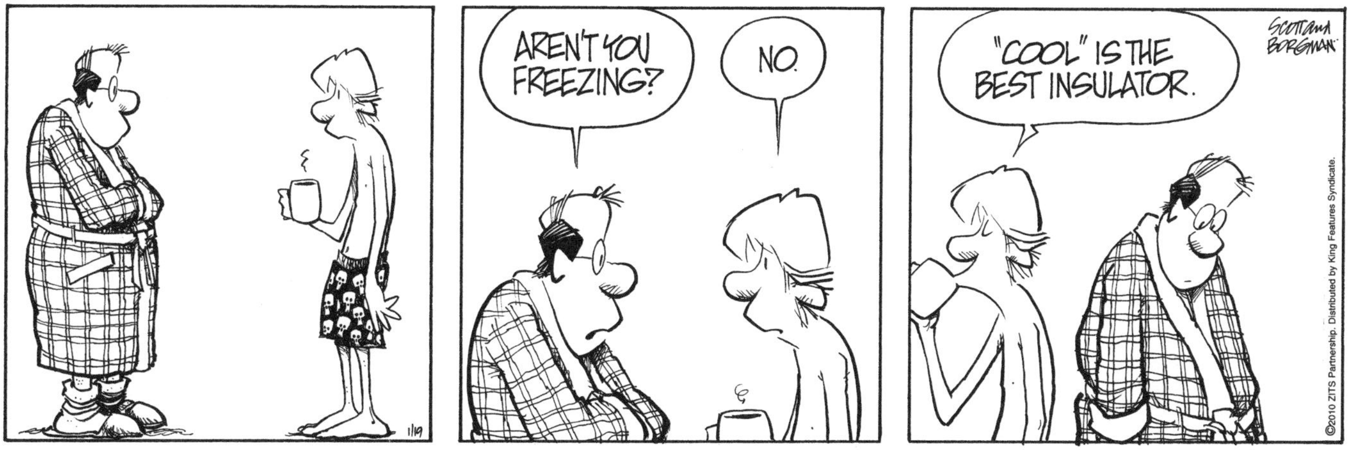
AREN'T YOU FREEZING?
NO.
"COOL" IS THE BEST INSULATOR.
©2010 ZITS Partnership. Distributed by King Features Syndicate.

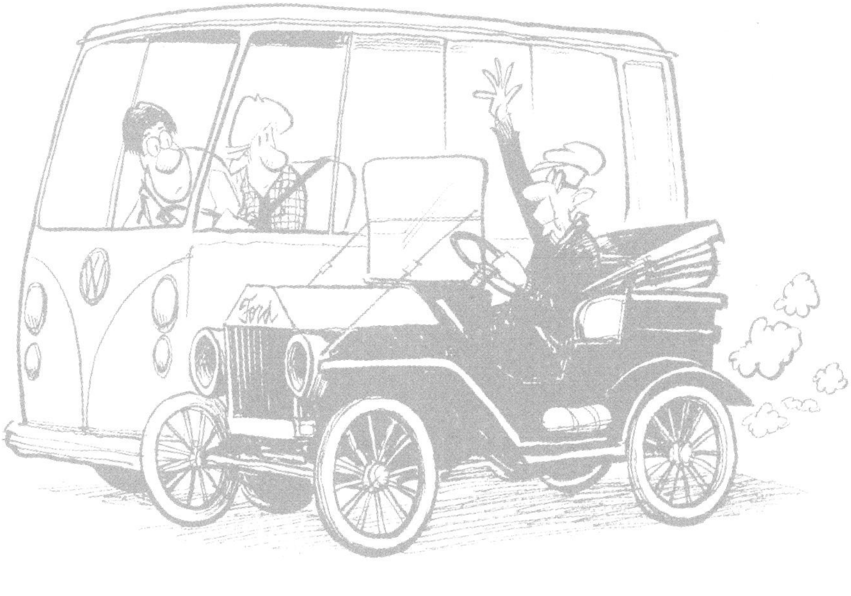

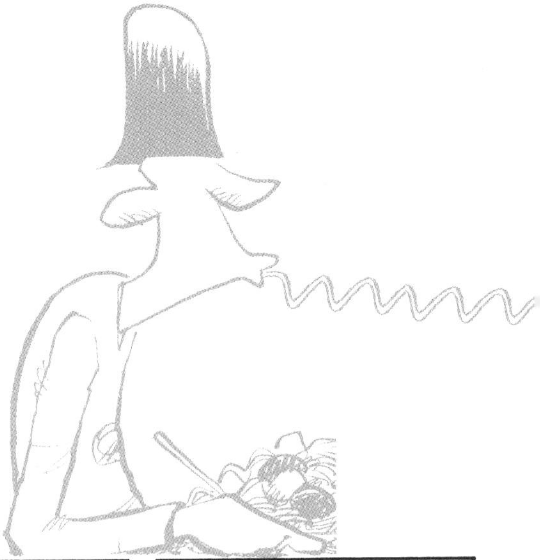

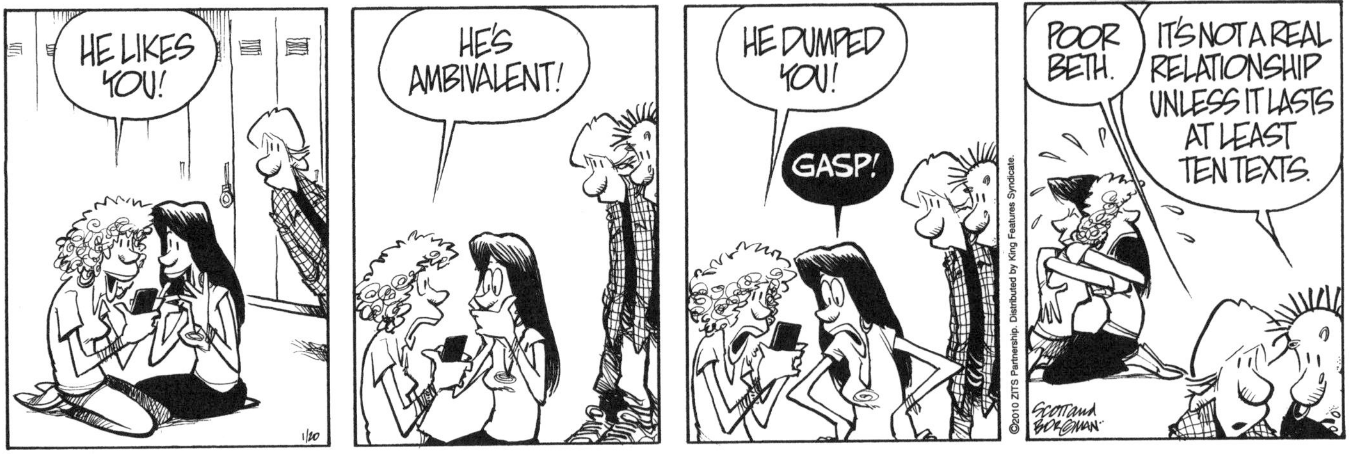
HE LIKES YOU!
HE'S AMBIVALENT!
HE DUMPED YOU!
GASP!
©2010 ZITS Partnership. Distributed by King Features Syndicate.
POOR BETH.
IT'S NOT A REAL RELATIONSHIP UNLESS IT LASTS AT LEAST TEN TEXTS.
SCOTT AND BORGMAN

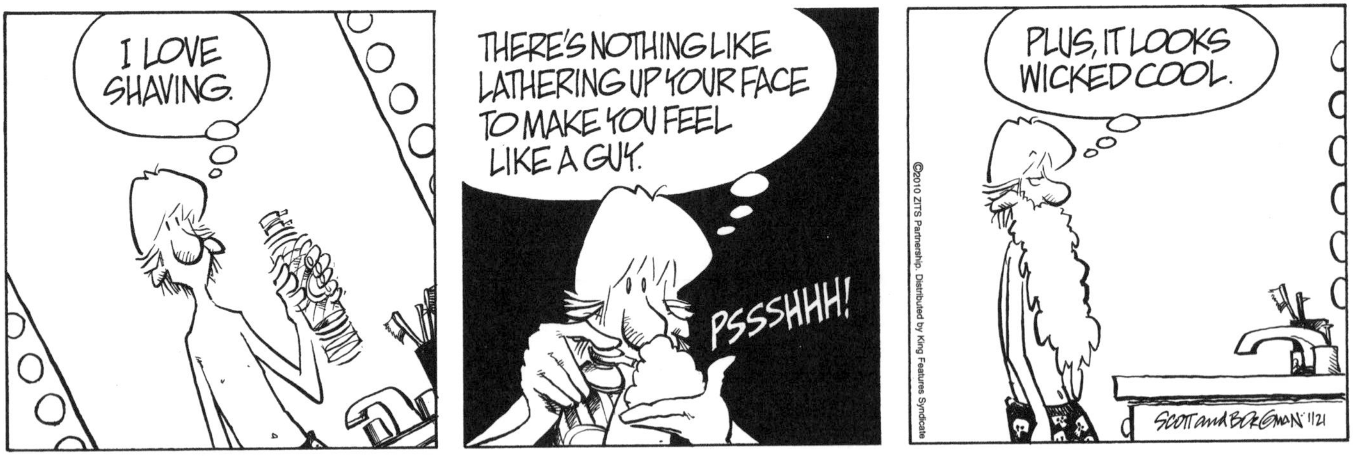
I LOVE SHAVING.
THERE'S NOTHING LIKE LATHERING UP YOUR FACE TO MAKE YOU FEEL LIKE A GUY.
PSSSHHH!
©2010 ZITS Partnership. Distributed by King Features Syndicate
PLUS, IT LOOKS WICKED COOL.
SCOTT AND BORGMAN

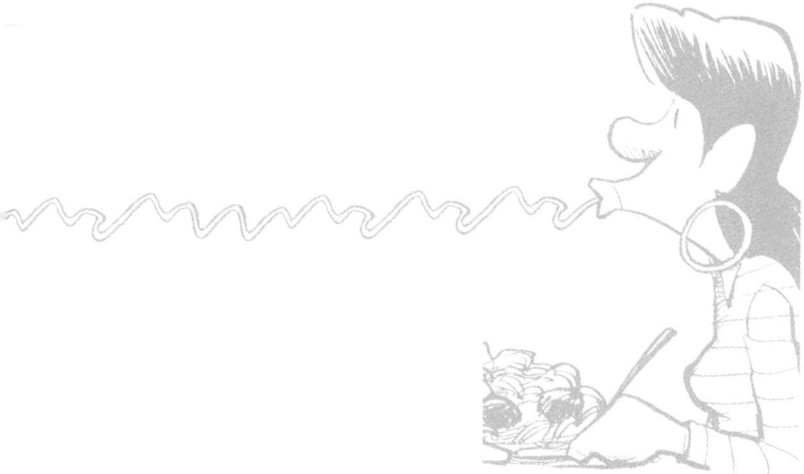

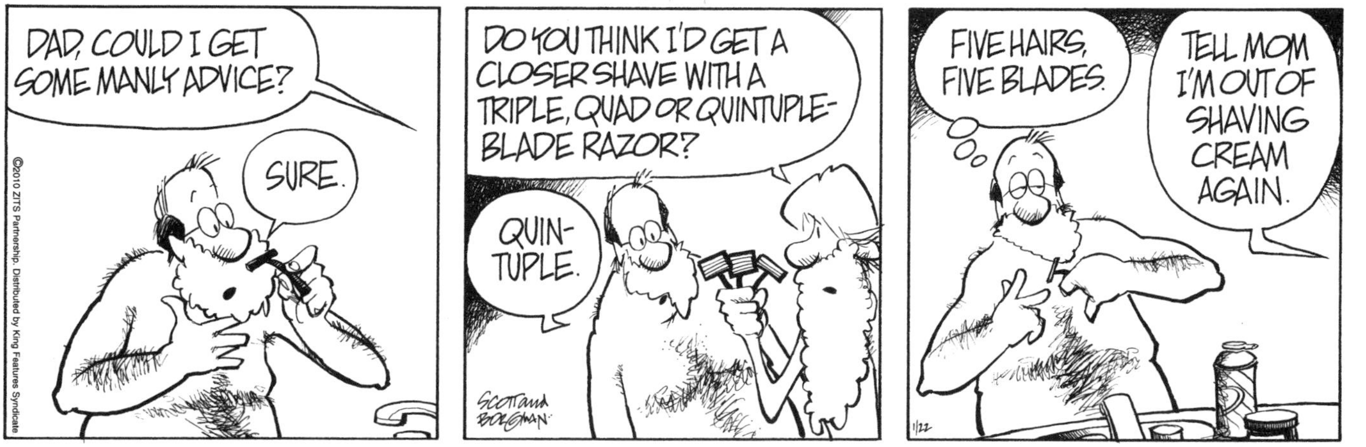
DAD, COULD I GET SOME MANLY ADVICE?
SURE.
©2010 ZITS Partnership. Distributed by King Features Syndicate
DO YOU THINK I'D GET A CLOSER SHAVE WITH A TRIPLE, QUAD OR QUINTUPLE-BLADE RAZOR?
QUINTUPLE.
SCOTT and BORGMAN
FIVE HAIRS, FIVE BLADES.
TELL MOM I'M OUT OF SHAVING CREAM AGAIN.
1/22

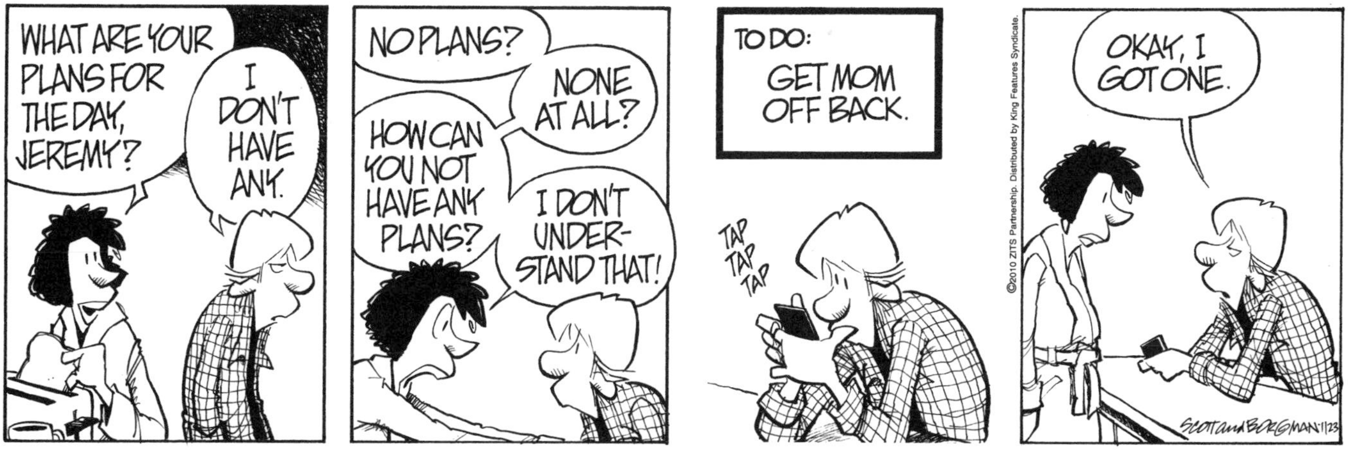
WHAT ARE YOUR PLANS FOR THE DAY, JEREMY?
I DON'T HAVE ANY.
NO PLANS?
NONE AT ALL?
HOW CAN YOU NOT HAVE ANY PLANS?
I DON'T UNDER-STAND THAT!
TO DO:
GET MOM OFF BACK.
TAP TAP TAP
©2010 ZITS Partnership. Distributed by King Features Syndicate.
OKAY, I GOT ONE.
SCOTT and BORGMAN 1/23

Zits
by
JERRY SCOTT and
JIM BORGMAN

BIP! BIP! BOOP! BIP! BIP!
BZZRT!
©2010 ZITS Partnership. Distributed by King Features Syndicate.
$ $ $
SCOTT and BORGMAN
YOU'RE EXAGGERATING.
WELL, THAT'S WHAT IT FEELS LIKE.

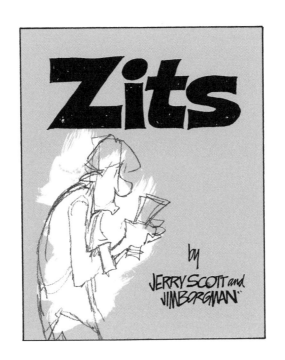

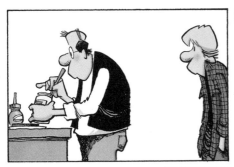

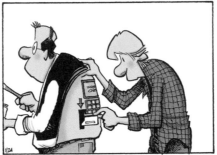

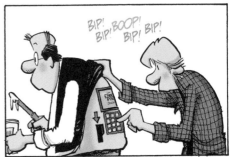

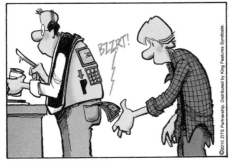

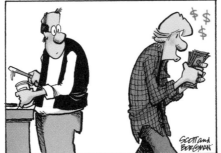

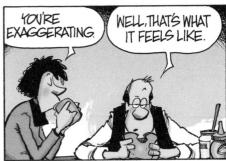

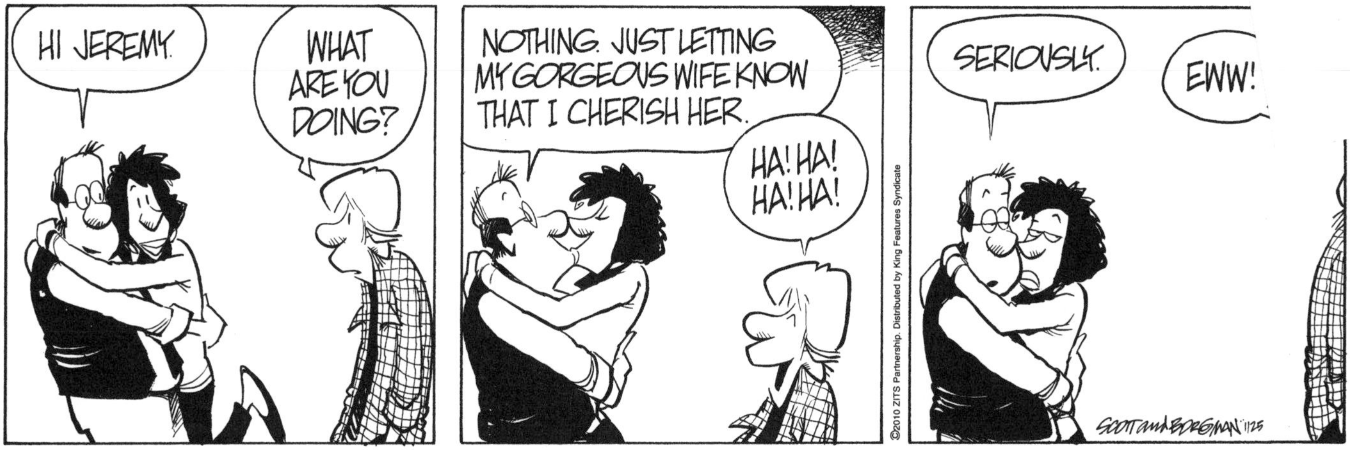
HI JEREMY.
WHAT ARE YOU DOING?
NOTHING. JUST LETTING MY GORGEOUS WIFE KNOW THAT I CHERISH HER.
HA! HA! HA! HA!
SERIOUSLY.
EWW!
©2010 ZITS Partnership. Distributed by King Features Syndicate
SCOTT and BORGMAN

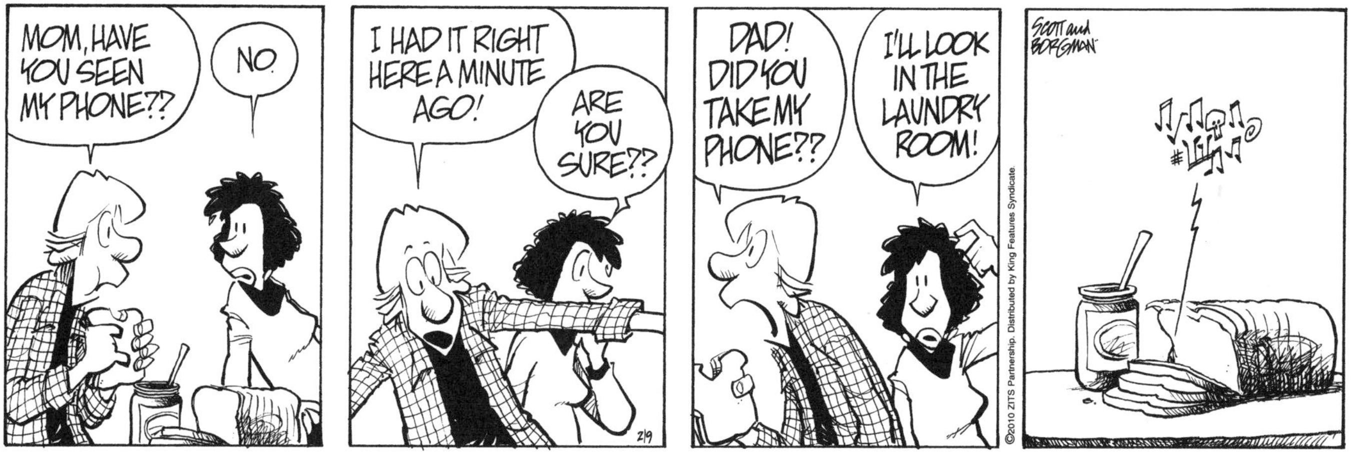
MOM, HAVE YOU SEEN MY PHONE??
NO.
I HAD IT RIGHT HERE A MINUTE AGO!
ARE YOU SURE??
DAD! DID YOU TAKE MY PHONE??
I'LL LOOK IN THE LAUNDRY ROOM!
©2010 ZITS Partnership. Distributed by King Features Syndicate.
SCOTT and BORGMAN

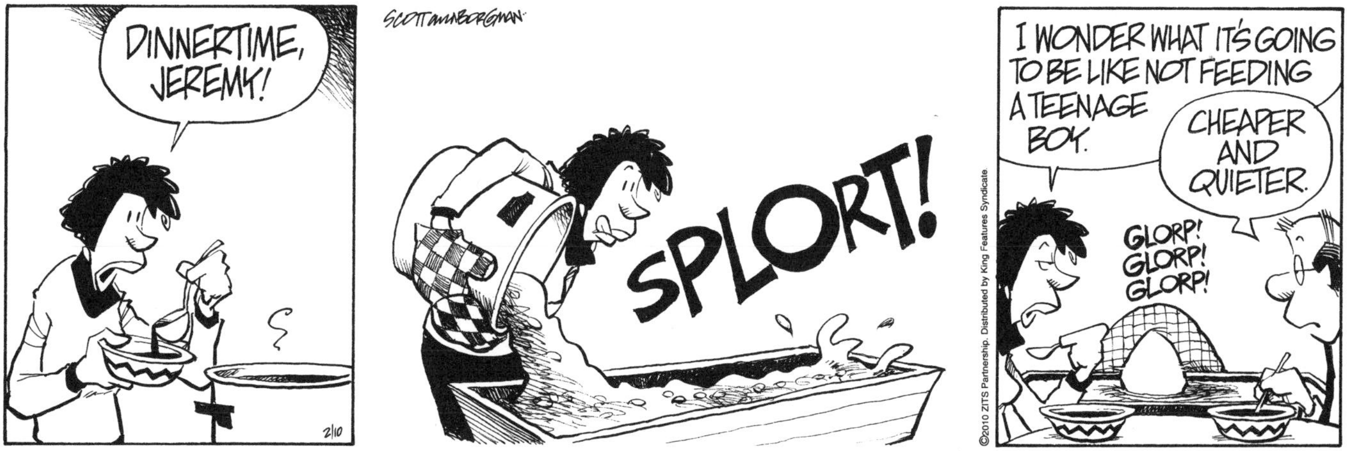
DINNERTIME, JEREMY!
SCOTT and BORGMAN
SPLORT!
I WONDER WHAT IT'S GOING TO BE LIKE NOT FEEDING A TEENAGE BOY.
CHEAPER AND QUIETER.
GLORP! GLORP! GLORP!
©2010 ZITS Partnership. Distributed by King Features Syndicate.

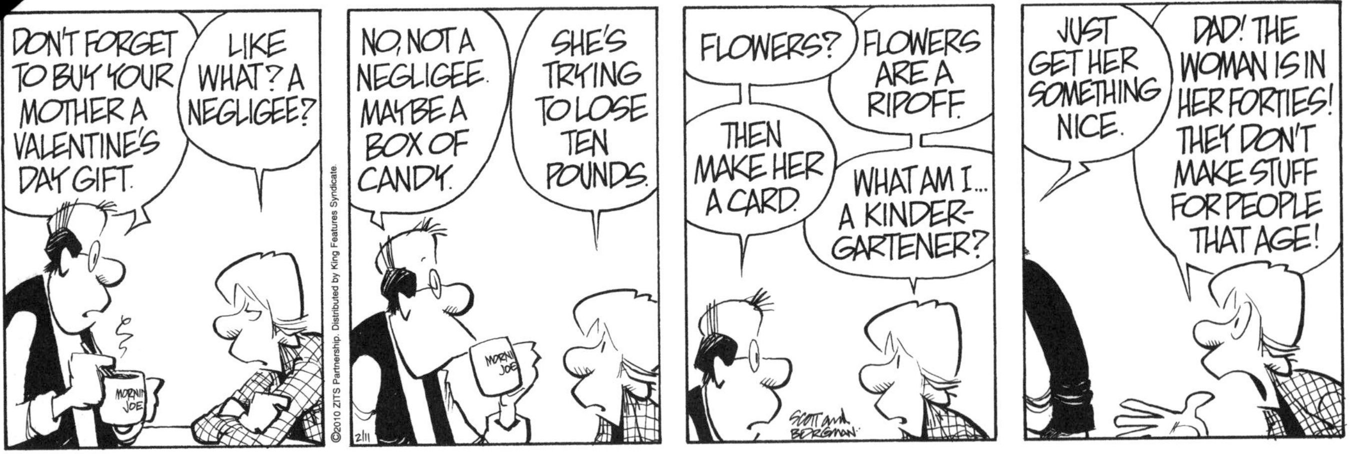
DON'T FORGET TO BUY YOUR MOTHER A VALENTINE'S DAY GIFT.
LIKE WHAT? A NEGLIGEE?
NO, NOT A NEGLIGEE. MAYBE A BOX OF CANDY.
SHE'S TRYING TO LOSE TEN POUNDS.
FLOWERS?
FLOWERS ARE A RIPOFF.
THEN MAKE HER A CARD.
WHAT AM I... A KINDER-GARTENER?
JUST GET HER SOMETHING NICE.
DAD! THE WOMAN IS IN HER FORTIES! THEY DON'T MAKE STUFF FOR PEOPLE THAT AGE!
©2010 ZITS Partnership. Distributed by King Features Syndicate.
SCOTT and BORGMAN

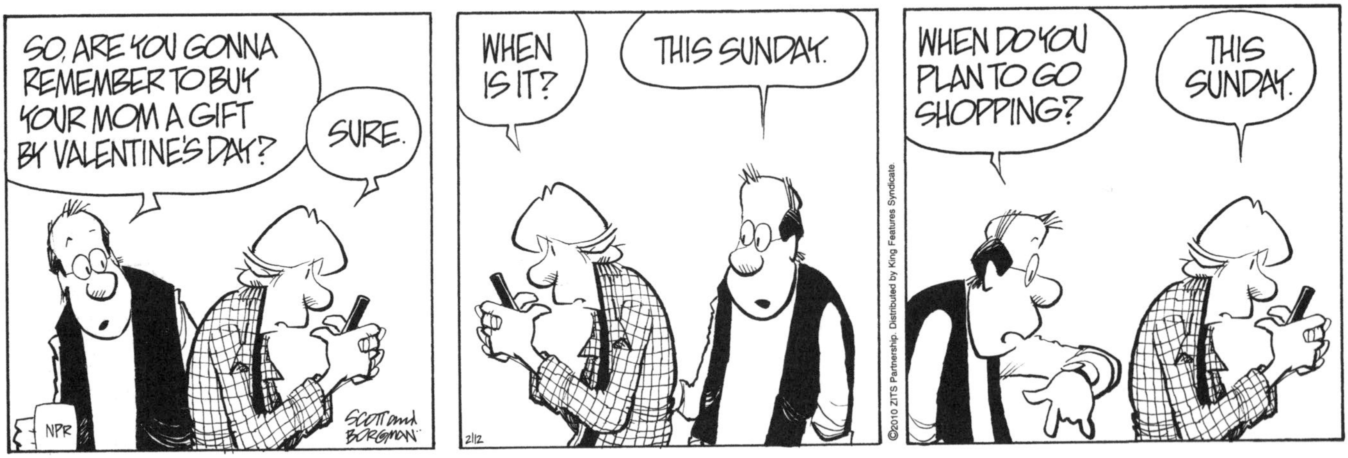
SO, ARE YOU GONNA REMEMBER TO BUY YOUR MOM A GIFT BY VALENTINE'S DAY?
SURE.
WHEN IS IT?
THIS SUNDAY.
WHEN DO YOU PLAN TO GO SHOPPING?
THIS SUNDAY.
NPR
SCOTT and BORGMAN
©2010 ZITS Partnership. Distributed by King Features Syndicate.

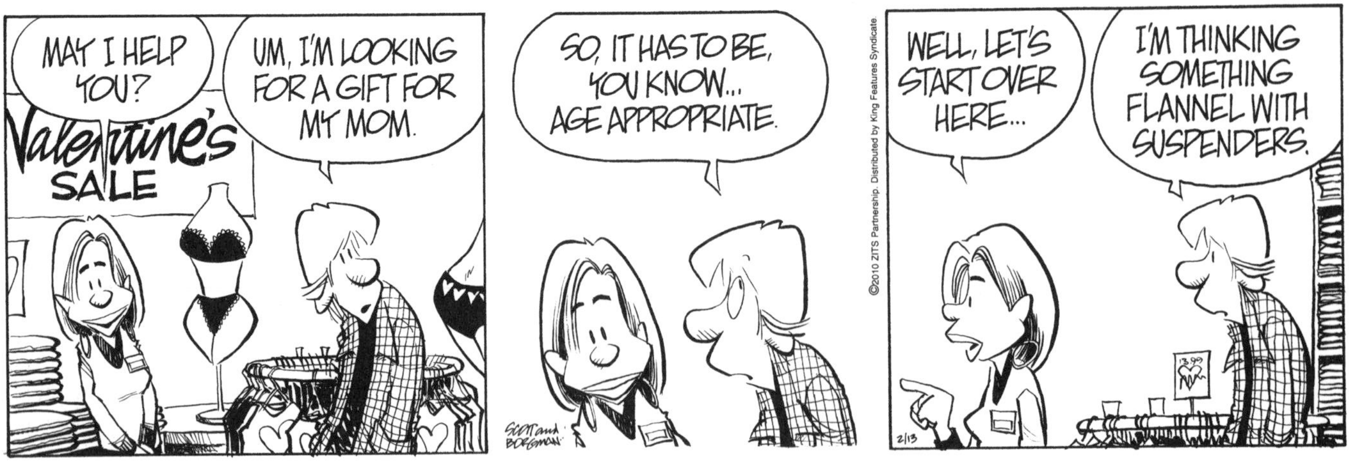
MAY I HELP YOU?
UM, I'M LOOKING FOR A GIFT FOR MY MOM.
Valentine's SALE
SO, IT HAS TO BE, YOU KNOW... AGE APPROPRIATE.
WELL, LET'S START OVER HERE...
I'M THINKING SOMETHING FLANNEL WITH SUSPENDERS.
SCOTT and BORGMAN
©2010 ZITS Partnership. Distributed by King Features Syndicate.

Zits
by JERRY SCOTT and JIM BORGMAN

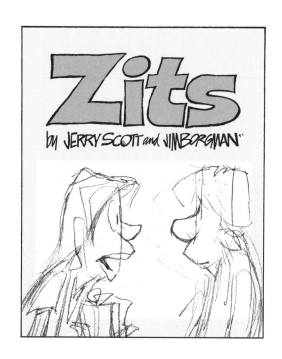

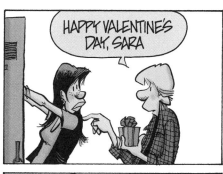

HAPPY VALENTINE'S DAY, SARA
OHMYGOSH! YOU GOT ME A GIFT!
THAT IS SO SWEET!
©2010 ZITS Partnership. Distributed by King Features Syndicate
IT'S JUST A LITTLE SOMETHING.
A KEYCHAIN! HOW CUTE!
2/14
SCOTT and BORGMAN
IS THAT AN OSTRICH OR A... DOLPHIN?
IT'S AN ALIEN DRAGON DEVOURING A HEART-SHAPED BOX OF DEAD RATS.
PIERCE HELPED ME PICK IT OUT.
WELL, EXCUSE US FOR BEING SENTIMENTAL!

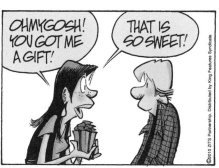

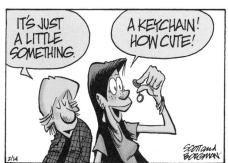

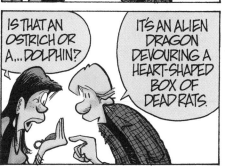

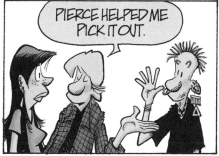

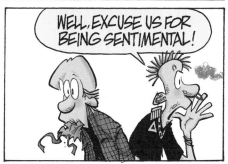

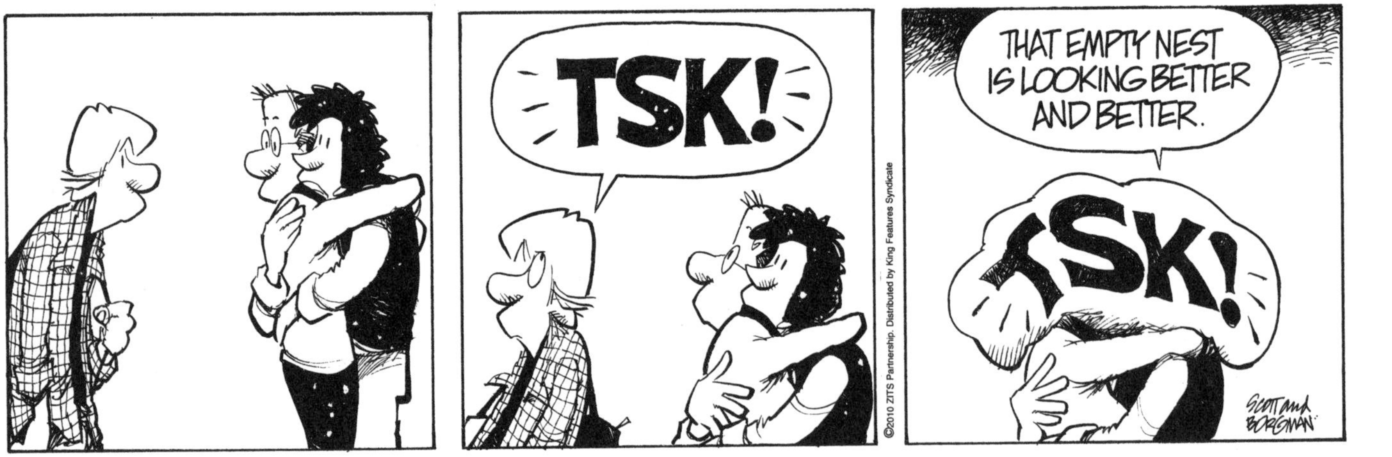
TSK!
©2010 ZITS Partnership. Distributed by King Features Syndicate
THAT EMPTY NEST IS LOOKING BETTER AND BETTER.
TSK!
SCOTT and BORGMAN

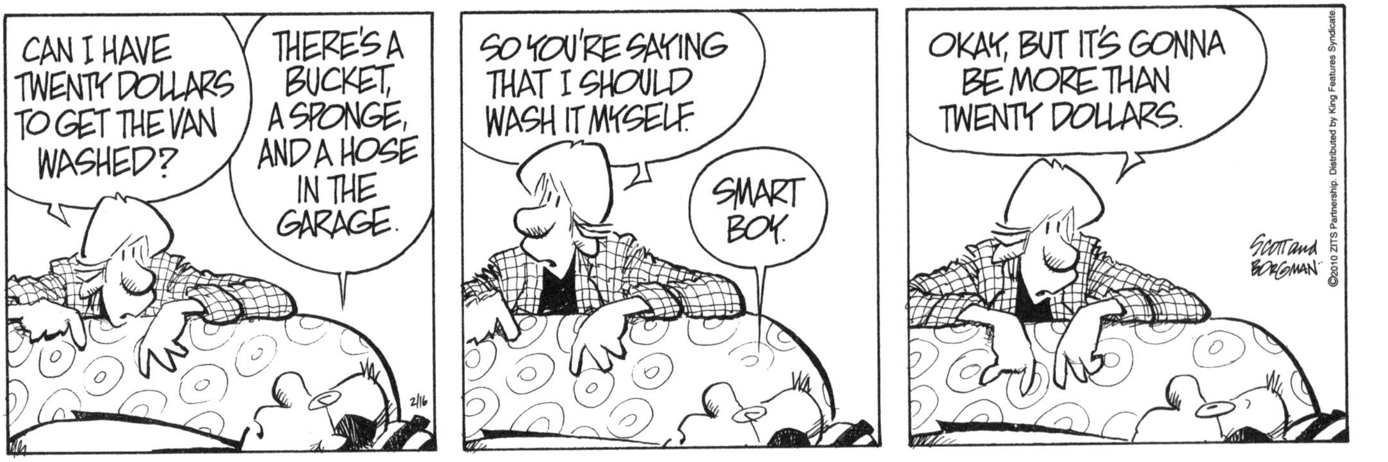
CAN I HAVE TWENTY DOLLARS TO GET THE VAN WASHED?
THERE'S A BUCKET, A SPONGE, AND A HOSE IN THE GARAGE.
2/16
SO YOU'RE SAYING THAT I SHOULD WASH IT MYSELF.
SMART BOY.
OKAY, BUT IT'S GONNA BE MORE THAN TWENTY DOLLARS.
SCOTT and BORGMAN
©2010 ZITS Partnership. Distributed by King Features Syndicate

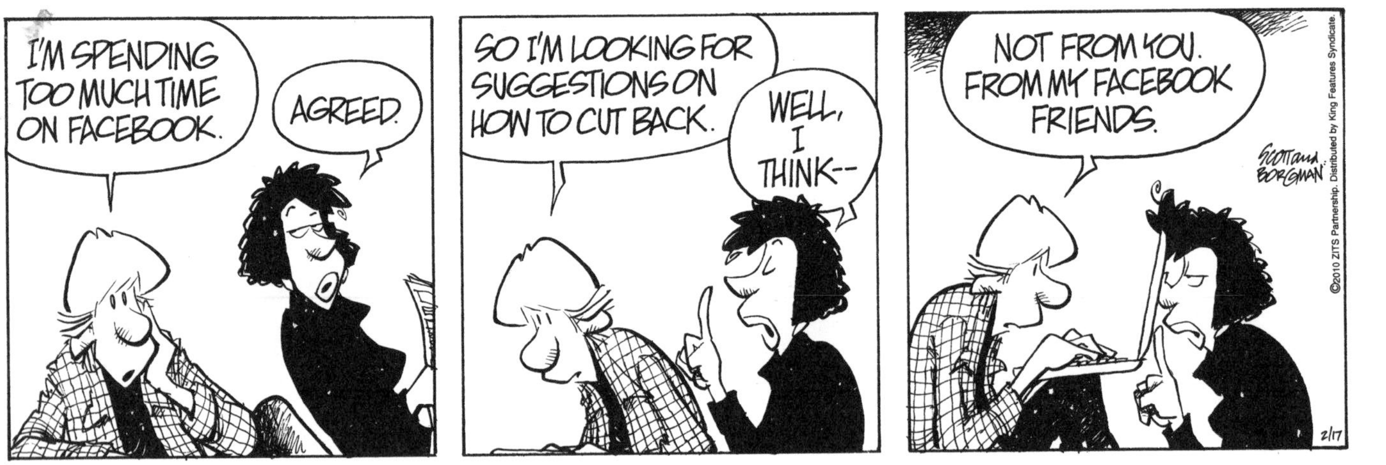
I'M SPENDING TOO MUCH TIME ON FACEBOOK.
AGREED.
SO I'M LOOKING FOR SUGGESTIONS ON HOW TO CUT BACK.
WELL, I THINK--
NOT FROM YOU. FROM MY FACEBOOK FRIENDS.
SCOTT and BORGMAN
©2010 ZITS Partnership. Distributed by King Features Syndicate.
2/17

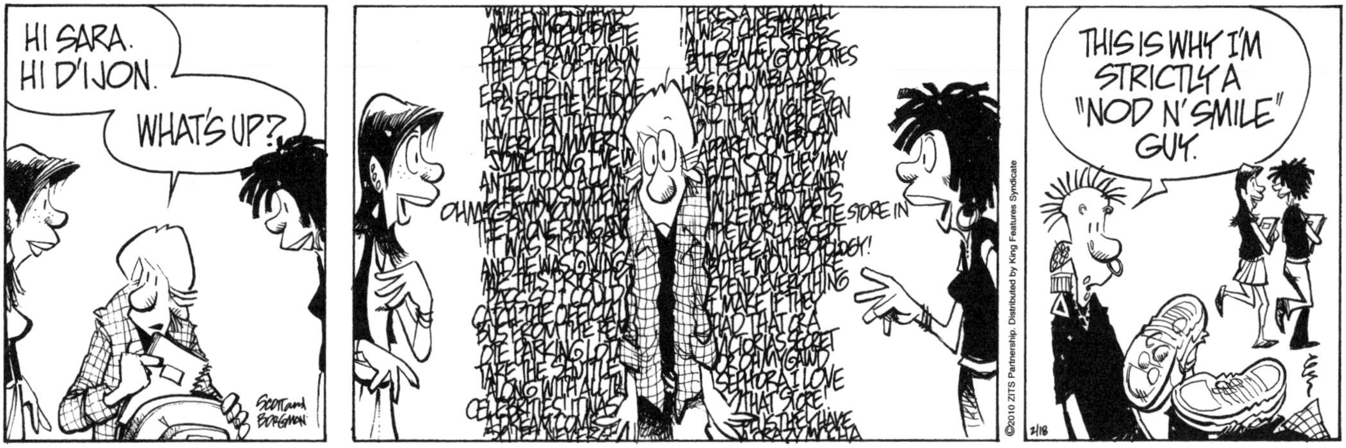
HI SARA.
HI D'IJON.
WHAT'S UP?
THIS IS WHY I'M STRICTLY A "NOD N' SMILE" GUY.
©2010 ZITS Partnership. Distributed by King Features Syndicate

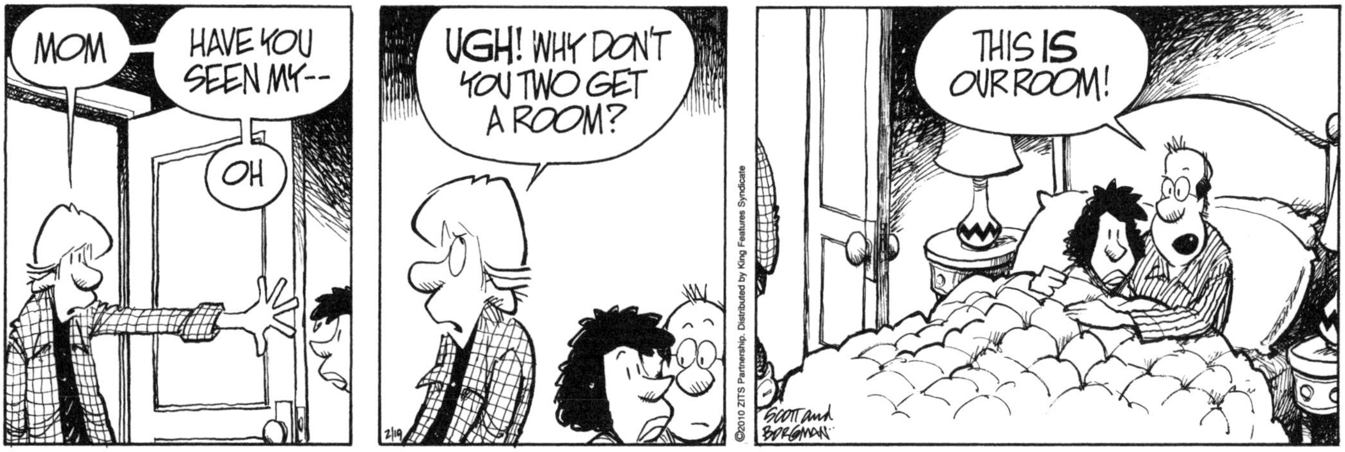
MOM
HAVE YOU SEEN MY--
OH
UGH! WHY DON'T YOU TWO GET A ROOM?
THIS IS OUR ROOM!
©2010 ZITS Partnership. Distributed by King Features Syndicate

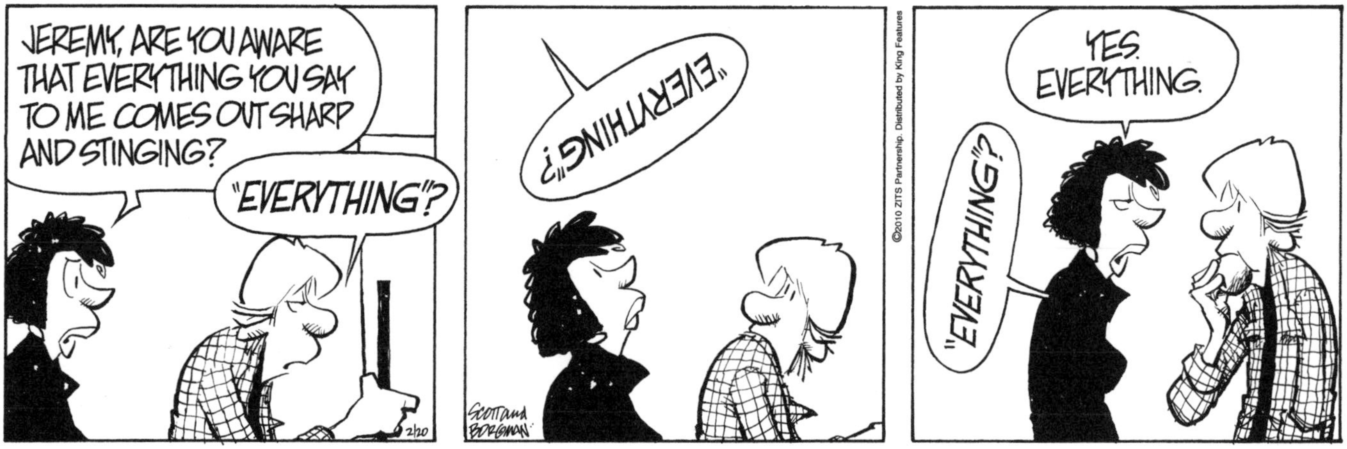
JEREMY, ARE YOU AWARE THAT EVERYTHING YOU SAY TO ME COMES OUT SHARP AND STINGING?
"EVERYTHING"?
"EVERYTHING"?
©2010 ZITS Partnership. Distributed by King Features
"EVERYTHING"?
YES. EVERYTHING.

Zits
by JERRY SCOTT and JIM BORGMAN

WE'RE NEVER GOING TO FIND THE RESTAURANT!
I GOT IT.
IT'S 515 FEET AHEAD ON THE RIGHT.
IT'S A RED BRICK BUILDING WITH A BLUE AWNING.
THE PARKING LOT IS RIGHT NEXT DOOR. THERE'S AN OPEN SPACE IN THE SECOND ROW NEXT TO THE 2006 SILVER BMW.
AND YOU'RE BOTH GOING TO ORDER THE HALIBUT.
SMART PHONES ARE GETTING A LITTLE TOO SMART, IF YOU ASK ME.
©2010 ZITS Partnership. Distributed by King Features Syndicate.
SCOTT and BORGMAN

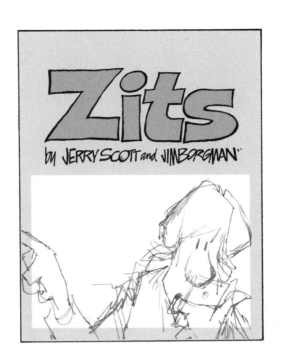

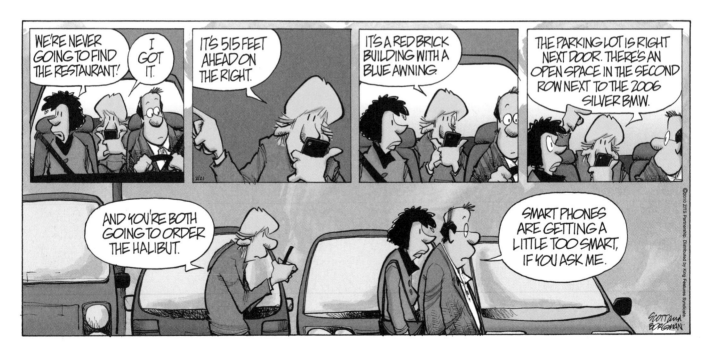

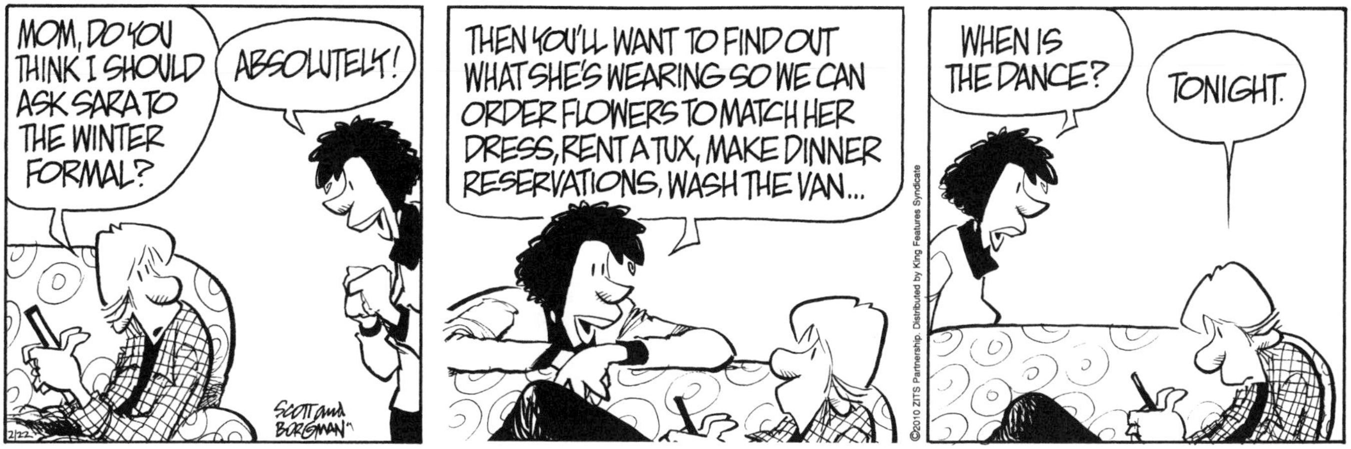
MOM, DO YOU THINK I SHOULD ASK SARA TO THE WINTER FORMAL?
ABSOLUTELY!
SCOTT and BORGMAN
THEN YOU'LL WANT TO FIND OUT WHAT SHE'S WEARING SO WE CAN ORDER FLOWERS TO MATCH HER DRESS, RENT A TUX, MAKE DINNER RESERVATIONS, WASH THE VAN...
©2010 ZITS Partnership. Distributed by King Features Syndicate
WHEN IS THE DANCE?
TONIGHT.

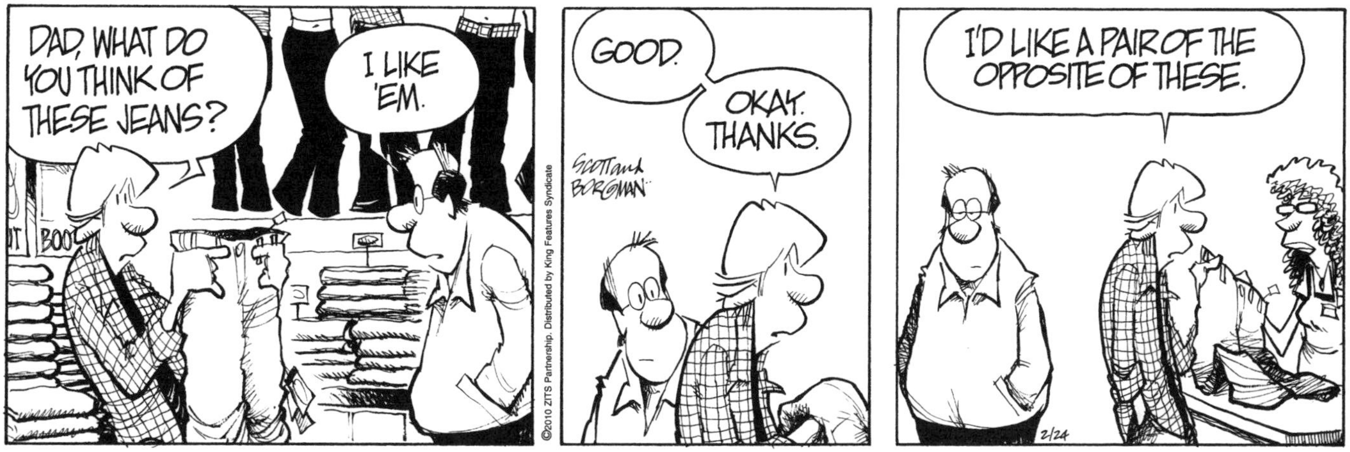
DAD, WHAT DO YOU THINK OF THESE JEANS?
I LIKE 'EM.
©2010 ZITS Partnership. Distributed by King Features Syndicate
GOOD.
OKAY. THANKS.
SCOTT and BORGMAN
I'D LIKE A PAIR OF THE OPPOSITE OF THESE.

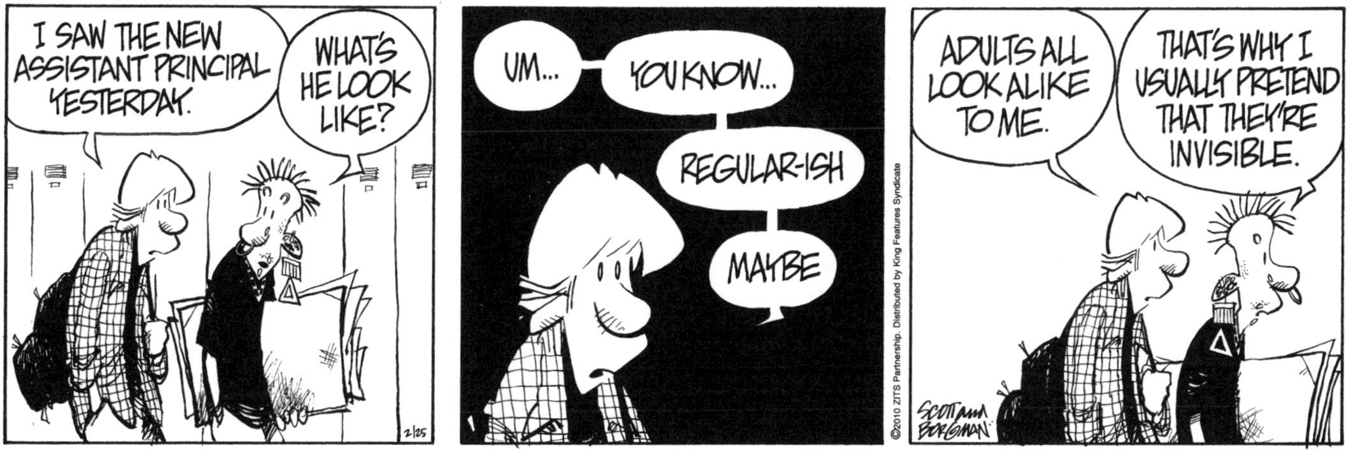
I SAW THE NEW ASSISTANT PRINCIPAL YESTERDAY.
WHAT'S HE LOOK LIKE?
UM...
YOU KNOW...
REGULAR-ISH
MAYBE
©2010 ZITS Partnership. Distributed by King Features Syndicate
ADULTS ALL LOOK ALIKE TO ME.
THAT'S WHY I USUALLY PRETEND THAT THEY'RE INVISIBLE.
SCOTT and BORGMAN

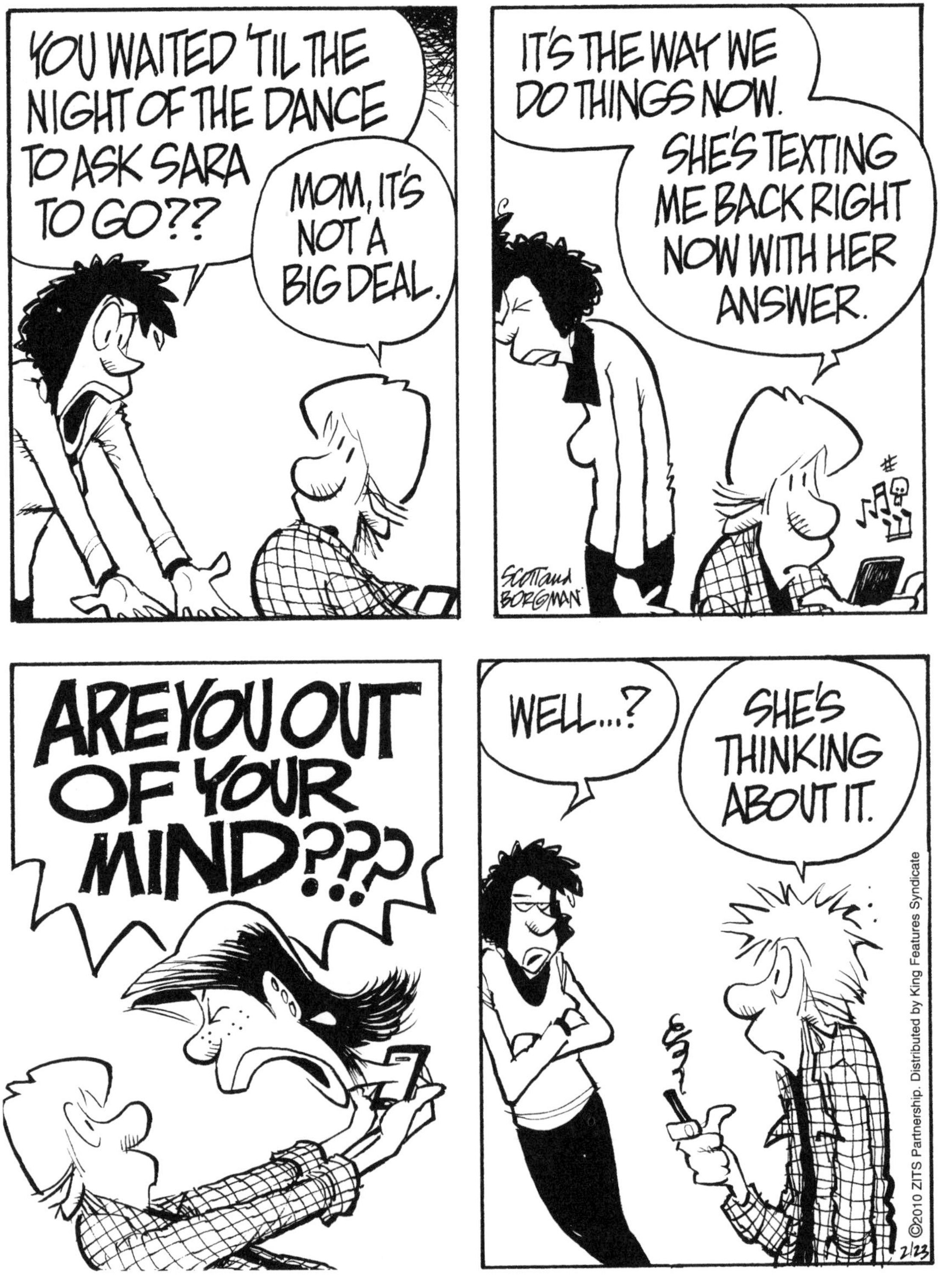
YOU WAITED 'TIL THE NIGHT OF THE DANCE TO ASK SARA TO GO??
MOM, IT'S NOT A BIG DEAL.
IT'S THE WAY WE DO THINGS NOW.
SHE'S TEXTING ME BACK RIGHT NOW WITH HER ANSWER.
SCOTT and BORGMAN
ARE YOU OUT OF YOUR MIND???
WELL...?
SHE'S THINKING ABOUT IT.
©2010 ZITS Partnership. Distributed by King Features Syndicate
2/23

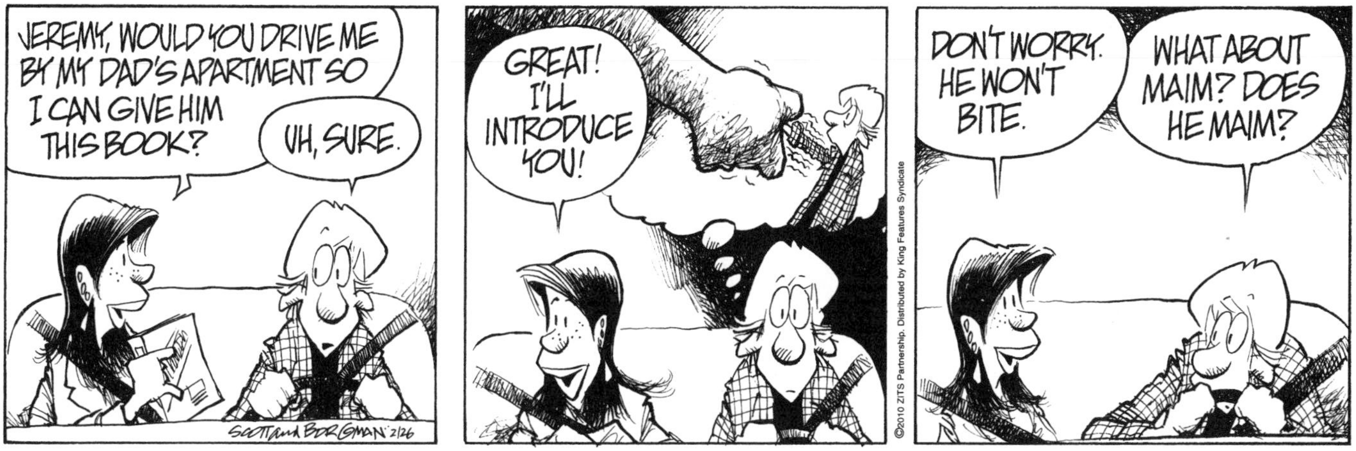
JEREMY, WOULD YOU DRIVE ME BY MY DAD'S APARTMENT SO I CAN GIVE HIM THIS BOOK?
UH, SURE.
SCOTT and BORGMAN 2/26
GREAT! I'LL INTRODUCE YOU!
©2010 ZITS Partnership. Distributed by King Features Syndicate
DON'T WORRY. HE WON'T BITE.
WHAT ABOUT MAIM? DOES HE MAIM?

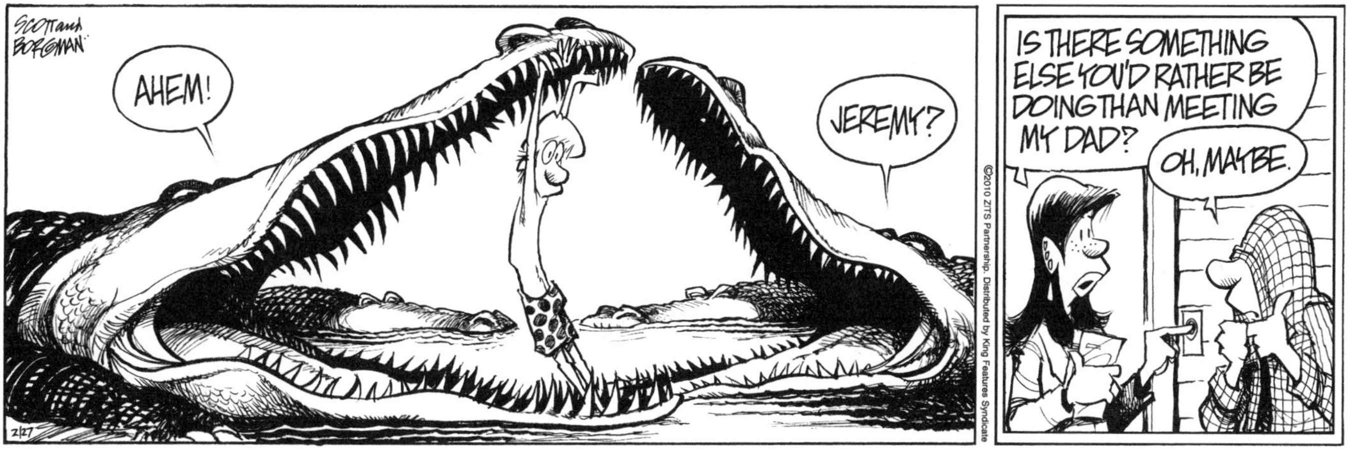
SCOTT and BORGMAN
AHEM!
JEREMY?
2/27
©2010 ZITS Partnership. Distributed by King Features Syndicate
IS THERE SOMETHING ELSE YOU'D RATHER BE DOING THAN MEETING MY DAD?
OH, MAYBE.

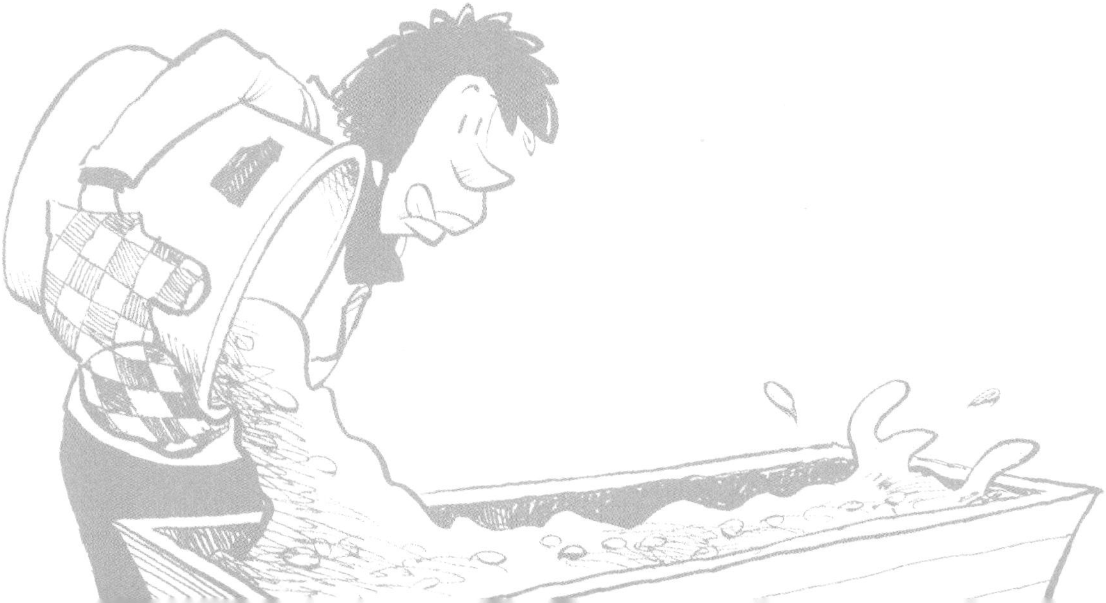

Zits
by JERRY SCOTT and JIM BORGMAN

CAN SOMEBODY REMIND ME HOW TO MAKE TOAST?
©2010 ZITS Partnership. Distributed by King Features Syndicate
SCOTT and BORGMAN

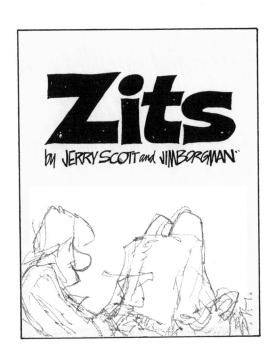

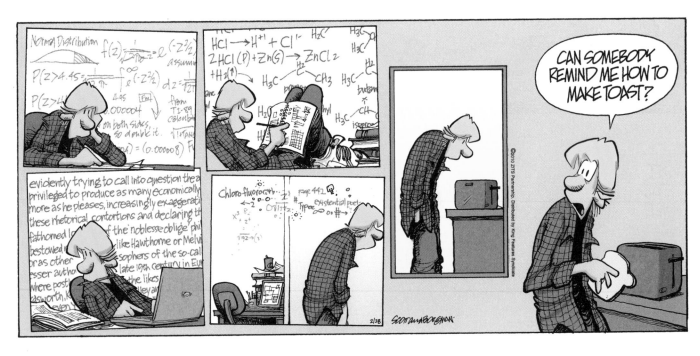

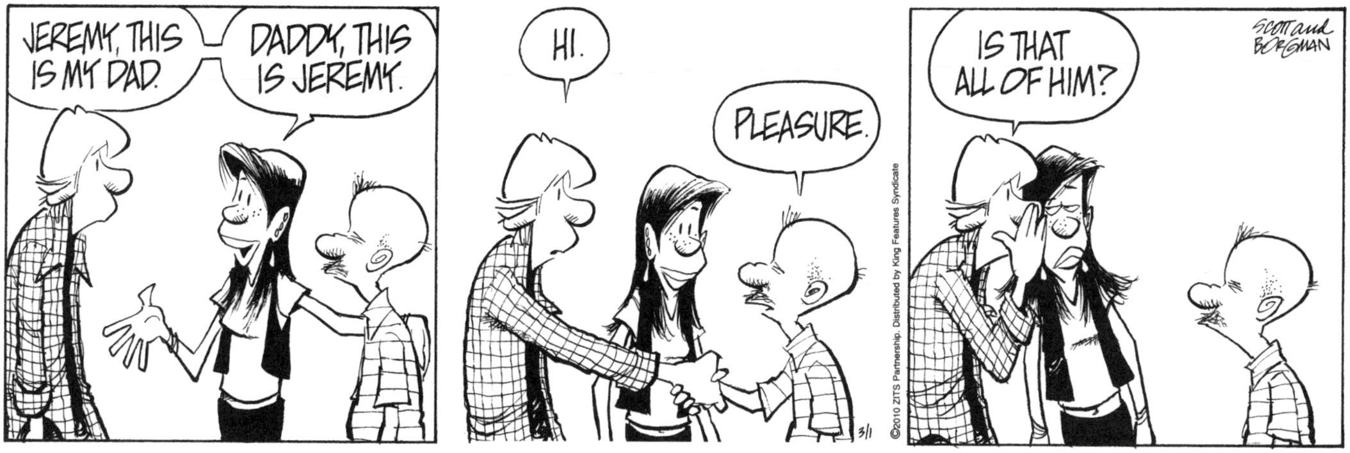
JEREMY, THIS IS MY DAD.
DADDY, THIS IS JEREMY.
HI.
PLEASURE.
IS THAT ALL OF HIM?
SCOTT and BORGMAN
3/1
©2010 ZITS Partnership. Distributed by King Features Syndicate

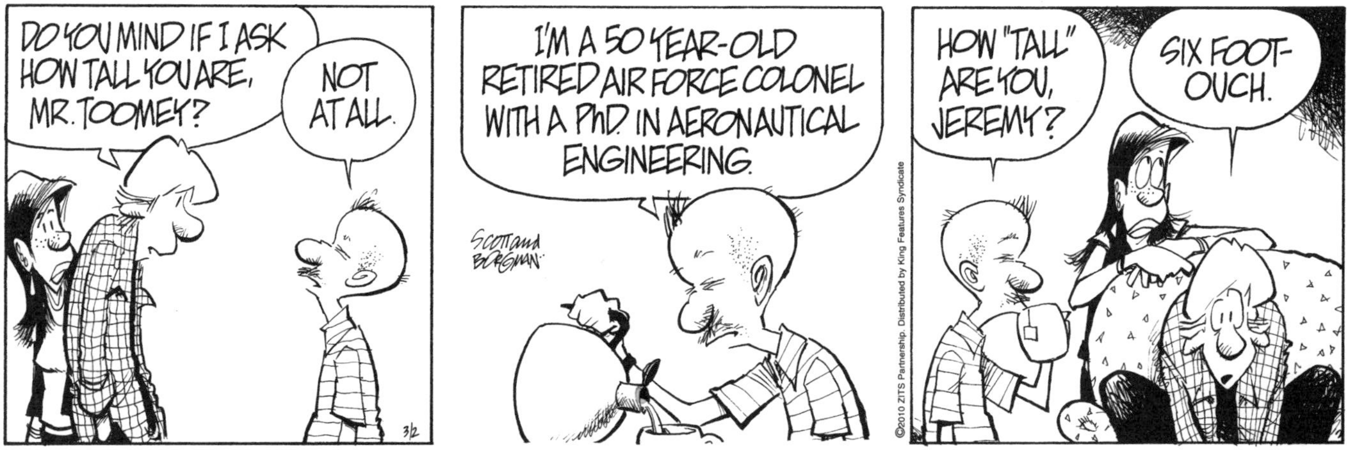
DO YOU MIND IF I ASK HOW TALL YOU ARE, MR. TOOMEY?
NOT AT ALL.
I'M A 50 YEAR-OLD RETIRED AIR FORCE COLONEL WITH A PhD. IN AERONAUTICAL ENGINEERING.
HOW "TALL" ARE YOU, JEREMY?
SIX FOOT-OUCH.
SCOTT and BORGMAN
3/2
©2010 ZITS Partnership. Distributed by King Features Syndicate

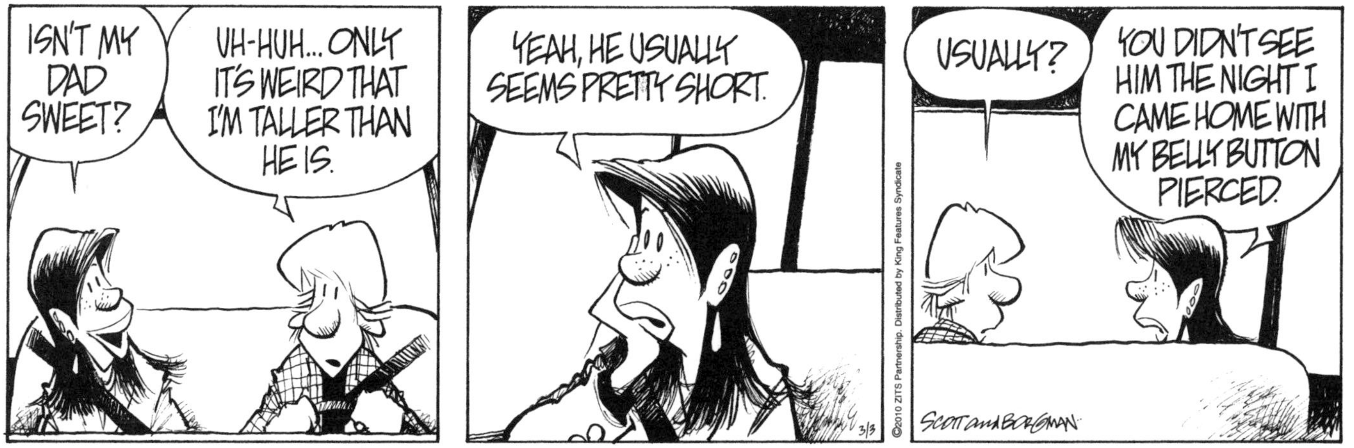
ISN'T MY DAD SWEET?
UH-HUH... ONLY IT'S WEIRD THAT I'M TALLER THAN HE IS.
YEAH, HE USUALLY SEEMS PRETTY SHORT.
USUALLY?
YOU DIDN'T SEE HIM THE NIGHT I CAME HOME WITH MY BELLY BUTTON PIERCED.
SCOTT and BORGMAN
3/3
©2010 ZITS Partnership. Distributed by King Features Syndicate

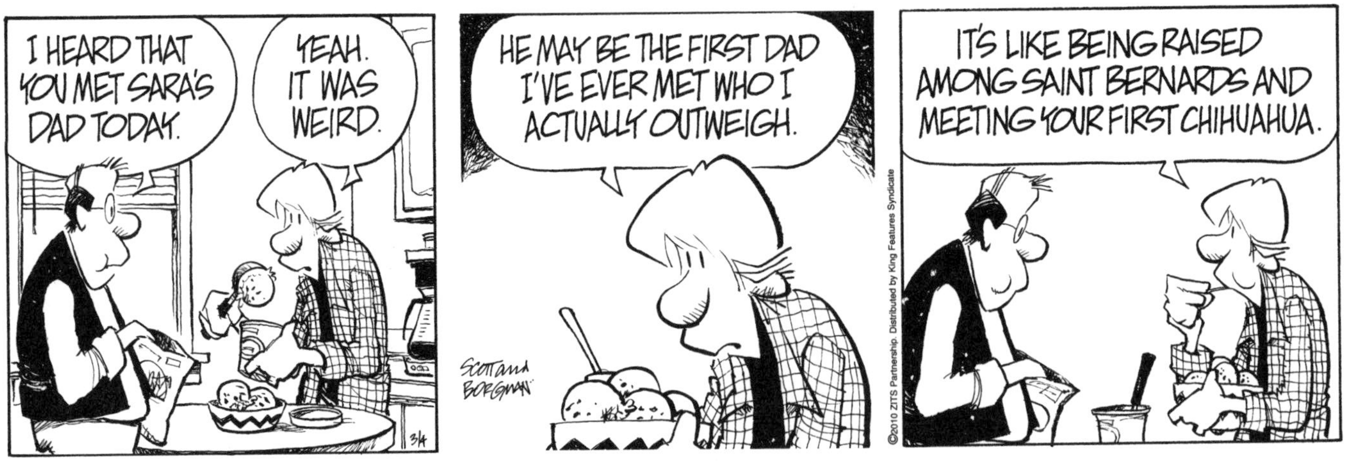
I HEARD THAT YOU MET SARA'S DAD TODAY.
YEAH. IT WAS WEIRD.
HE MAY BE THE FIRST DAD I'VE EVER MET WHO I ACTUALLY OUTWEIGH.
IT'S LIKE BEING RAISED AMONG SAINT BERNARDS AND MEETING YOUR FIRST CHIHUAHUA.
3/4
SCOTT and BORGMAN
©2010 ZITS Partnership. Distributed by King Features Syndicate

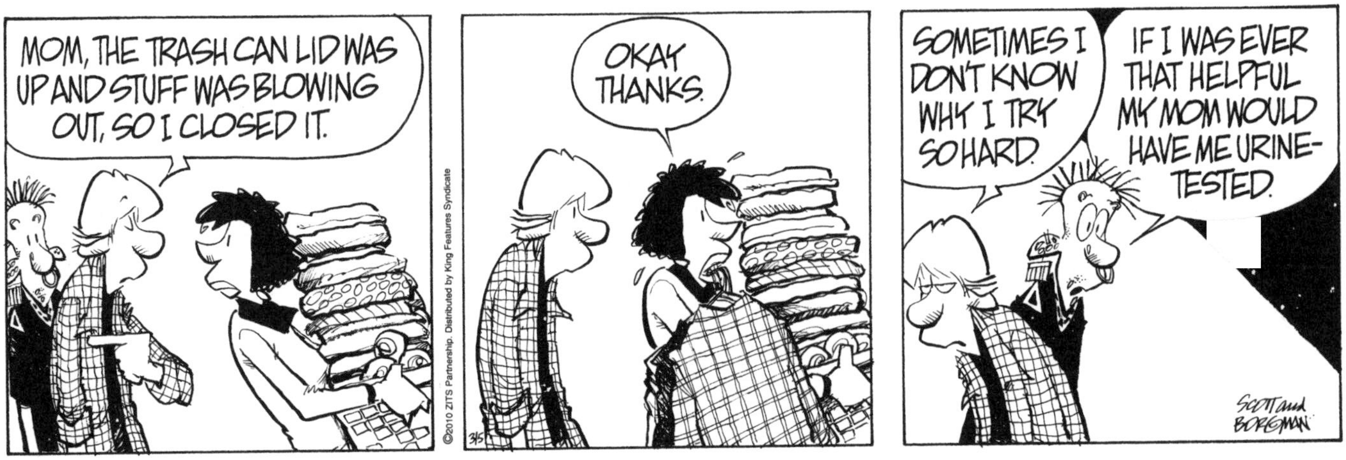
MOM, THE TRASH CAN LID WAS UP AND STUFF WAS BLOWING OUT, SO I CLOSED IT.
OKAY THANKS.
SOMETIMES I DON'T KNOW WHY I TRY SO HARD.
IF I WAS EVER THAT HELPFUL MY MOM WOULD HAVE ME URINE-TESTED.
3/5
SCOTT and BORGMAN
©2010 ZITS Partnership. Distributed by King Features Syndicate

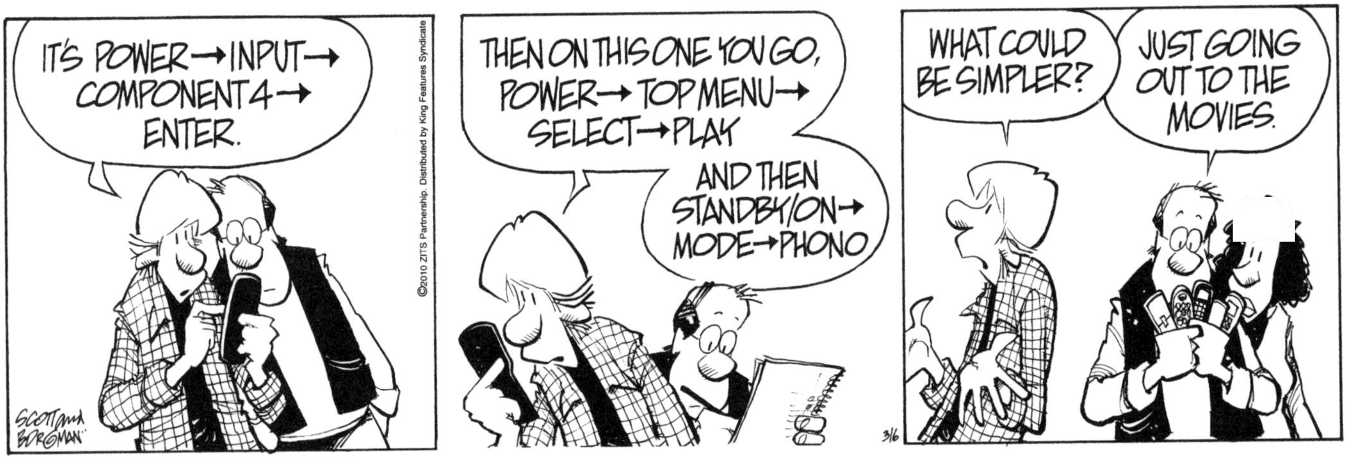
IT'S POWER→INPUT→ COMPONENT 4→ ENTER.
THEN ON THIS ONE YOU GO, POWER→TOP MENU→ SELECT→PLAY
AND THEN STANDBY/ON→ MODE→PHONO
WHAT COULD BE SIMPLER?
JUST GOING OUT TO THE MOVIES.
3/6
SCOTT and BORGMAN
©2010 ZITS Partnership. Distributed by King Features Syndicate

Zits
by JERRY SCOTT and JIM BORGMAN

MOM, HAVE YOU SEEN MY PHONE?
NO...
...BUT I'LL DIAL YOUR NUMBER SO YOU CAN--
FORGET IT. THE BATTERY WAS ALMOST DEAD.
THE CHANCES THAT IT'LL RING ARE LIKE, A TRILLION TO ONE!
OH.
THEN I GUESS YOU'LL JUST HAVE TO SEARCH YOUR ROOM.
ON SECOND THOUGHT, LET'S GIVE THAT NUMBER A TRY.
OUT!
SCOTT and BORGMAN 3/7
©2010 ZITS Partnership. Distributed by King Features Syndicate

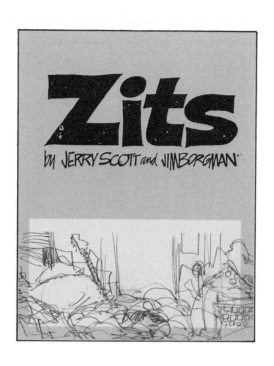

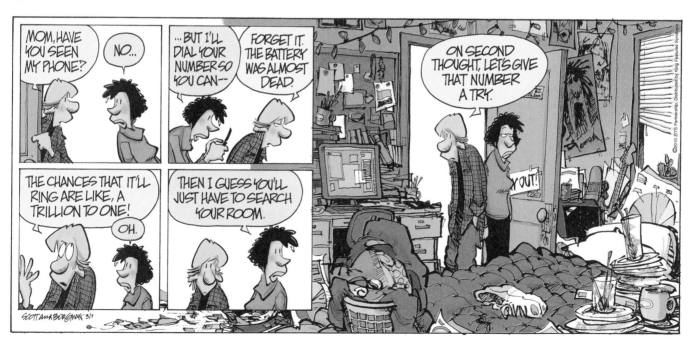

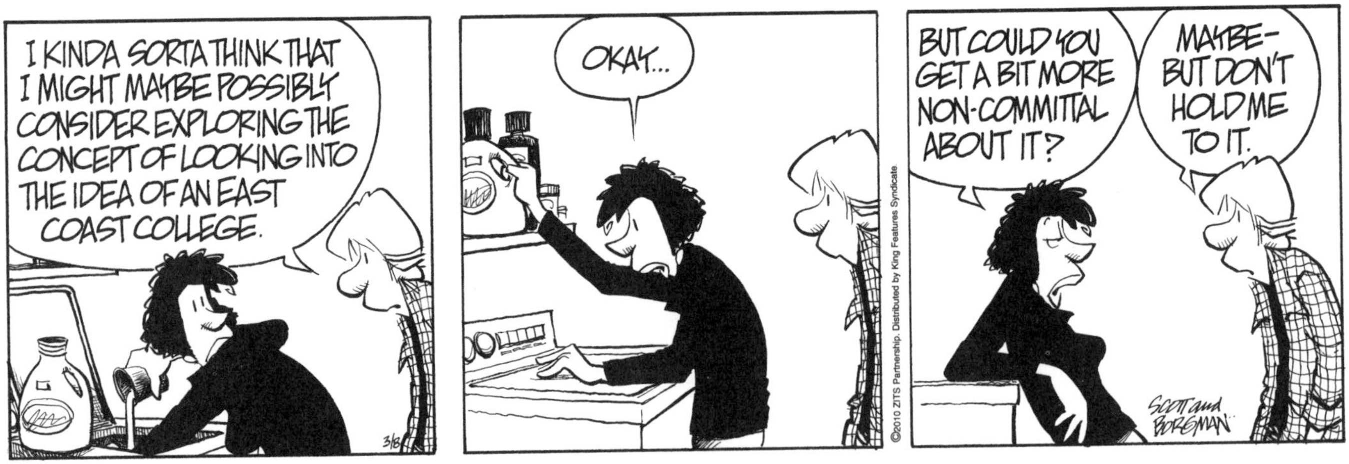
I KINDA SORTA THINK THAT I MIGHT MAYBE POSSIBLY CONSIDER EXPLORING THE CONCEPT OF LOOKING INTO THE IDEA OF AN EAST COAST COLLEGE.
3/8
OKAY...
©2010 ZITS Partnership. Distributed by King Features Syndicate.
BUT COULD YOU GET A BIT MORE NON-COMMITTAL ABOUT IT?
MAYBE- BUT DON'T HOLD ME TO IT.
SCOTT and BORGMAN

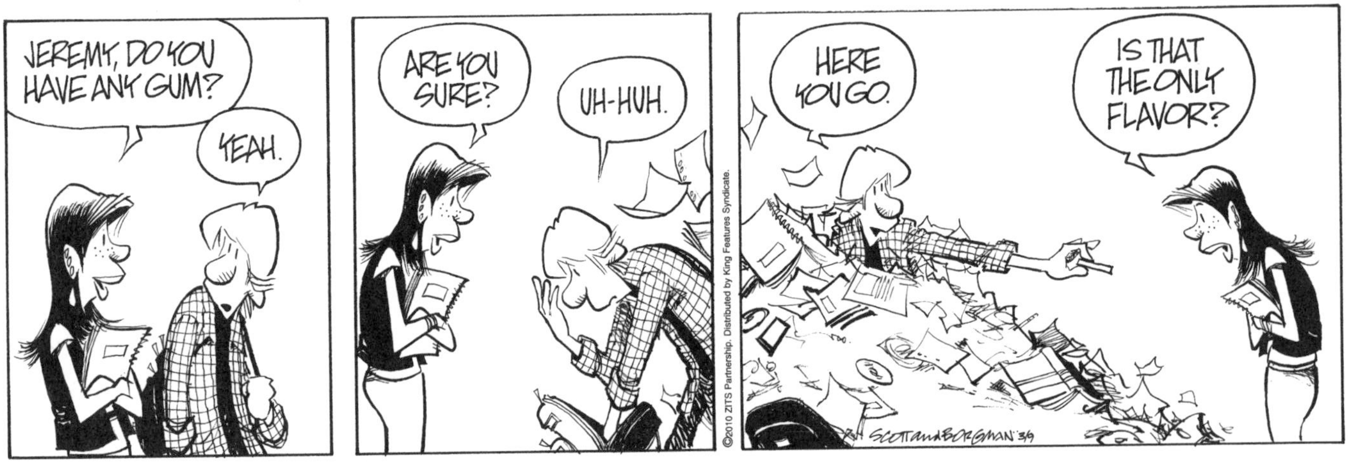
JEREMY, DO YOU HAVE ANY GUM?
YEAH.
ARE YOU SURE?
UH-HUH.
©2010 ZITS Partnership. Distributed by King Features Syndicate.
HERE YOU GO.
IS THAT THE ONLY FLAVOR?
SCOTT and BORGMAN 3/9

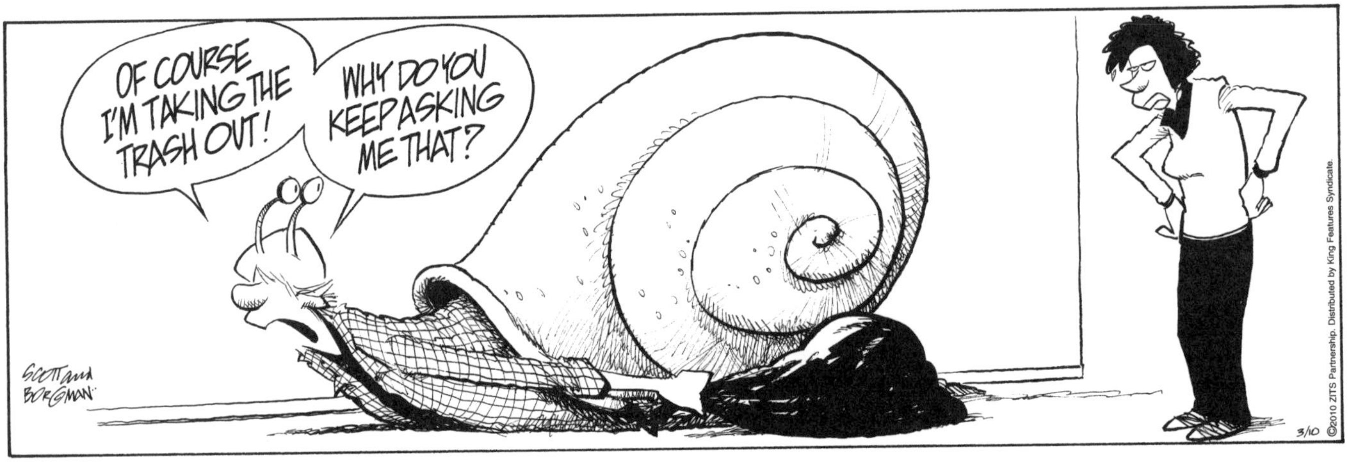
OF COURSE I'M TAKING THE TRASH OUT!
WHY DO YOU KEEP ASKING ME THAT?
SCOTT and BORGMAN
3/10
©2010 ZITS Partnership. Distributed by King Features Syndicate.

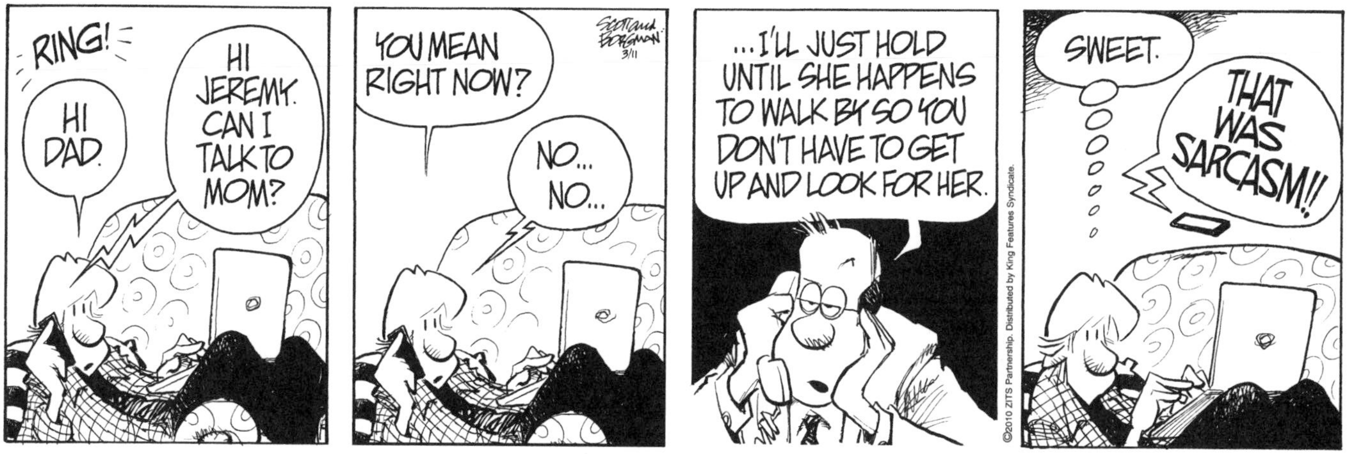
RING!
HI DAD.
HI JEREMY. CAN I TALK TO MOM?
SCOTT and BORGMAN 3/11
YOU MEAN RIGHT NOW?
NO... NO...
...I'LL JUST HOLD UNTIL SHE HAPPENS TO WALK BY SO YOU DON'T HAVE TO GET UP AND LOOK FOR HER.
©2010 ZITS Partnership. Distributed by King Features Syndicate.
SWEET.
THAT WAS SARCASM!!

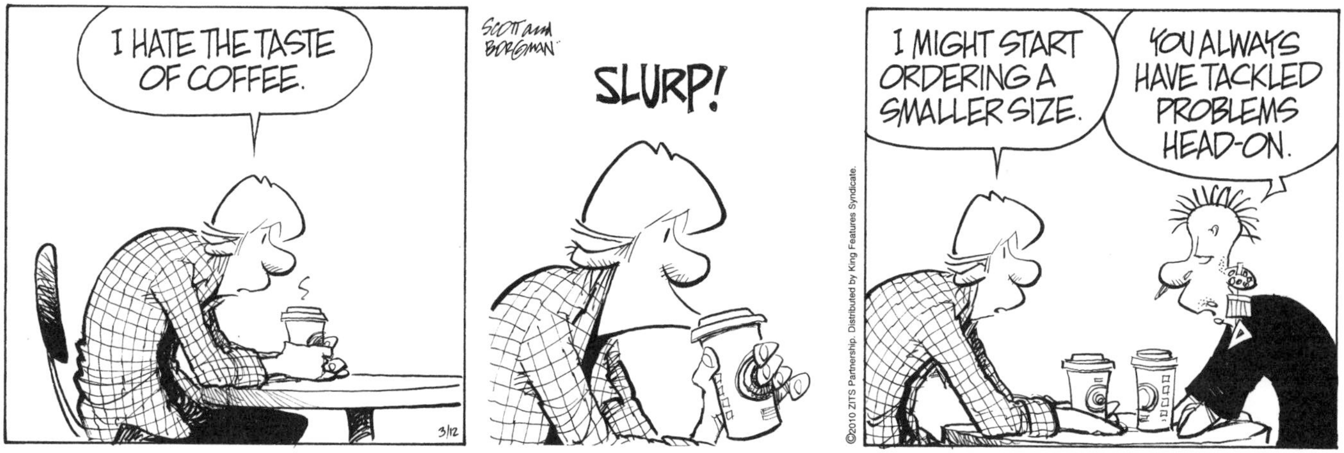
I HATE THE TASTE OF COFFEE.
3/12
SCOTT and BORGMAN
SLURP!
©2010 ZITS Partnership. Distributed by King Features Syndicate.
I MIGHT START ORDERING A SMALLER SIZE.
YOU ALWAYS HAVE TACKLED PROBLEMS HEAD-ON.

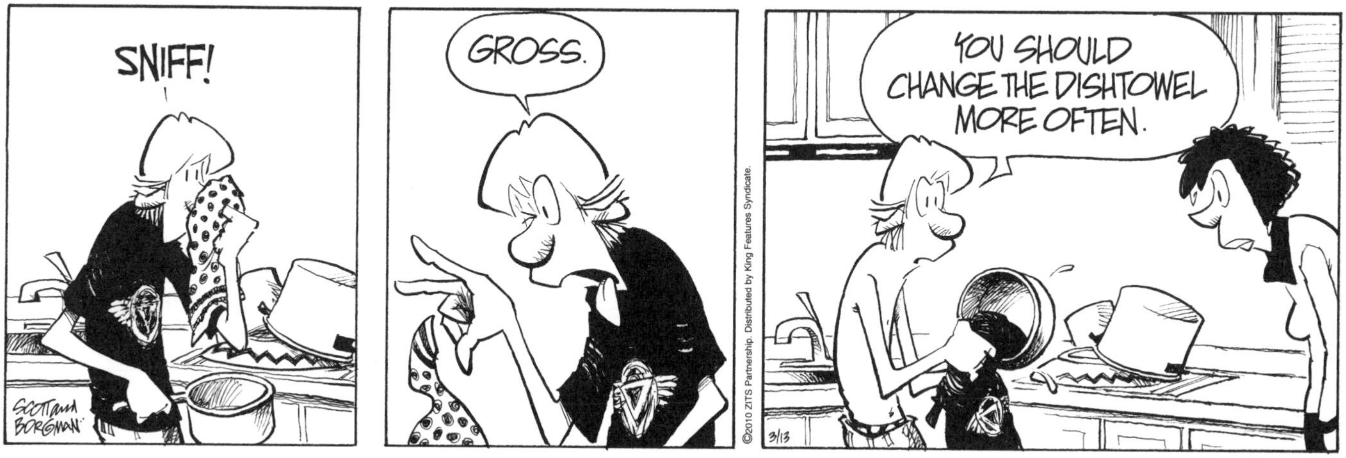
SNIFF!
SCOTT and BORGMAN
GROSS.
©2010 ZITS Partnership. Distributed by King Features Syndicate.
YOU SHOULD CHANGE THE DISHTOWEL MORE OFTEN.
3/13

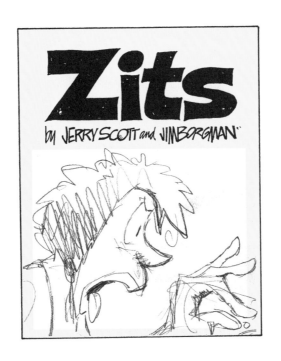

Zits
by JERRY SCOTT and JIM BORGMAN

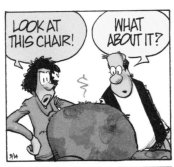

LOOK AT THIS CHAIR!
WHAT ABOUT IT?
3/14
IT'S COVERED WITH FOOD STAINS, DRINK RINGS, SHOE PRINTS AND CRUMBS!
HOW DID IT GET SO DISGUSTING?
SCOTT and BORGMAN
ON THE OTHER HAND, HOW HAS IT STAYED THIS NICE?
©2010 ZITS Partnership. Distributed by King Features Syndicate

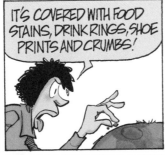

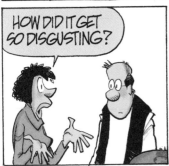

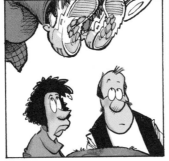

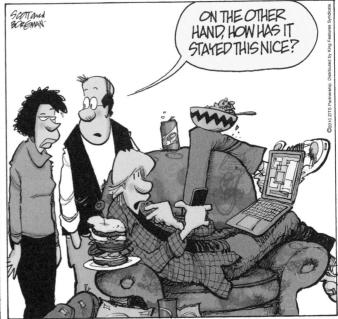

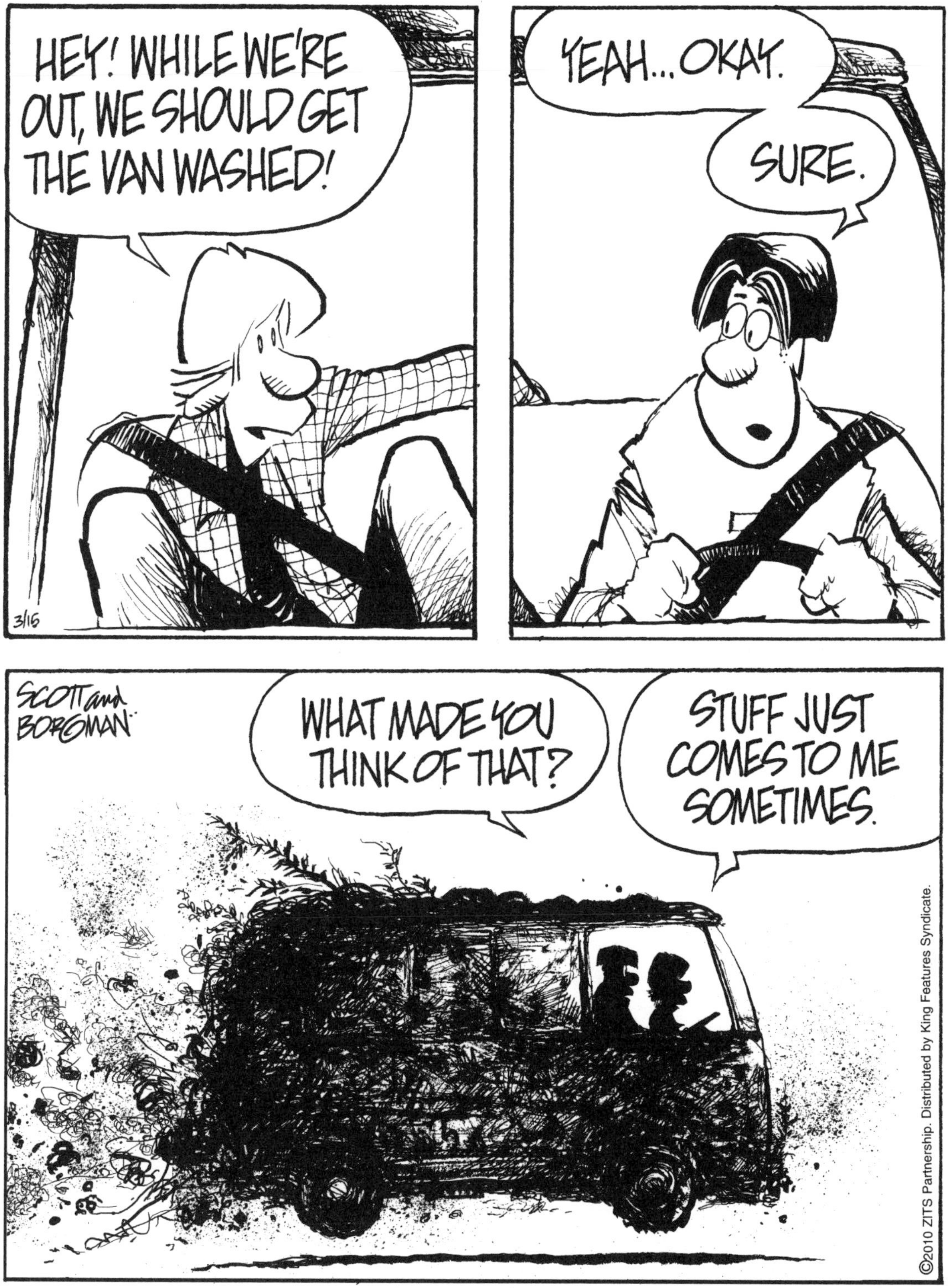
HEY! WHILE WE'RE OUT, WE SHOULD GET THE VAN WASHED!
YEAH... OKAY.
SURE.
3/15
SCOTT and BORGMAN
WHAT MADE YOU THINK OF THAT?
STUFF JUST COMES TO ME SOMETIMES.
©2010 ZITS Partnership. Distributed by King Features Syndicate.

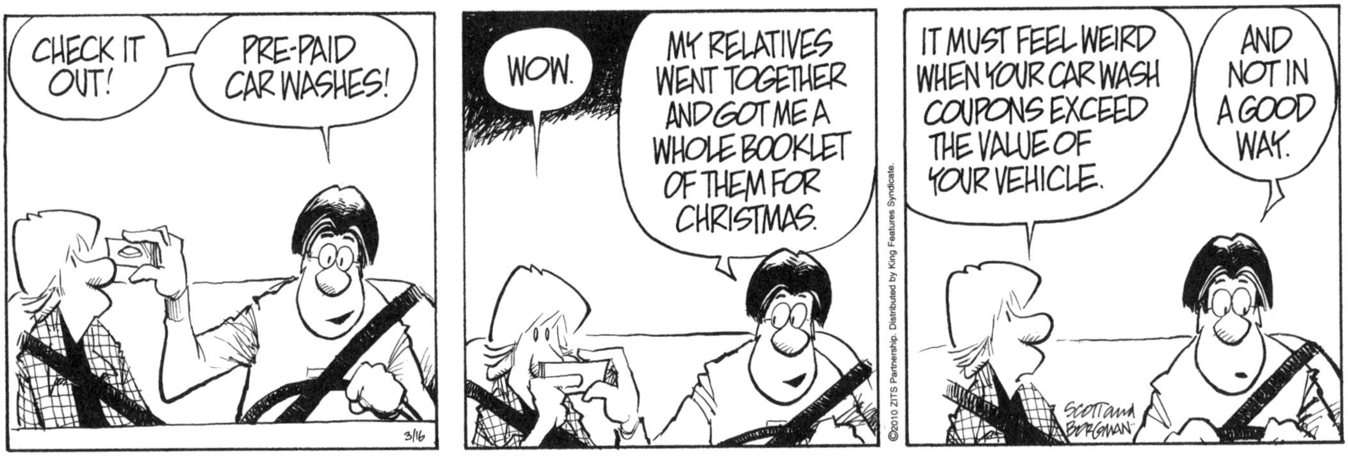
CHECK IT OUT!
PRE-PAID CAR WASHES!
WOW.
MY RELATIVES WENT TOGETHER AND GOT ME A WHOLE BOOKLET OF THEM FOR CHRISTMAS.
IT MUST FEEL WEIRD WHEN YOUR CAR WASH COUPONS EXCEED THE VALUE OF YOUR VEHICLE.
AND NOT IN A GOOD WAY.
SCOTT and BORGMAN
3/16
©2010 ZITS Partnership. Distributed by King Features Syndicate.

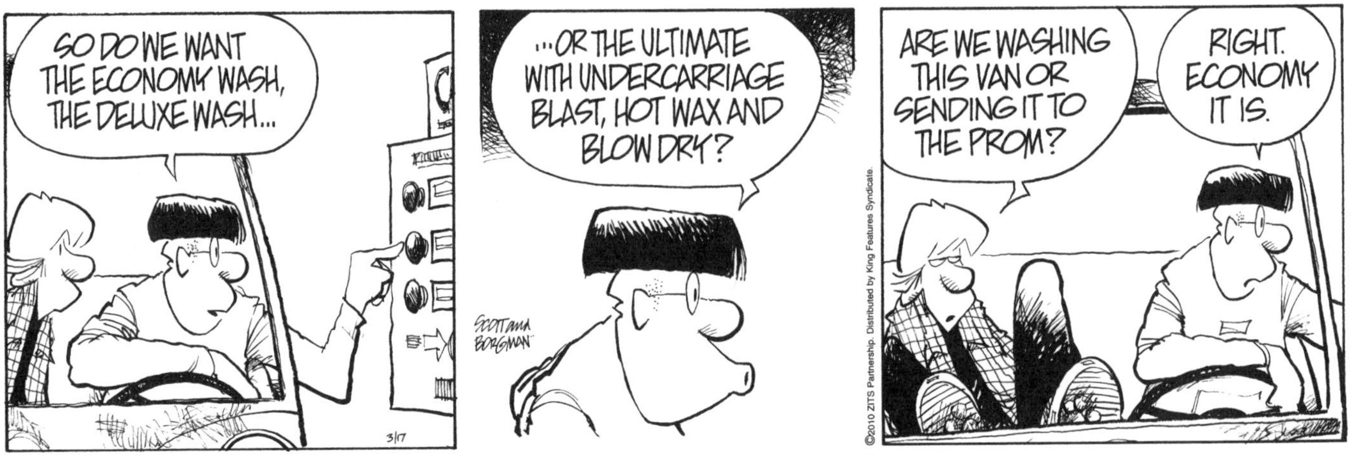
SO DO WE WANT THE ECONOMY WASH, THE DELUXE WASH...
...OR THE ULTIMATE WITH UNDERCARRIAGE BLAST, HOT WAX AND BLOW DRY?
ARE WE WASHING THIS VAN OR SENDING IT TO THE PROM?
RIGHT. ECONOMY IT IS.
SCOTT and BORGMAN
3/17
©2010 ZITS Partnership. Distributed by King Features Syndicate.

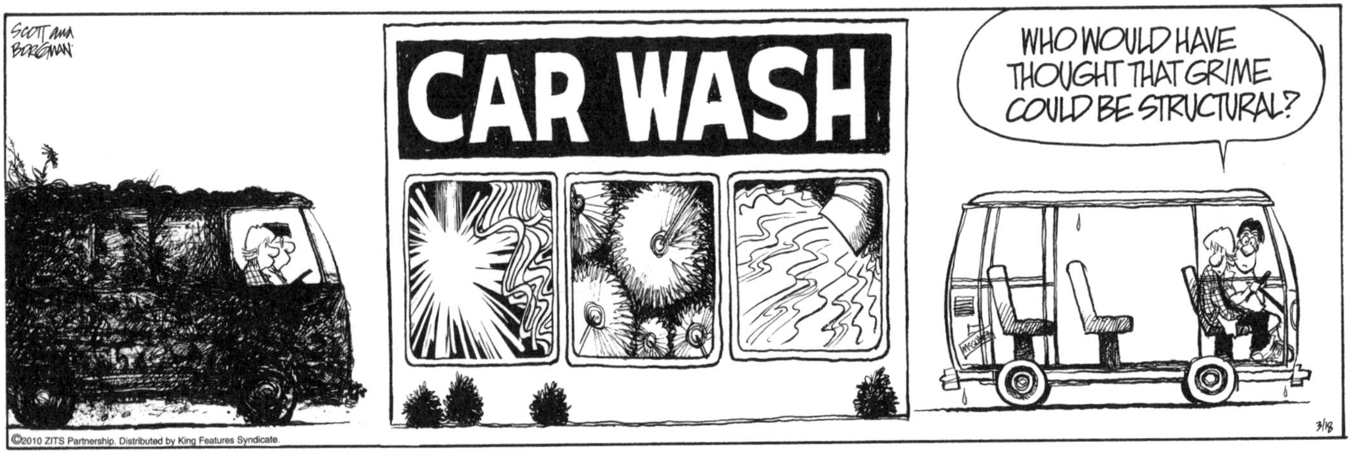
SCOTT and BORGMAN
CAR WASH
WHO WOULD HAVE THOUGHT THAT GRIME COULD BE STRUCTURAL?
3/18
©2010 ZITS Partnership. Distributed by King Features Syndicate.

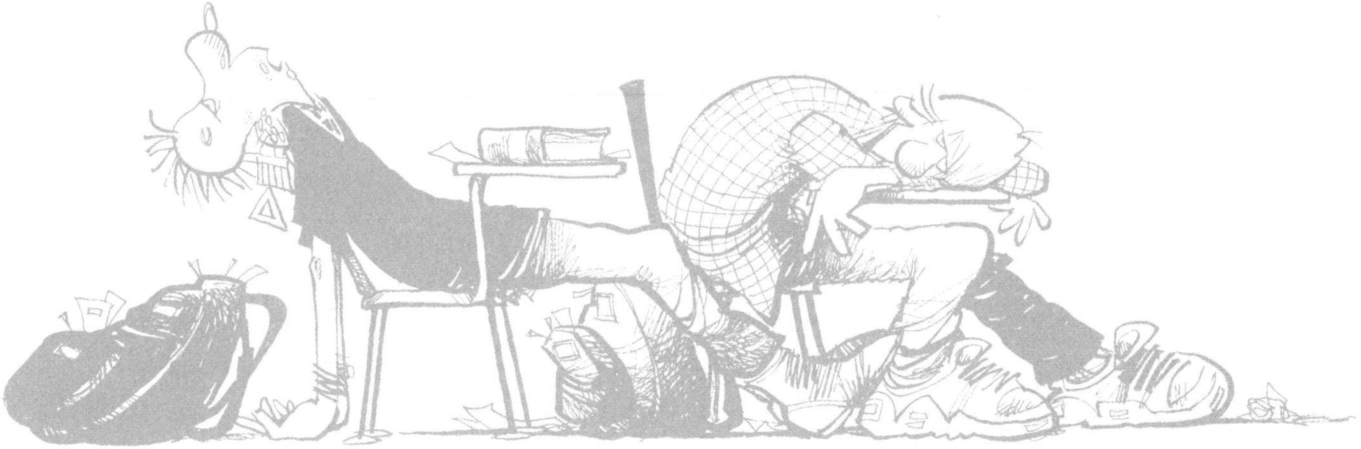

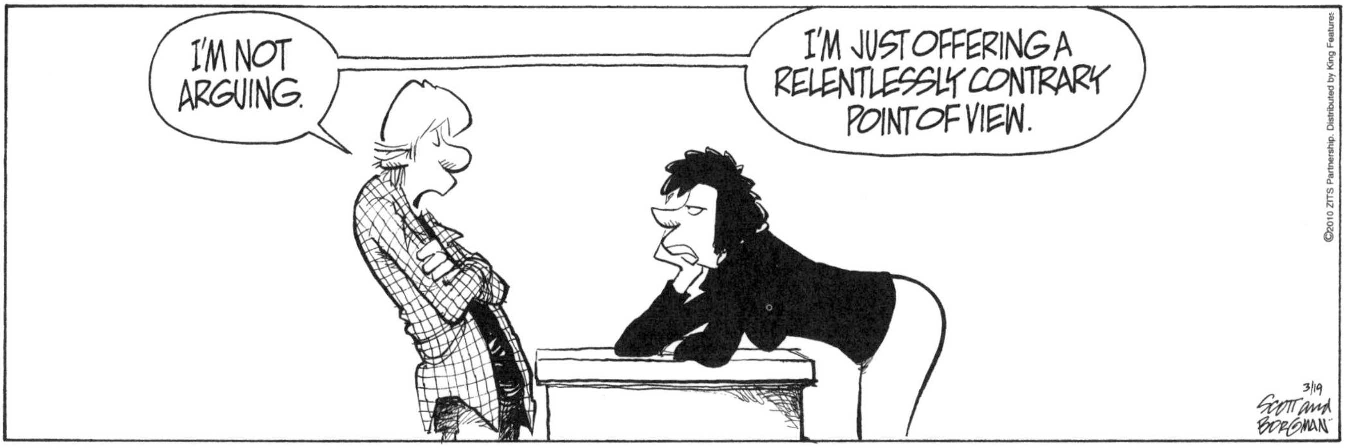
I'M NOT ARGUING.
I'M JUST OFFERING A RELENTLESSLY CONTRARY POINT OF VIEW.
©2010 ZITS Partnership. Distributed by King Features
3/19
SCOTT and BORGMAN

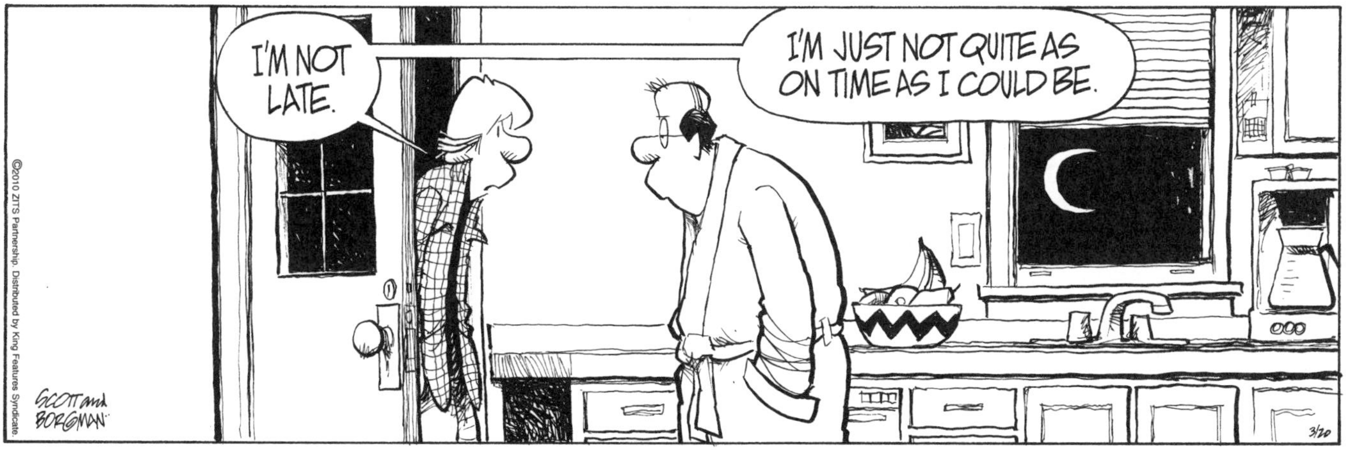
I'M NOT LATE.
I'M JUST NOT QUITE AS ON TIME AS I COULD BE.
©2010 ZITS Partnership. Distributed by King Features Syndicate.
SCOTT and BORGMAN
3/20

Zits
by JERRY SCOTT and JIM BORGMAN

NOW THAT'S JUST DESPERATE.
AH, BUT YOU'RE TALKING TO ME!
HI JEREMY. HOW WAS YOUR DAY?
STAY OUT
SCOTT and BORGMAN
©2010 ZITS Partnership. Distributed by King Features Syndicate.
3/21

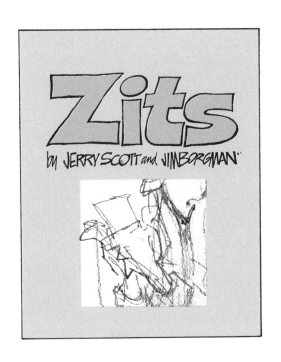

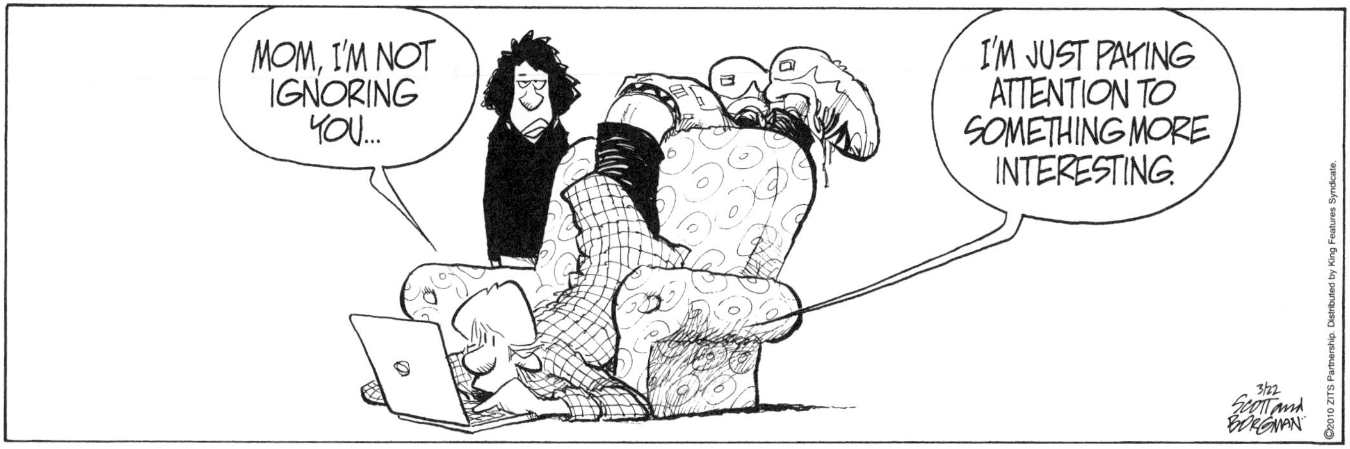
MOM, I'M NOT IGNORING YOU...
I'M JUST PAYING ATTENTION TO SOMETHING MORE INTERESTING.
3/22 SCOTT and BORGMAN
©2010 ZITS Partnership. Distributed by King Features Syndicate.

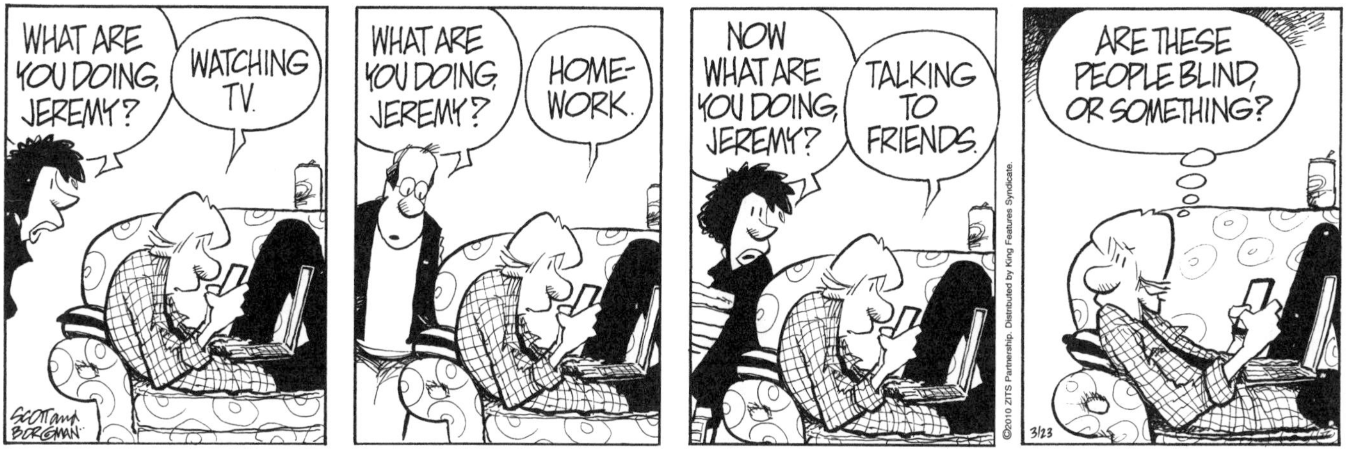
WHAT ARE YOU DOING, JEREMY?
WATCHING TV.
SCOTT and BORGMAN
WHAT ARE YOU DOING, JEREMY?
HOME-WORK.
NOW WHAT ARE YOU DOING, JEREMY?
TALKING TO FRIENDS.
©2010 ZITS Partnership. Distributed by King Features Syndicate.
ARE THESE PEOPLE BLIND, OR SOMETHING?
3/23

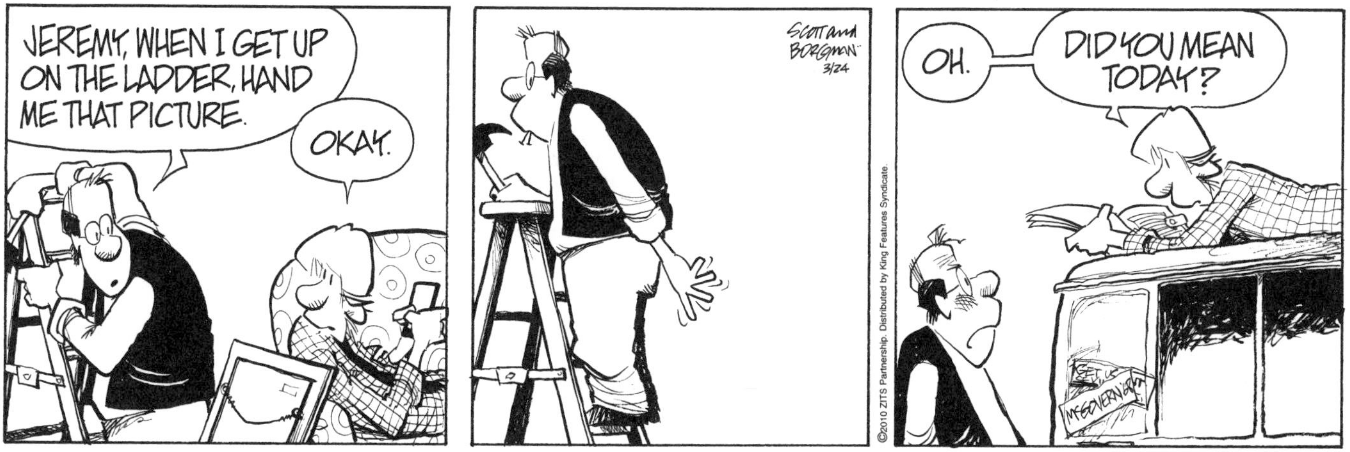
JEREMY, WHEN I GET UP ON THE LADDER, HAND ME THAT PICTURE.
OKAY.
SCOTT and BORGMAN 3/24
©2010 ZITS Partnership. Distributed by King Features Syndicate.
OH.
DID YOU MEAN TODAY?

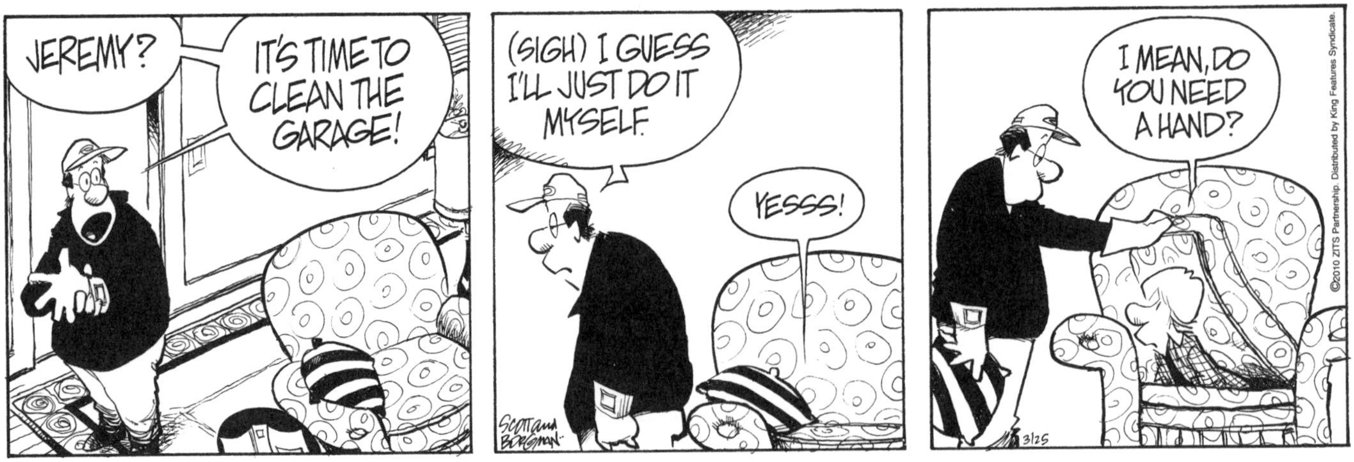
JEREMY?
IT'S TIME TO CLEAN THE GARAGE!
(SIGH) I GUESS I'LL JUST DO IT MYSELF.
YESSS!
I MEAN, DO YOU NEED A HAND?
SCOTT and BORGMAN
3/25
©2010 ZITS Partnership. Distributed by King Features Syndicate.

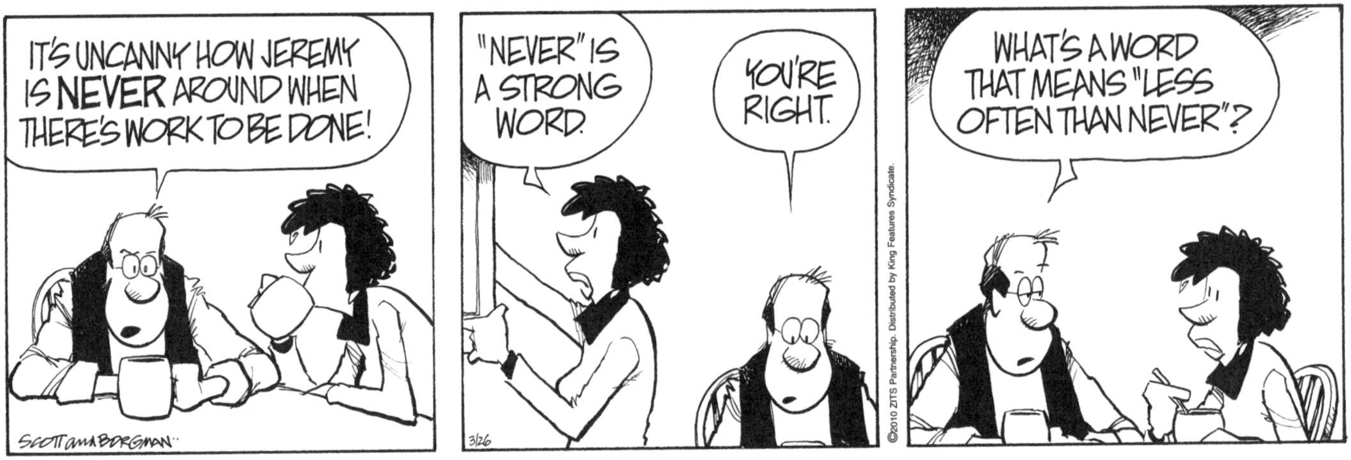
IT'S UNCANNY HOW JEREMY IS NEVER AROUND WHEN THERE'S WORK TO BE DONE!
"NEVER" IS A STRONG WORD.
YOU'RE RIGHT.
WHAT'S A WORD THAT MEANS "LESS OFTEN THAN NEVER"?
SCOTT and BORGMAN
3/26
©2010 ZITS Partnership. Distributed by King Features Syndicate.

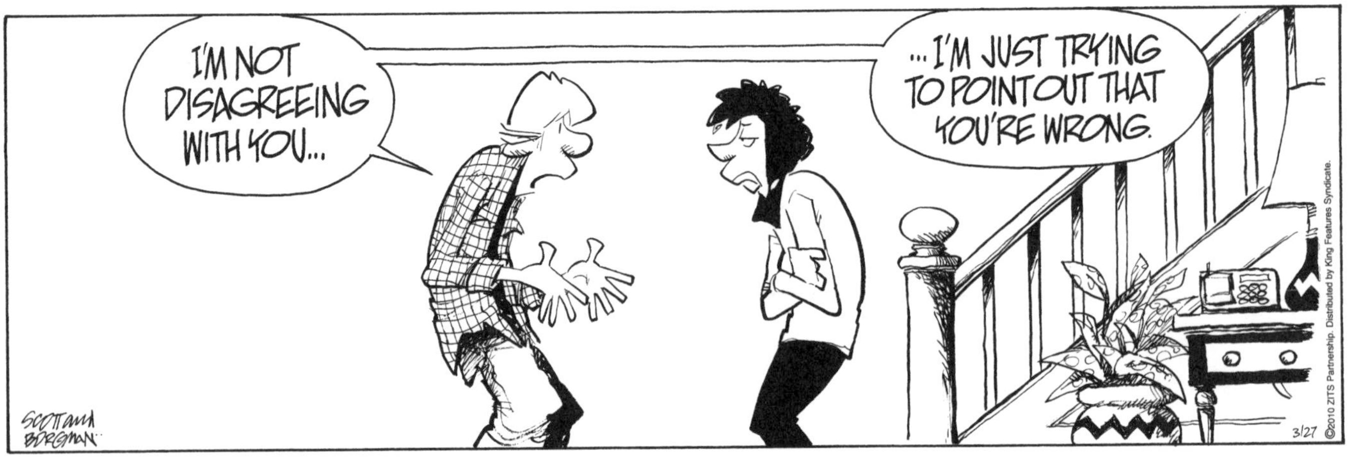
I'M NOT DISAGREEING WITH YOU...
...I'M JUST TRYING TO POINT OUT THAT YOU'RE WRONG.
SCOTT and BORGMAN
3/27
©2010 ZITS Partnership. Distributed by King Features Syndicate.

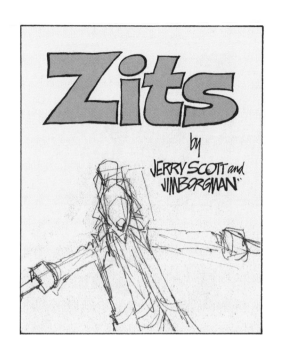

Zits
by
JERRY SCOTT and
JIM BORGMAN

3/28
I'VE GOT NOPLACE TO GO, NOBODY TO SEE, ALL OF MY FRIENDS ARE BUSY...
...AND I'M STUCK HERE AT HOME WITH NOTHING TO DO!
SCOTT AND BORGMAN
THROW IN A FOOT RUB AND HE'S DESCRIBED MY IDEA OF THE PERFECT EVENING.
TAKE OFF YOUR SOCKS.
©2010 ZITS Partnership. Distributed by King Features Syndicate.

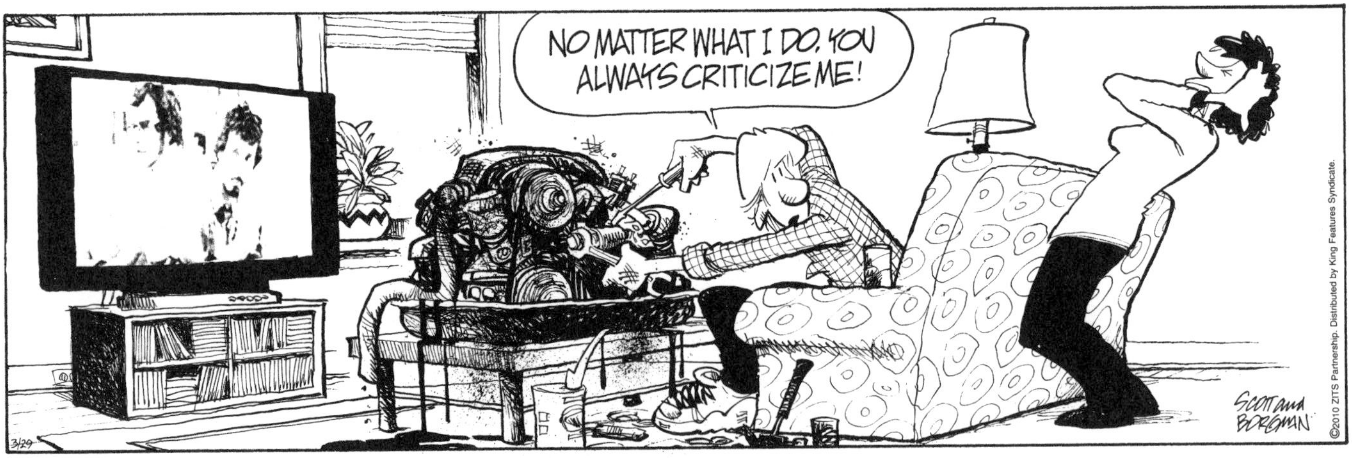
NO MATTER WHAT I DO, YOU ALWAYS CRITICIZE ME!
SCOTT and BORGMAN
3/29
©2010 ZITS Partnership. Distributed by King Features Syndicate.

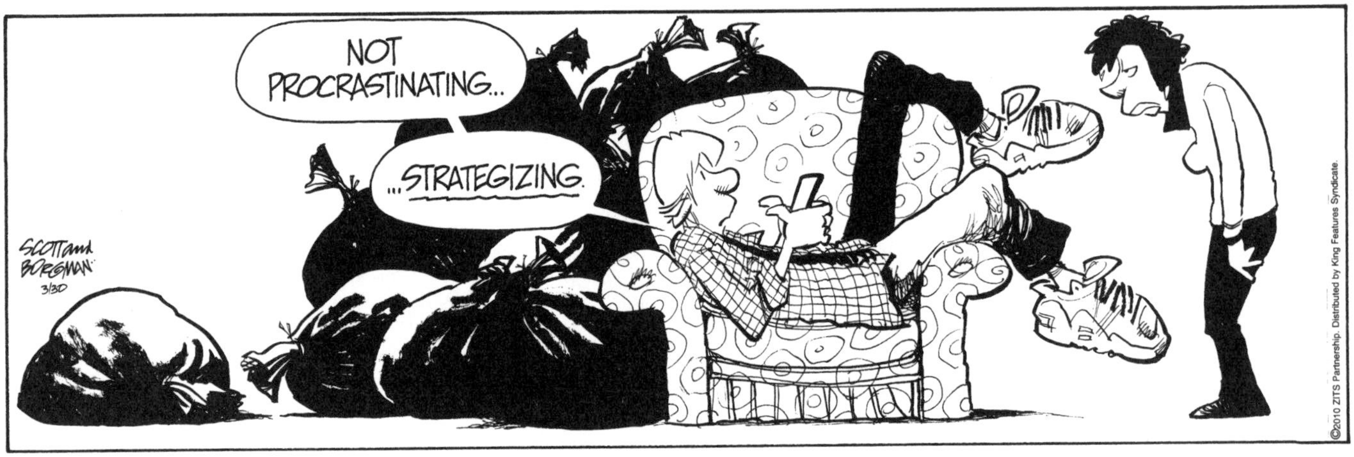
NOT PROCRASTINATING...
...STRATEGIZING.
SCOTT and BORGMAN
3/30
©2010 ZITS Partnership. Distributed by King Features Syndicate.

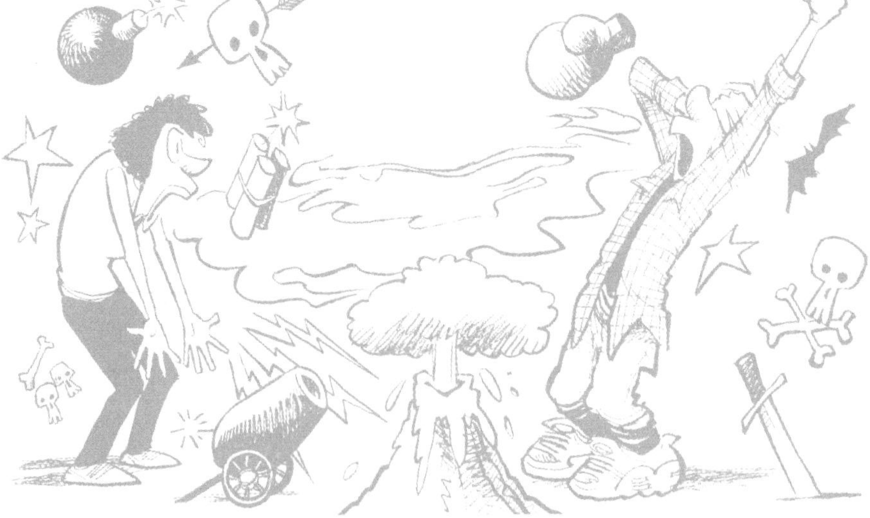

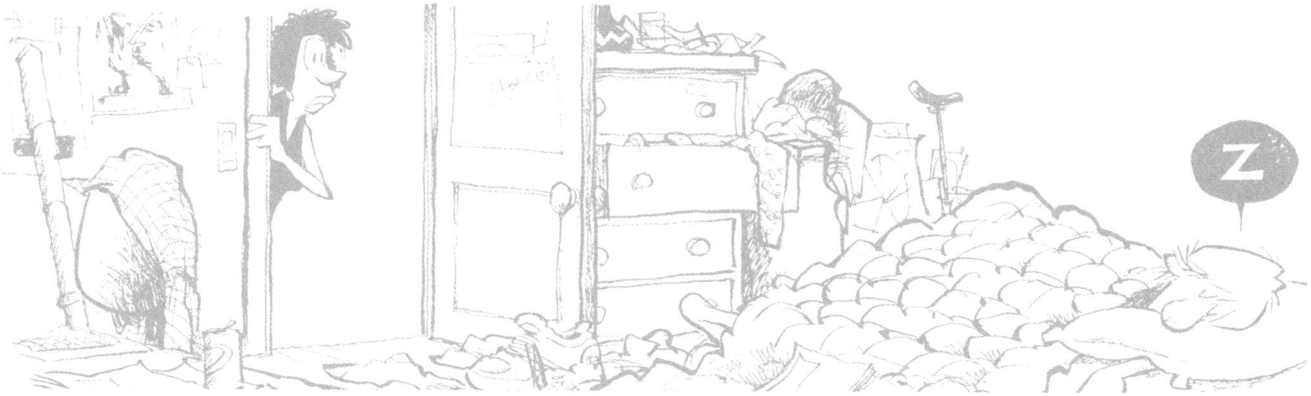
Z

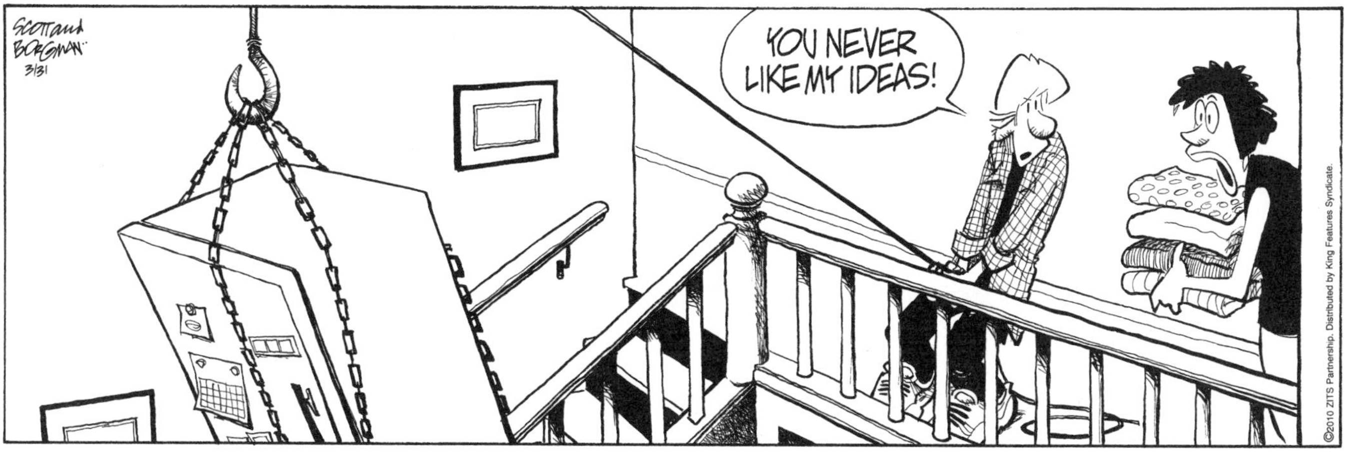
SCOTT and BORGMAN 3/31
YOU NEVER LIKE MY IDEAS!
©2010 ZITS Partnership. Distributed by King Features Syndicate.

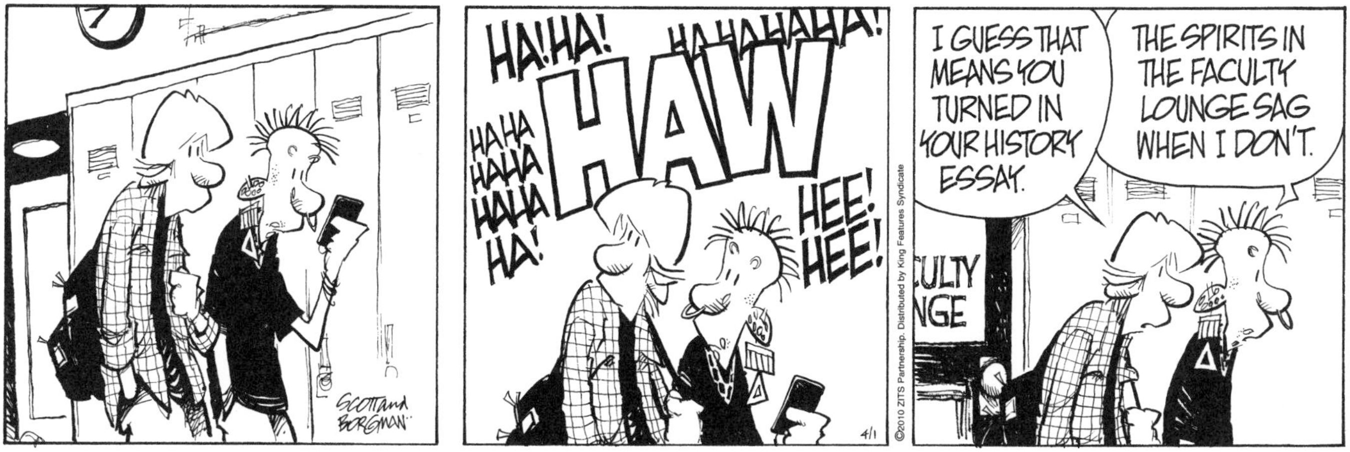
SCOTT and BORGMAN
HA! HA!
HA HA HA HA HA!
HA HA HA HA HA HA HA!
HAW
HEE! HEE!
4/1
©2010 ZITS Partnership. Distributed by King Features Syndicate
I GUESS THAT MEANS YOU TURNED IN YOUR HISTORY ESSAY.
THE SPIRITS IN THE FACULTY LOUNGE SAG WHEN I DON'T.

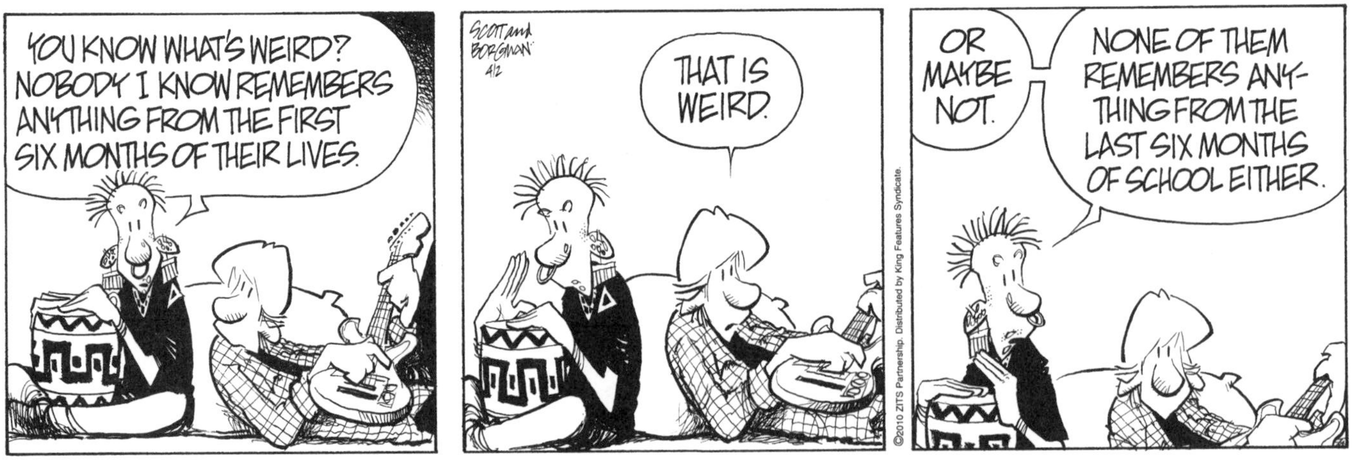
YOU KNOW WHAT'S WEIRD? NOBODY I KNOW REMEMBERS ANYTHING FROM THE FIRST SIX MONTHS OF THEIR LIVES.
THAT IS WEIRD.
OR MAYBE NOT.
NONE OF THEM REMEMBERS ANYTHING FROM THE LAST SIX MONTHS OF SCHOOL EITHER.
©2010 ZITS Partnership. Distributed by King Features Syndicate.

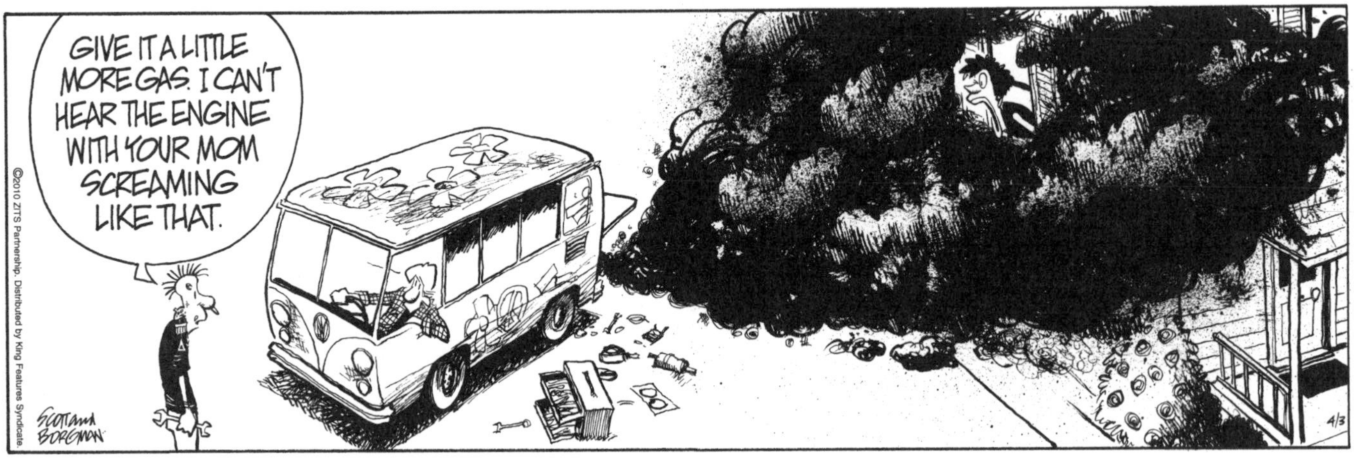
GIVE IT A LITTLE MORE GAS. I CAN'T HEAR THE ENGINE WITH YOUR MOM SCREAMING LIKE THAT.
©2010 ZITS Partnership. Distributed by King Features Syndicate.

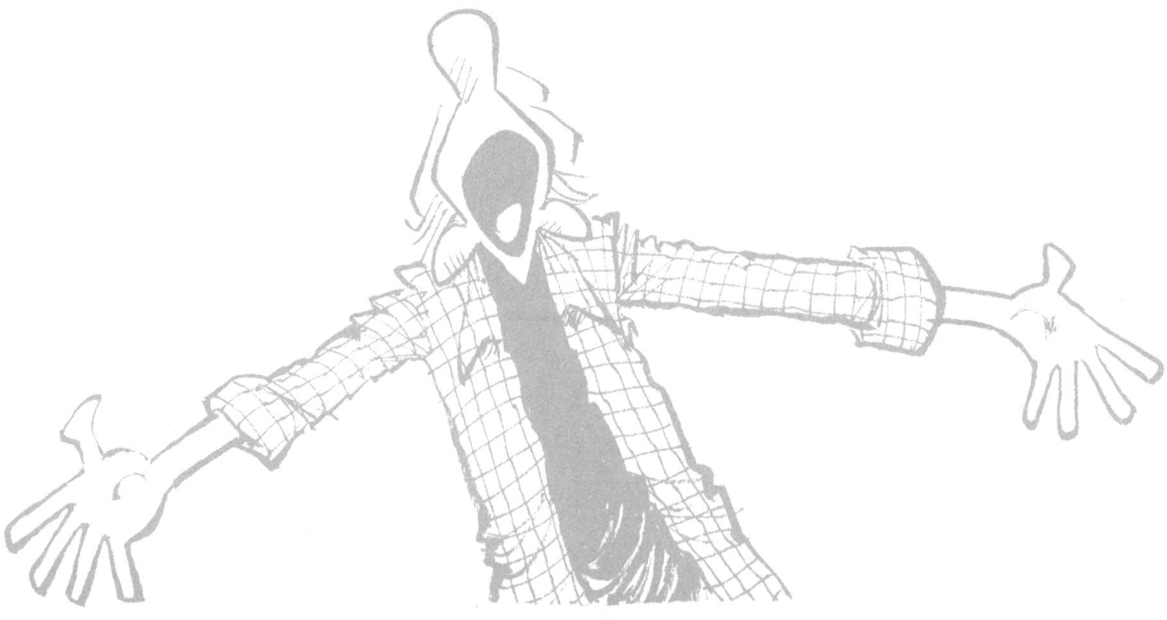

Zits
by JERRY SCOTT and JIM BORGMAN

GET UP.
GET UP.
GET UP!
GET UP?
DID YOU SAY SOMETHING?
SCOTT and BORGMAN
4/4
©2010 ZITS Partnership. Distributed by King Features Syndicate.

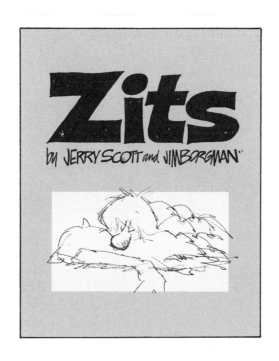

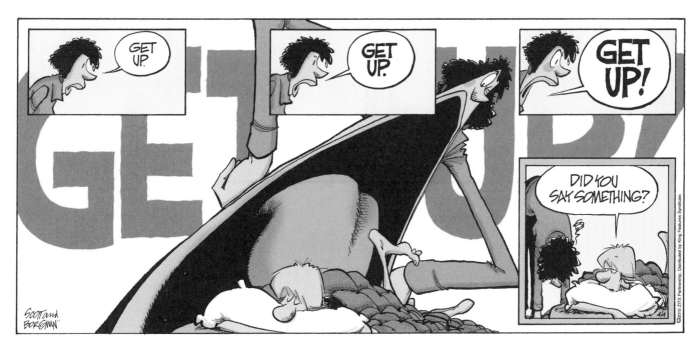

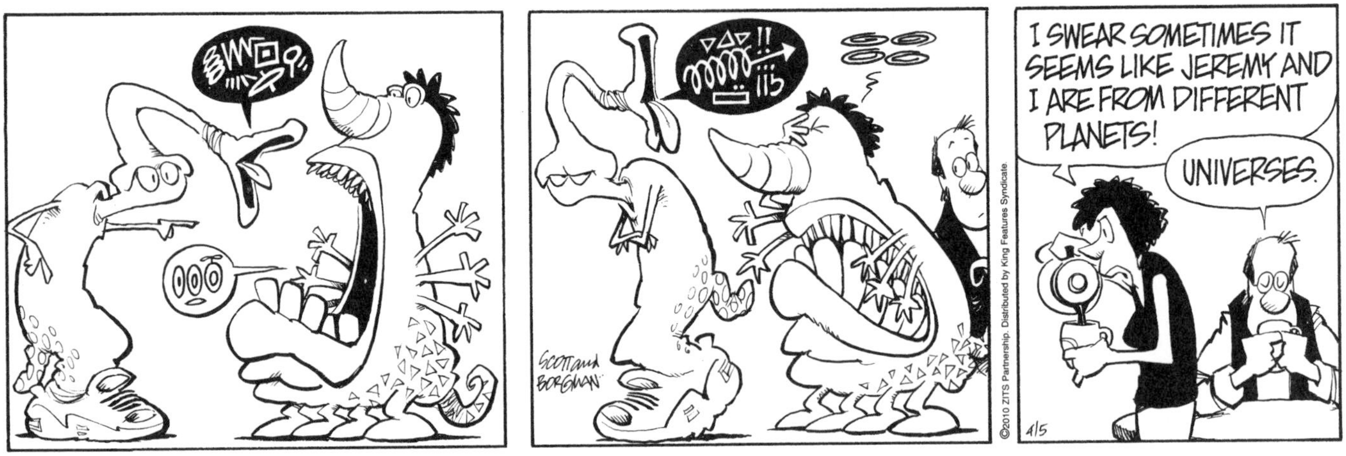
SCOTT and BORGMAN
I SWEAR SOMETIMES IT SEEMS LIKE JEREMY AND I ARE FROM DIFFERENT PLANETS!
UNIVERSES.
©2010 ZITS Partnership. Distributed by King Features Syndicate.
4/5

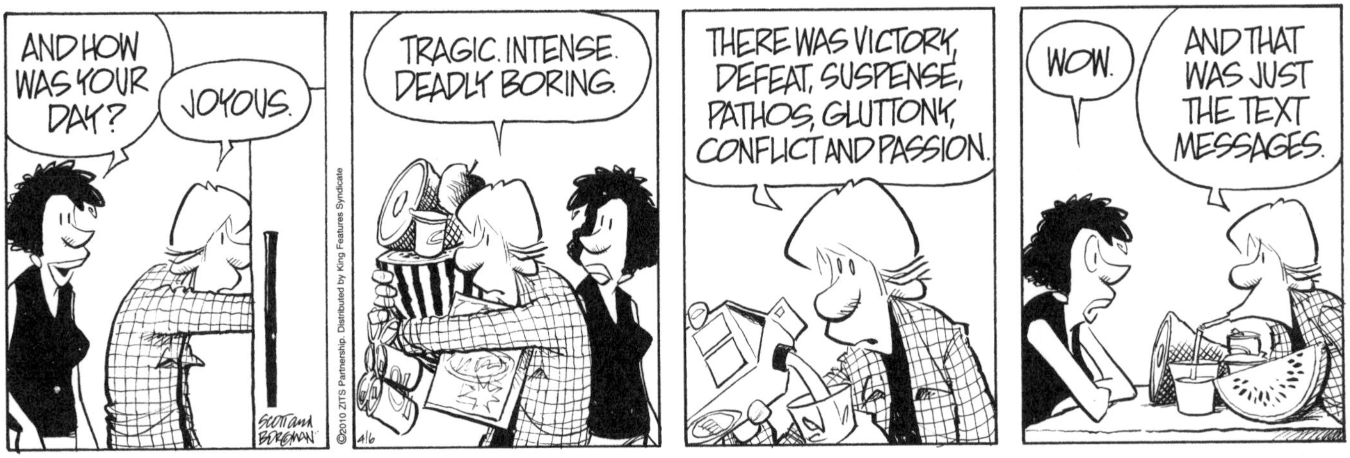
AND HOW WAS YOUR DAY?
JOYOUS.
SCOTT and BORGMAN
©2010 ZITS Partnership. Distributed by King Features Syndicate
4/6
TRAGIC. INTENSE. DEADLY BORING.
THERE WAS VICTORY, DEFEAT, SUSPENSE, PATHOS, GLUTTONY, CONFLICT AND PASSION.
WOW.
AND THAT WAS JUST THE TEXT MESSAGES.

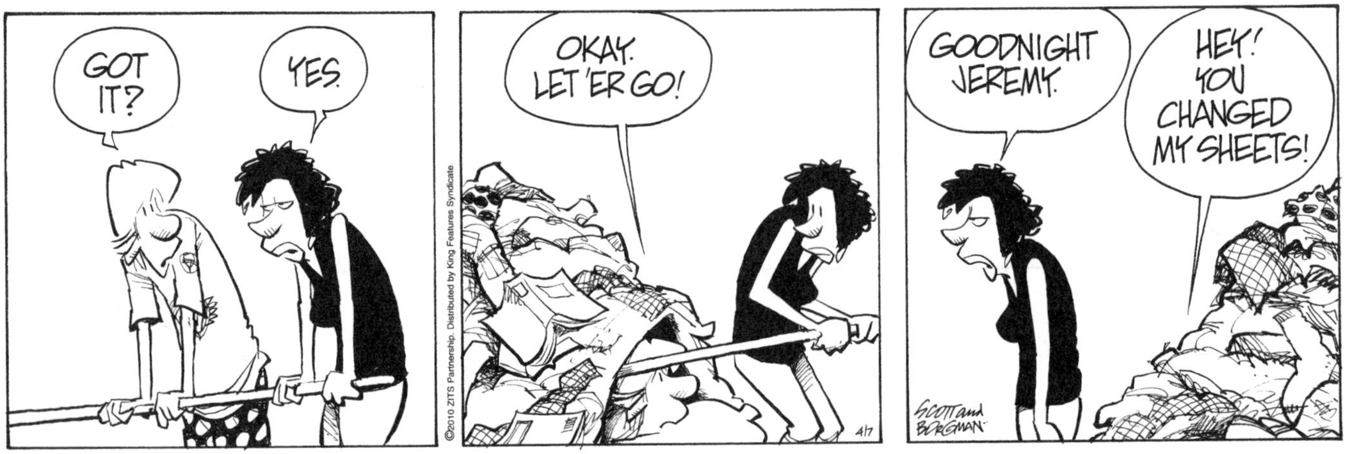
GOT IT?
YES.
©2010 ZITS Partnership. Distributed by King Features Syndicate.
OKAY. LET 'ER GO!
4/7
GOODNIGHT JEREMY.
HEY! YOU CHANGED MY SHEETS!
SCOTT and BORGMAN

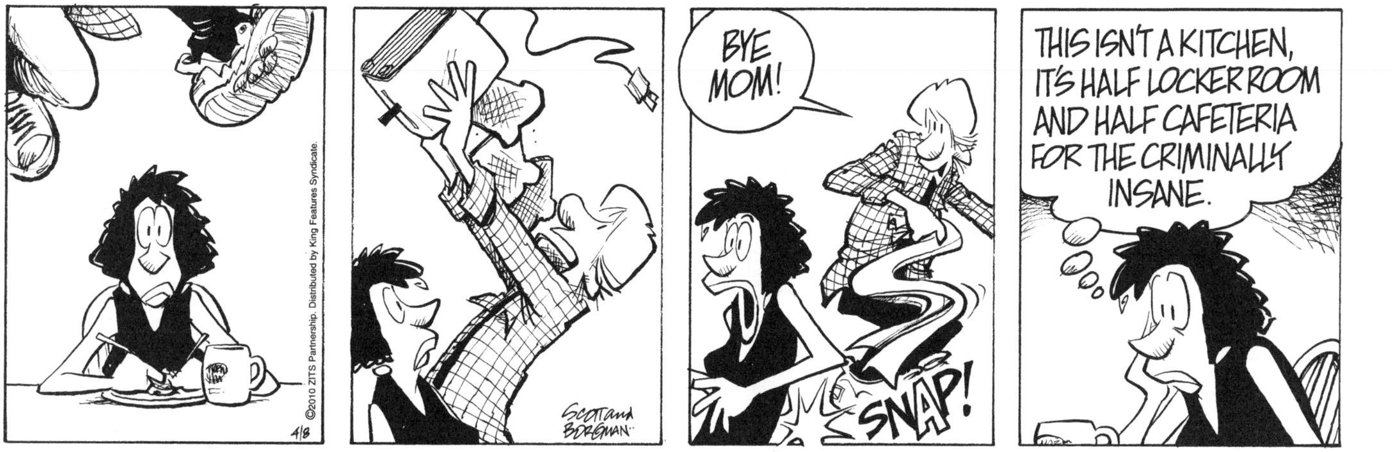
©2010 ZITS Partnership. Distributed by King Features Syndicate.
4/8
SCOTT and BORGMAN
BYE MOM!
SNAP!
THIS ISN'T A KITCHEN, IT'S HALF LOCKER ROOM AND HALF CAFETERIA FOR THE CRIMINALLY INSANE.

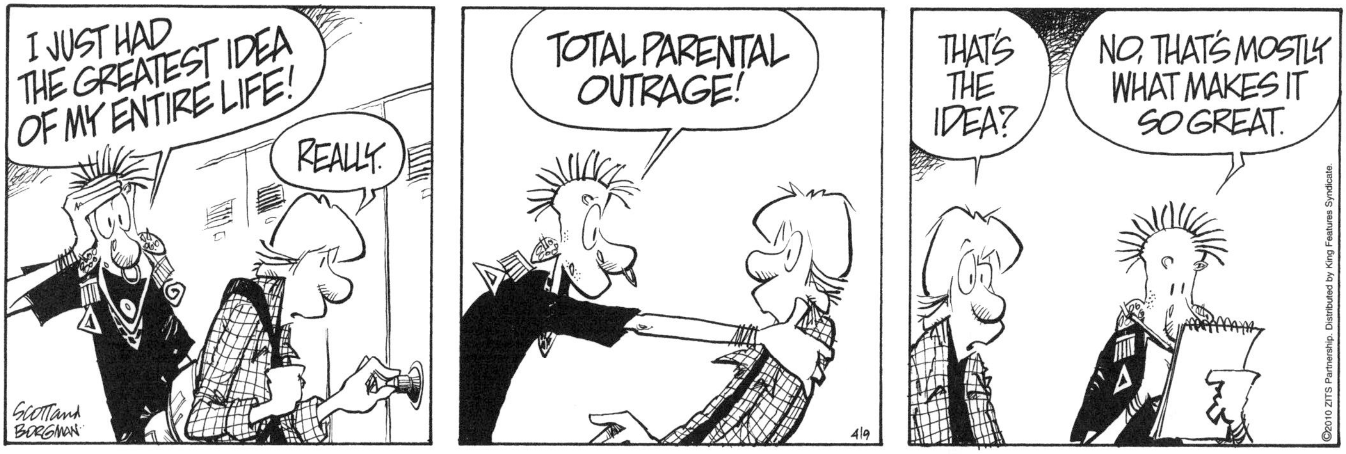
I JUST HAD THE GREATEST IDEA OF MY ENTIRE LIFE!
REALLY.
SCOTT and BORGMAN
TOTAL PARENTAL OUTRAGE!
4/9
THAT'S THE IDEA?
NO, THAT'S MOSTLY WHAT MAKES IT SO GREAT.
©2010 ZITS Partnership. Distributed by King Features Syndicate.

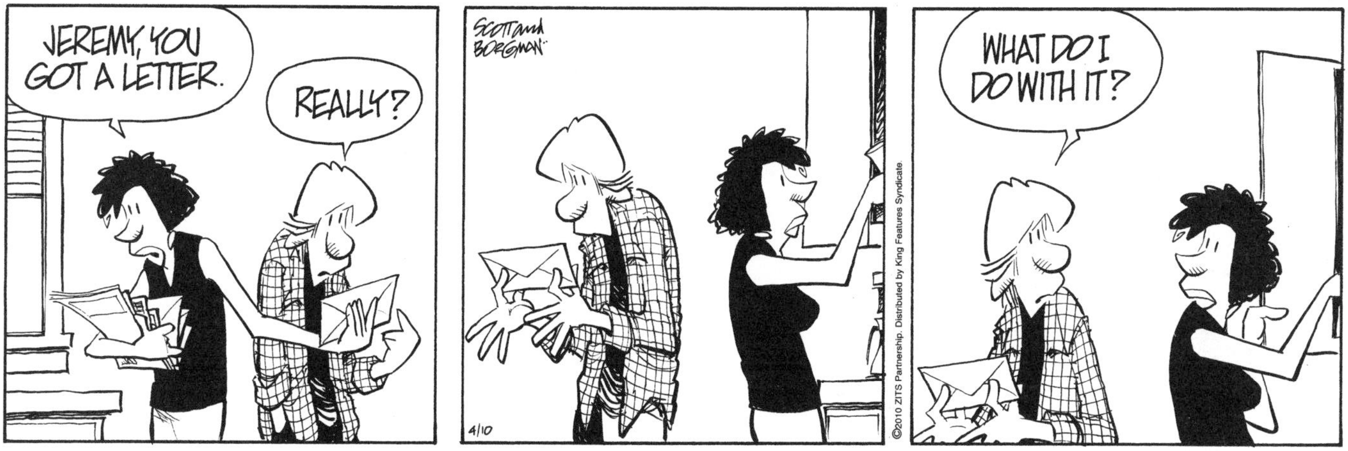
JEREMY, YOU GOT A LETTER.
REALLY?
SCOTT and BORGMAN
4/10
©2010 ZITS Partnership. Distributed by King Features Syndicate.
WHAT DO I DO WITH IT?

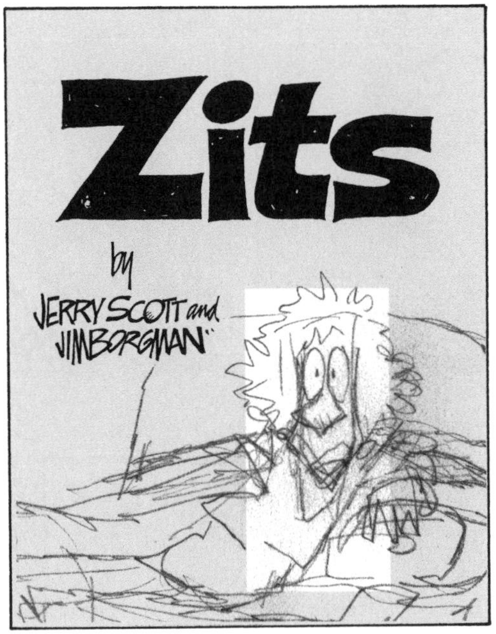
Zits
by
JERRY SCOTT and
JIM BORGMAN

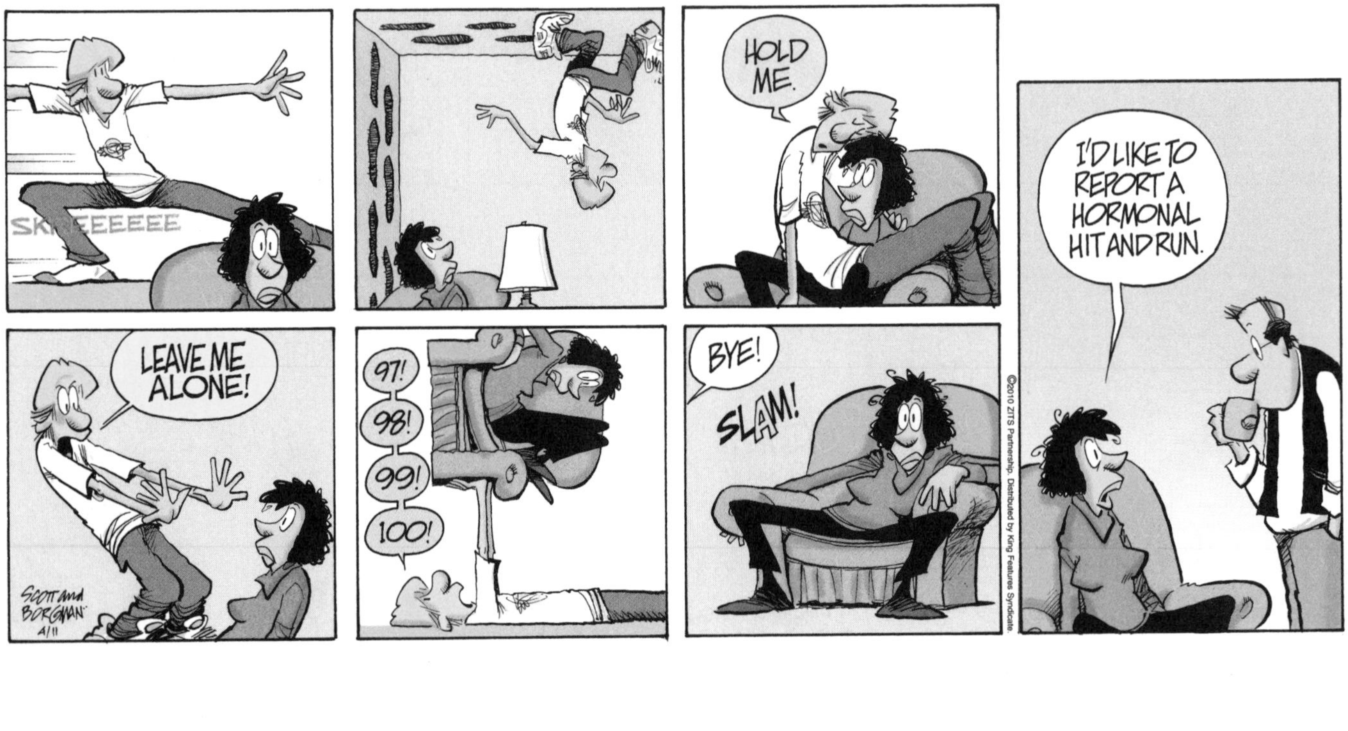
SKREEEEEEE
HOLD ME.
LEAVE ME ALONE!
SCOTT and BORGMAN
4/11
97!
98!
99!
100!
BYE!
SLAM!
©2010 ZITS Partnership. Distributed by King Features Syndicate.
I'D LIKE TO REPORT A HORMONAL HIT AND RUN.

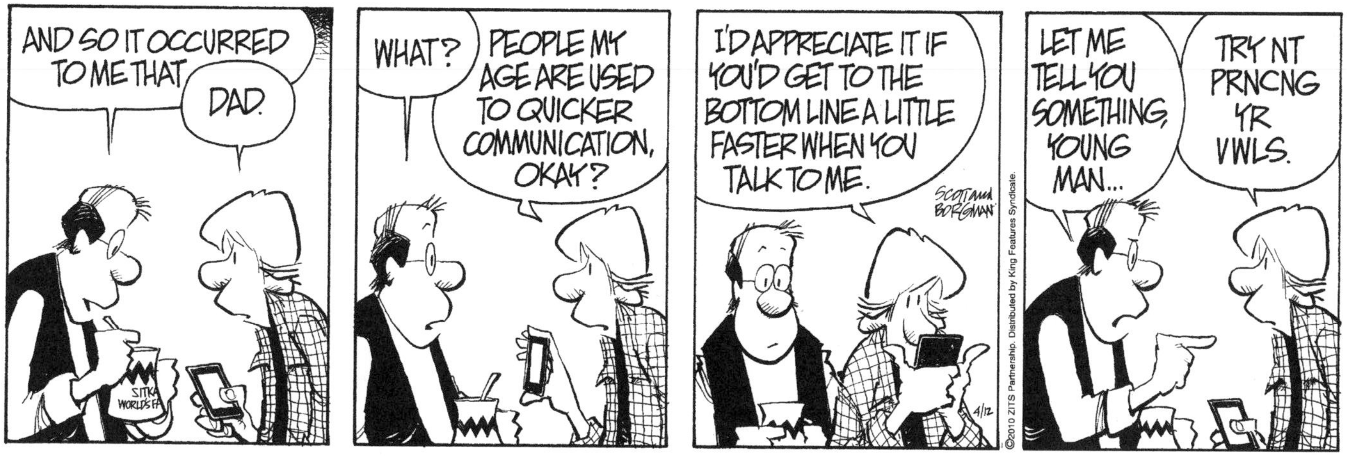
AND SO IT OCCURRED TO ME THAT
DAD.
SITKA WORLD'S FA
WHAT?
PEOPLE MY AGE ARE USED TO QUICKER COMMUNICATION, OKAY?
I'D APPRECIATE IT IF YOU'D GET TO THE BOTTOM LINE A LITTLE FASTER WHEN YOU TALK TO ME.
SCOTT and BORGMAN
4/12
LET ME TELL YOU SOMETHING, YOUNG MAN...
TRY NT PRNCNG YR VWLS.
©2010 ZITS Partnership. Distributed by King Features Syndicate.

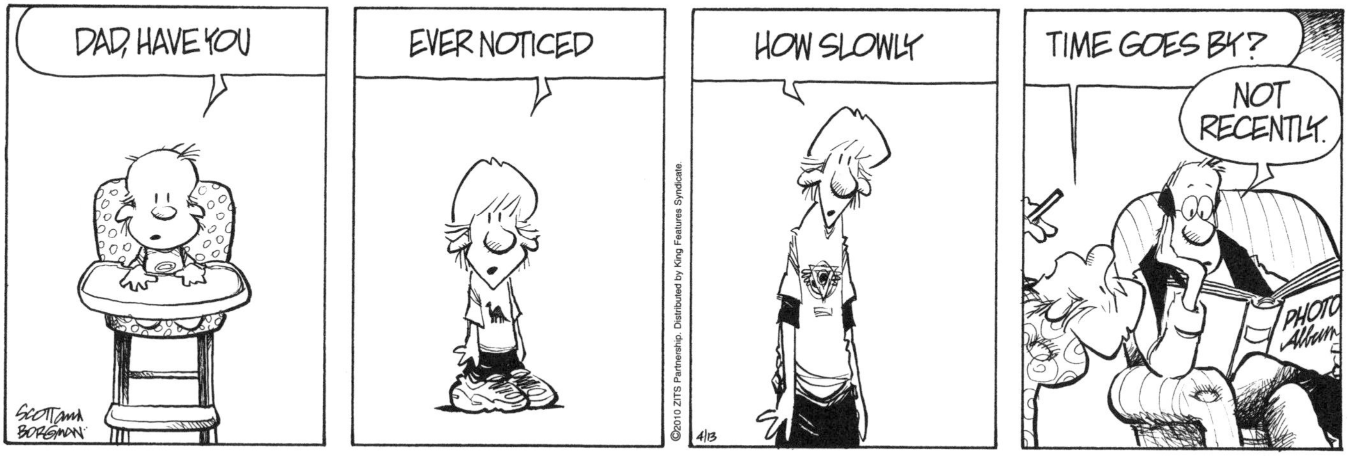
DAD, HAVE YOU
SCOTT and BORGMAN
EVER NOTICED
©2010 ZITS Partnership. Distributed by King Features Syndicate.
HOW SLOWLY
4/13
TIME GOES BY?
NOT RECENTLY.
PHOTO Album

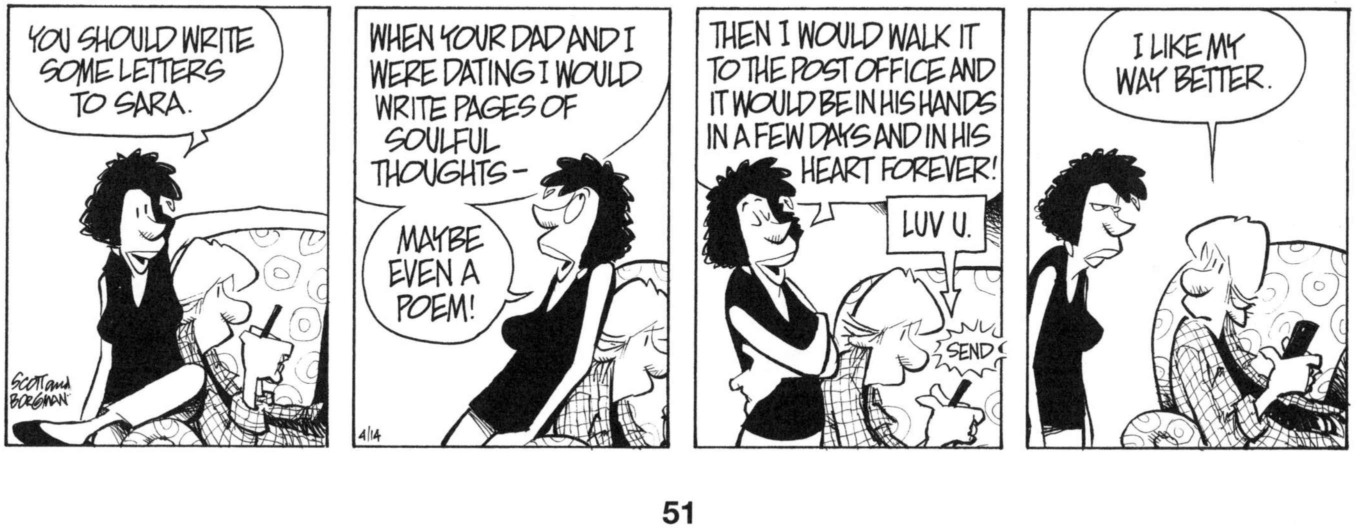
YOU SHOULD WRITE SOME LETTERS TO SARA.
SCOTT and BORGMAN
4/14
WHEN YOUR DAD AND I WERE DATING I WOULD WRITE PAGES OF SOULFUL THOUGHTS -
MAYBE EVEN A POEM!
THEN I WOULD WALK IT TO THE POST OFFICE AND IT WOULD BE IN HIS HANDS IN A FEW DAYS AND IN HIS HEART FOREVER!
LUV U.
SEND
I LIKE MY WAY BETTER.

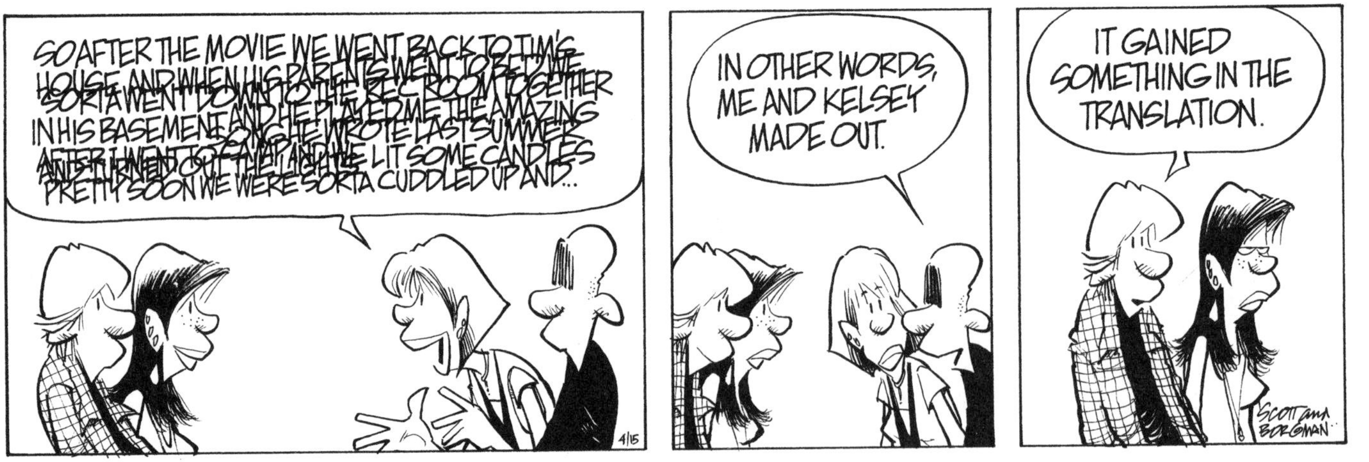
SO AFTER THE MOVIE WE WENT BACK TO TIM'S HOUSE AND WHEN HIS PARENTS WENT TO BED WE SORTA WENT DOWN TO THE REC ROOM TOGETHER IN HIS BASEMENT AND HE PLAYED ME THE AMAZING SONG HE WROTE LAST SUMMER AFTER I WENT TO CAMP AND WE LIT SOME CANDLES AND TURNED OUT THE LIGHTS PRETTY SOON WE WERE SORTA CUDDLED UP AND...
4/15
IN OTHER WORDS, ME AND KELSEY MADE OUT.
IT GAINED SOMETHING IN THE TRANSLATION.
SCOTT and BORGMAN

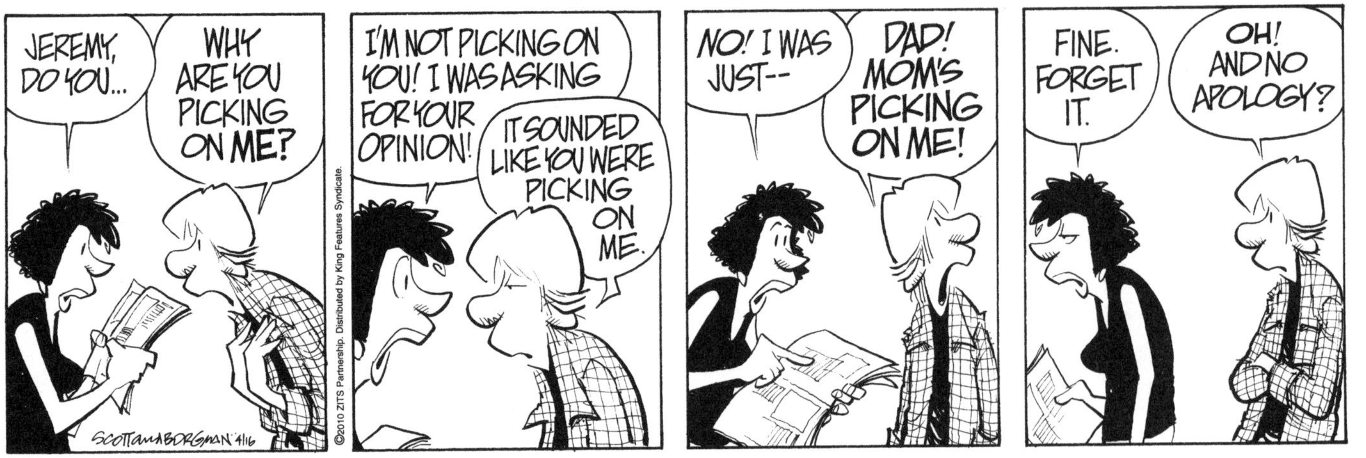
JEREMY, DO YOU...
WHY ARE YOU PICKING ON ME?
SCOTT and BORGMAN 4/16
©2010 ZITS Partnership. Distributed by King Features Syndicate.
I'M NOT PICKING ON YOU! I WAS ASKING FOR YOUR OPINION!
IT SOUNDED LIKE YOU WERE PICKING ON ME.
NO! I WAS JUST--
DAD! MOM'S PICKING ON ME!
FINE. FORGET IT.
OH! AND NO APOLOGY?

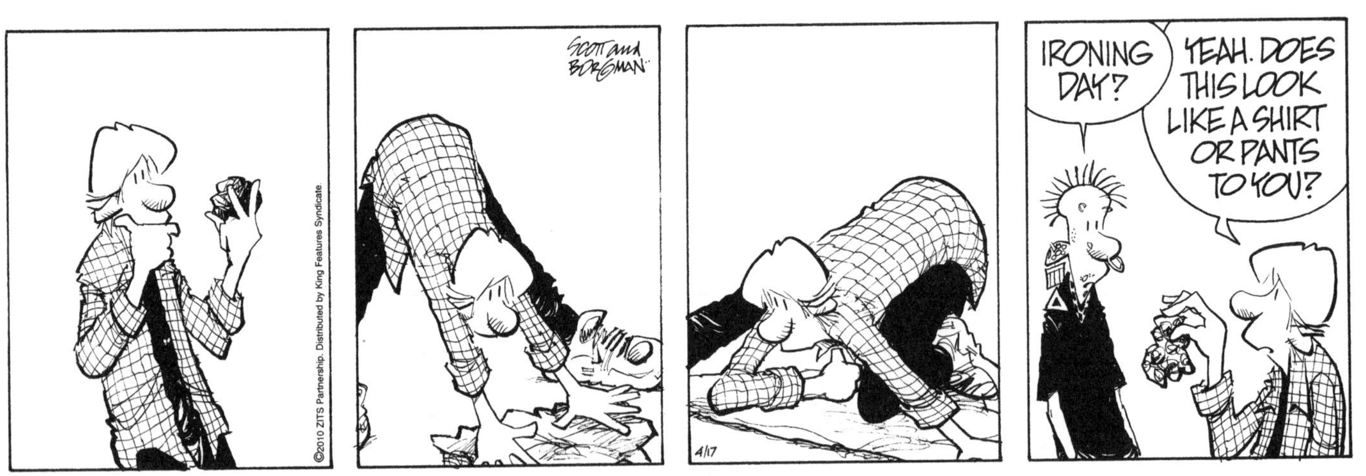
©2010 ZITS Partnership. Distributed by King Features Syndicate.
SCOTT and BORGMAN
4/17
IRONING DAY?
YEAH. DOES THIS LOOK LIKE A SHIRT OR PANTS TO YOU?

Zits
by JERRY SCOTT and JIM BORGMAN

PROFOUNDLY BORED.
WHAT ABOUT YOU?
SAME.
SCOTT and BORGMAN
©2010 ZITS Partnership. Distributed by King Features Syndicate.

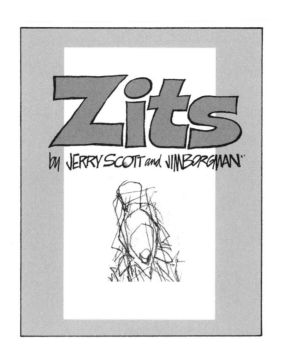

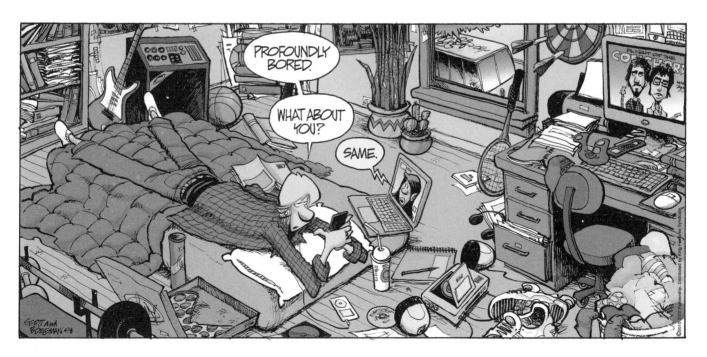

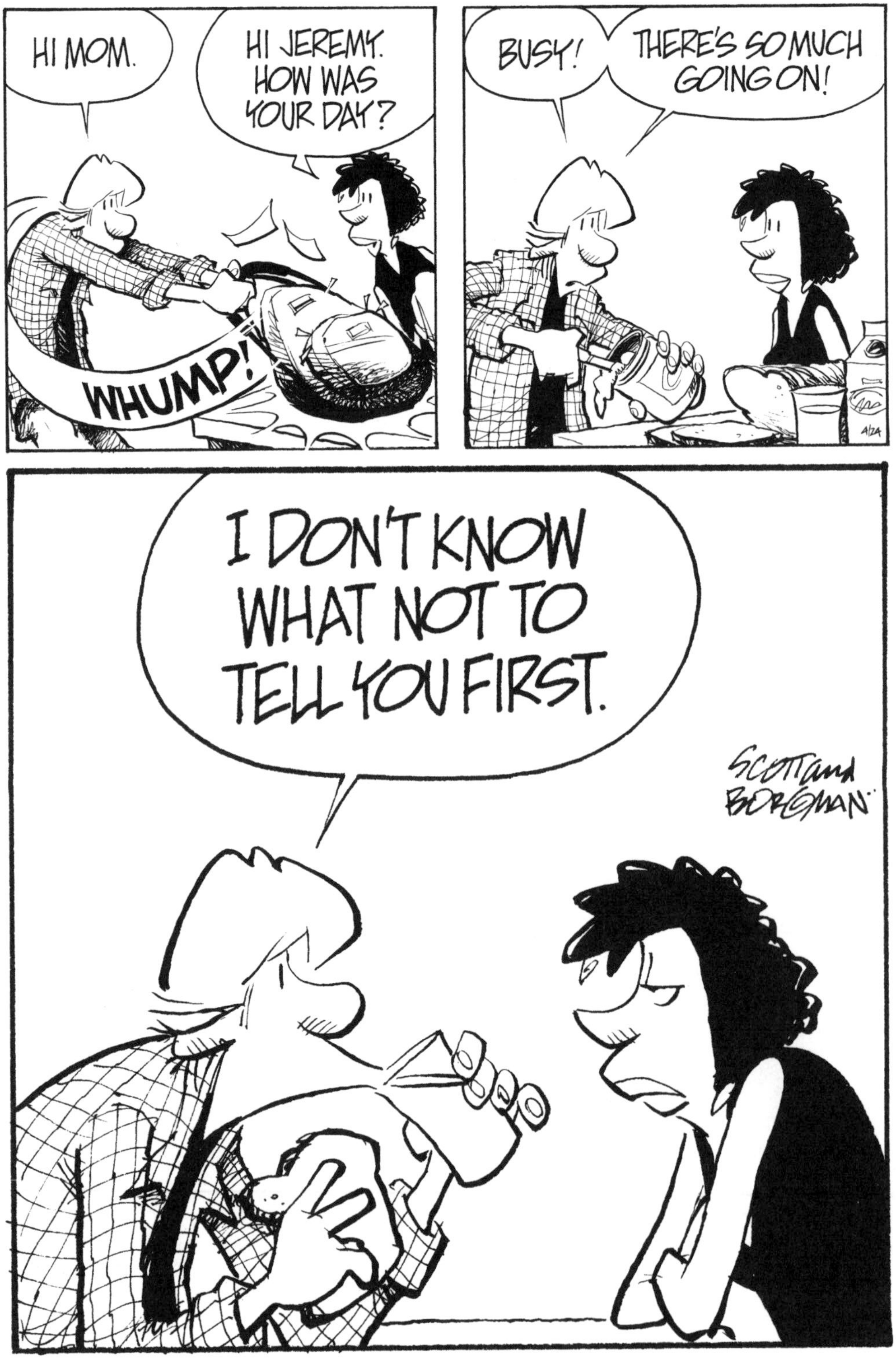
HI MOM.
HI JEREMY. HOW WAS YOUR DAY?
WHUMP!
BUSY!
THERE'S SO MUCH GOING ON!
I DON'T KNOW WHAT NOT TO TELL YOU FIRST.
SCOTT and BORGMAN

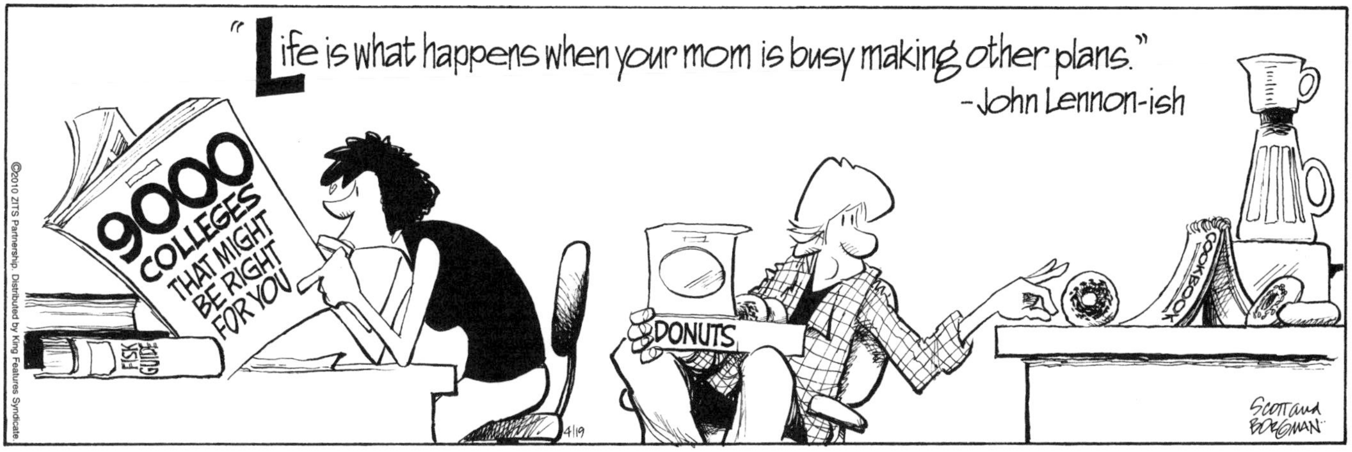
"Life is what happens when your mom is busy making other plans."
-John Lennon-ish
9000 COLLEGES THAT MIGHT BE RIGHT FOR YOU
FISKE GUIDE
DONUTS
COOKBOOK
4/19
SCOTT and BORGMAN
©2010 ZITS Partnership. Distributed by King Features Syndicate.

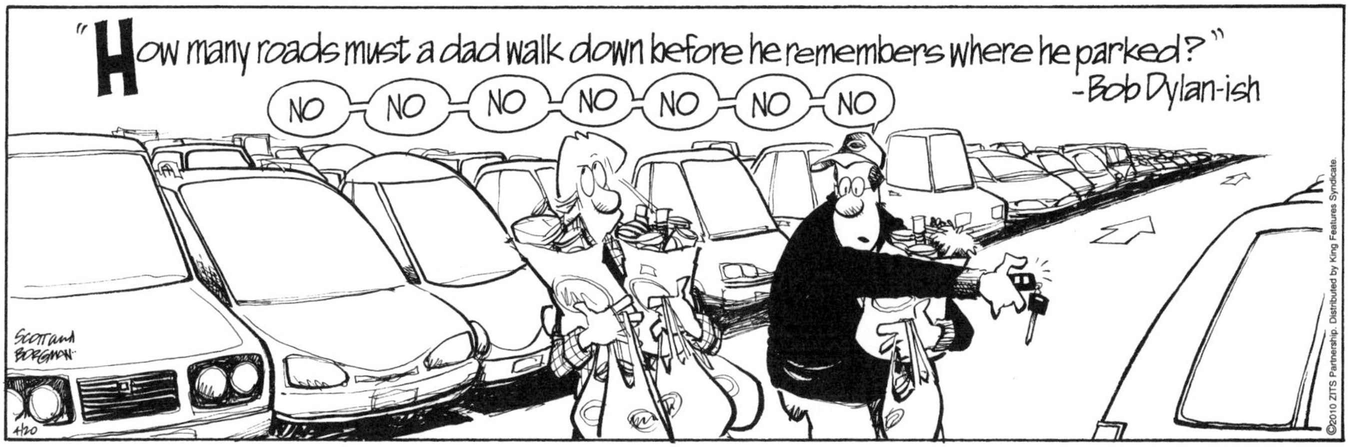
"How many roads must a dad walk down before he remembers where he parked?"
-Bob Dylan-ish
NO
NO
NO
NO
NO
NO
NO
SCOTT and BORGMAN
4/20
©2010 ZITS Partnership. Distributed by King Features Syndicate.

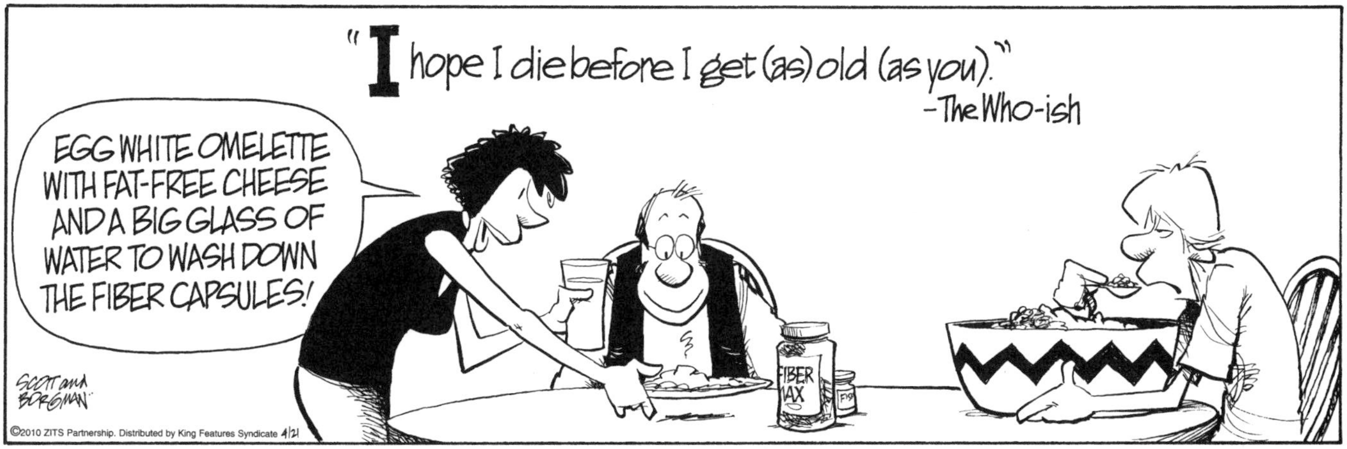
"I hope I die before I get (as) old (as you)."
-The Who-ish
EGG WHITE OMELETTE WITH FAT-FREE CHEESE AND A BIG GLASS OF WATER TO WASH DOWN THE FIBER CAPSULES!
FIBER LAX
SCOTT and BORGMAN
©2010 ZITS Partnership. Distributed by King Features Syndicate 4/21

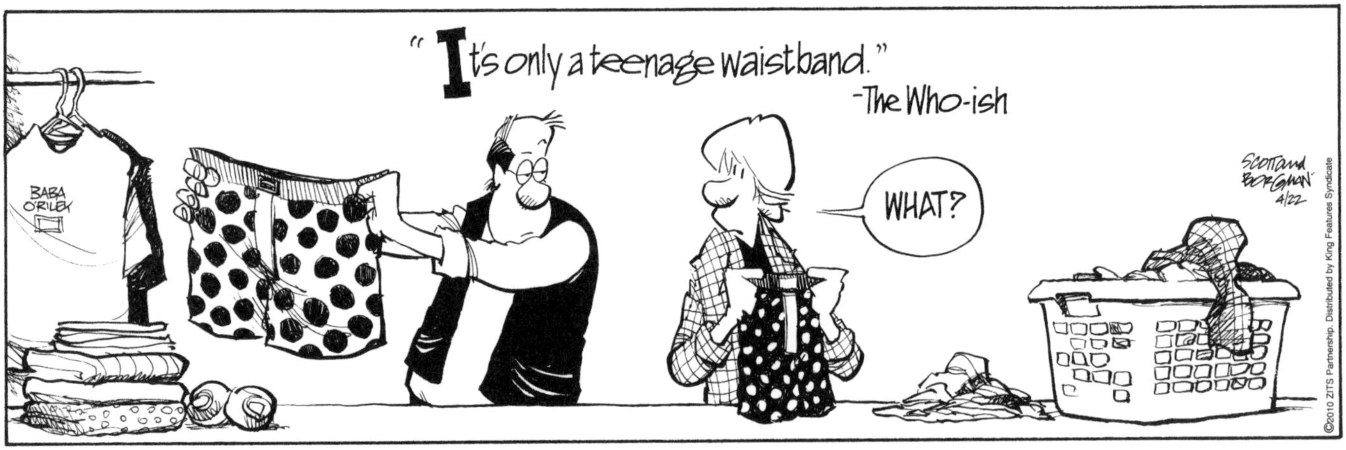
"It's only a teenage waistband."
-The Who-ish
BABA O'RILEY
WHAT?
SCOTT and BORGMAN 4/22
©2010 ZITS Partnership. Distributed by King Features Syndicate

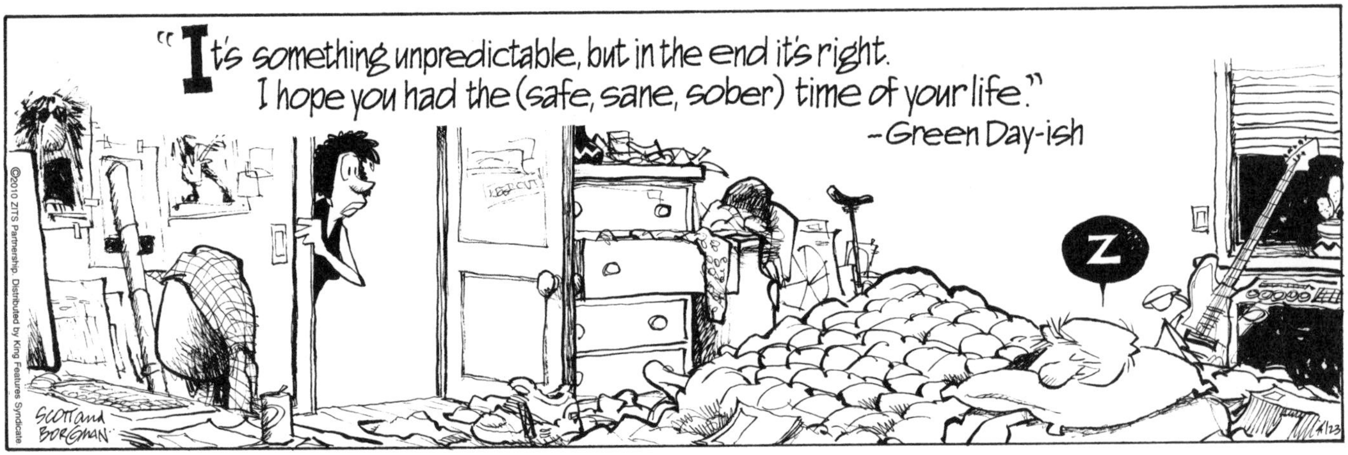
"It's something unpredictable, but in the end it's right.
I hope you had the (safe, sane, sober) time of your life."
-Green Day-ish
Z
SCOTT and BORGMAN
4/23
©2010 ZITS Partnership. Distributed by King Features Syndicate

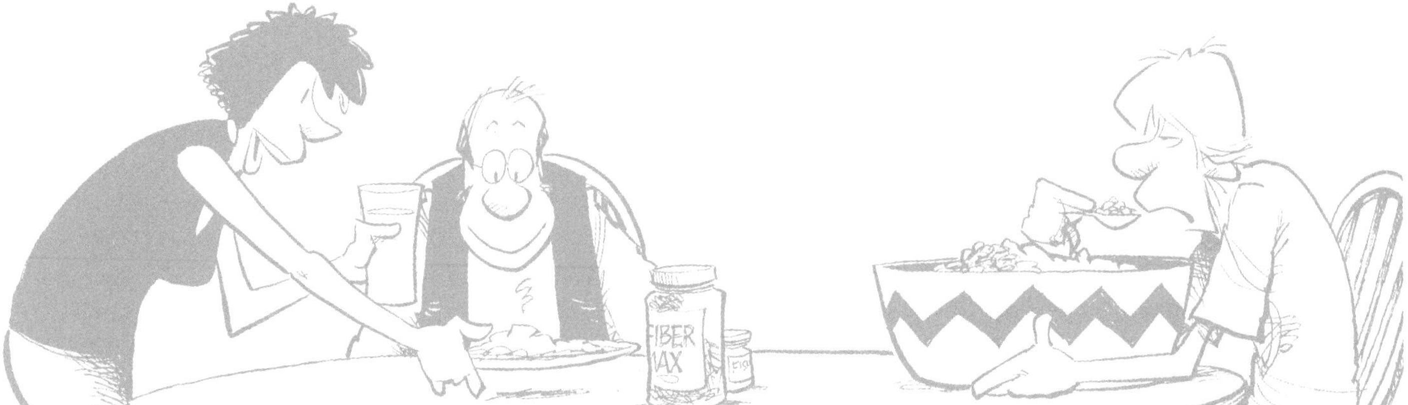
FIBER MAX

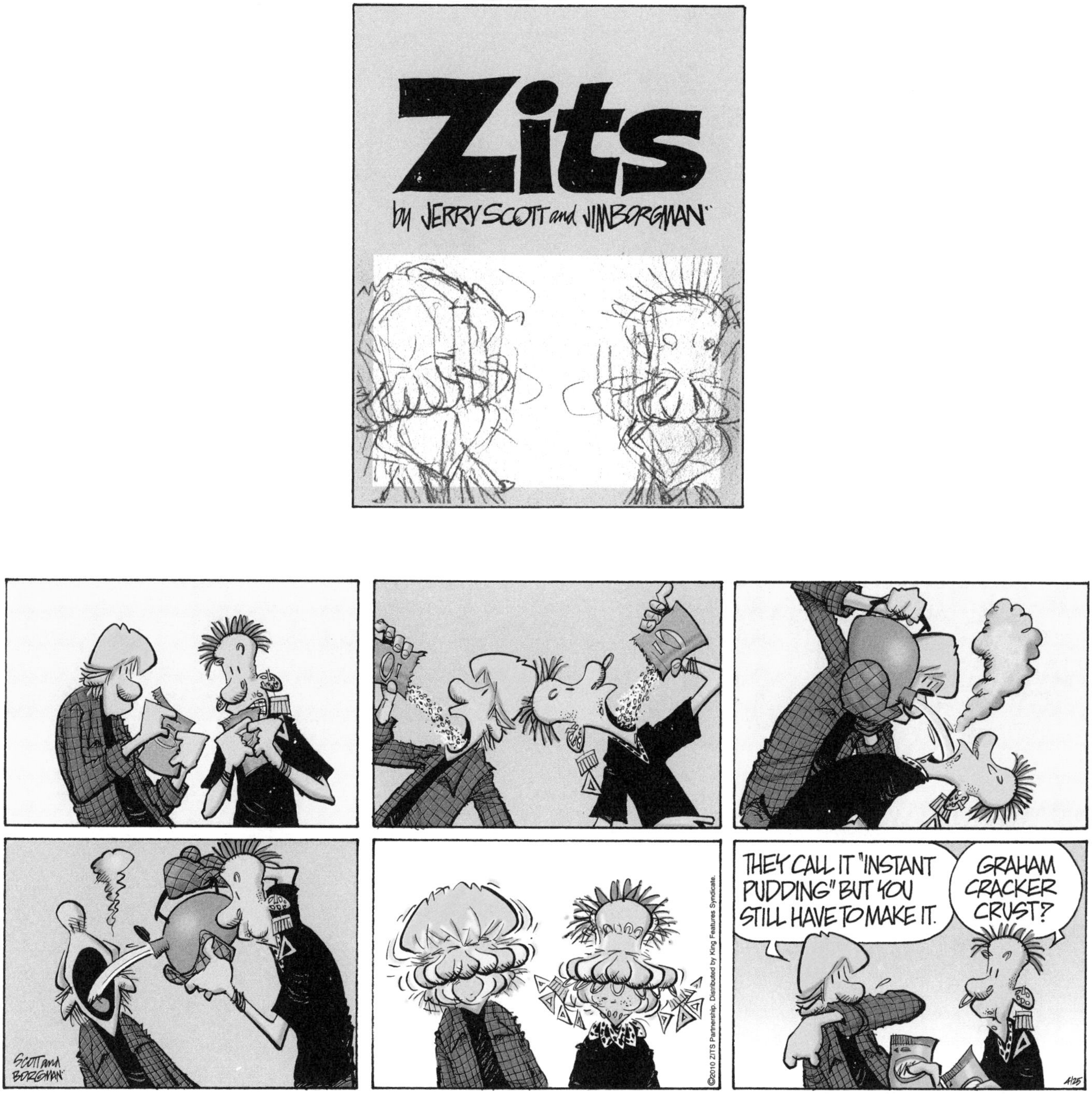
Zits
by JERRY SCOTT and JIM BORGMAN
SCOTT and BORGMAN
©2010 ZITS Partnership. Distributed by King Features Syndicate.
THEY CALL IT "INSTANT PUDDING" BUT YOU STILL HAVE TO MAKE IT.
GRAHAM CRACKER CRUST?
4/25

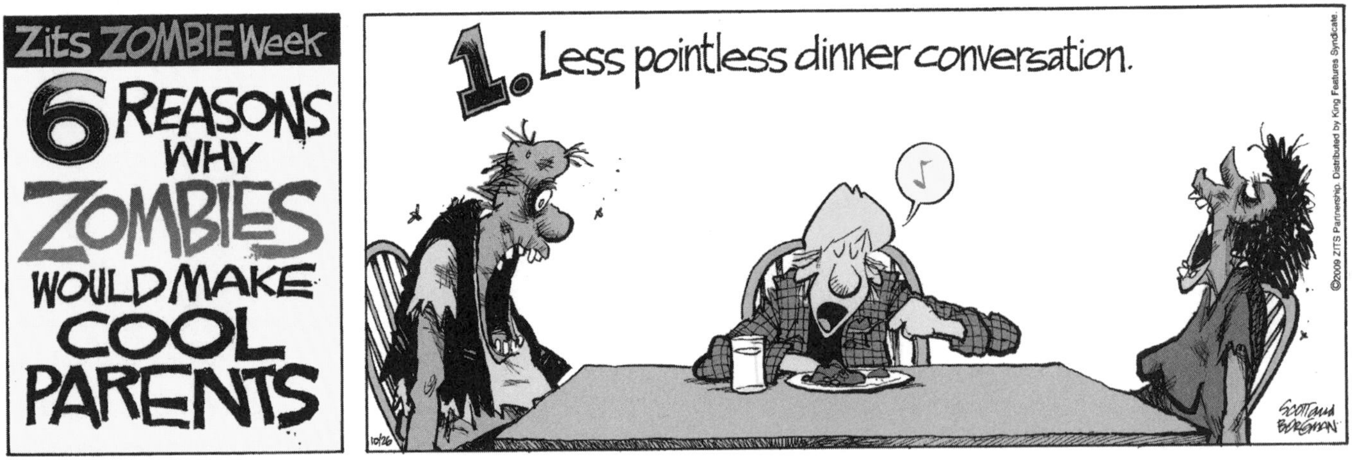
Zits ZOMBIE Week
6 REASONS WHY ZOMBIES WOULD MAKE COOL PARENTS
1. Less pointless dinner conversation.
©2009 ZITS Partnership. Distributed by King Features Syndicate.

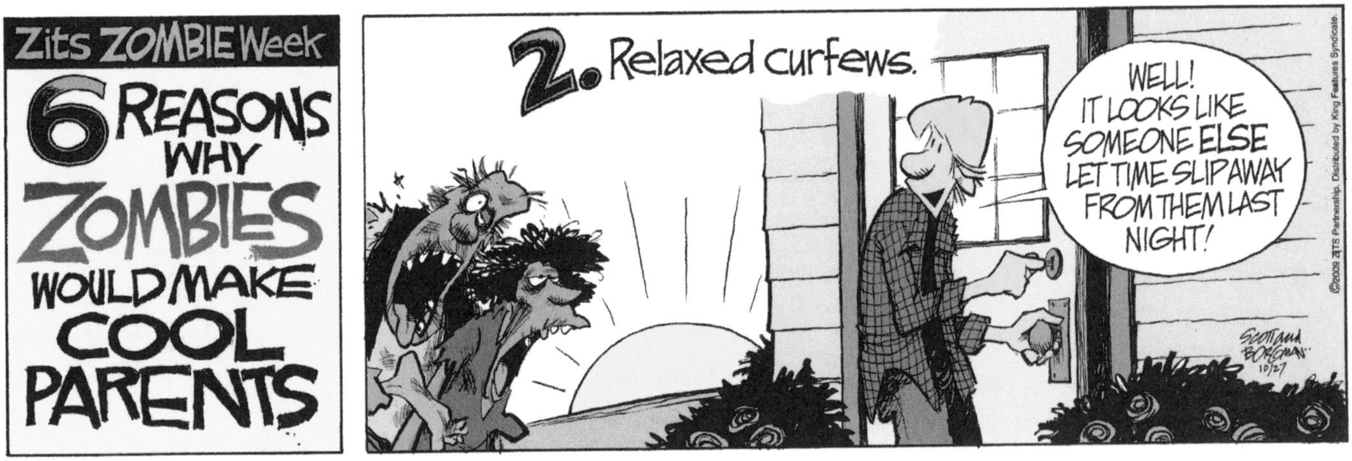
Zits ZOMBIE Week
6 REASONS WHY ZOMBIES WOULD MAKE COOL PARENTS
2. Relaxed curfews.
WELL! IT LOOKS LIKE SOMEONE ELSE LET TIME SLIP AWAY FROM THEM LAST NIGHT!
©2009 ZITS Partnership. Distributed by King Features Syndicate.

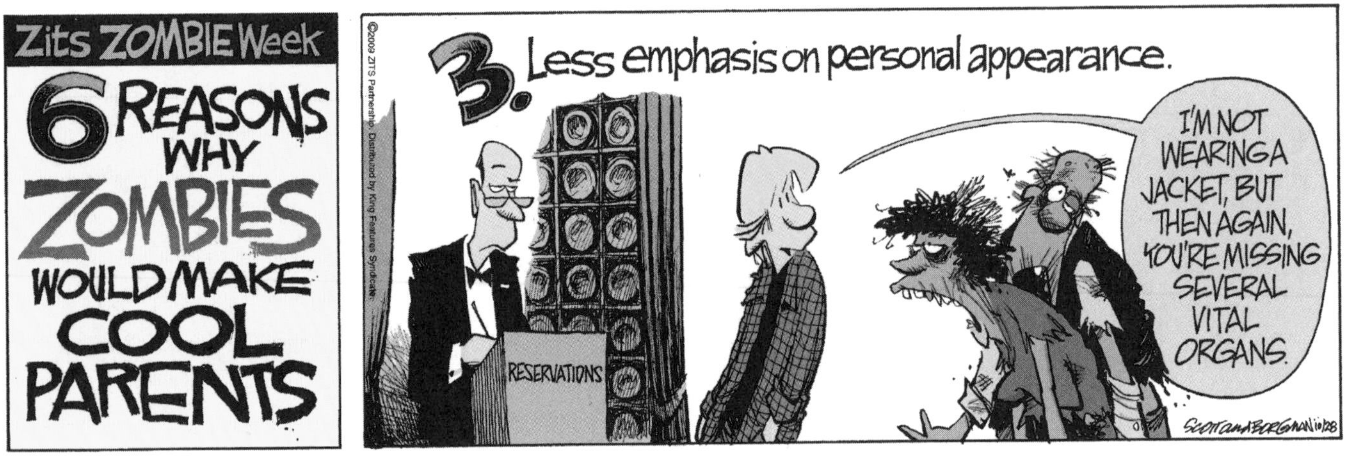
Zits ZOMBIE Week
6 REASONS WHY ZOMBIES WOULD MAKE COOL PARENTS
3. Less emphasis on personal appearance.
RESERVATIONS
I'M NOT WEARING A JACKET, BUT THEN AGAIN, YOU'RE MISSING SEVERAL VITAL ORGANS.
©2009 ZITS Partnership. Distributed by King Features Syndicate.

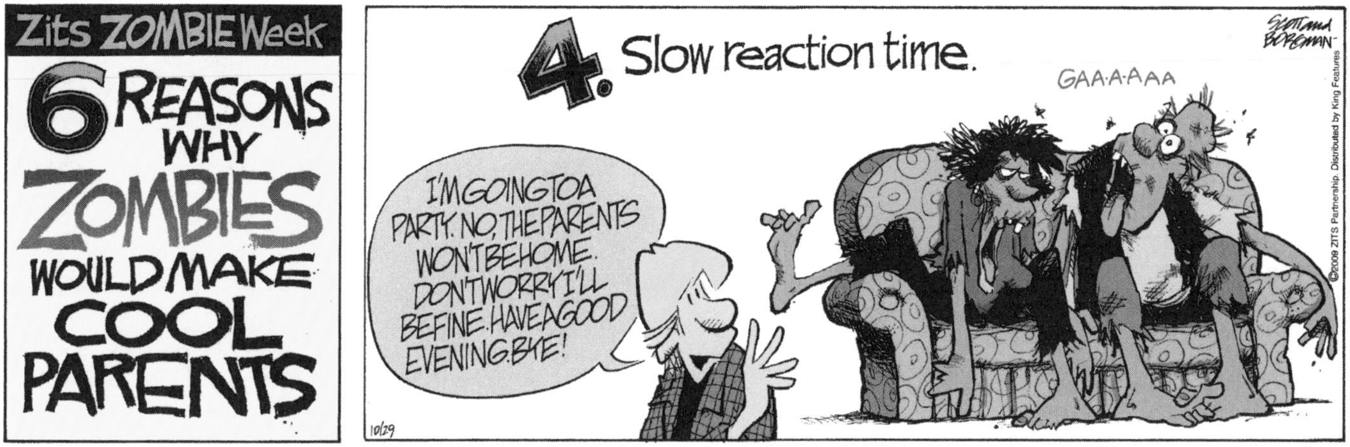
Zits ZOMBIE Week
6 REASONS WHY ZOMBIES WOULD MAKE COOL PARENTS
4. Slow reaction time.
I'M GOING TO A PARTY. NO, THE PARENTS WON'T BE HOME. DON'T WORRY I'LL BE FINE. HAVE A GOOD EVENING. BYE!
GAA-A-AAA
SCOTT AND BORGMAN
©2009 ZITS Partnership. Distributed by King Features
10/29

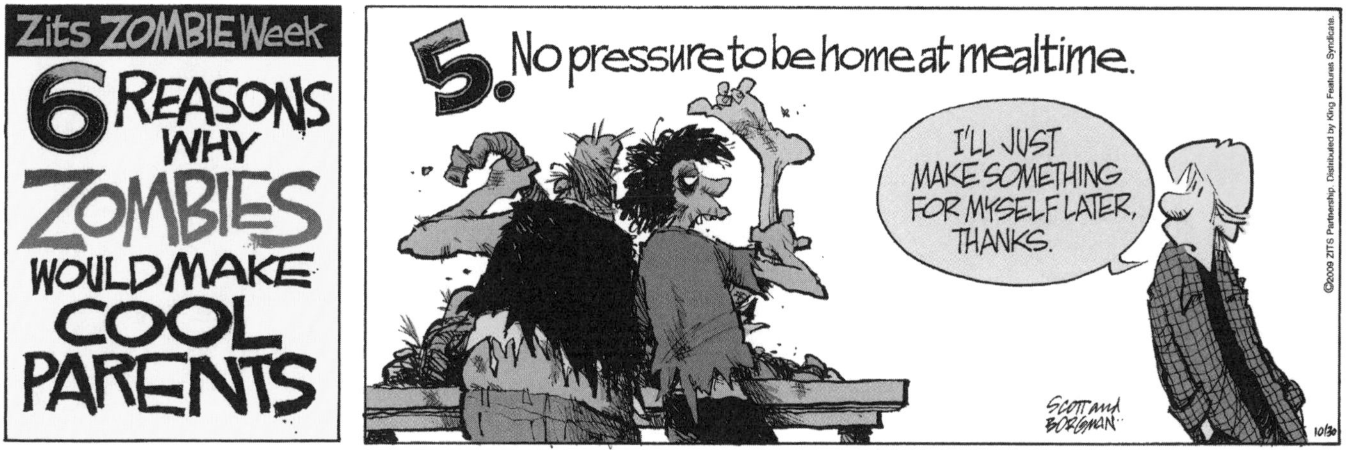
Zits ZOMBIE Week
6 REASONS WHY ZOMBIES WOULD MAKE COOL PARENTS
5. No pressure to be home at mealtime.
I'LL JUST MAKE SOMETHING FOR MYSELF LATER, THANKS.
SCOTT AND BORGMAN
©2009 ZITS Partnership. Distributed by King Features Syndicate.
10/30

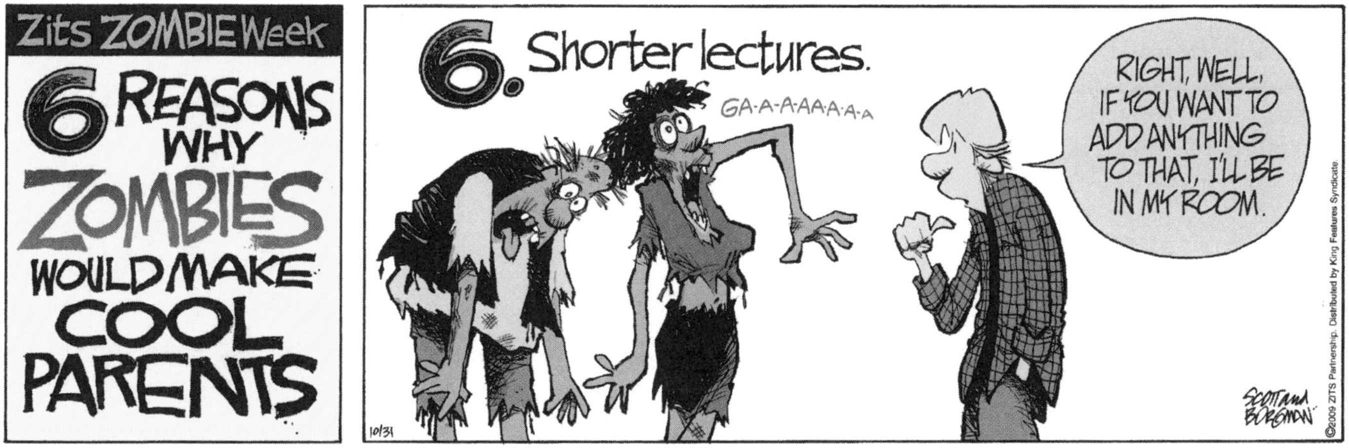
Zits ZOMBIE Week
6 REASONS WHY ZOMBIES WOULD MAKE COOL PARENTS
6. Shorter lectures.
GA-A-A-AAA-A-A-A
RIGHT, WELL, IF YOU WANT TO ADD ANYTHING TO THAT, I'LL BE IN MY ROOM.
SCOTT AND BORGMAN
©2009 ZITS Partnership. Distributed by King Features Syndicate.
10/31

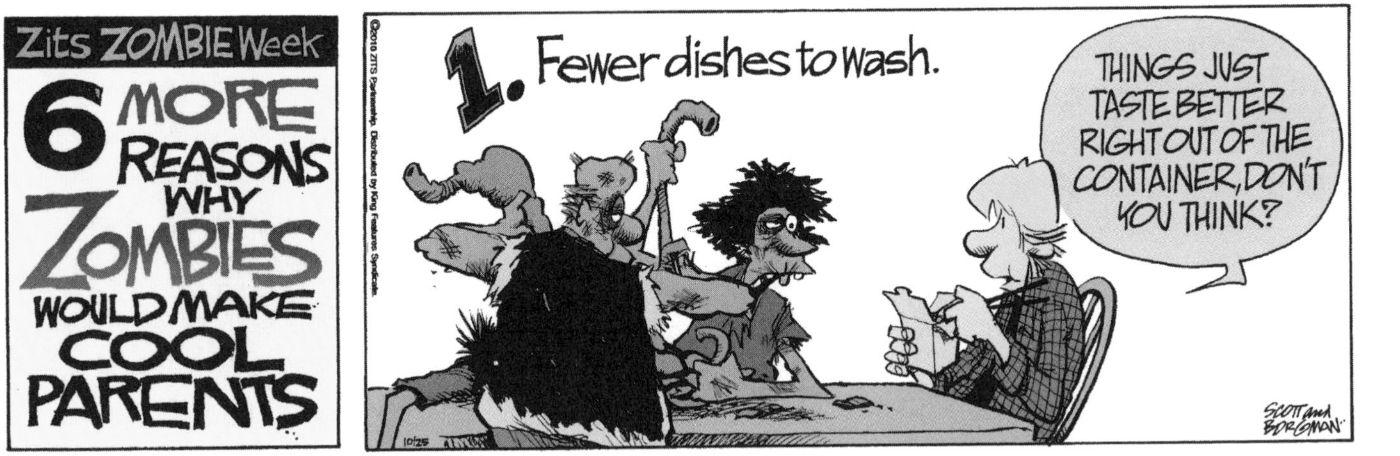
Zits ZOMBIE Week
6 MORE REASONS WHY ZOMBIES WOULD MAKE COOL PARENTS
1. Fewer dishes to wash.
THINGS JUST TASTE BETTER RIGHT OUT OF THE CONTAINER, DON'T YOU THINK?
©2010 ZITS Partnership. Distributed by King Features Syndicate.
SCOTT and BORGMAN

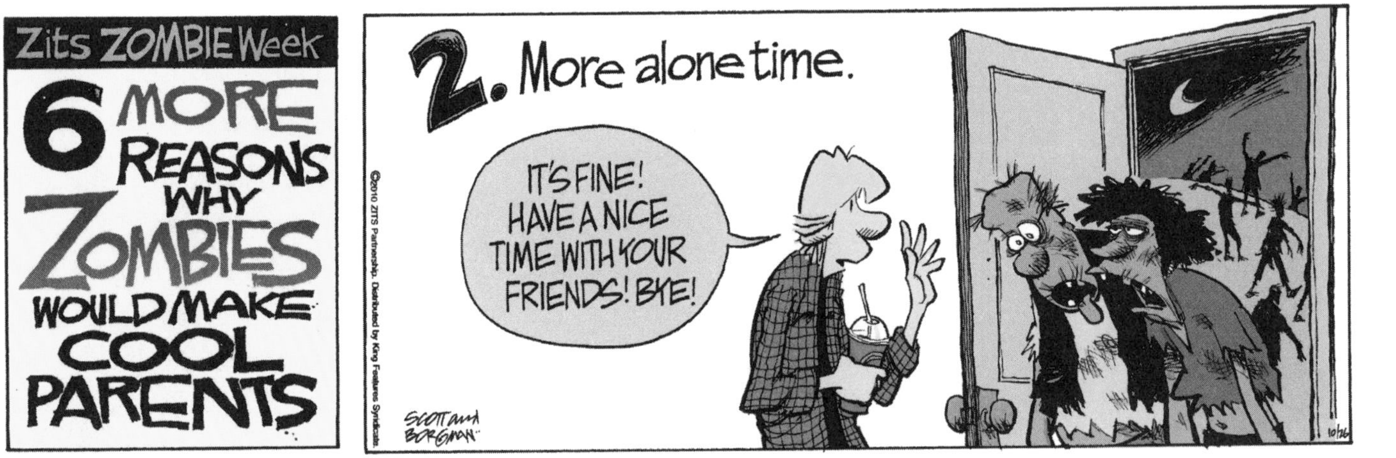
Zits ZOMBIE Week
6 MORE REASONS WHY ZOMBIES WOULD MAKE COOL PARENTS
2. More alone time.
IT'S FINE! HAVE A NICE TIME WITH YOUR FRIENDS! BYE!
©2010 ZITS Partnership. Distributed by King Features Syndicate.
SCOTT and BORGMAN

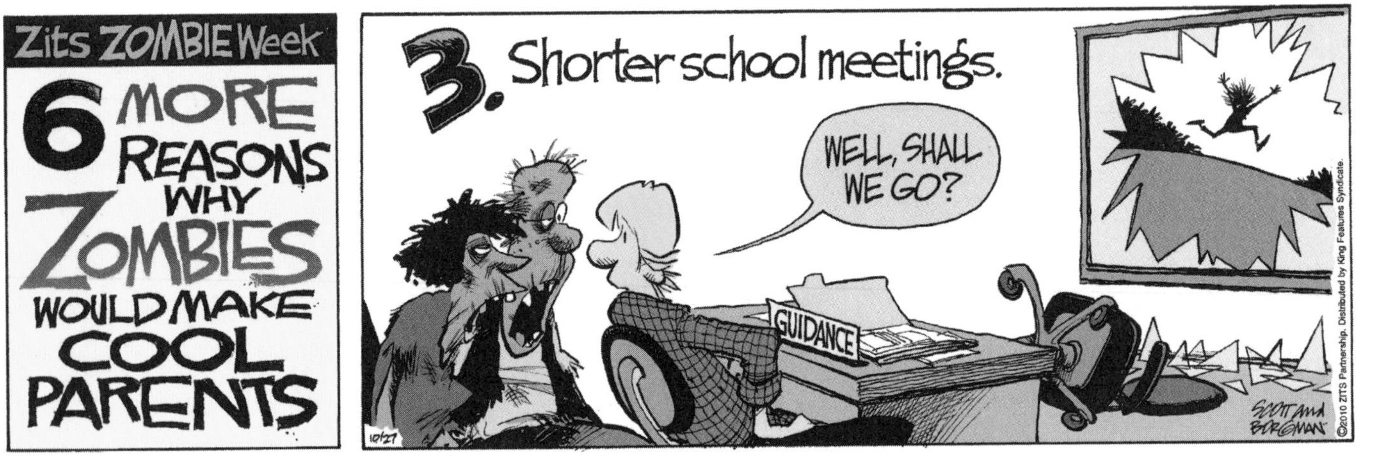
Zits ZOMBIE Week
6 MORE REASONS WHY ZOMBIES WOULD MAKE COOL PARENTS
3. Shorter school meetings.
WELL, SHALL WE GO?
GUIDANCE
©2010 ZITS Partnership. Distributed by King Features Syndicate.
SCOTT and BORGMAN

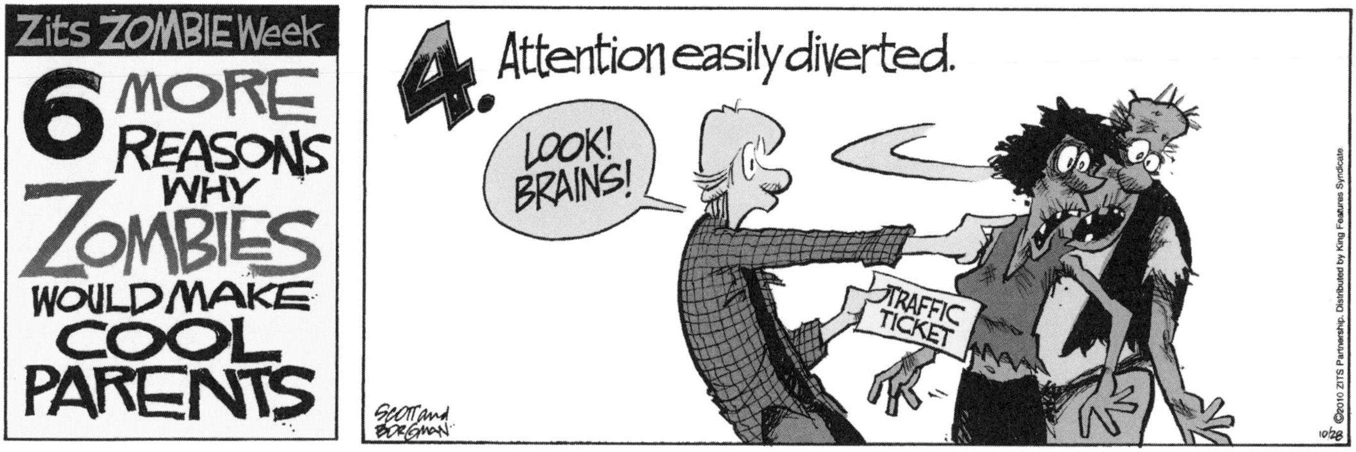
Zits ZOMBIE Week
6 MORE REASONS WHY ZOMBIES WOULD MAKE COOL PARENTS
4. Attention easily diverted.
LOOK! BRAINS!
TRAFFIC TICKET
SCOTT and BORGMAN
©2010 ZITS Partnership. Distributed by King Features Syndicate
10/28

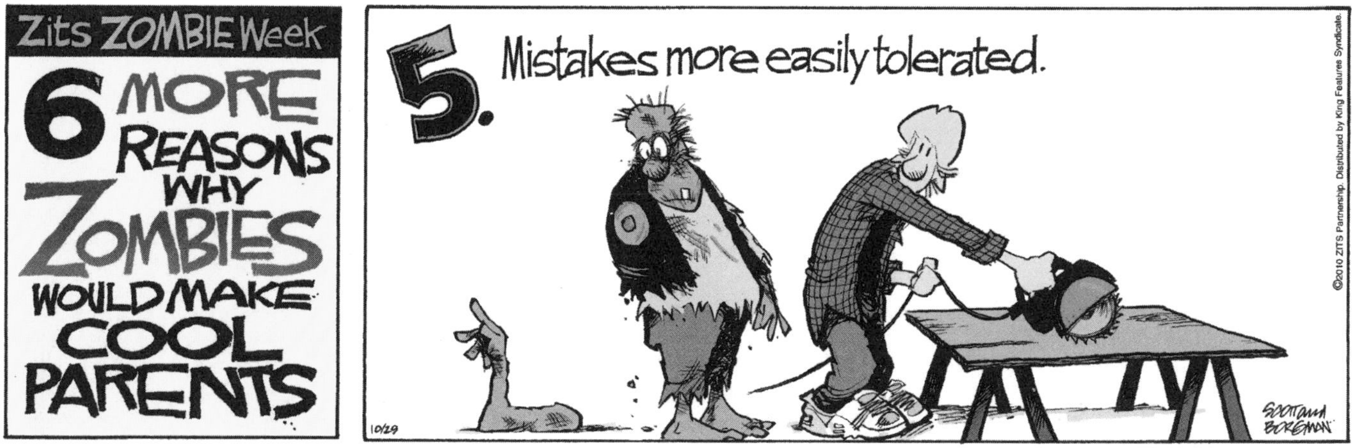
Zits ZOMBIE Week
6 MORE REASONS WHY ZOMBIES WOULD MAKE COOL PARENTS
5. Mistakes more easily tolerated.
©2010 ZITS Partnership. Distributed by King Features Syndicate.
10/29
SCOTT and BORGMAN

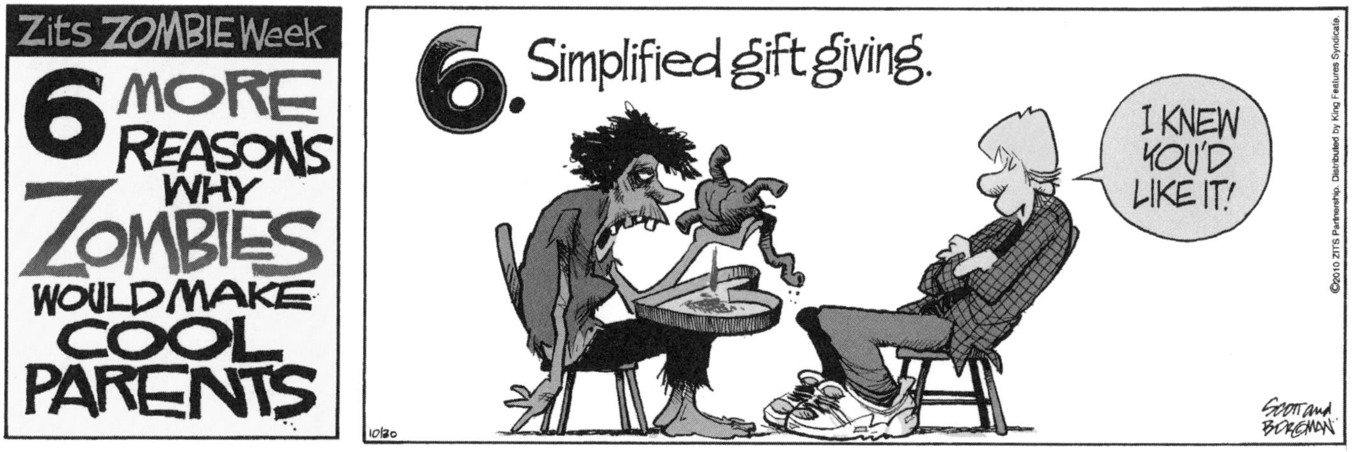
Zits ZOMBIE Week
6 MORE REASONS WHY ZOMBIES WOULD MAKE COOL PARENTS
6. Simplified gift giving.
I KNEW YOU'D LIKE IT!
©2010 ZITS Partnership. Distributed by King Features Syndicate.
10/30
SCOTT and BORGMAN

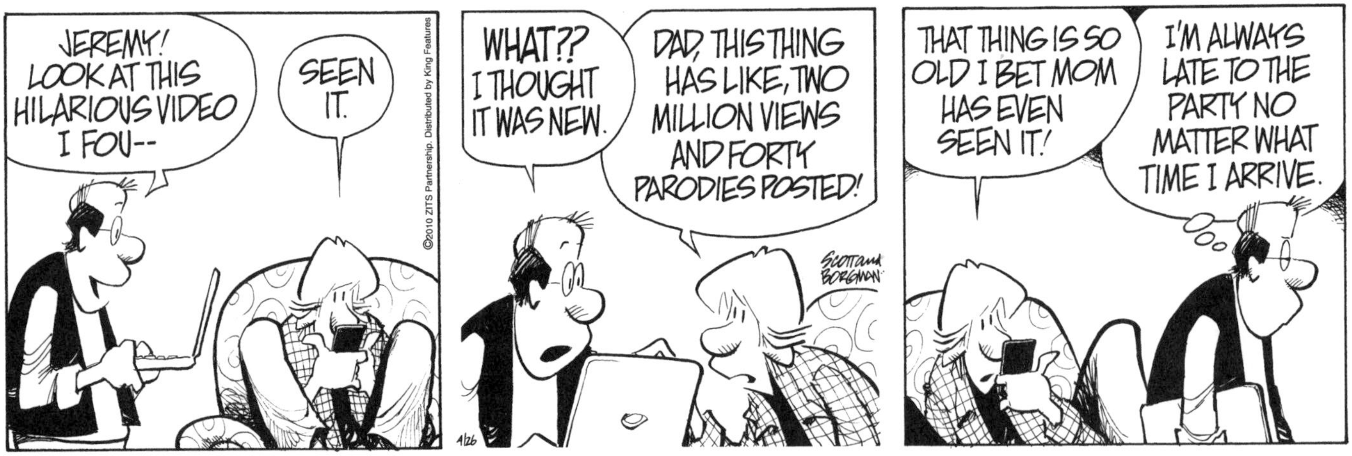
JEREMY! LOOK AT THIS HILARIOUS VIDEO I FOU--
SEEN IT.
©2010 ZITS Partnership. Distributed by King Features
WHAT?? I THOUGHT IT WAS NEW.
DAD, THIS THING HAS LIKE, TWO MILLION VIEWS AND FORTY PARODIES POSTED!
THAT THING IS SO OLD I BET MOM HAS EVEN SEEN IT!
I'M ALWAYS LATE TO THE PARTY NO MATTER WHAT TIME I ARRIVE.

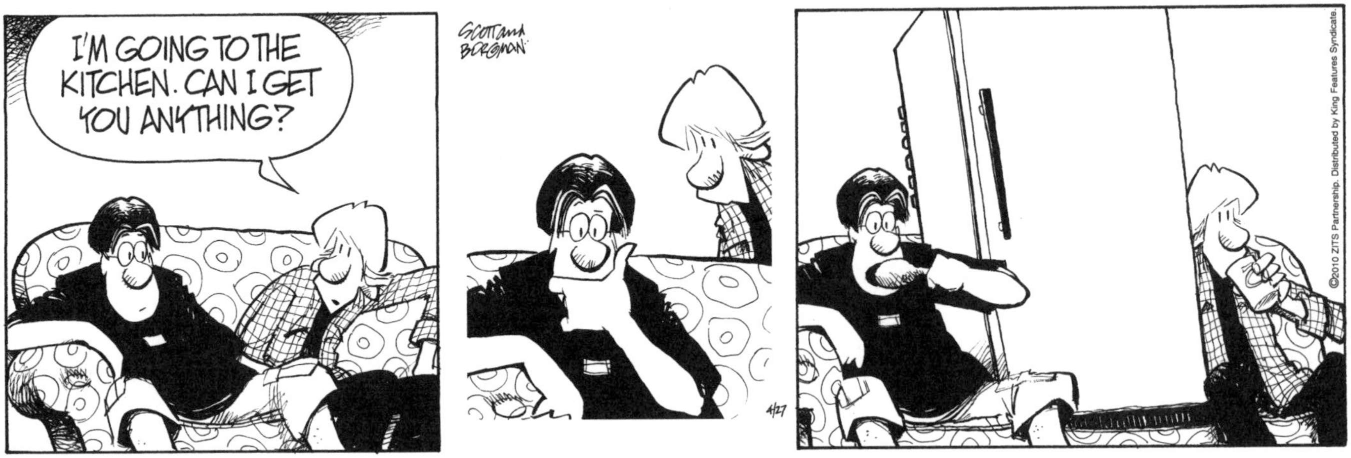
I'M GOING TO THE KITCHEN. CAN I GET YOU ANYTHING?
©2010 ZITS Partnership. Distributed by King Features Syndicate.

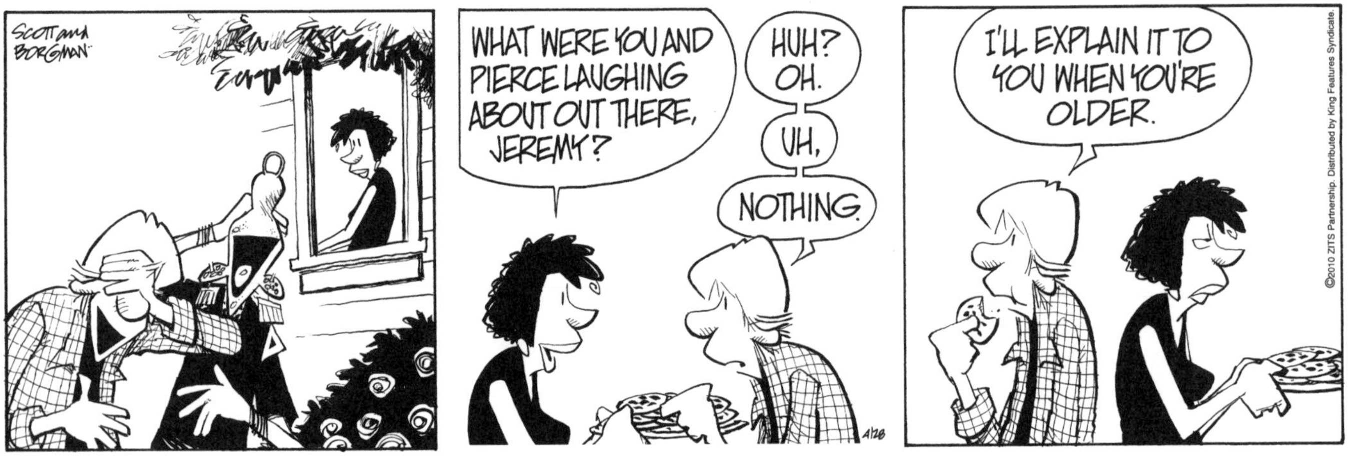
WHAT WERE YOU AND PIERCE LAUGHING ABOUT OUT THERE, JEREMY?
HUH? OH.
UH,
NOTHING.
I'LL EXPLAIN IT TO YOU WHEN YOU'RE OLDER.
©2010 ZITS Partnership. Distributed by King Features Syndicate.

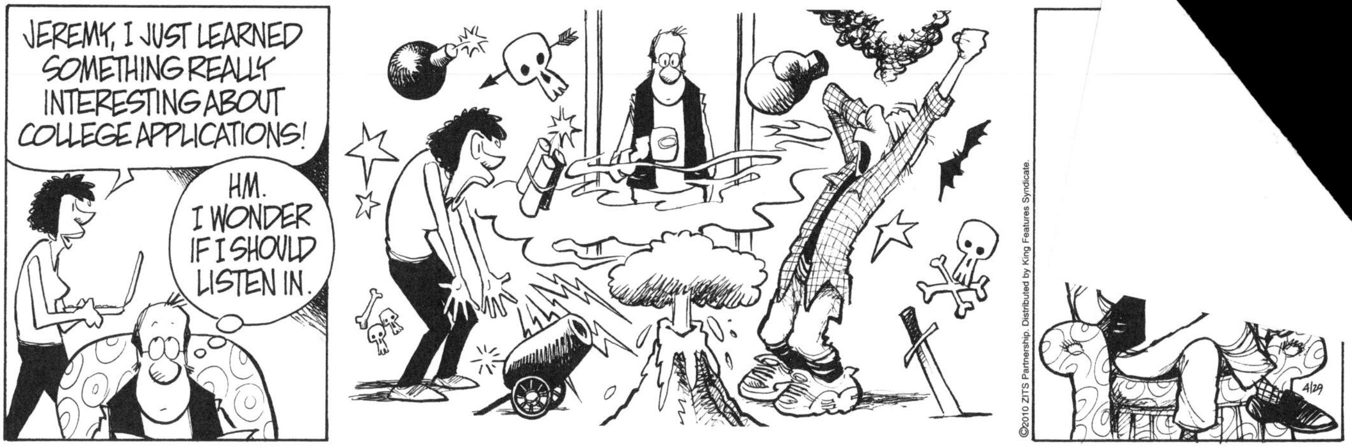
JEREMY, I JUST LEARNED SOMETHING REALLY INTERESTING ABOUT COLLEGE APPLICATIONS!
HM. I WONDER IF I SHOULD LISTEN IN.
4/29
©2010 ZITS Partnership. Distributed by King Features Syndicate.

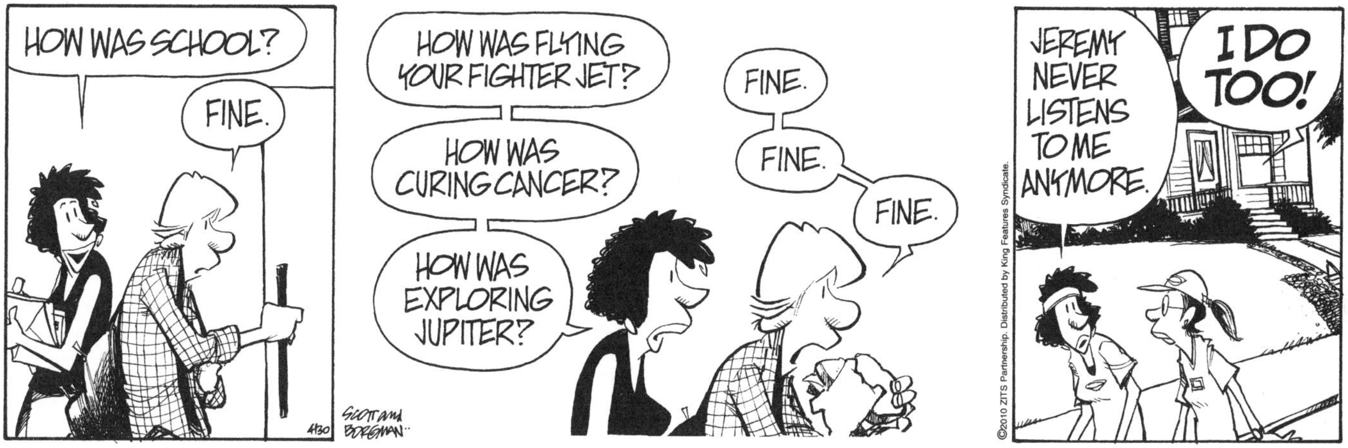
HOW WAS SCHOOL?
FINE.
4/30
SCOTT AND BORGMAN
HOW WAS FLYING YOUR FIGHTER JET?
FINE.
HOW WAS CURING CANCER?
FINE.
HOW WAS EXPLORING JUPITER?
FINE.
JEREMY NEVER LISTENS TO ME ANYMORE.
I DO TOO!
©2010 ZITS Partnership. Distributed by King Features Syndicate.

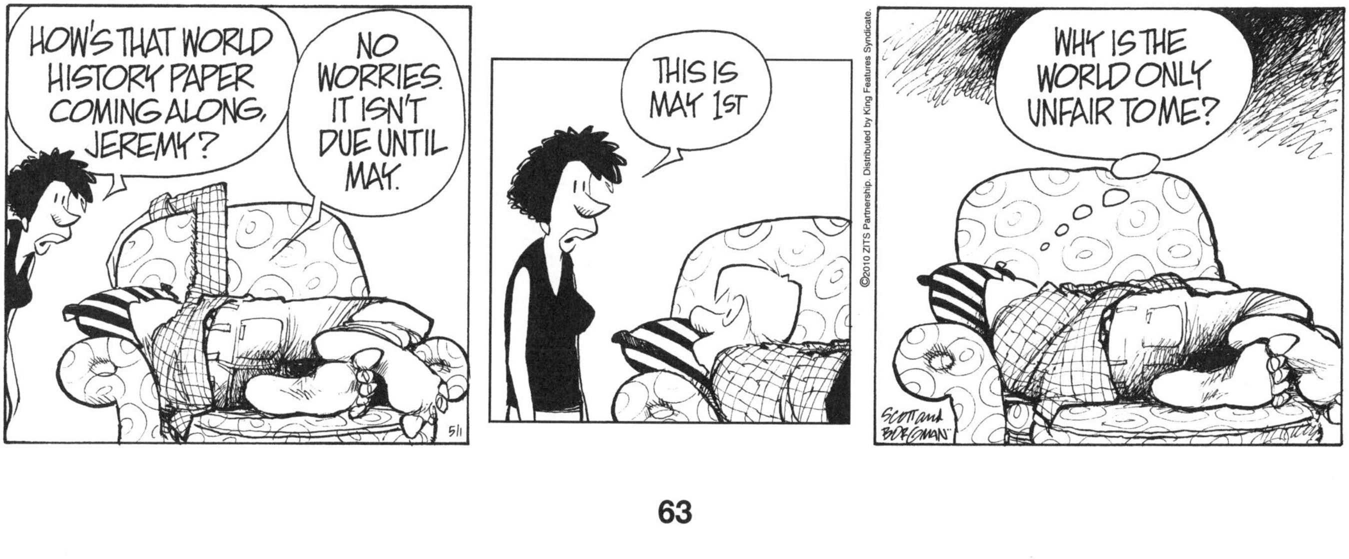
HOW'S THAT WORLD HISTORY PAPER COMING ALONG, JEREMY?
NO WORRIES. IT ISN'T DUE UNTIL MAY.
5/1
THIS IS MAY 1ST
©2010 ZITS Partnership. Distributed by King Features Syndicate.
WHY IS THE WORLD ONLY UNFAIR TO ME?
SCOTT AND BORGMAN

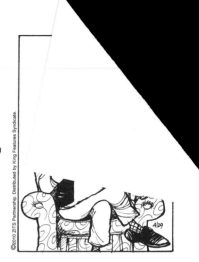

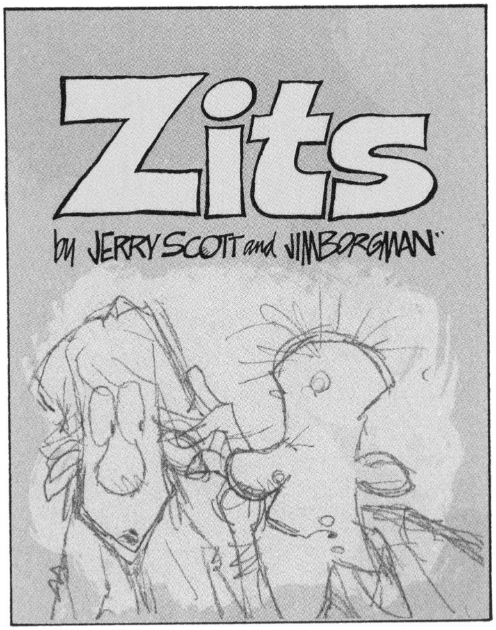
Zits
by JERRY SCOTT and JIM BORGMAN

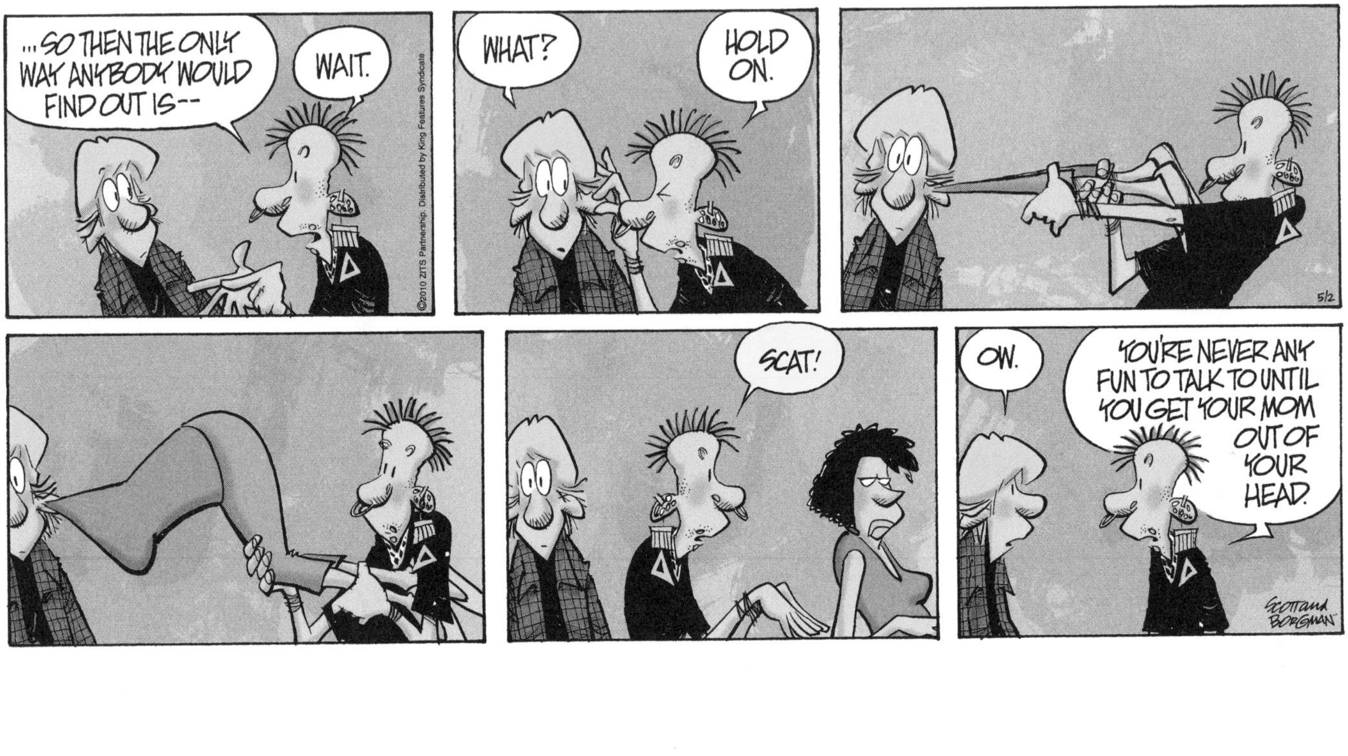
...SO THEN THE ONLY WAY ANYBODY WOULD FIND OUT IS--
WAIT.
©2010 ZITS Partnership. Distributed by King Features Syndicate
WHAT?
HOLD ON.
5/2
SCAT!
OW.
YOU'RE NEVER ANY FUN TO TALK TO UNTIL YOU GET YOUR MOM OUT OF YOUR HEAD.
SCOTT and BORGMAN

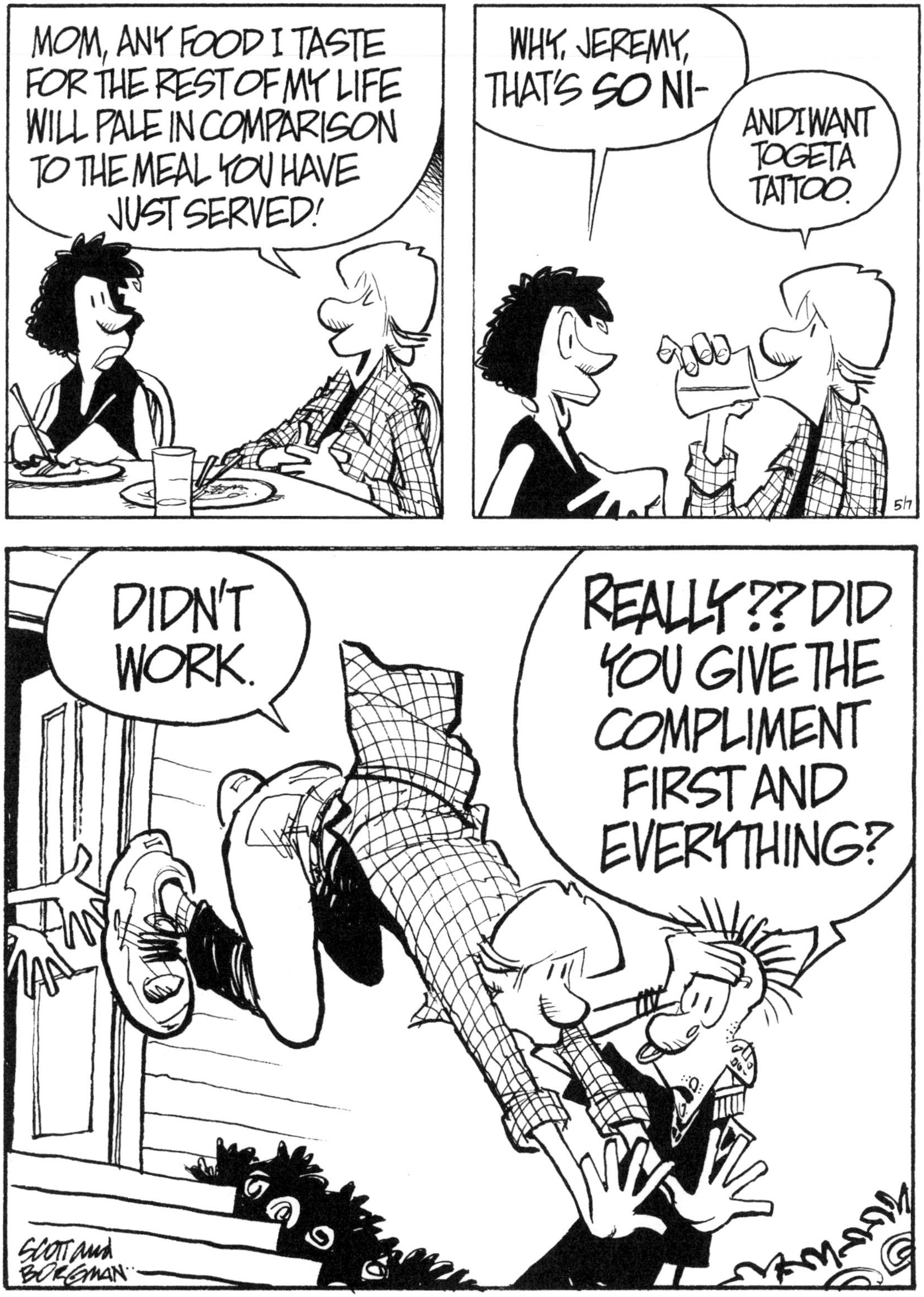
MOM, ANY FOOD I TASTE FOR THE REST OF MY LIFE WILL PALE IN COMPARISON TO THE MEAL YOU HAVE JUST SERVED!
WHY, JEREMY, THAT'S SO NI-
AND I WANT TO GET A TATTOO.
5/7
DIDN'T WORK.
REALLY?? DID YOU GIVE THE COMPLIMENT FIRST AND EVERYTHING?
SCOTT and BORGMAN

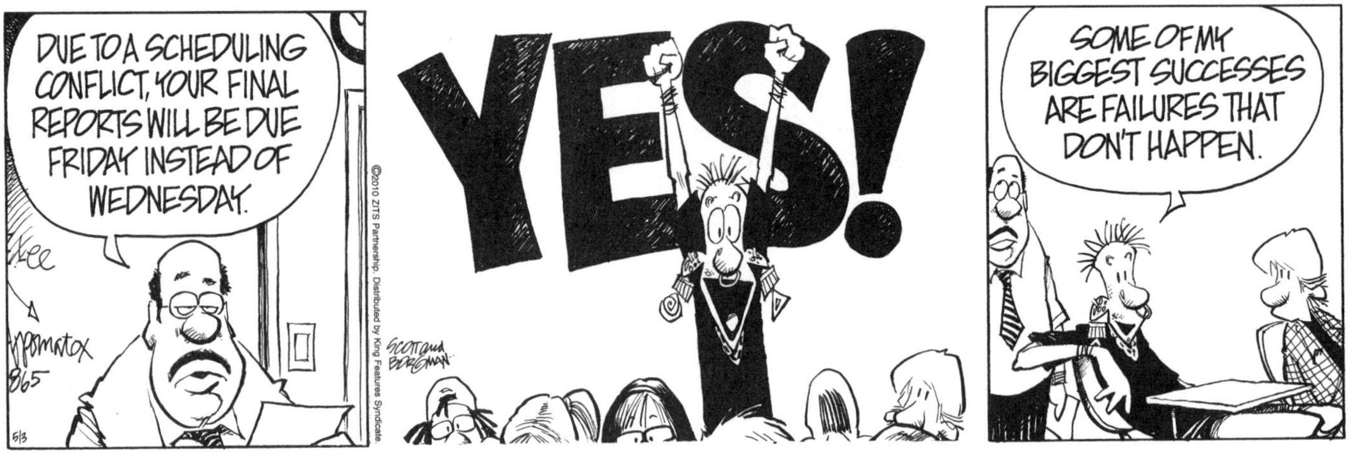
DUE TO A SCHEDULING CONFLICT, YOUR FINAL REPORTS WILL BE DUE FRIDAY INSTEAD OF WEDNESDAY.
5/3
©2010 ZITS Partnership. Distributed by King Features Syndicate.
YES!
SCOTT and BORGMAN
SOME OF MY BIGGEST SUCCESSES ARE FAILURES THAT DON'T HAPPEN.

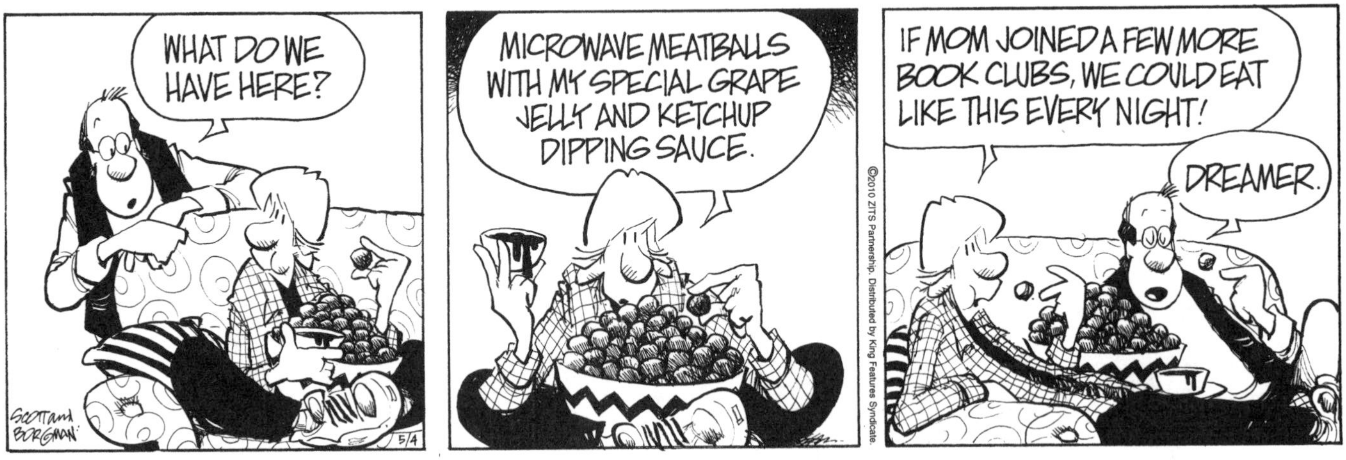
WHAT DO WE HAVE HERE?
SCOTT and BORGMAN
5/4
MICROWAVE MEATBALLS WITH MY SPECIAL GRAPE JELLY AND KETCHUP DIPPING SAUCE.
©2010 ZITS Partnership. Distributed by King Features Syndicate.
IF MOM JOINED A FEW MORE BOOK CLUBS, WE COULD EAT LIKE THIS EVERY NIGHT!
DREAMER.

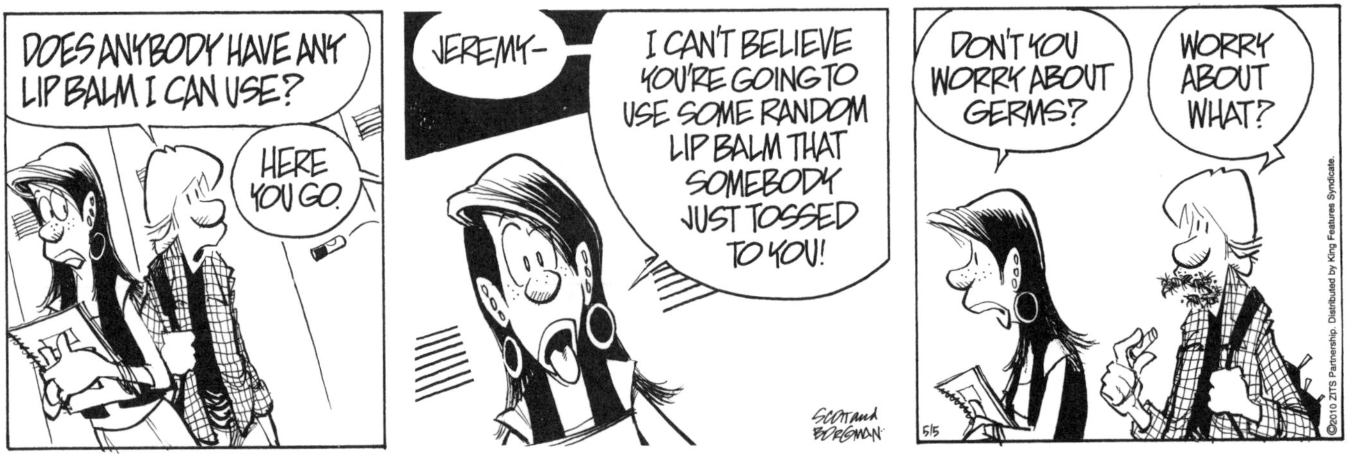
DOES ANYBODY HAVE ANY LIP BALM I CAN USE?
HERE YOU GO.
JEREMY-
I CAN'T BELIEVE YOU'RE GOING TO USE SOME RANDOM LIP BALM THAT SOMEBODY JUST TOSSED TO YOU!
SCOTT and BORGMAN
DON'T YOU WORRY ABOUT GERMS?
WORRY ABOUT WHAT?
5/5
©2010 ZITS Partnership. Distributed by King Features Syndicate.

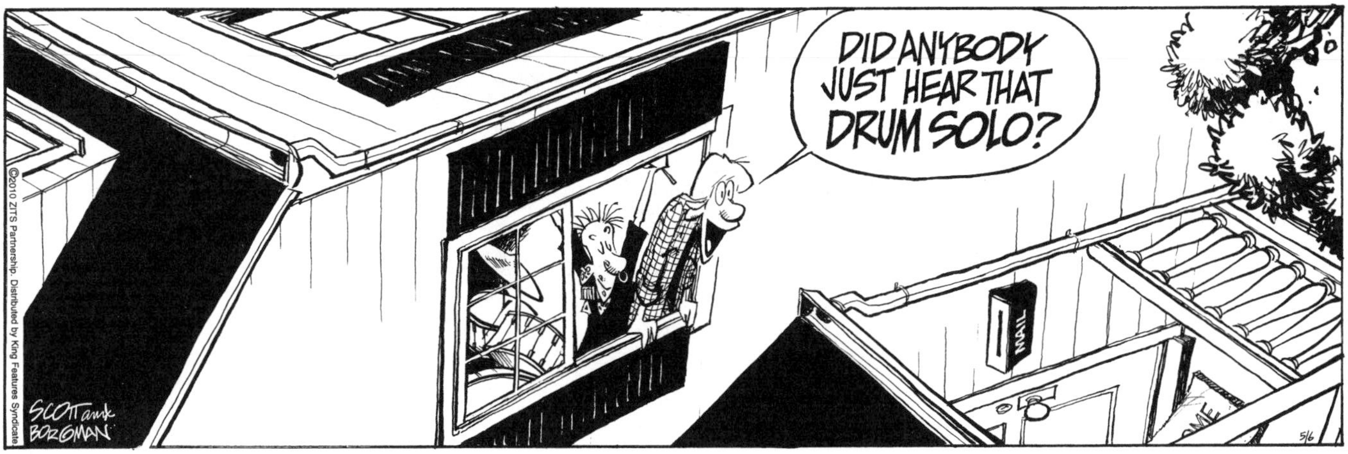
DID ANYBODY JUST HEAR THAT DRUM SOLO?
MAIL
©2010 ZITS Partnership. Distributed by King Features Syndicate.
SCOTT and BORGMAN
5/6

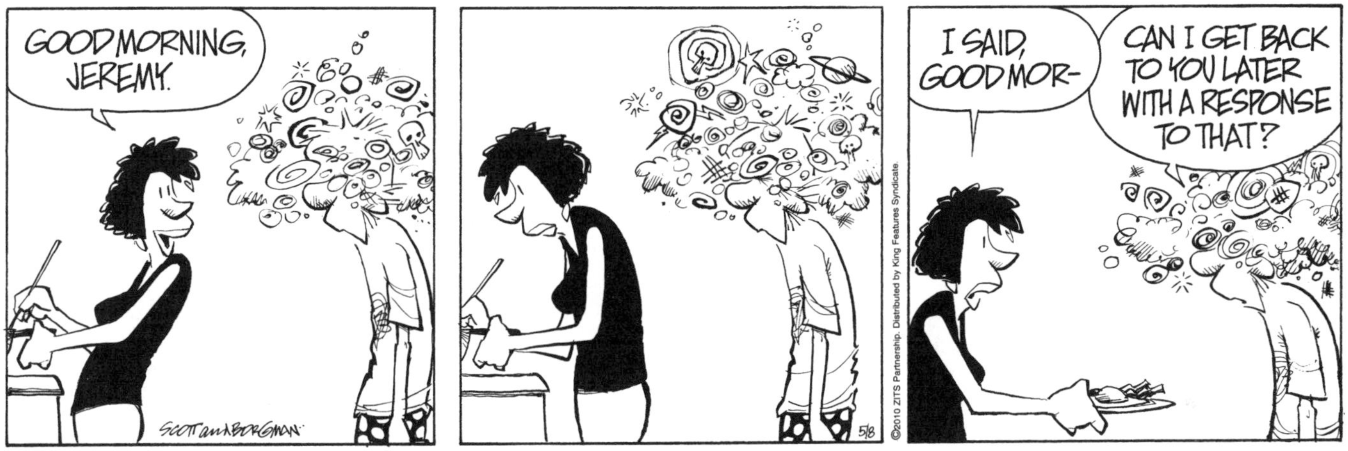
GOOD MORNING, JEREMY.
SCOTT and BORGMAN
5/8
©2010 ZITS Partnership. Distributed by King Features Syndicate.
I SAID, GOOD MOR-
CAN I GET BACK TO YOU LATER WITH A RESPONSE TO THAT?

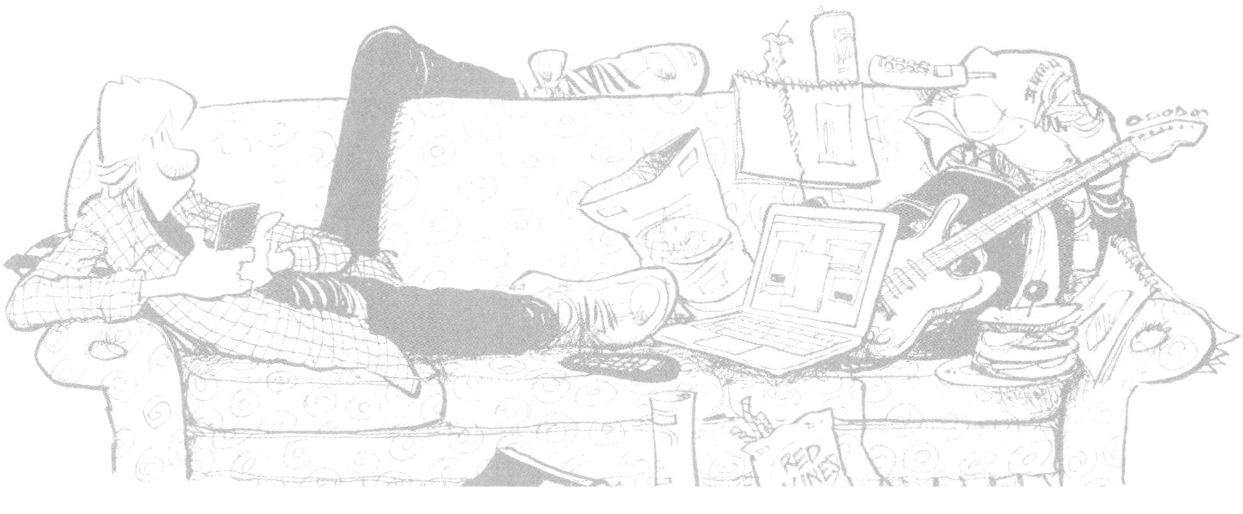
RED VINES

Zits
by
JERRY SCOTT and
JIM BORGMAN

JEREMY, IS THAT THE WAY YOU ALWAYS HOLD A PENCIL?
YEAH, WHY?
YOUR HAND LOOKS LIKE A CLAW ALL TWISTED UP LIKE THAT!
©2010 ZITS Partnership. Distributed by King Features Syndicate
IT DOES?
YES!
I CAN'T IMAGINE WHAT IT MUST FEEL LIKE TO WRITE LIKE THAT FOR VERY LONG.
THAT MAKES TWO OF US.
SCOTT and BORGMAN
5/9

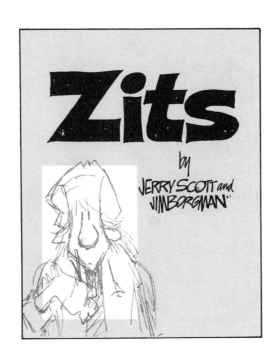

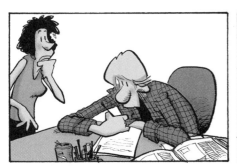

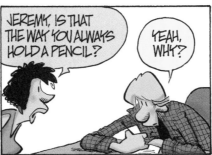

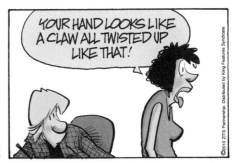

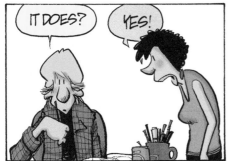

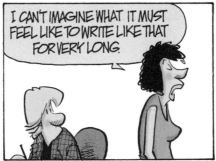

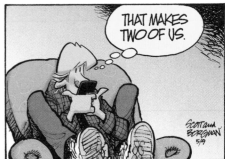

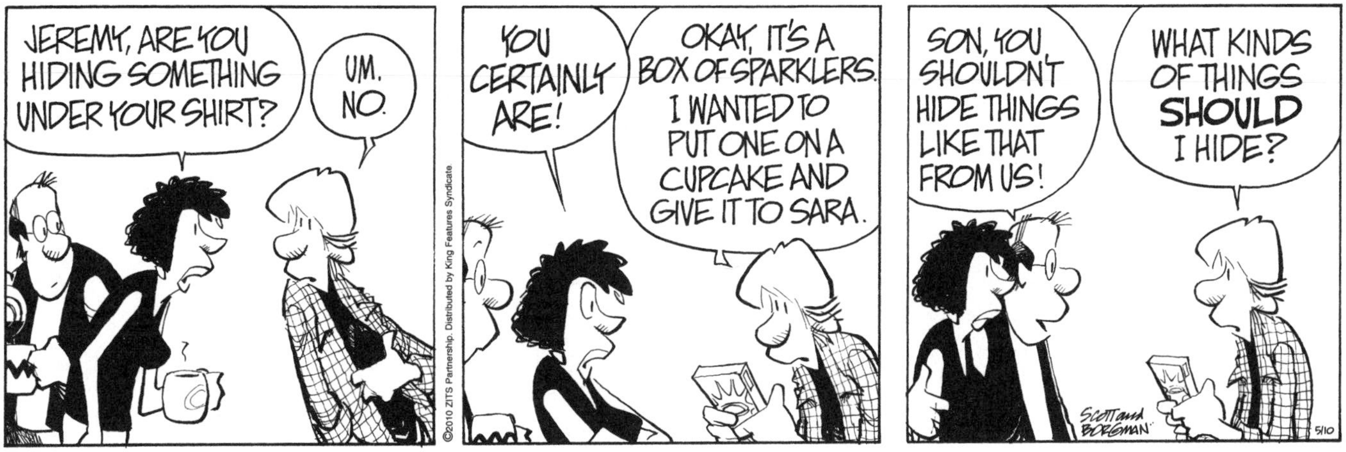
JEREMY, ARE YOU HIDING SOMETHING UNDER YOUR SHIRT?
UM. NO.
YOU CERTAINLY ARE!
OKAY, IT'S A BOX OF SPARKLERS. I WANTED TO PUT ONE ON A CUPCAKE AND GIVE IT TO SARA.
SON, YOU SHOULDN'T HIDE THINGS LIKE THAT FROM US!
WHAT KINDS OF THINGS **SHOULD** I HIDE?
SCOTT and BORGMAN
5/10

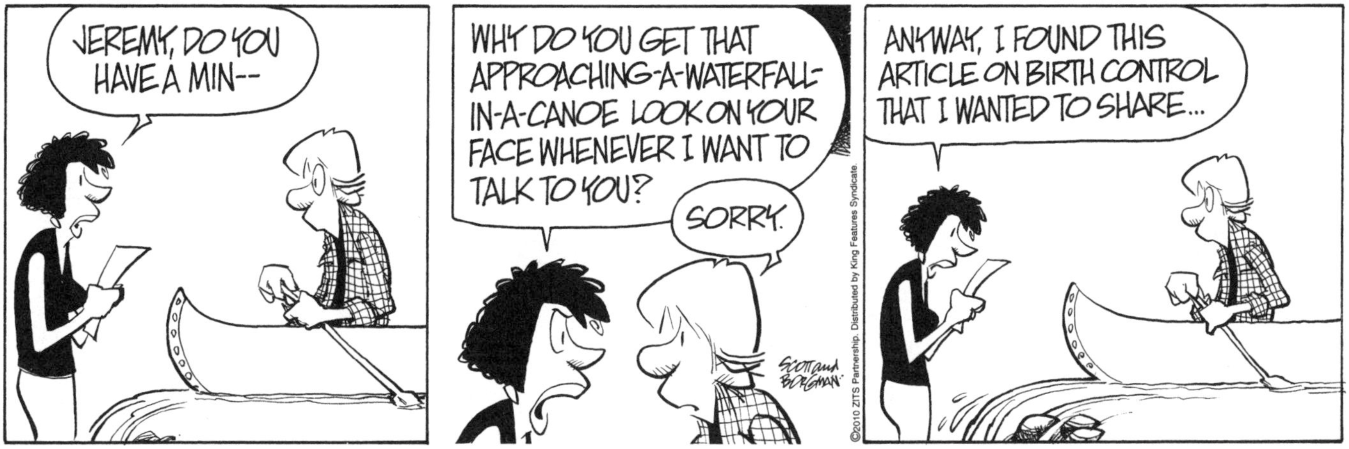
JEREMY, DO YOU HAVE A MIN--
WHY DO YOU GET THAT APPROACHING-A-WATERFALL-IN-A-CANOE LOOK ON YOUR FACE WHENEVER I WANT TO TALK TO YOU?
SORRY.
SCOTT and BORGMAN
ANYWAY, I FOUND THIS ARTICLE ON BIRTH CONTROL THAT I WANTED TO SHARE...

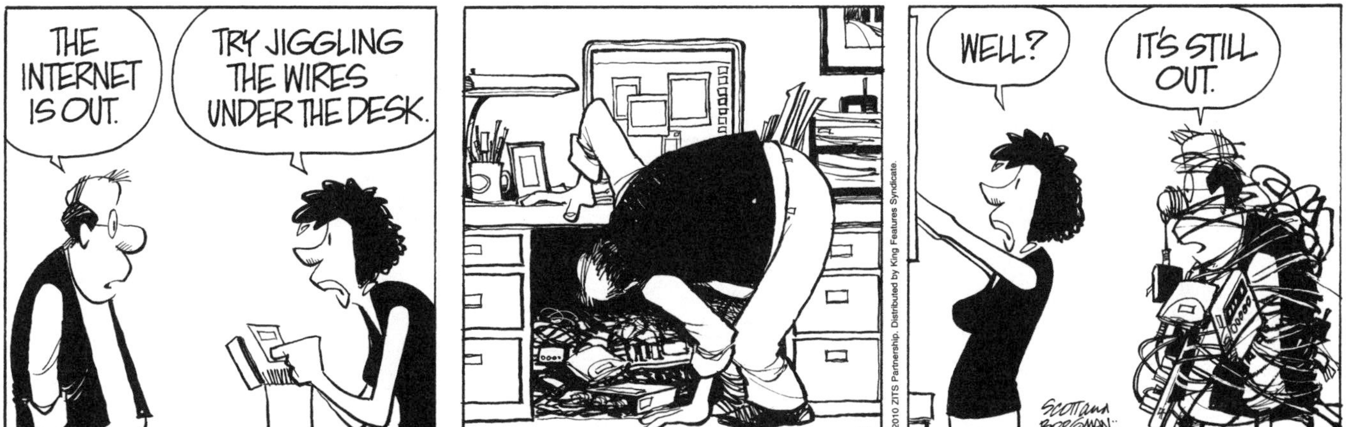
THE INTERNET IS OUT.
TRY JIGGLING THE WIRES UNDER THE DESK.
5/12
WELL?
IT'S STILL OUT.
SCOTT and BORGMAN

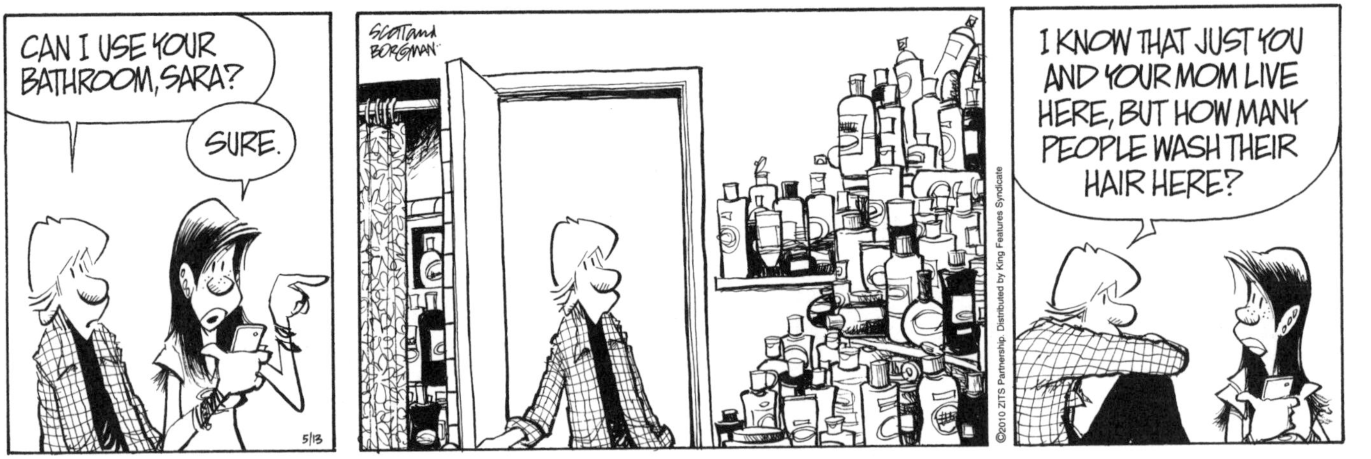
CAN I USE YOUR BATHROOM, SARA?
SURE.
I KNOW THAT JUST YOU AND YOUR MOM LIVE HERE, BUT HOW MANY PEOPLE WASH THEIR HAIR HERE?
©2010 ZITS Partnership. Distributed by King Features Syndicate

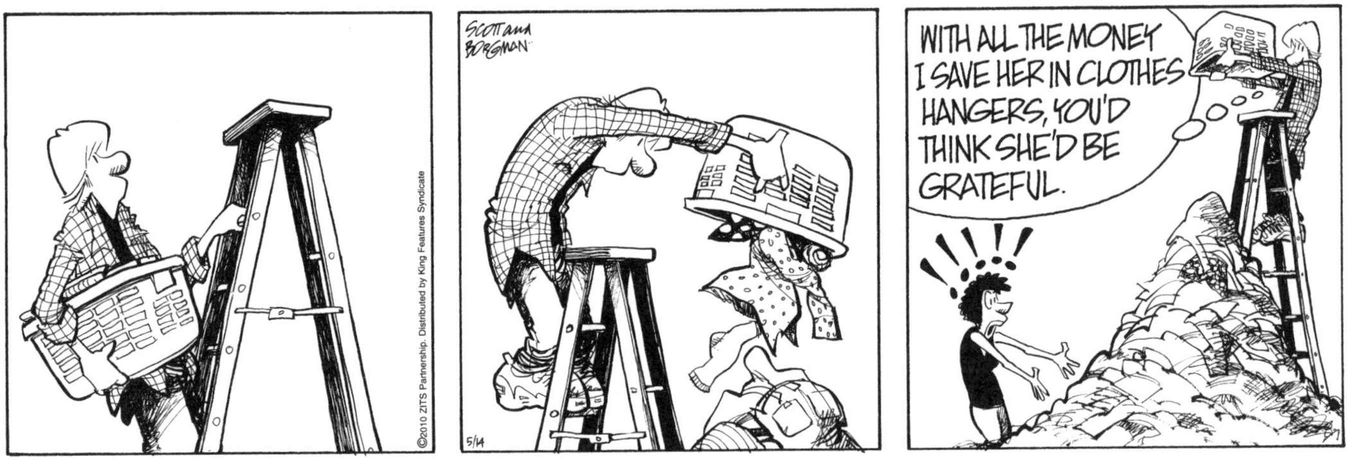
©2010 ZITS Partnership. Distributed by King Features Syndicate
WITH ALL THE MONEY I SAVE HER IN CLOTHES HANGERS, YOU'D THINK SHE'D BE GRATEFUL.

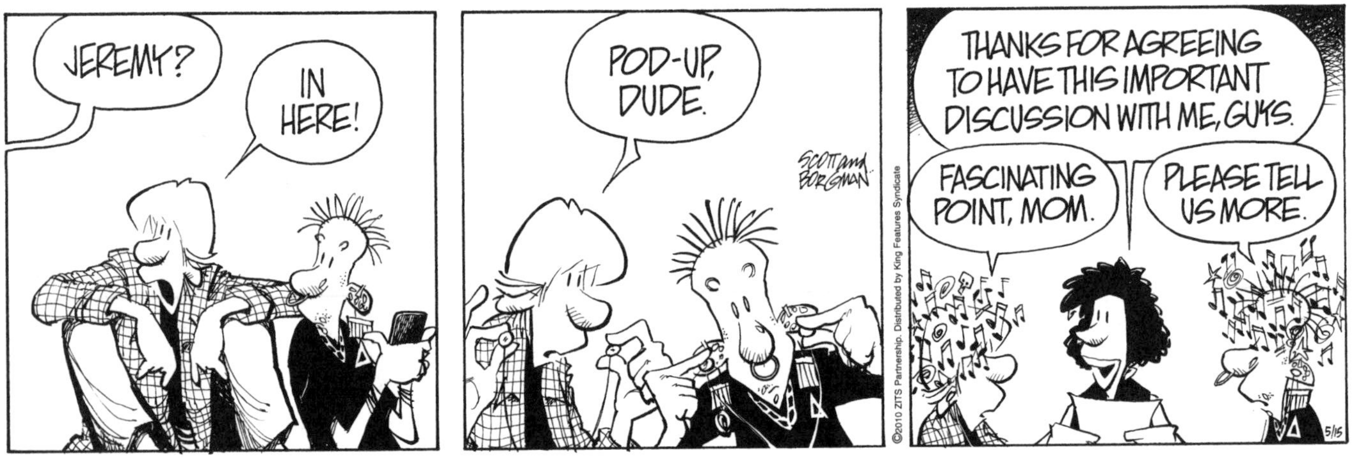
JEREMY?
IN HERE!
POD-UP, DUDE.
©2010 ZITS Partnership. Distributed by King Features Syndicate
THANKS FOR AGREEING TO HAVE THIS IMPORTANT DISCUSSION WITH ME, GUYS.
FASCINATING POINT, MOM.
PLEASE TELL US MORE.

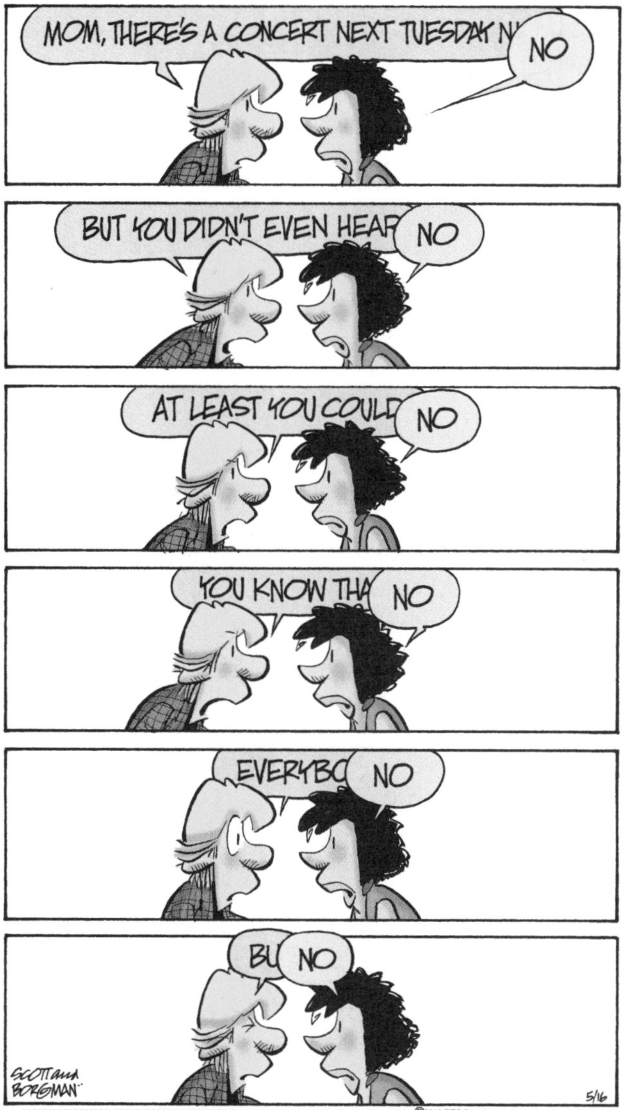
MOM, THERE'S A CONCERT NEXT TUESDAY N
NO
BUT YOU DIDN'T EVEN HEAR
NO
AT LEAST YOU COULD
NO
YOU KNOW THA
NO
EVERYBO
NO
BU
NO
SCOTT and BORGMAN
5/16

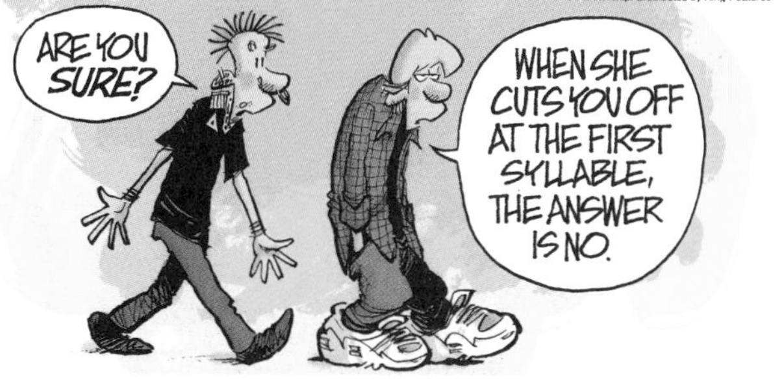
ARE YOU *SURE?*
WHEN SHE CUTS YOU OFF AT THE FIRST SYLLABLE, THE ANSWER IS NO.

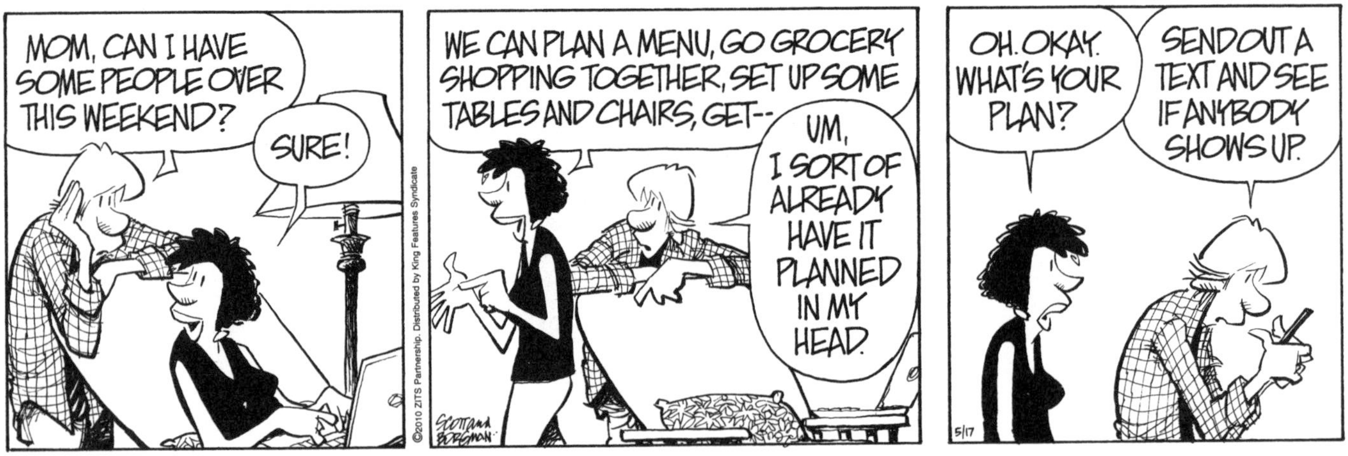
MOM, CAN I HAVE SOME PEOPLE OVER THIS WEEKEND?
SURE!
©2010 ZITS Partnership. Distributed by King Features Syndicate
WE CAN PLAN A MENU, GO GROCERY SHOPPING TOGETHER, SET UP SOME TABLES AND CHAIRS, GET--
UM, I SORT OF ALREADY HAVE IT PLANNED IN MY HEAD.
OH. OKAY. WHAT'S YOUR PLAN?
SEND OUT A TEXT AND SEE IF ANYBODY SHOWS UP.
5/17

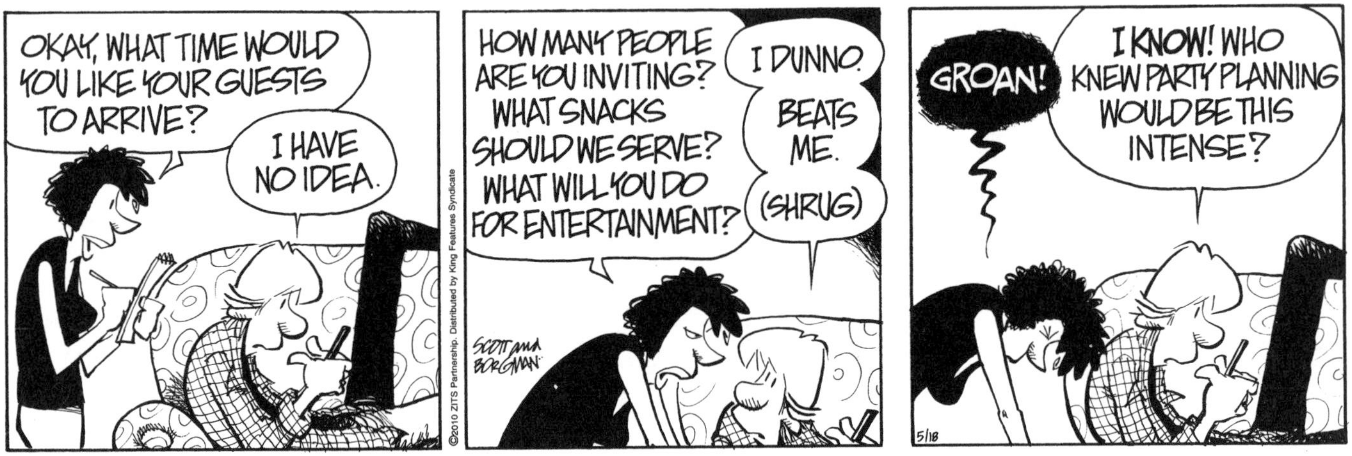
OKAY, WHAT TIME WOULD YOU LIKE YOUR GUESTS TO ARRIVE?
I HAVE NO IDEA.
©2010 ZITS Partnership. Distributed by King Features Syndicate
HOW MANY PEOPLE ARE YOU INVITING? WHAT SNACKS SHOULD WE SERVE? WHAT WILL YOU DO FOR ENTERTAINMENT?
I DUNNO.
BEATS ME.
(SHRUG)
GROAN!
I KNOW! WHO KNEW PARTY PLANNING WOULD BE THIS INTENSE?
5/18

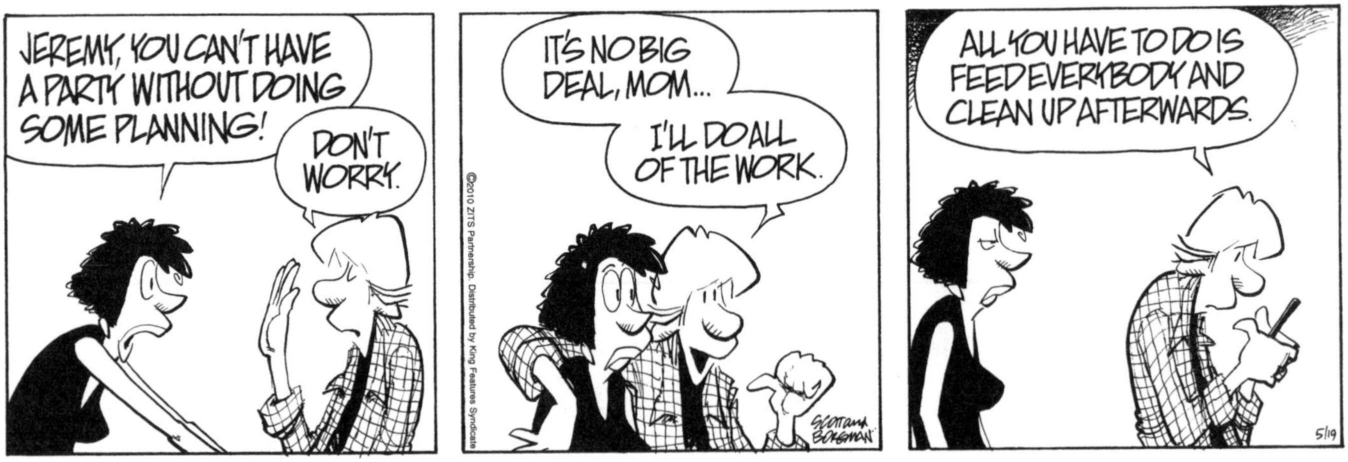
JEREMY, YOU CAN'T HAVE A PARTY WITHOUT DOING SOME PLANNING!
DON'T WORRY.
©2010 ZITS Partnership. Distributed by King Features Syndicate
IT'S NO BIG DEAL, MOM...
I'LL DO ALL OF THE WORK.
ALL YOU HAVE TO DO IS FEED EVERYBODY AND CLEAN UP AFTERWARDS.
5/19

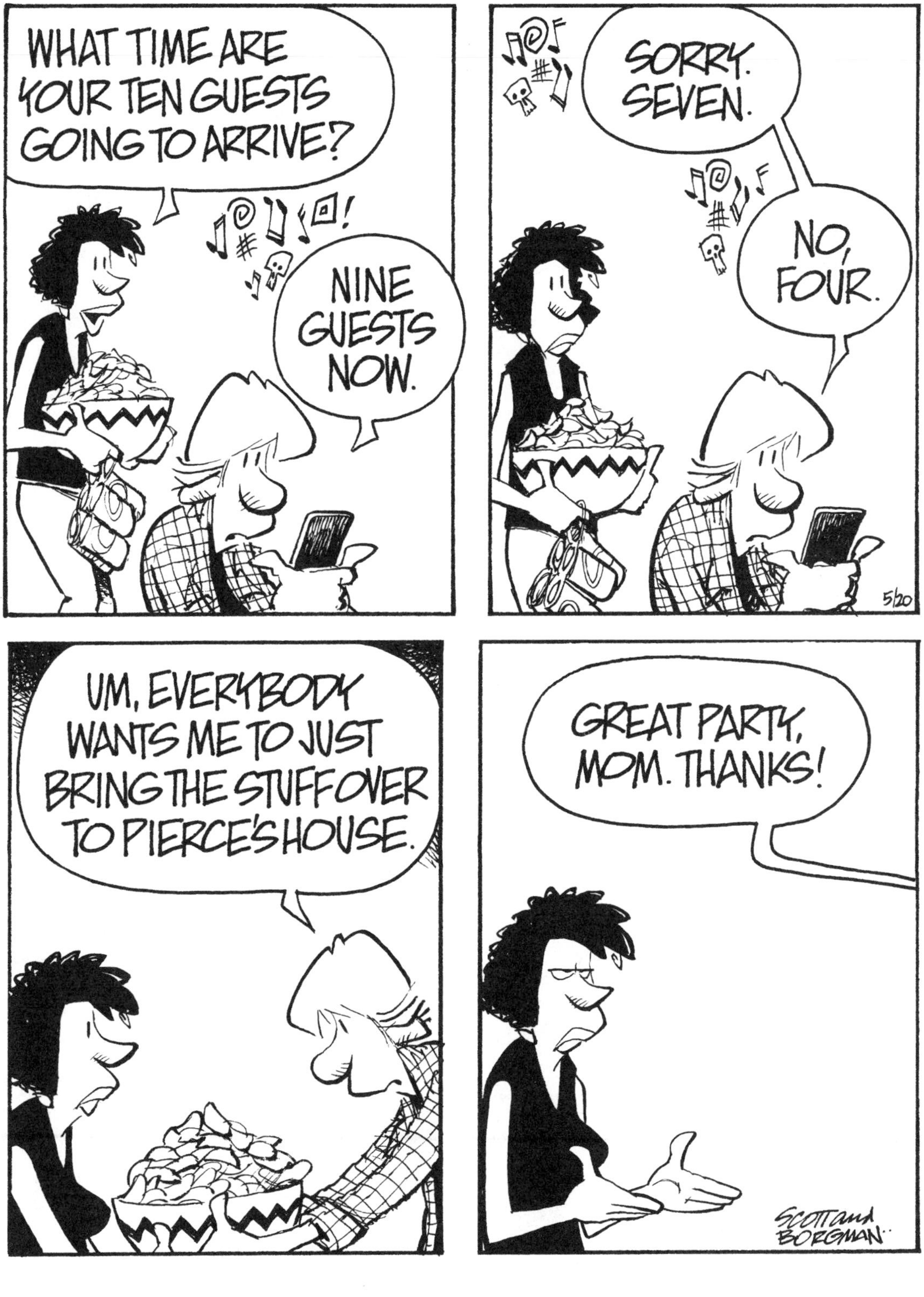
WHAT TIME ARE YOUR TEN GUESTS GOING TO ARRIVE?
NINE GUESTS NOW.
SORRY. SEVEN.
NO, FOUR.
5/20
UM, EVERYBODY WANTS ME TO JUST BRING THE STUFF OVER TO PIERCE'S HOUSE.
GREAT PARTY, MOM. THANKS!
SCOTT and BORGMAN

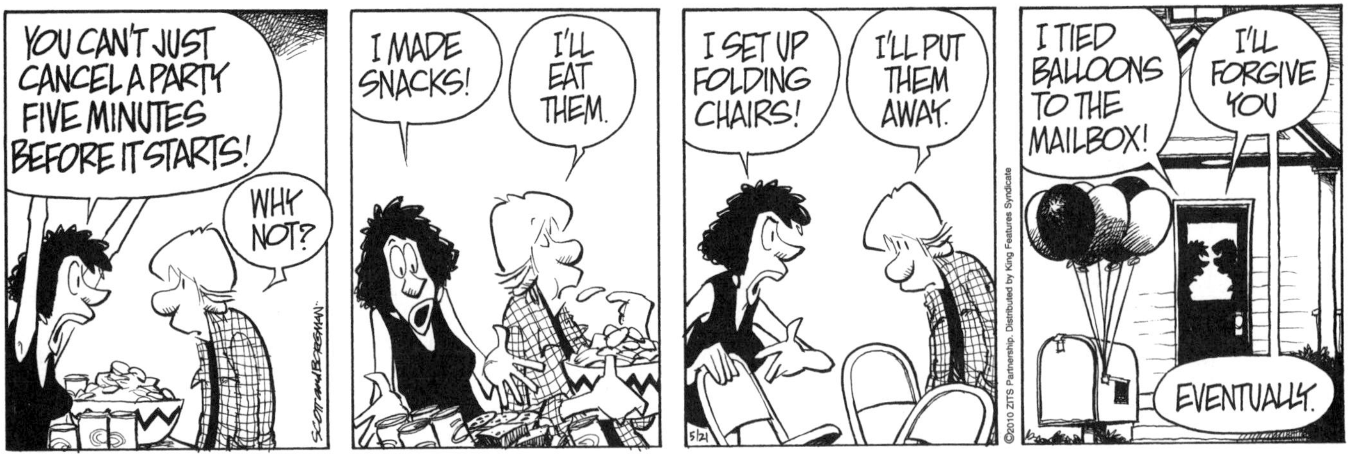
YOU CAN'T JUST CANCEL A PARTY FIVE MINUTES BEFORE IT STARTS!
WHY NOT?
I MADE SNACKS!
I'LL EAT THEM.
I SET UP FOLDING CHAIRS!
I'LL PUT THEM AWAY.
I TIED BALLOONS TO THE MAILBOX!
I'LL FORGIVE YOU
EVENTUALLY.
SCOTT and BORGMAN
5/21
©2010 ZITS Partnership. Distributed by King Features Syndicate

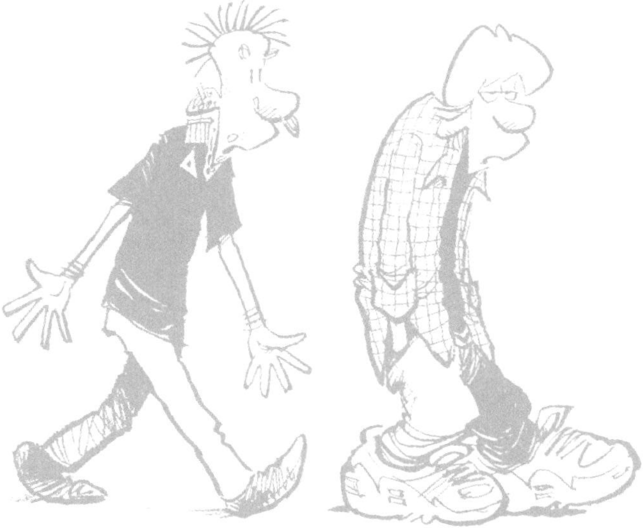

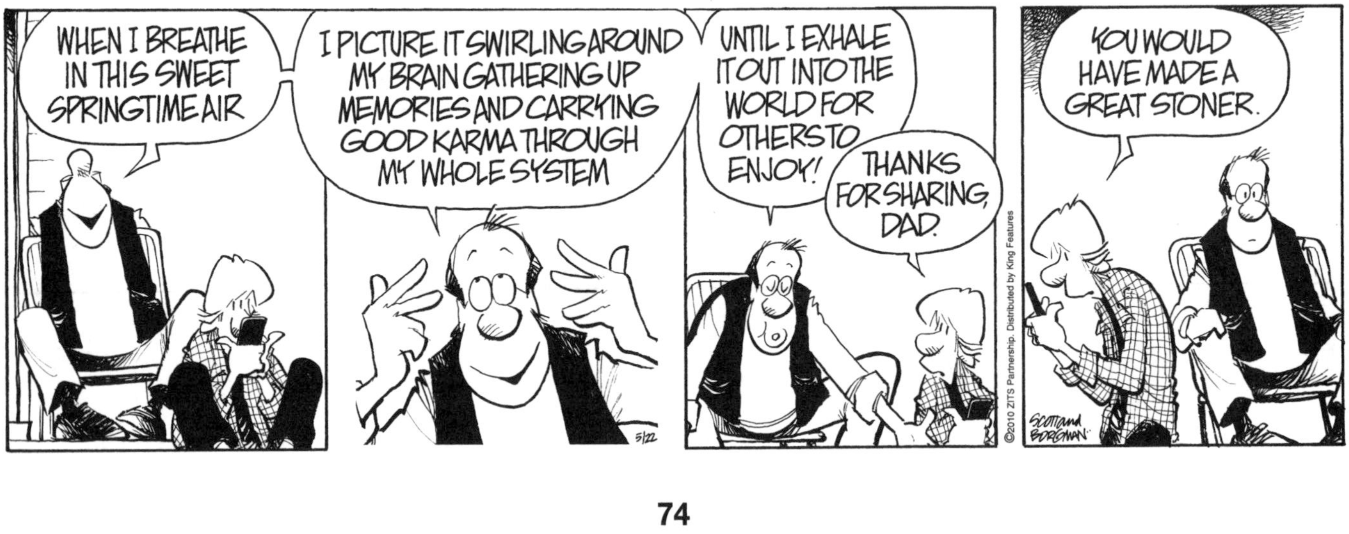
WHEN I BREATHE IN THIS SWEET SPRINGTIME AIR
I PICTURE IT SWIRLING AROUND MY BRAIN GATHERING UP MEMORIES AND CARRYING GOOD KARMA THROUGH MY WHOLE SYSTEM
UNTIL I EXHALE IT OUT INTO THE WORLD FOR OTHERS TO ENJOY!
THANKS FOR SHARING, DAD.
YOU WOULD HAVE MADE A GREAT STONER.
5/22
©2010 ZITS Partnership. Distributed by King Features
SCOTT and BORGMAN

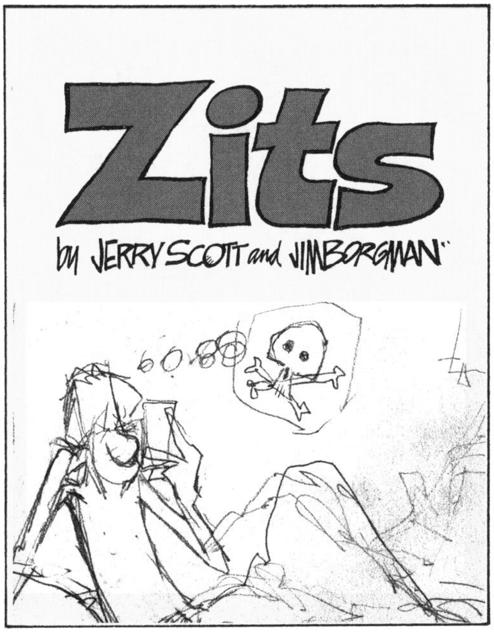
Zits
by JERRY SCOTT and JIM BORGMAN

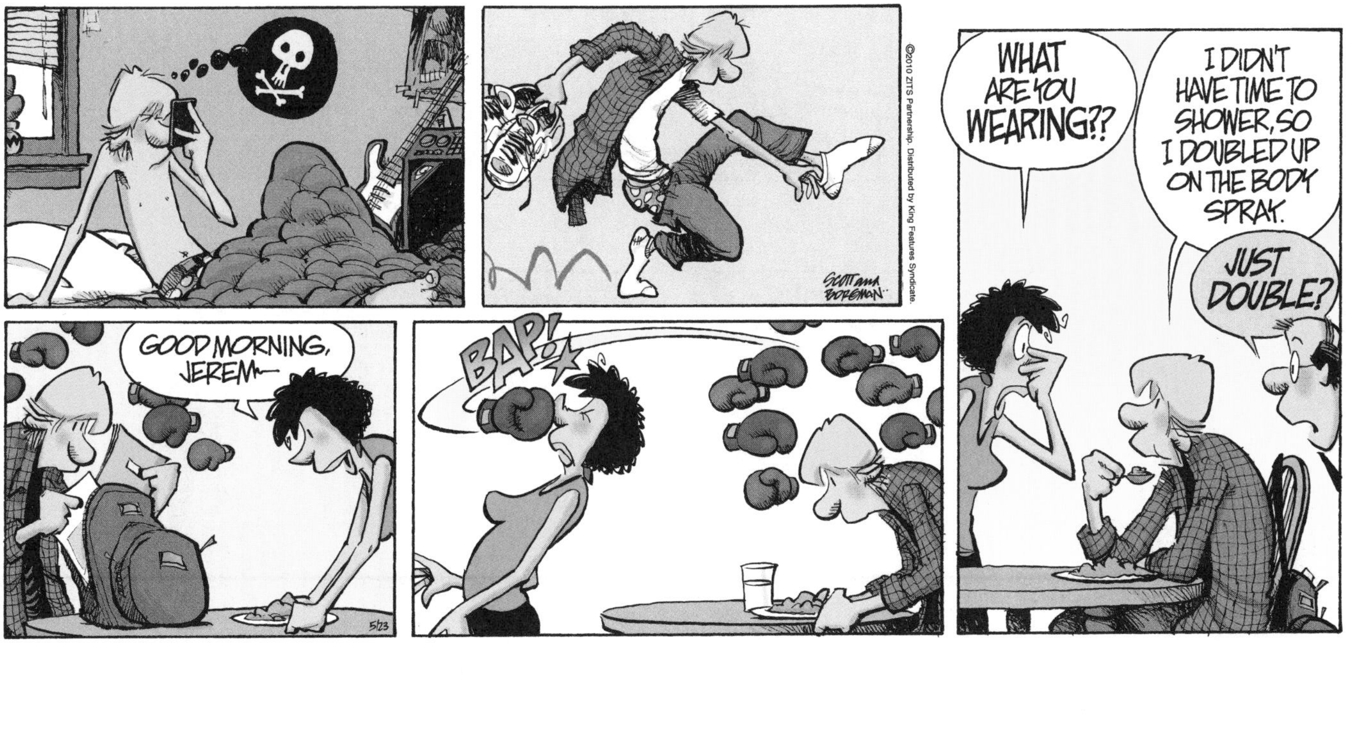
©2010 ZITS Partnership. Distributed by King Features Syndicate.
SCOTT and BORGMAN
GOOD MORNING, JEREM–
5/23
BAP!
WHAT ARE YOU WEARING??
I DIDN'T HAVE TIME TO SHOWER, SO I DOUBLED UP ON THE BODY SPRAY.
JUST DOUBLE?

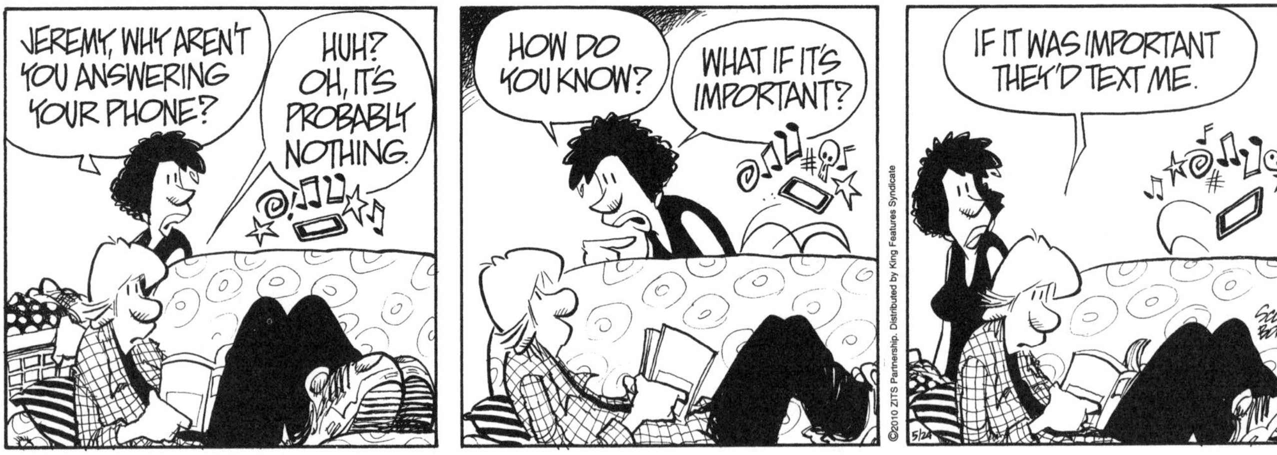
JEREMY, WHY AREN'T YOU ANSWERING YOUR PHONE?
HUH? OH, IT'S PROBABLY NOTHING.
HOW DO YOU KNOW?
WHAT IF IT'S IMPORTANT?
IF IT WAS IMPORTANT THEY'D TEXT ME.
©2010 ZITS Partnership. Distributed by King Features Syndicate.
5/24
SCOTT and BORGMAN

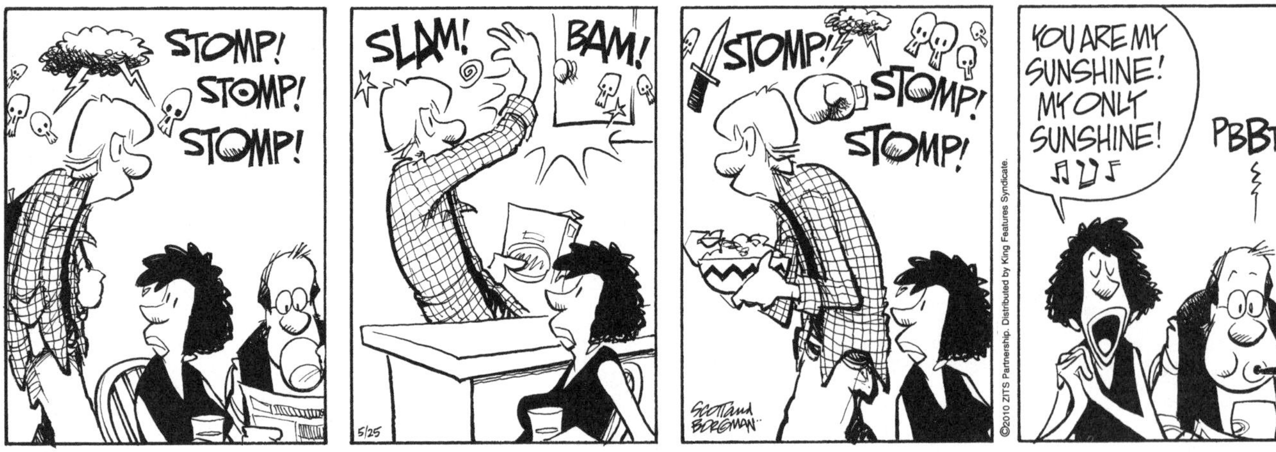
STOMP! STOMP! STOMP!
SLAM!
BAM!
5/25
STOMP! STOMP! STOMP!
SCOTT and BORGMAN
©2010 ZITS Partnership. Distributed by King Features Syndicate.
YOU ARE MY SUNSHINE! MY ONLY SUNSHINE!
PBBTH!

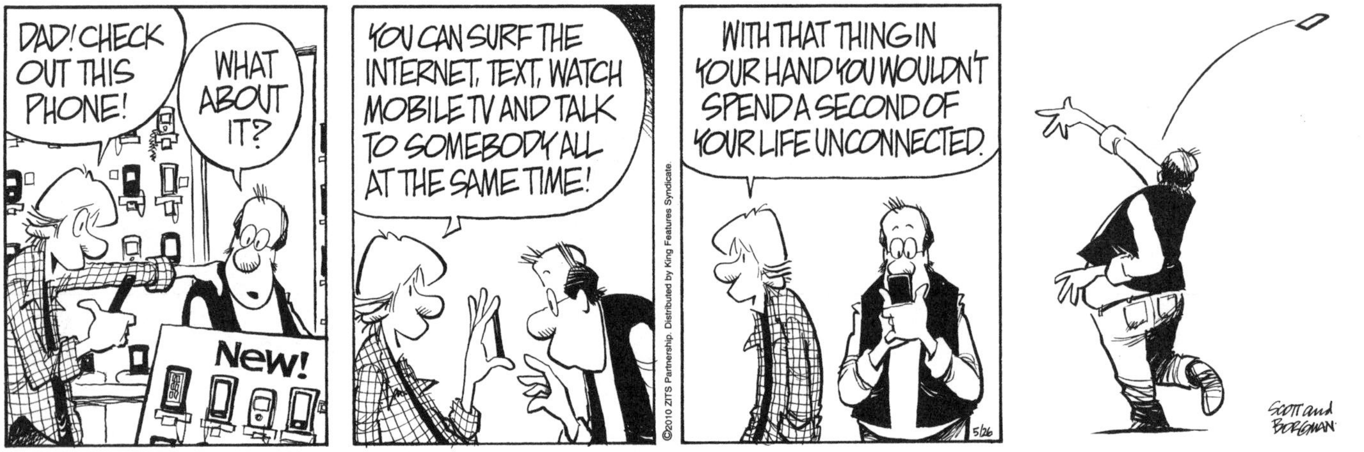
DAD! CHECK OUT THIS PHONE!
WHAT ABOUT IT?
New!
YOU CAN SURF THE INTERNET, TEXT, WATCH MOBILE TV AND TALK TO SOMEBODY ALL AT THE SAME TIME!
©2010 ZITS Partnership. Distributed by King Features Syndicate.
WITH THAT THING IN YOUR HAND YOU WOULDN'T SPEND A SECOND OF YOUR LIFE UNCONNECTED.
5/26
SCOTT and BORGMAN

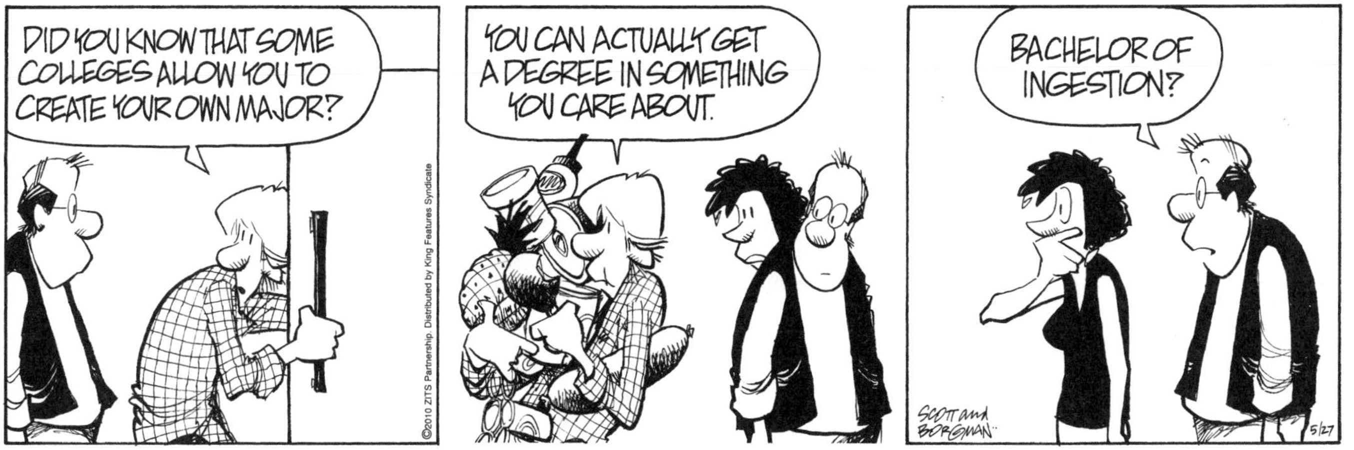
DID YOU KNOW THAT SOME COLLEGES ALLOW YOU TO CREATE YOUR OWN MAJOR?
YOU CAN ACTUALLY GET A DEGREE IN SOMETHING YOU CARE ABOUT.
BACHELOR OF INGESTION?
©2010 ZITS Partnership. Distributed by King Features Syndicate
SCOTT and BORGMAN
5/27

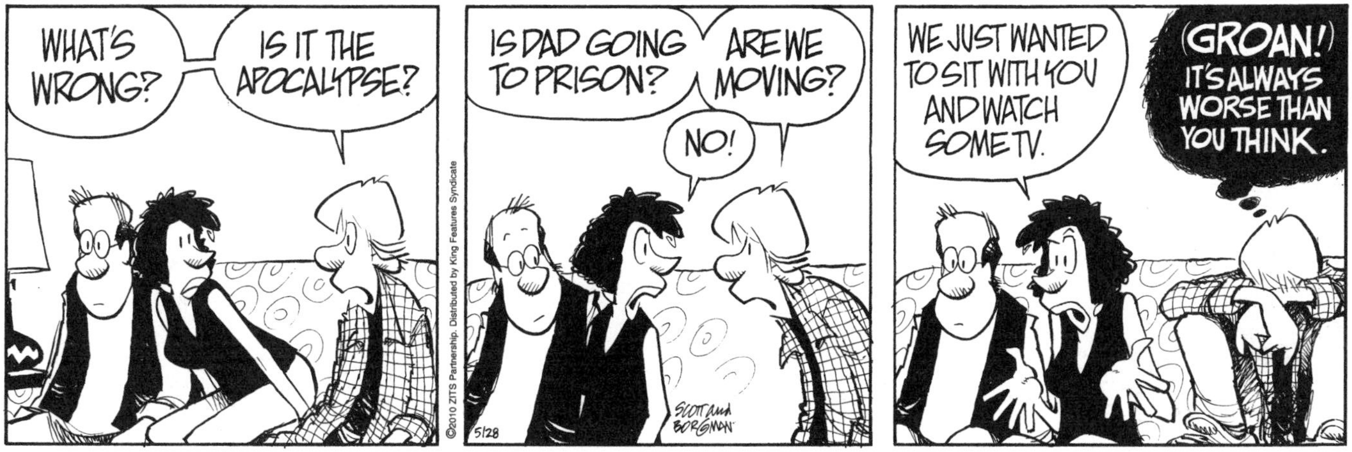
WHAT'S WRONG?
IS IT THE APOCALYPSE?
IS DAD GOING TO PRISON?
ARE WE MOVING?
NO!
WE JUST WANTED TO SIT WITH YOU AND WATCH SOME TV.
(GROAN!) IT'S ALWAYS WORSE THAN YOU THINK.
©2010 ZITS Partnership. Distributed by King Features Syndicate
5/28
SCOTT and BORGMAN

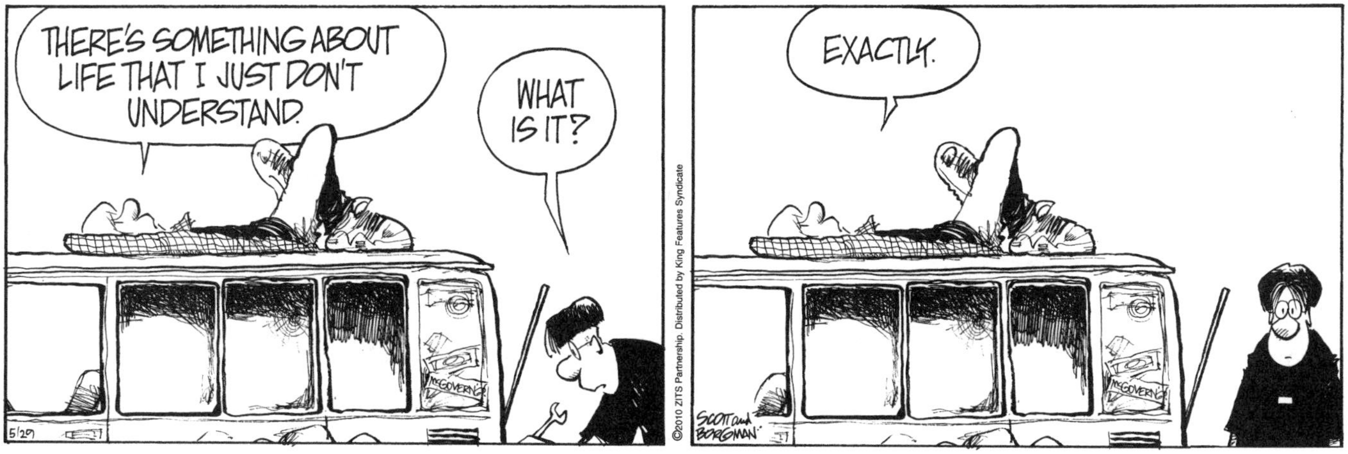
THERE'S SOMETHING ABOUT LIFE THAT I JUST DON'T UNDERSTAND.
WHAT IS IT?
EXACTLY.
McGOVERN
5/29
©2010 ZITS Partnership. Distributed by King Features Syndicate
SCOTT and BORGMAN

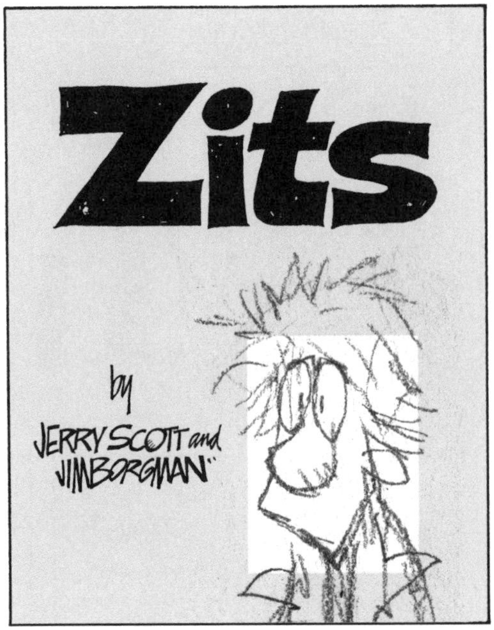
Zits
by
JERRY SCOTT and JIM BORGMAN

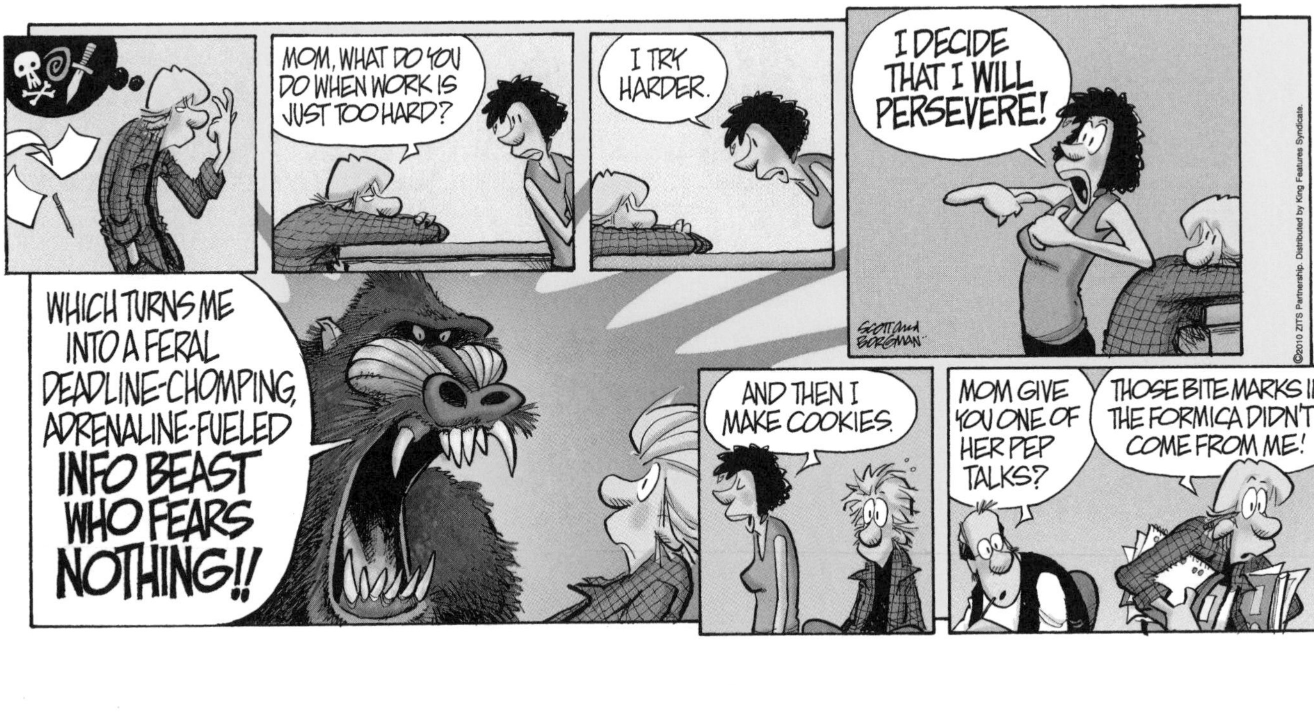
MOM, WHAT DO YOU DO WHEN WORK IS JUST TOO HARD?
I TRY HARDER.
I DECIDE THAT I WILL PERSEVERE!
SCOTT and BORGMAN
©2010 ZITS Partnership. Distributed by King Features Syndicate.
WHICH TURNS ME INTO A FERAL DEADLINE-CHOMPING, ADRENALINE-FUELED INFO BEAST WHO FEARS NOTHING!!
AND THEN I MAKE COOKIES.
MOM GIVE YOU ONE OF HER PEP TALKS?
THOSE BITE MARKS IN THE FORMICA DIDN'T COME FROM ME!
5/30

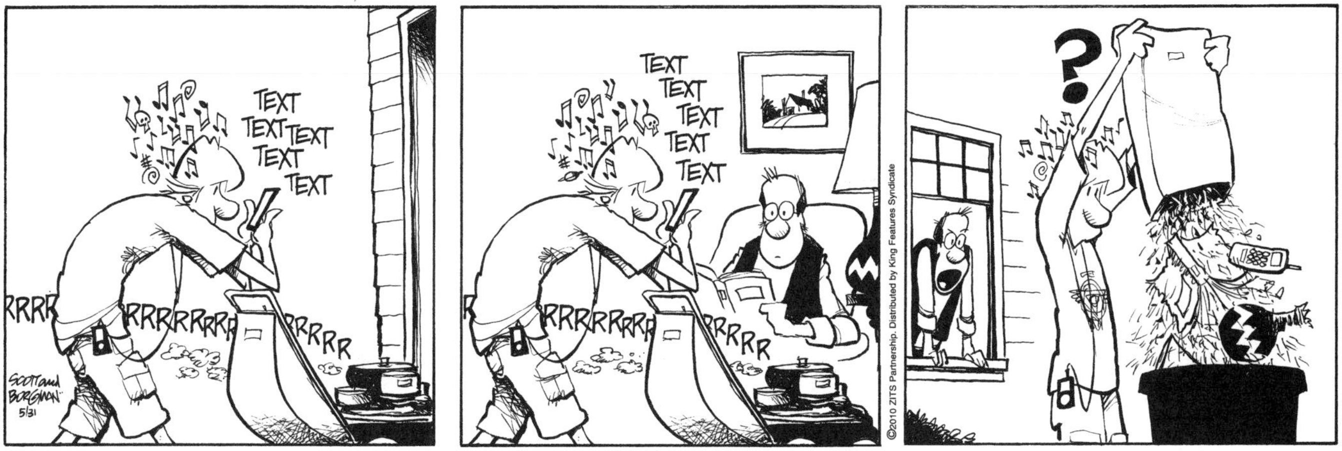
TEXT
TEXT TEXT
TEXT
TEXT
RRRR
RRRRRRRR
RRRRR
SCOTT and BORGMAN 5/31
TEXT
TEXT
TEXT
TEXT
TEXT
?
©2010 ZITS Partnership. Distributed by King Features Syndicate

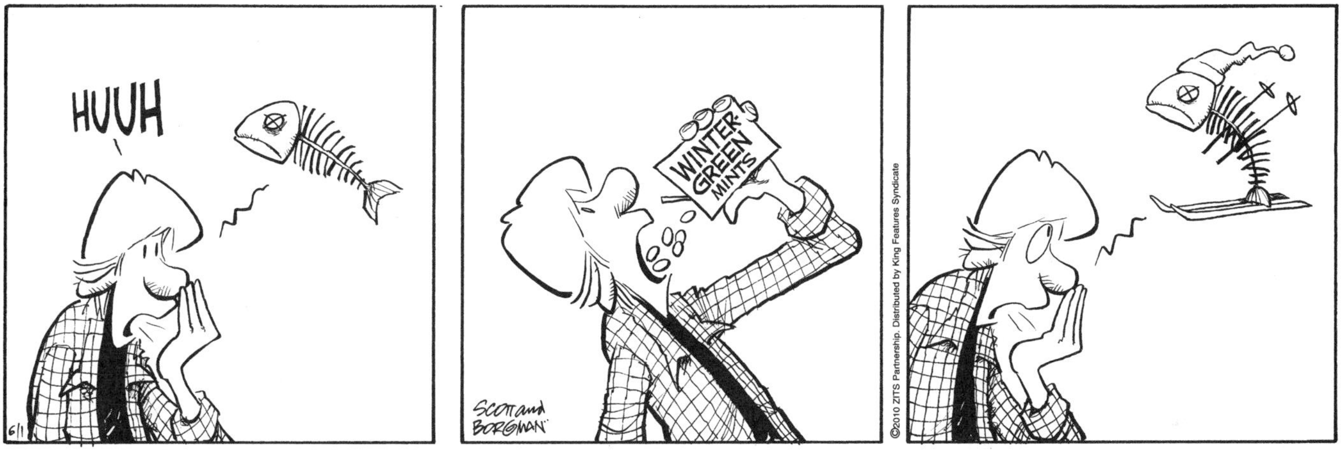
HUUH
6/1
WINTER GREEN MINTS
SCOTT and BORGMAN
©2010 ZITS Partnership. Distributed by King Features Syndicate

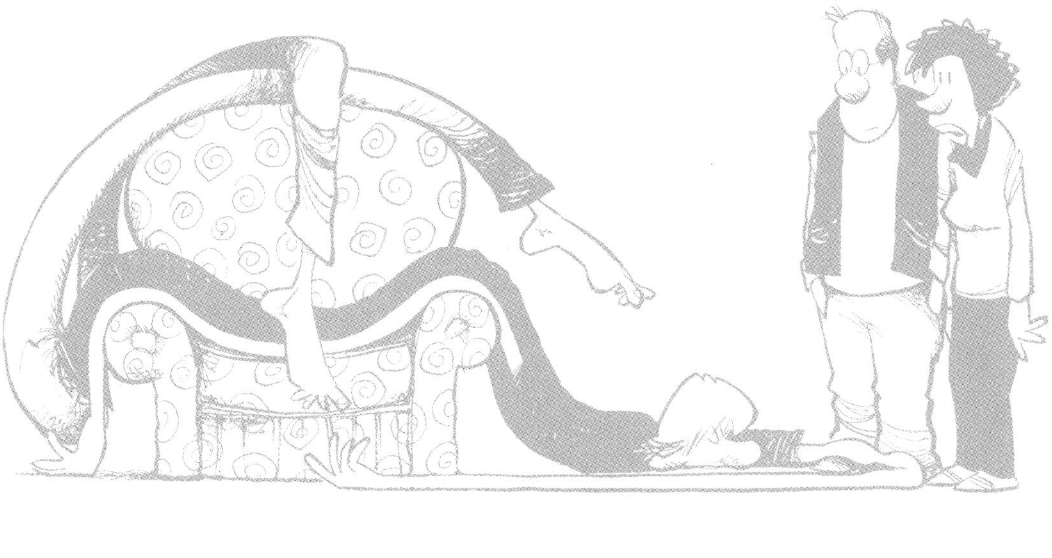

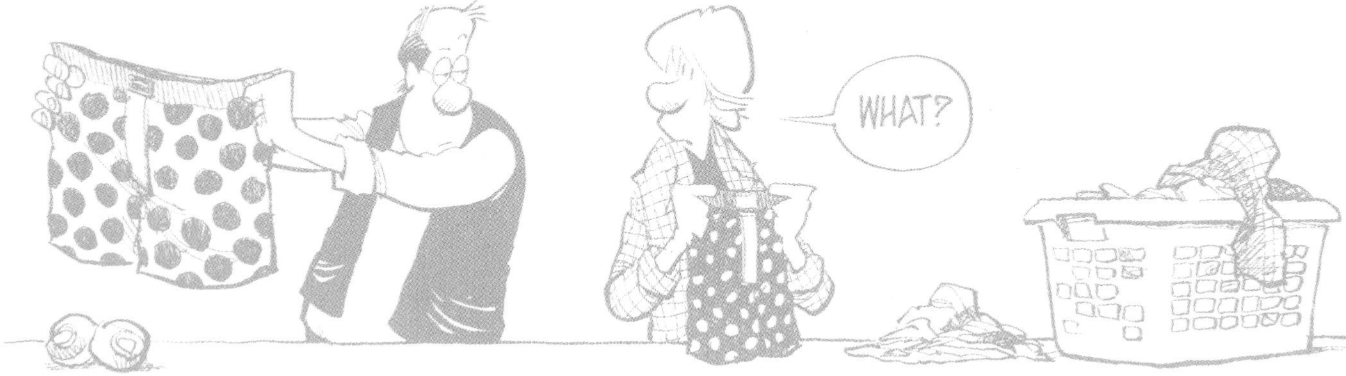
WHAT?

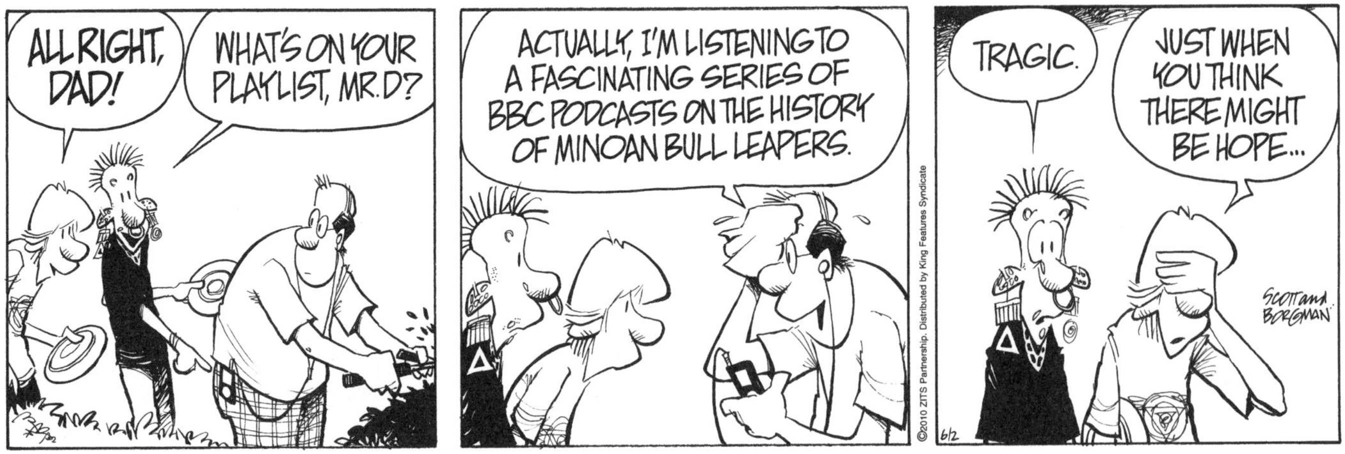
ALL RIGHT, DAD!
WHAT'S ON YOUR PLAYLIST, MR. D?
ACTUALLY, I'M LISTENING TO A FASCINATING SERIES OF BBC PODCASTS ON THE HISTORY OF MINOAN BULL LEAPERS.
©2010 ZITS Partnership. Distributed by King Features Syndicate
6/2
TRAGIC.
JUST WHEN YOU THINK THERE MIGHT BE HOPE...
SCOTT AND BORGMAN

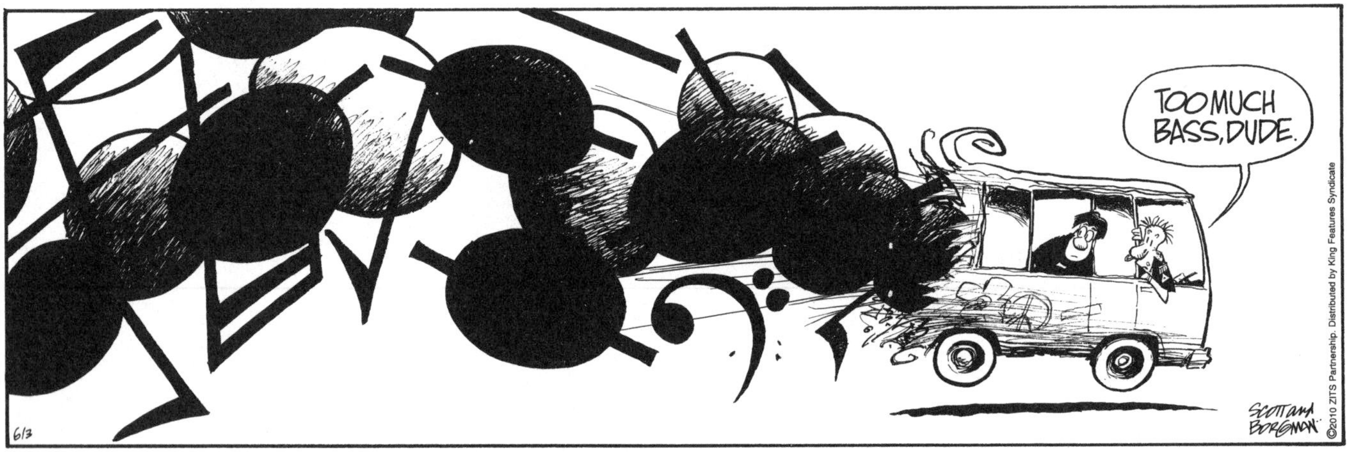
TOO MUCH BASS, DUDE.
6/3
SCOTT AND BORGMAN
©2010 ZITS Partnership. Distributed by King Features Syndicate

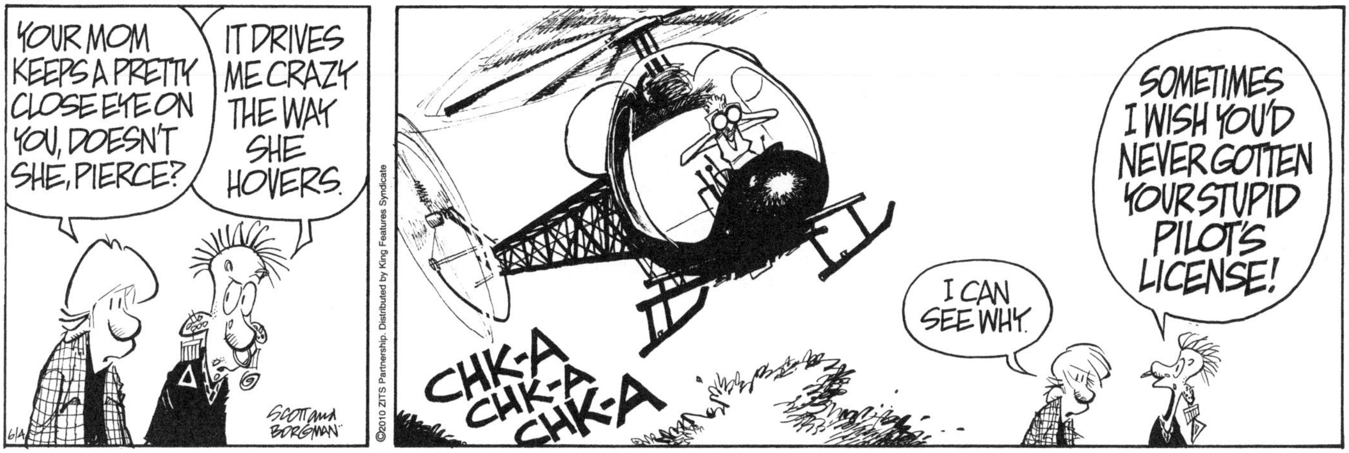
YOUR MOM KEEPS A PRETTY CLOSE EYE ON YOU, DOESN'T SHE, PIERCE?
IT DRIVES ME CRAZY THE WAY SHE HOVERS.
CHK-A CHK-A CHK-A
I CAN SEE WHY.
SOMETIMES I WISH YOU'D NEVER GOTTEN YOUR STUPID PILOT'S LICENSE!
©2010 ZITS Partnership. Distributed by King Features Syndicate

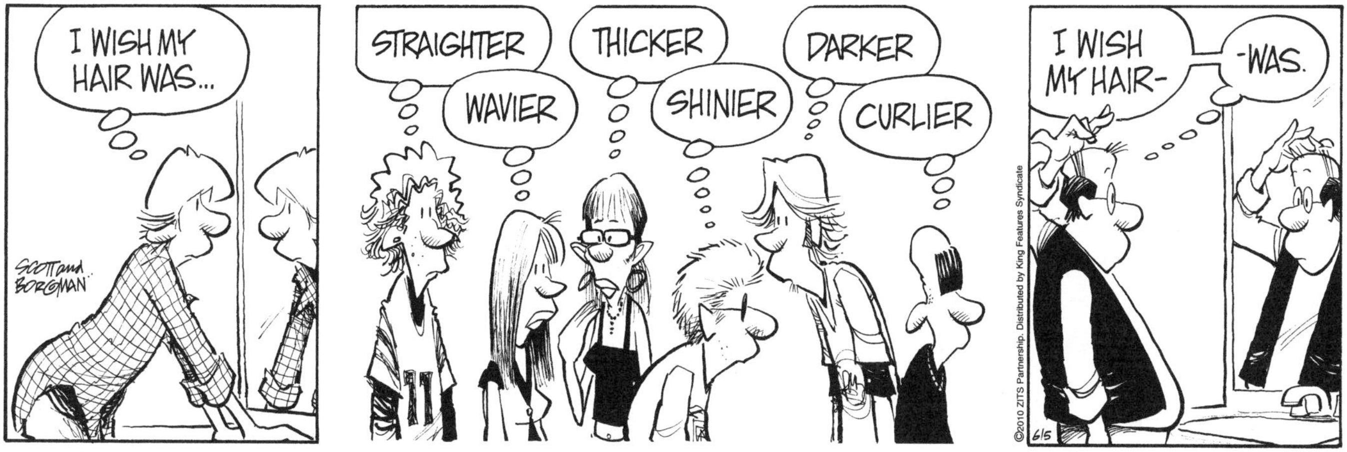
I WISH MY HAIR WAS...
STRAIGHTER
WAVIER
THICKER
SHINIER
DARKER
CURLIER
I WISH MY HAIR-
-WAS.
©2010 ZITS Partnership. Distributed by King Features Syndicate

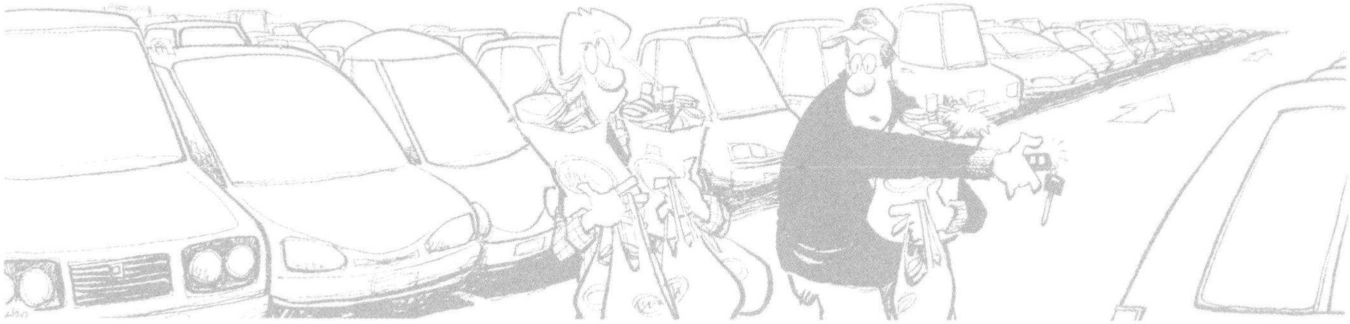

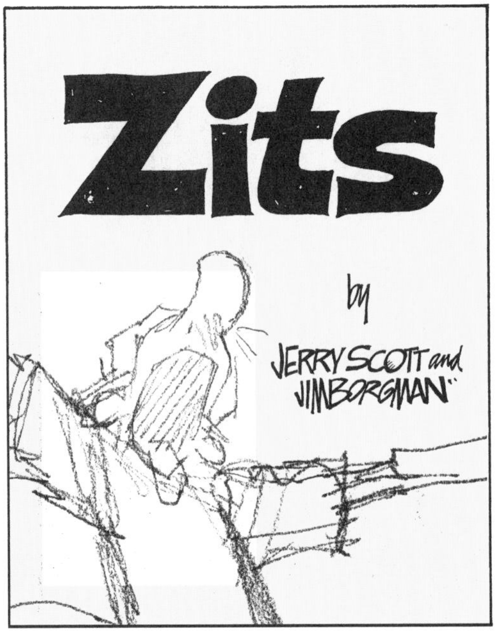
Zits
by
JERRY SCOTT and
JIM BORGMAN

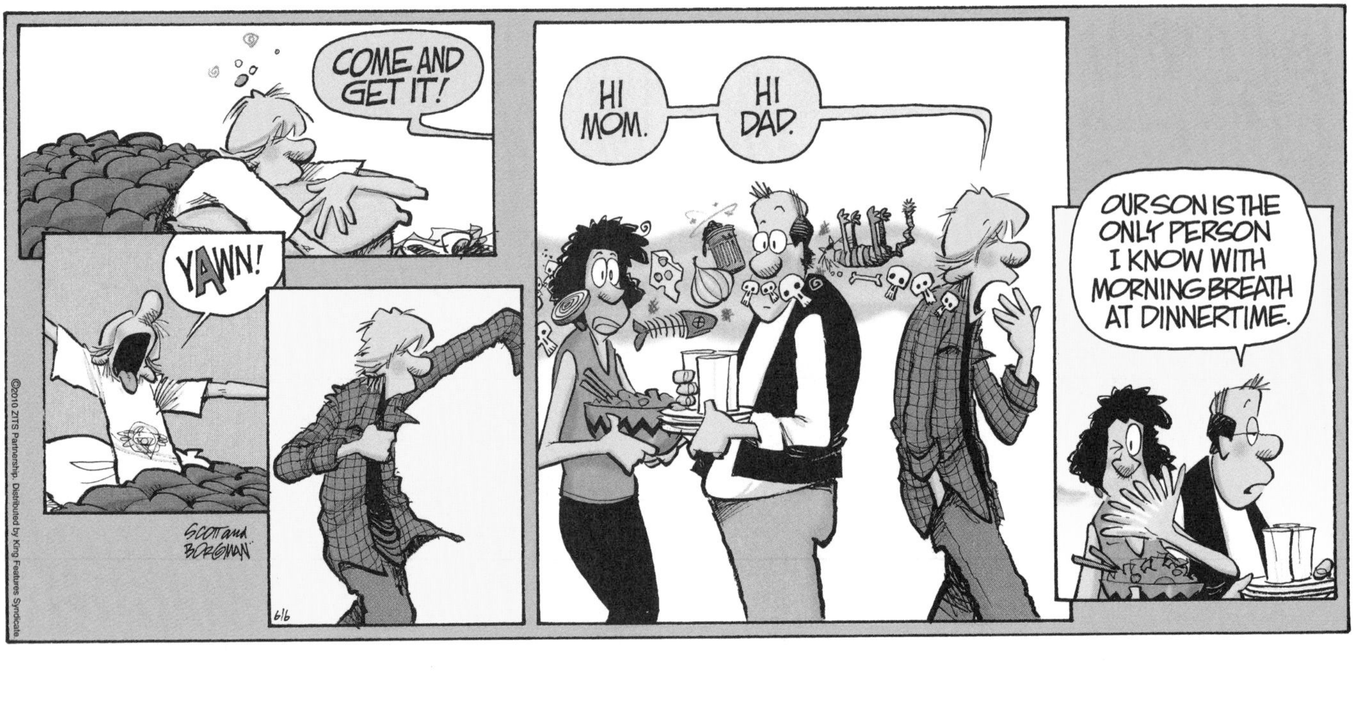
COME AND GET IT!
YAWN!
HI MOM.
HI DAD.
OUR SON IS THE ONLY PERSON I KNOW WITH MORNING BREATH AT DINNERTIME.
SCOTT and BORGMAN
6/6
©2010 ZITS Partnership. Distributed by King Features Syndicate

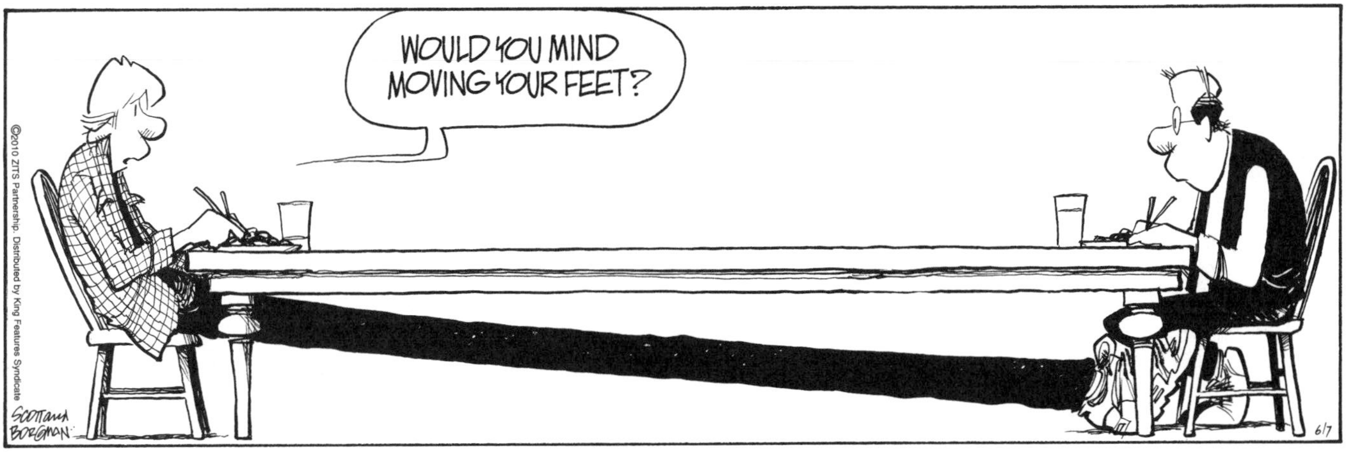
WOULD YOU MIND MOVING YOUR FEET?
©2010 ZITS Partnership. Distributed by King Features Syndicate
SCOTT and BORGMAN
6/7

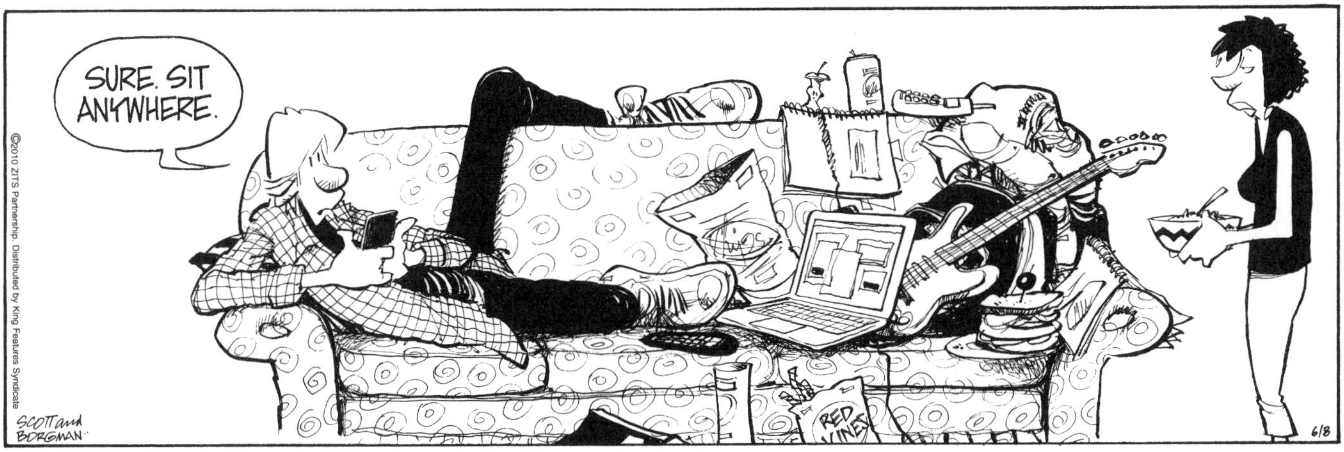
SURE. SIT ANYWHERE.
©2010 ZITS Partnership. Distributed by King Features Syndicate
SCOTT and BORGMAN
RED VINES
6/8

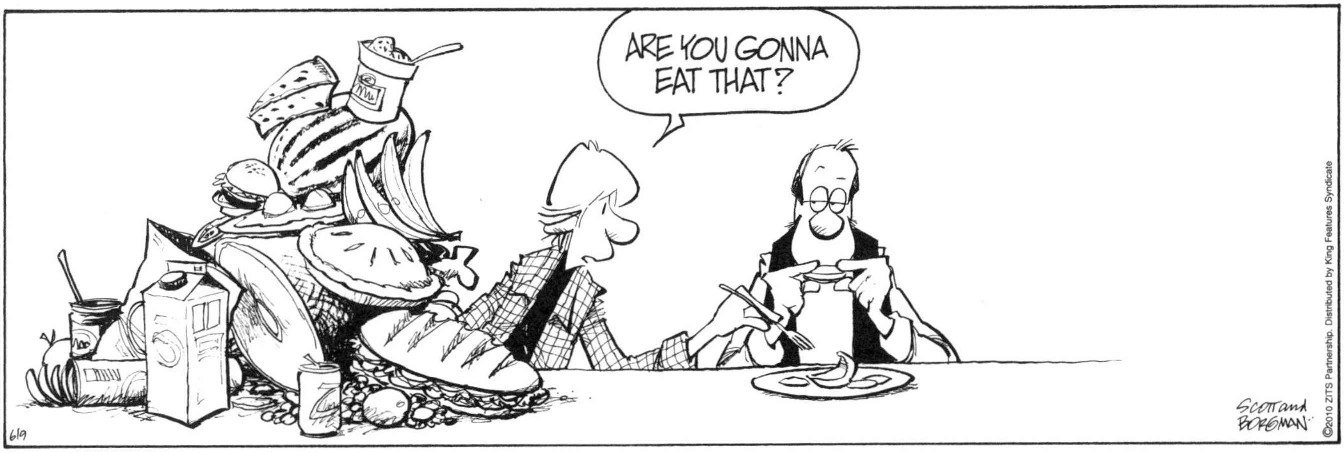
ARE YOU GONNA EAT THAT?
©2010 ZITS Partnership. Distributed by King Features Syndicate
SCOTT and BORGMAN
6/9

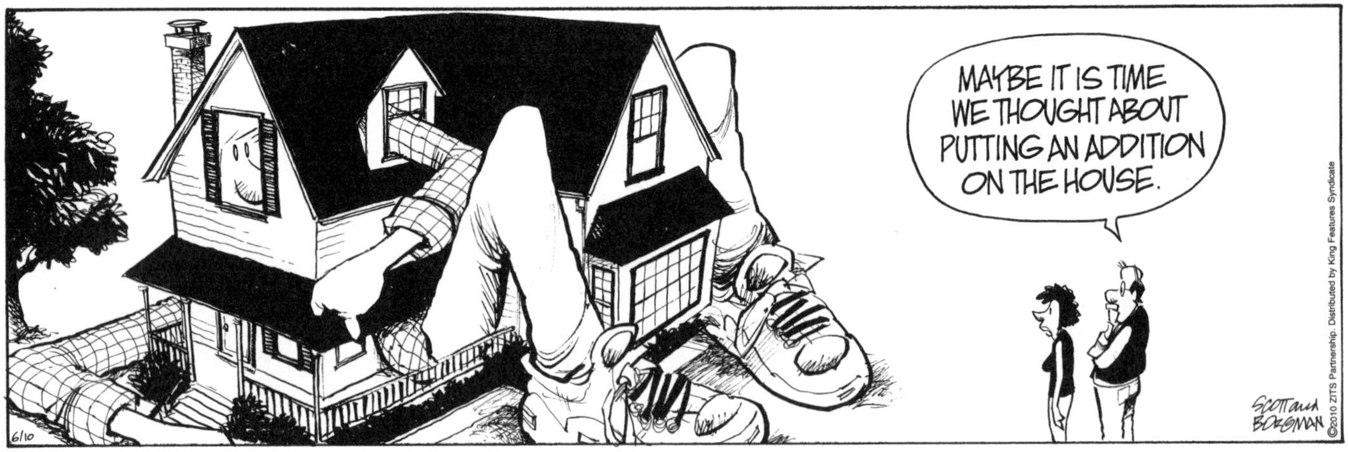
6/10
MAYBE IT IS TIME WE THOUGHT ABOUT PUTTING AN ADDITION ON THE HOUSE.
SCOTT and BORGMAN
©2010 ZITS Partnership. Distributed by King Features Syndicate

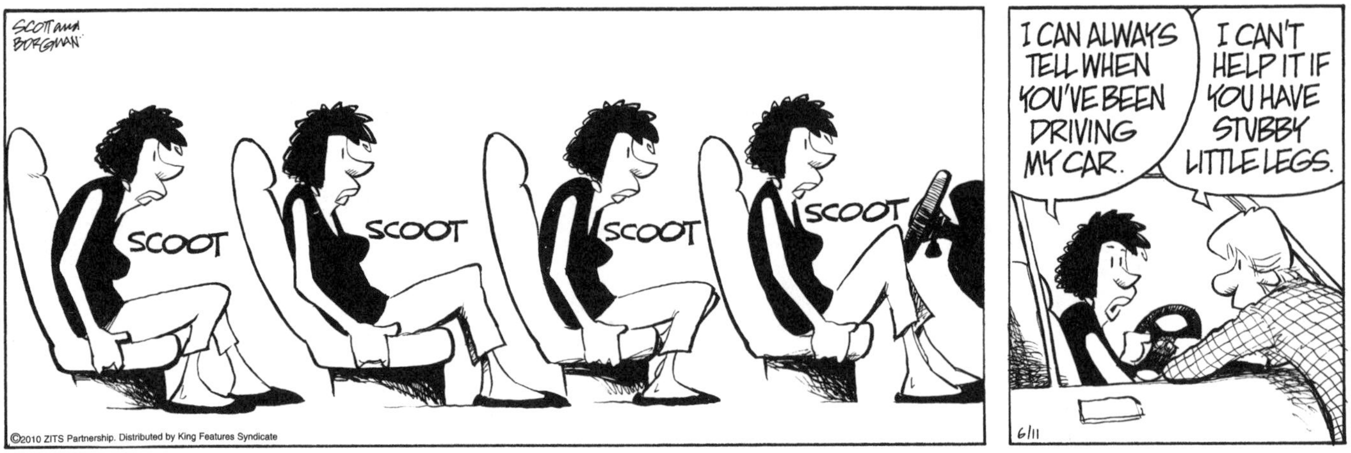
SCOTT and BORGMAN
SCOOT
SCOOT
SCOOT
SCOOT
I CAN ALWAYS TELL WHEN YOU'VE BEEN DRIVING MY CAR.
I CAN'T HELP IT IF YOU HAVE STUBBY LITTLE LEGS.
6/11
©2010 ZITS Partnership. Distributed by King Features Syndicate

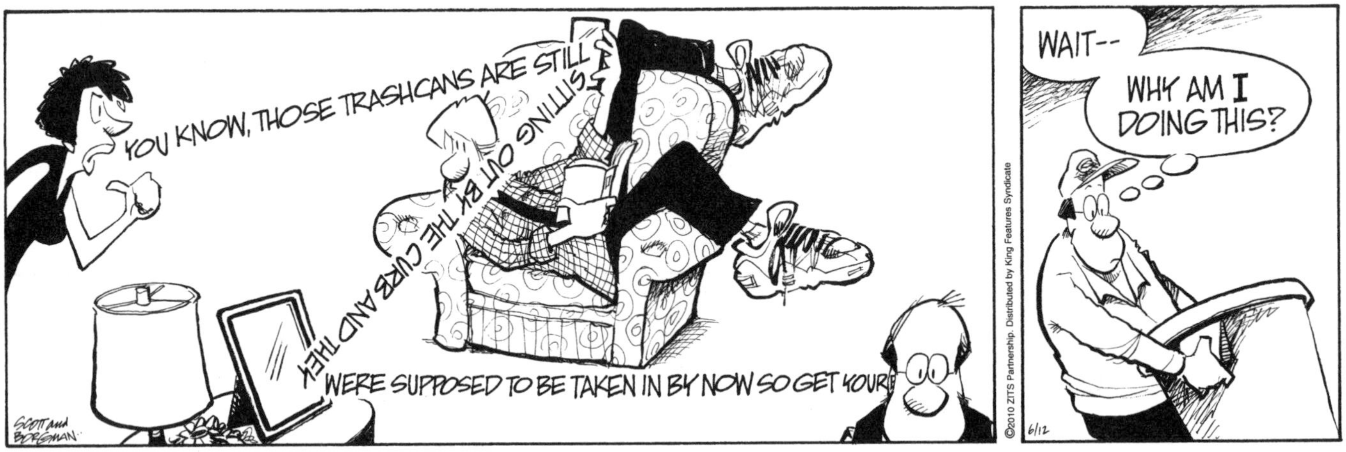
YOU KNOW, THOSE TRASHCANS ARE STILL SITTING OUT BY THE CURB AND THEY WERE SUPPOSED TO BE TAKEN IN BY NOW SO GET YOUR
SCOTT and BORGMAN
©2010 ZITS Partnership. Distributed by King Features Syndicate
WAIT--
WHY AM **I** DOING THIS?
6/12

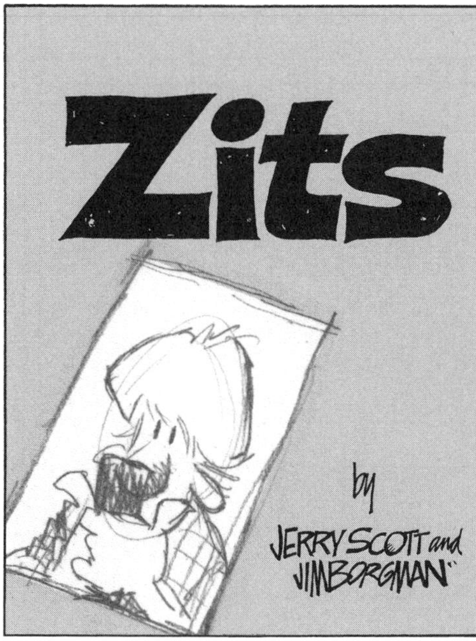
Zits
by
JERRY SCOTT and
JIM BORGMAN

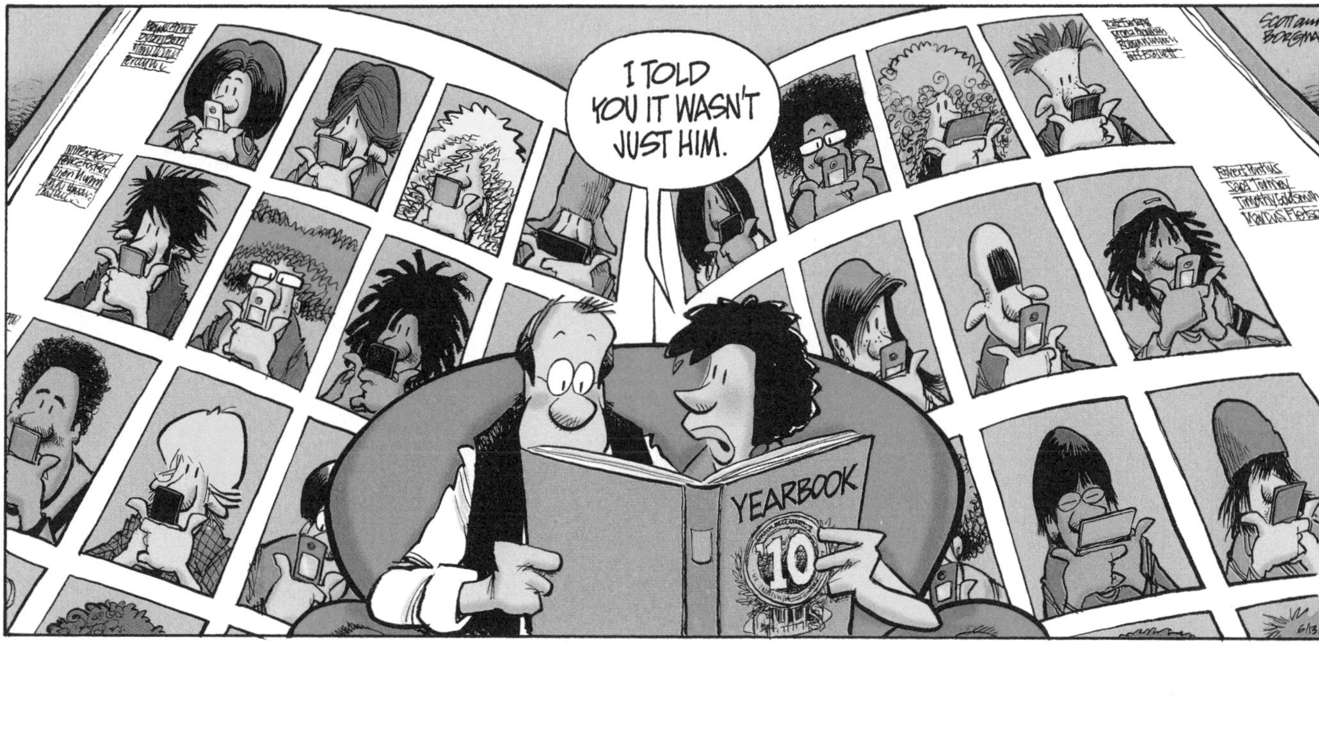
SCOTT and BORGMAN
I TOLD YOU IT WASN'T JUST HIM.
YEARBOOK
10
©2010 ZITS Partnership. Distributed by King Features Syndicate.

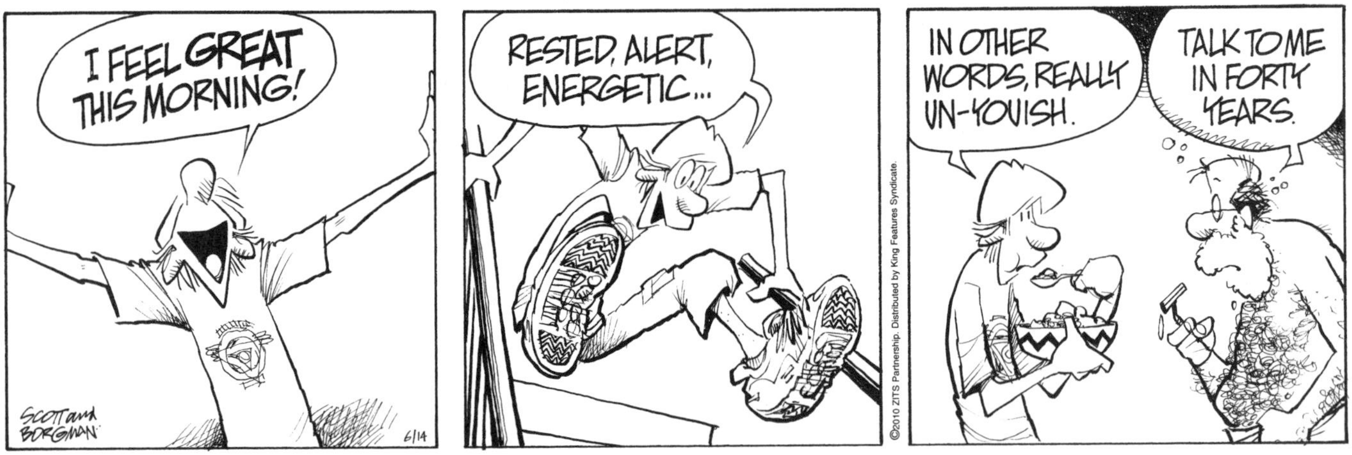
I FEEL GREAT THIS MORNING!
SCOTT and BORGMAN
6/14
RESTED, ALERT, ENERGETIC...
©2010 ZITS Partnership. Distributed by King Features Syndicate.
IN OTHER WORDS, REALLY UN-YOUISH.
TALK TO ME IN FORTY YEARS.

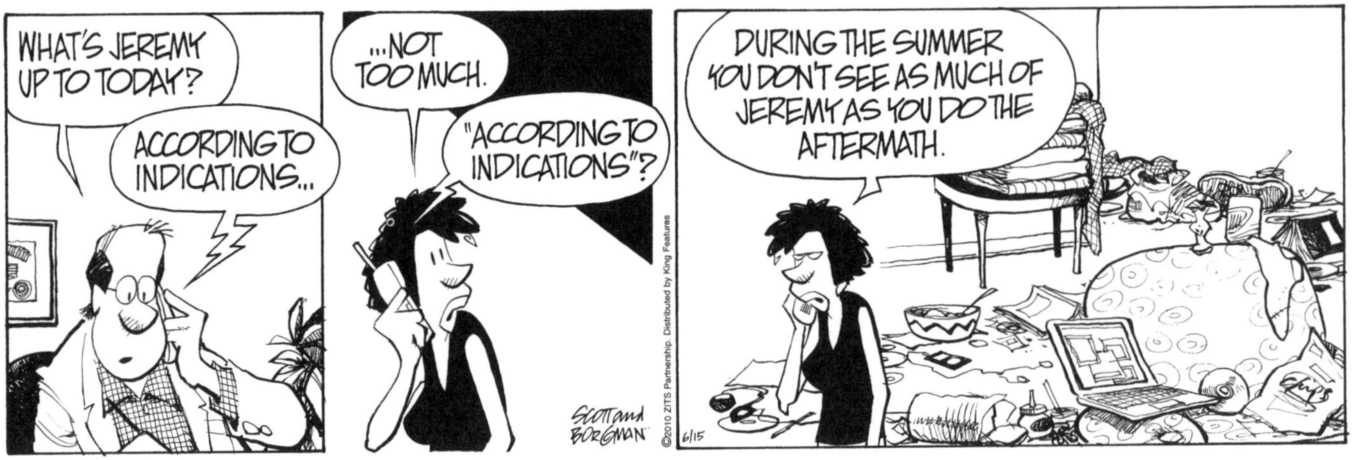
WHAT'S JEREMY UP TO TODAY?
ACCORDING TO INDICATIONS...
...NOT TOO MUCH.
"ACCORDING TO INDICATIONS"?
SCOTT and BORGMAN
©2010 ZITS Partnership. Distributed by King Features
6/15
DURING THE SUMMER YOU DON'T SEE AS MUCH OF JEREMY AS YOU DO THE AFTERMATH.

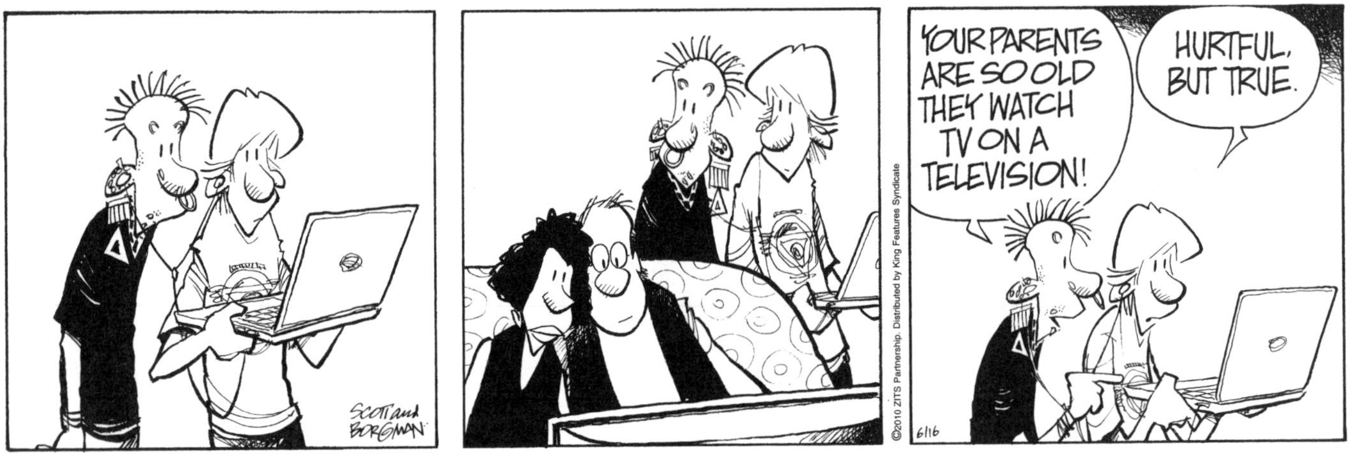
SCOTT and BORGMAN
©2010 ZITS Partnership. Distributed by King Features Syndicate
6/16
YOUR PARENTS ARE SO OLD THEY WATCH TV ON A TELEVISION!
HURTFUL, BUT TRUE.

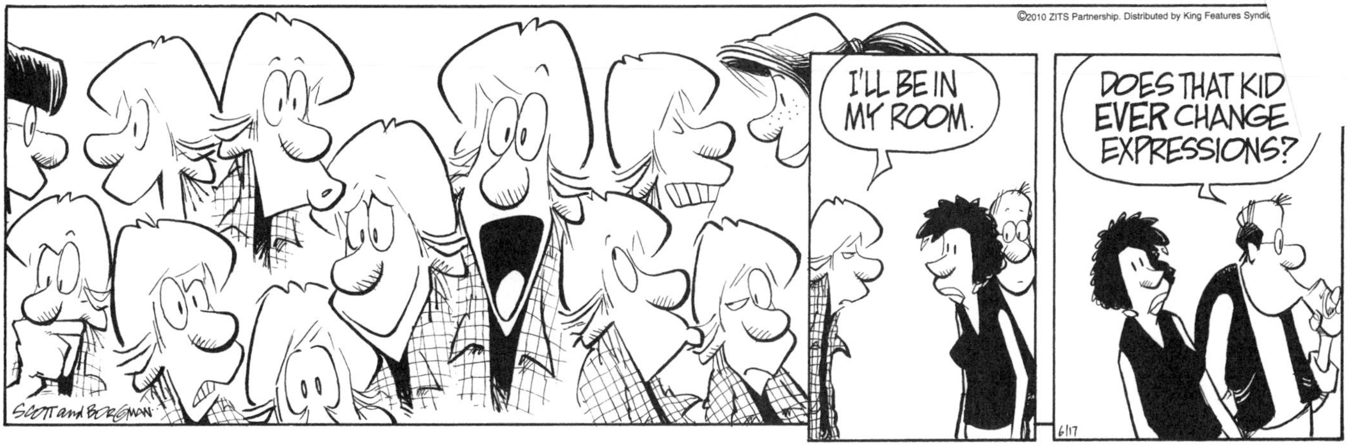
©2010 ZITS Partnership. Distributed by King Features Syndic
SCOTT and BORGMAN
I'LL BE IN MY ROOM.
DOES THAT KID EVER CHANGE EXPRESSIONS?
6/17

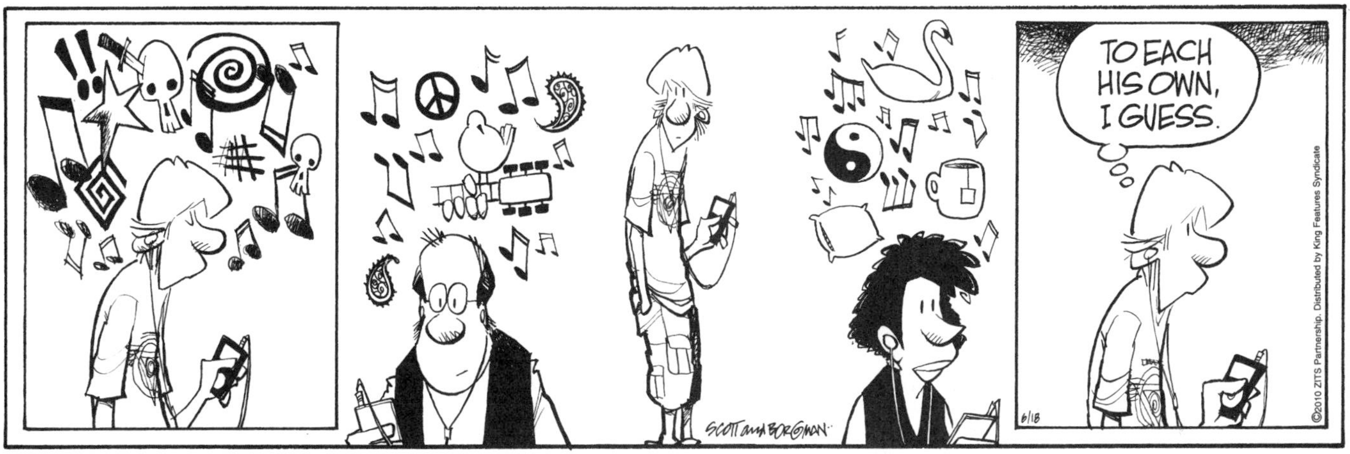
SCOTT and BORGMAN
TO EACH HIS OWN, I GUESS.
6/18
©2010 ZITS Partnership. Distributed by King Features Syndicate

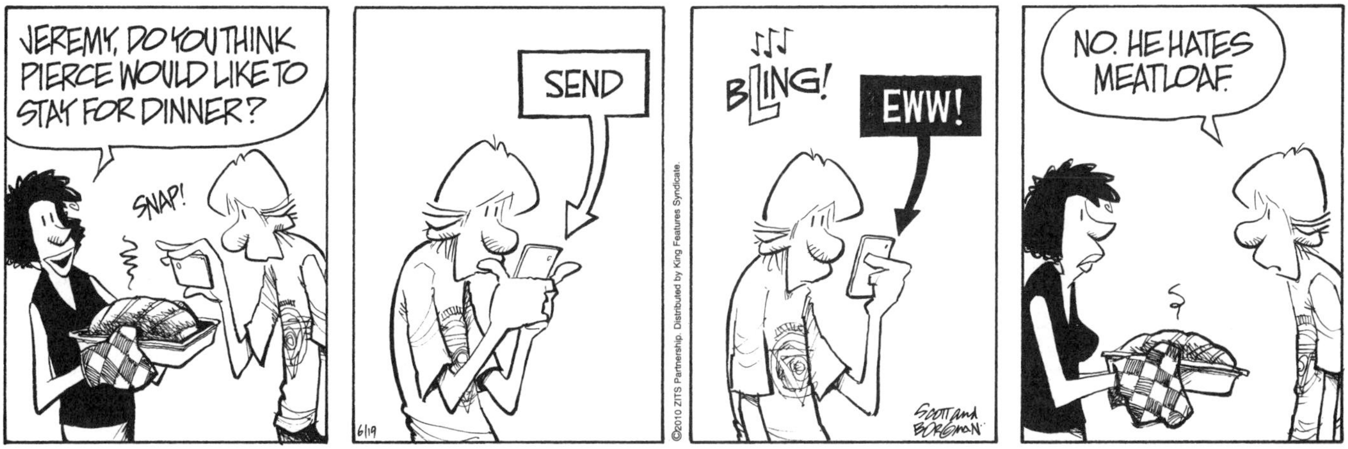
JEREMY, DO YOU THINK PIERCE WOULD LIKE TO STAY FOR DINNER?
SNAP!
SEND
6/19
©2010 ZITS Partnership. Distributed by King Features Syndicate.
BLING!
EWW!
SCOTT and BORGMAN
NO. HE HATES MEATLOAF.

Zits
by JERRY SCOTT and JIM BORGMAN
TAP!

JEREMY AND HIS FRIENDS WERE UP LATE LAST NIGHT.
LET'S TRY TO BE QUIET SO HE CAN SLEEP.
'K.
6/20
8 AM
TAP!
SHH!
10 AM
©2010 ZITS Partnership. Distributed by King Features
12 PM
AHEM!
2 PM
OOPS!
FLICK!
THUD!
SCOTT and BORGMAN
6 PM
WHAT DO YOU THINK... IS FIFTEEN HOURS ENOUGH REST?
LET THE GRACE PERIOD EXPIRE!

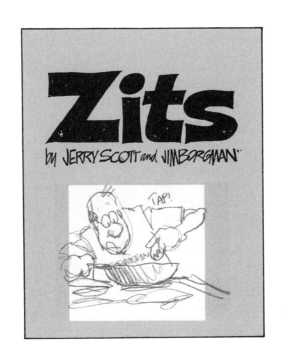

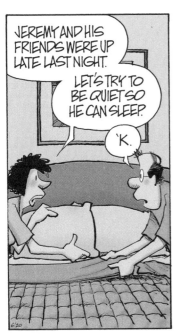

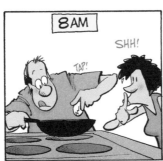

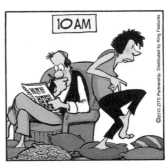

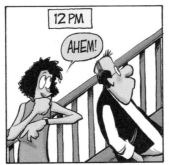

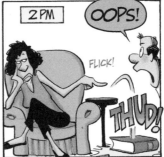

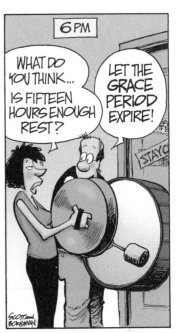

SCOTT and BORGMAN
SLAM!
SLAM!
SLAM!
6/23
KEEP OUT
SLAM!
FOUR SLAMS AND ALL'S WELL.
I MISS WORDS. DO YOU EVER MISS WORDS?

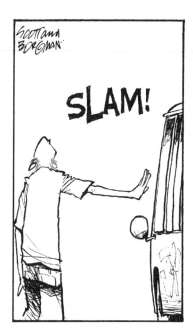

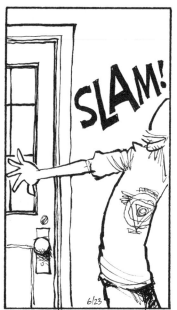

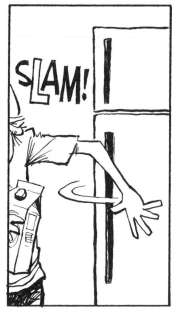

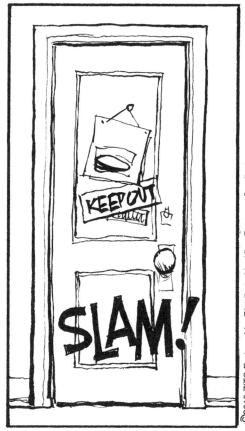

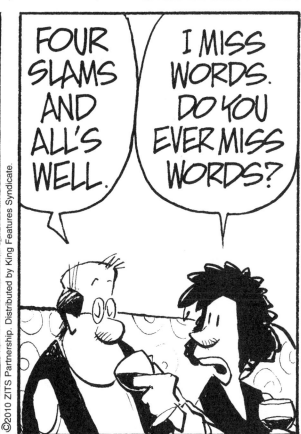

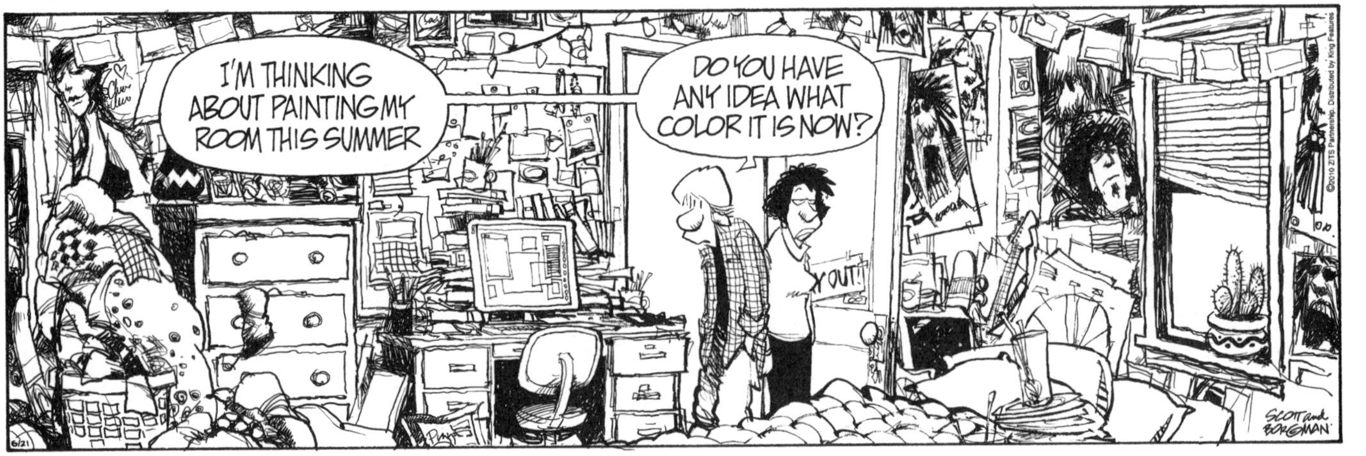
I'M THINKING ABOUT PAINTING MY ROOM THIS SUMMER
DO YOU HAVE ANY IDEA WHAT COLOR IT IS NOW?
OUT!
©2010 ZITS Partnership. Distributed by King Features
SCOTT and BORGMAN

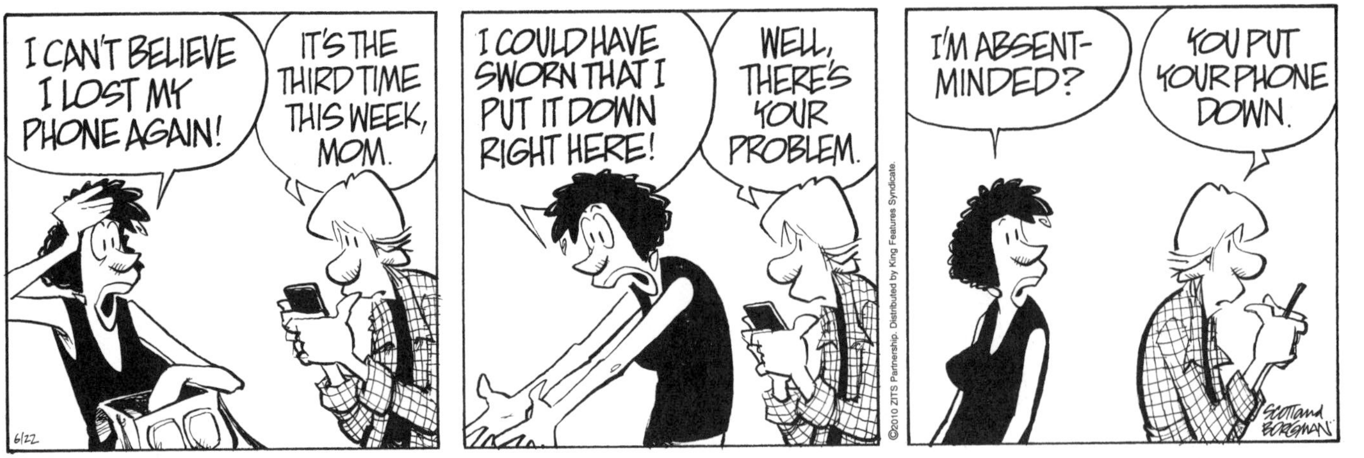
I CAN'T BELIEVE I LOST MY PHONE AGAIN!
IT'S THE THIRD TIME THIS WEEK, MOM.
I COULD HAVE SWORN THAT I PUT IT DOWN RIGHT HERE!
WELL, THERE'S YOUR PROBLEM.
©2010 ZITS Partnership. Distributed by King Features Syndicate.
I'M ABSENT-MINDED?
YOU PUT YOUR PHONE DOWN.
SCOTT and BORGMAN

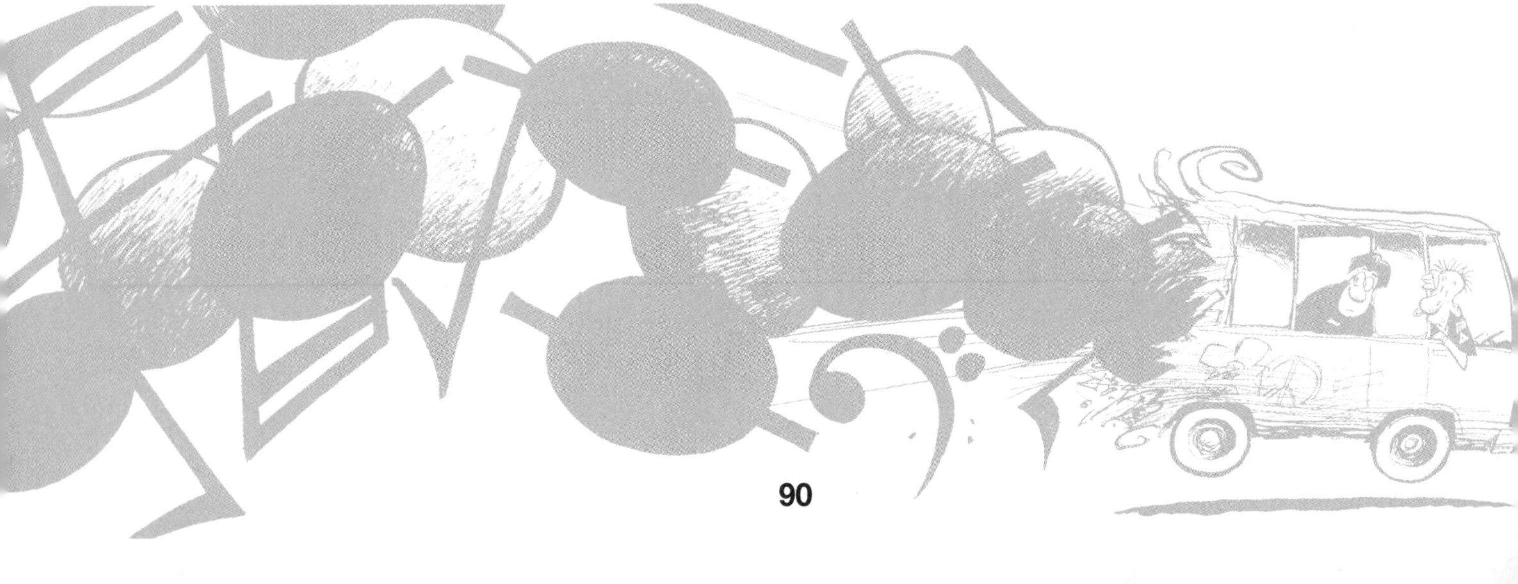

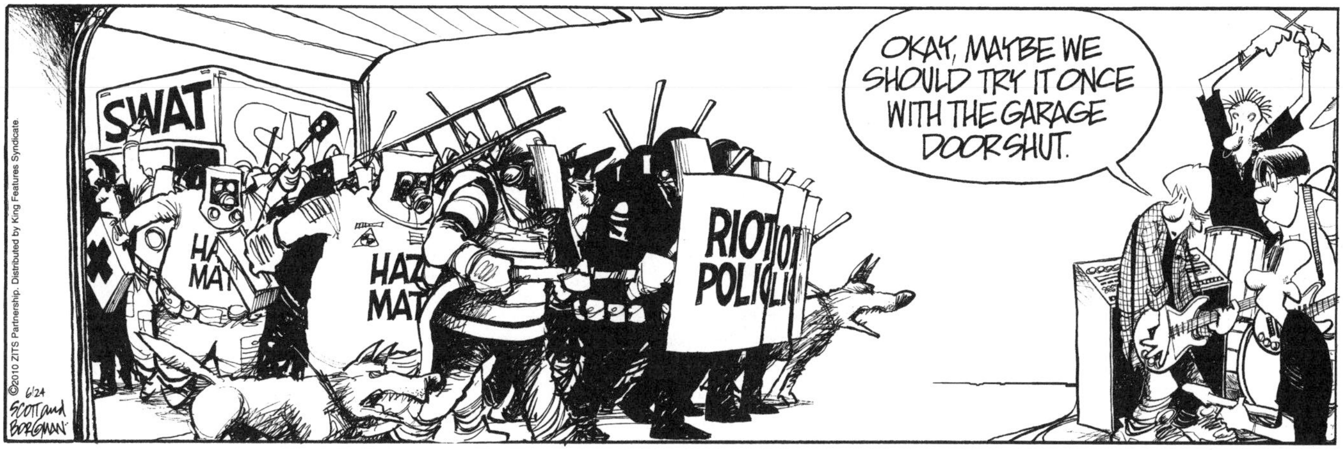
©2010 ZITS Partnership. Distributed by King Features Syndicate.
6/24
SCOTT and BORGMAN
SWAT
HAZ MAT
HAZ MAT
RIOT POLICE
OKAY, MAYBE WE SHOULD TRY IT ONCE WITH THE GARAGE DOOR SHUT.

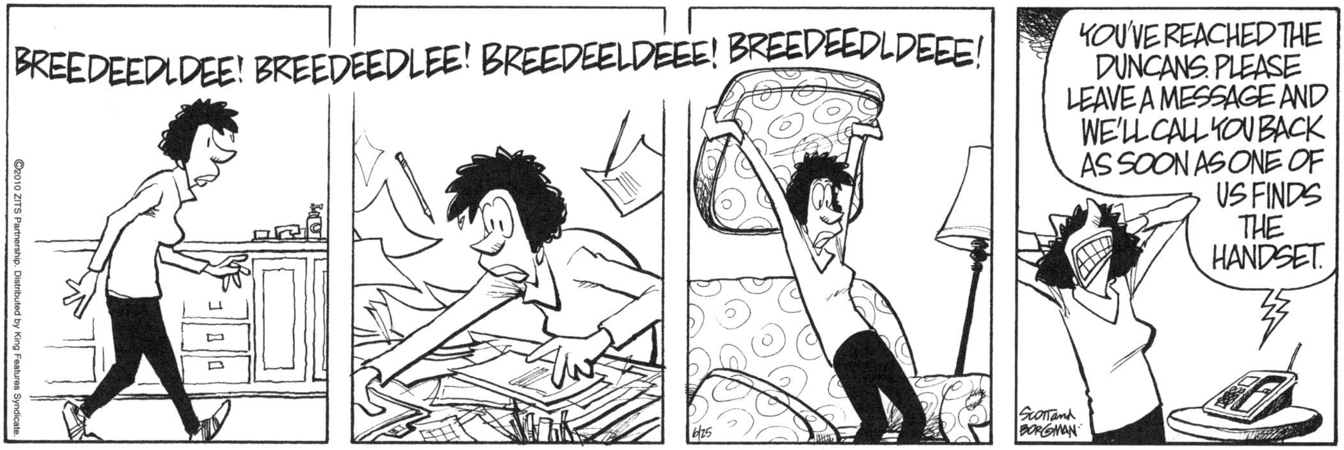
©2010 ZITS Partnership. Distributed by King Features Syndicate.
BREEDEEDLDEE!
BREEDEEDLEE!
BREEDEELDEEE!
BREEDEEDLDEEE!
6/25
YOU'VE REACHED THE DUNCANS. PLEASE LEAVE A MESSAGE AND WE'LL CALL YOU BACK AS SOON AS ONE OF US FINDS THE HANDSET.
SCOTT and BORGMAN

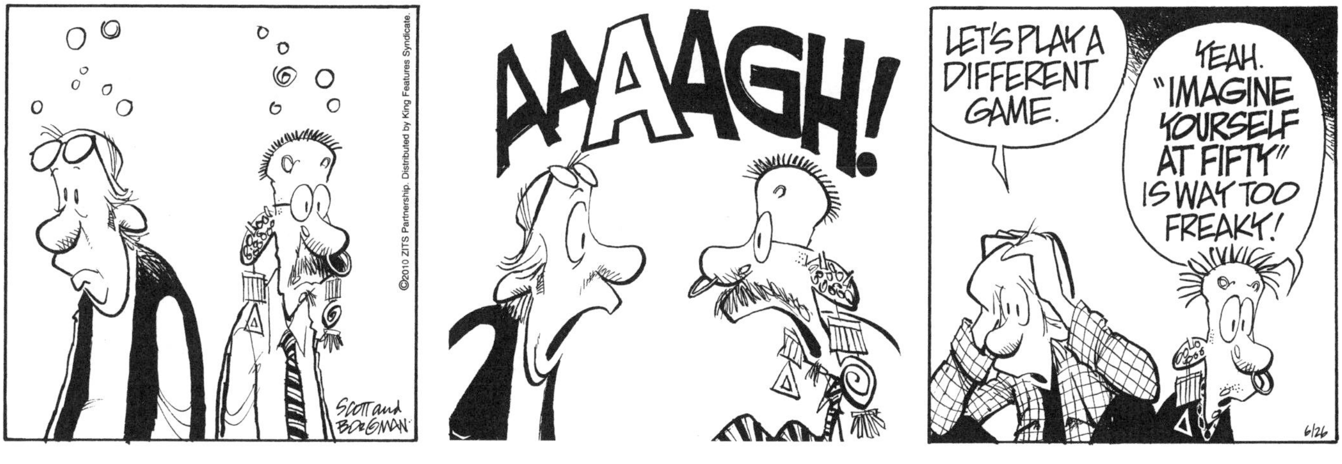
©2010 ZITS Partnership. Distributed by King Features Syndicate.
SCOTT and BORGMAN
AAAAGH!
LET'S PLAY A DIFFERENT GAME.
YEAH. "IMAGINE YOURSELF AT FIFTY" IS WAY TOO FREAKY!
6/26

Zits
by JERRY SCOTT and JIM BORGMAN

TRY IT ONE MORE TIME!
©2010 ZITS Partnership. Distributed by King Features Syndicate
DUDE, IT'S NOT STARTING.
I GUESS WE'D BETTER GET THE HOSE.
ARE YOU SURE?
WHAT CHOICE DO WE HAVE?
WE'RE EITHER STUCK HERE ALL DAY, OR WE DO A LITTLE SIPHONING.
BZZZZZZ
AND IT'S COOL WITH YOUR DAD?
I THINK HE'S COME TO EXPECT IT.
SCOTT and BORGMAN

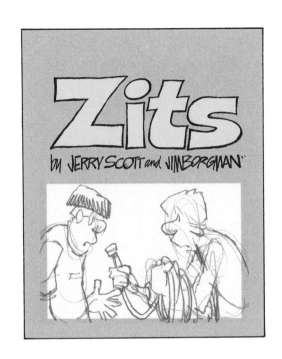

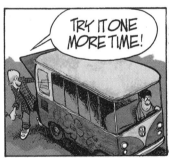

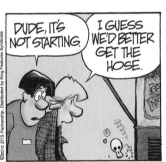

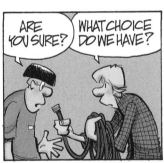

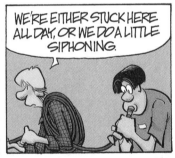

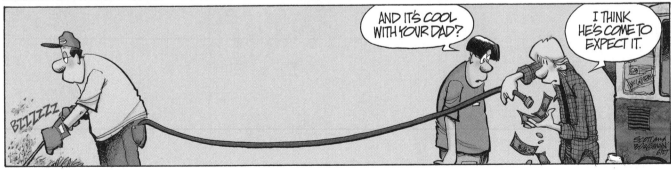

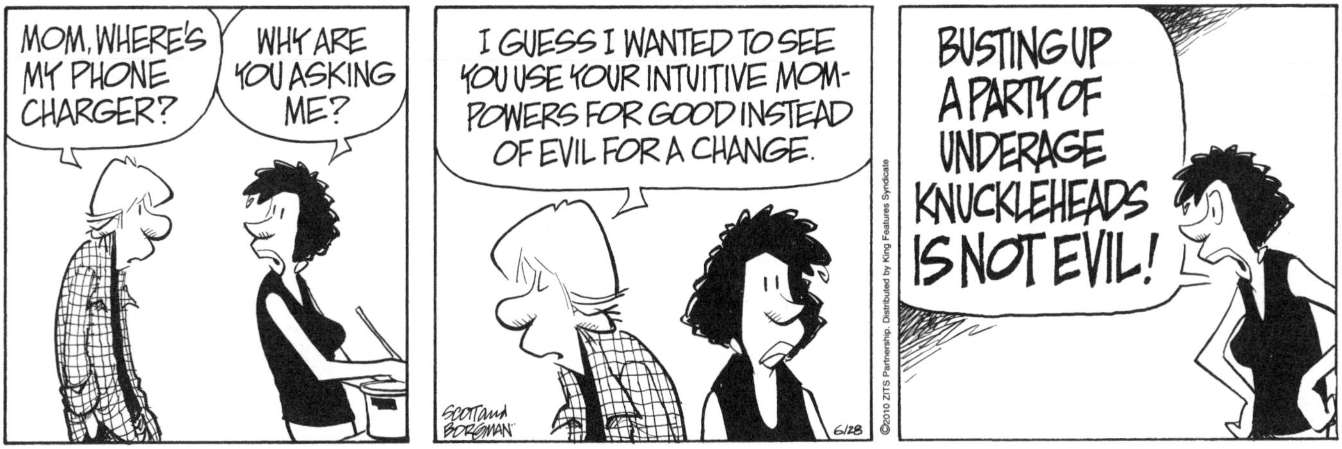
MOM, WHERE'S MY PHONE CHARGER?
WHY ARE YOU ASKING ME?
I GUESS I WANTED TO SEE YOU USE YOUR INTUITIVE MOM-POWERS FOR GOOD INSTEAD OF EVIL FOR A CHANGE.
SCOTT and BORGMAN
6/28
BUSTING UP A PARTY OF UNDERAGE KNUCKLEHEADS IS NOT EVIL!
©2010 ZITS Partnership. Distributed by King Features Syndicate

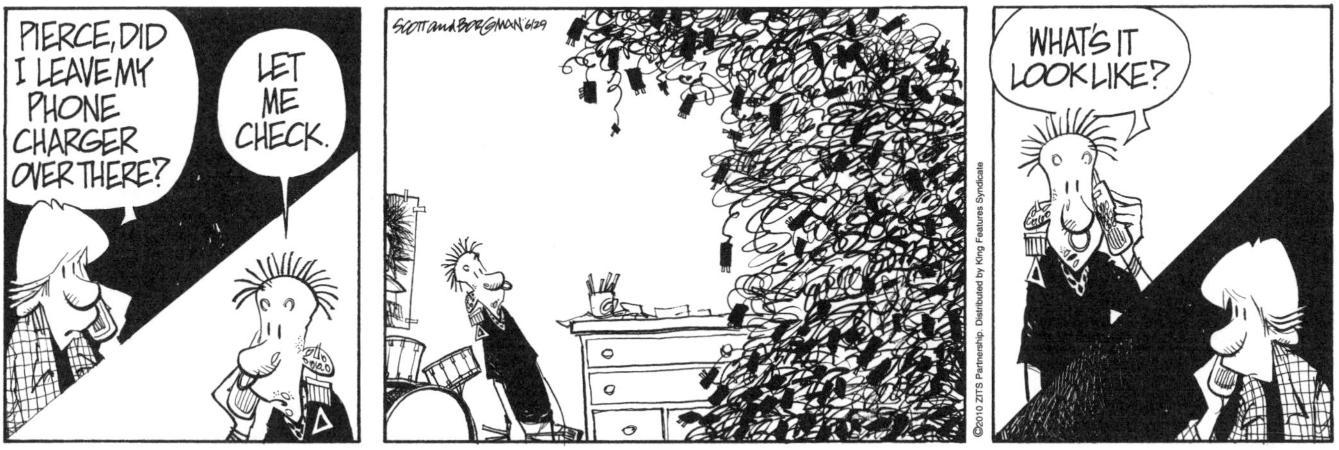
PIERCE, DID I LEAVE MY PHONE CHARGER OVER THERE?
LET ME CHECK.
SCOTT and BORGMAN 6/29
WHAT'S IT LOOK LIKE?
©2010 ZITS Partnership. Distributed by King Features Syndicate

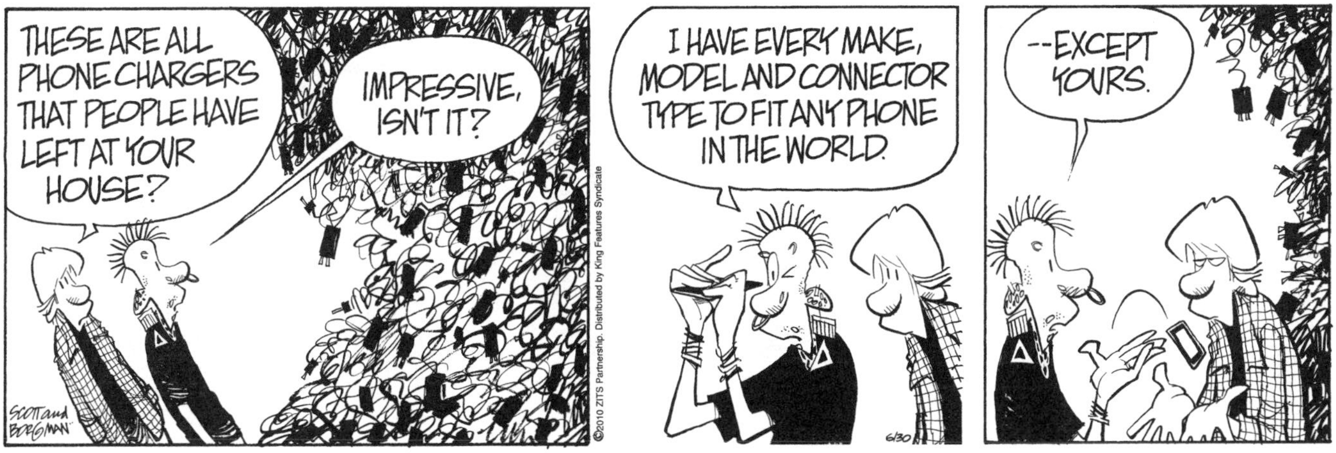
THESE ARE ALL PHONE CHARGERS THAT PEOPLE HAVE LEFT AT YOUR HOUSE?
IMPRESSIVE, ISN'T IT?
SCOTT and BORGMAN
©2010 ZITS Partnership. Distributed by King Features Syndicate
I HAVE EVERY MAKE, MODEL AND CONNECTOR TYPE TO FIT ANY PHONE IN THE WORLD.
6/30
--EXCEPT YOURS.

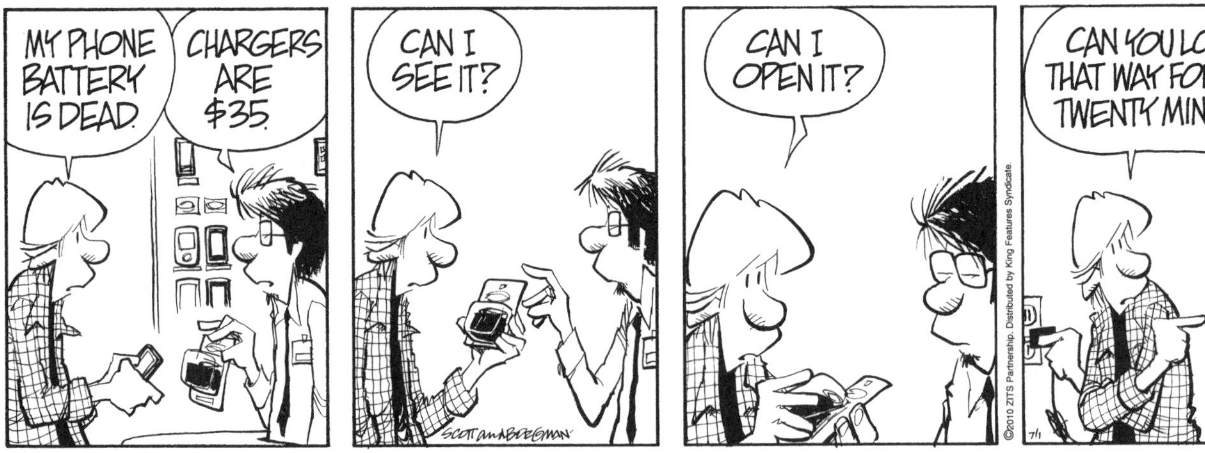
MY PHONE BATTERY IS DEAD.
CHARGERS ARE $35.
CAN I SEE IT?
CAN I OPEN IT?
CAN YOU LOOK THAT WAY FOR ABOUT TWENTY MINUTES?
SCOTT and BORGMAN
©2010 ZITS Partnership. Distributed by King Features Syndicate.
7/1

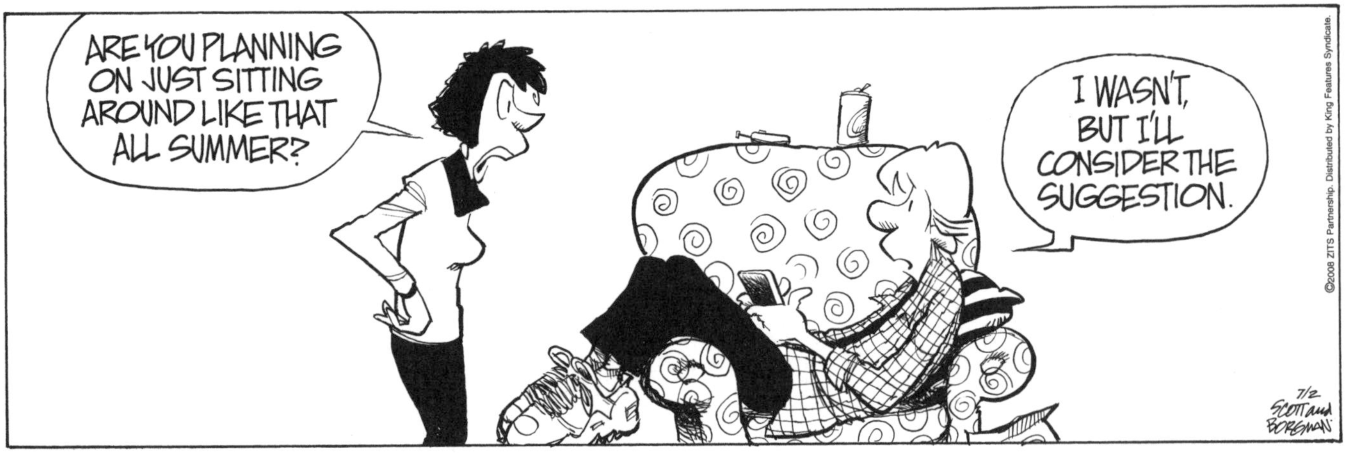
ARE YOU PLANNING ON JUST SITTING AROUND LIKE THAT ALL SUMMER?
I WASN'T, BUT I'LL CONSIDER THE SUGGESTION.
©2008 ZITS Partnership. Distributed by King Features Syndicate.
7/2
SCOTT and BORGMAN

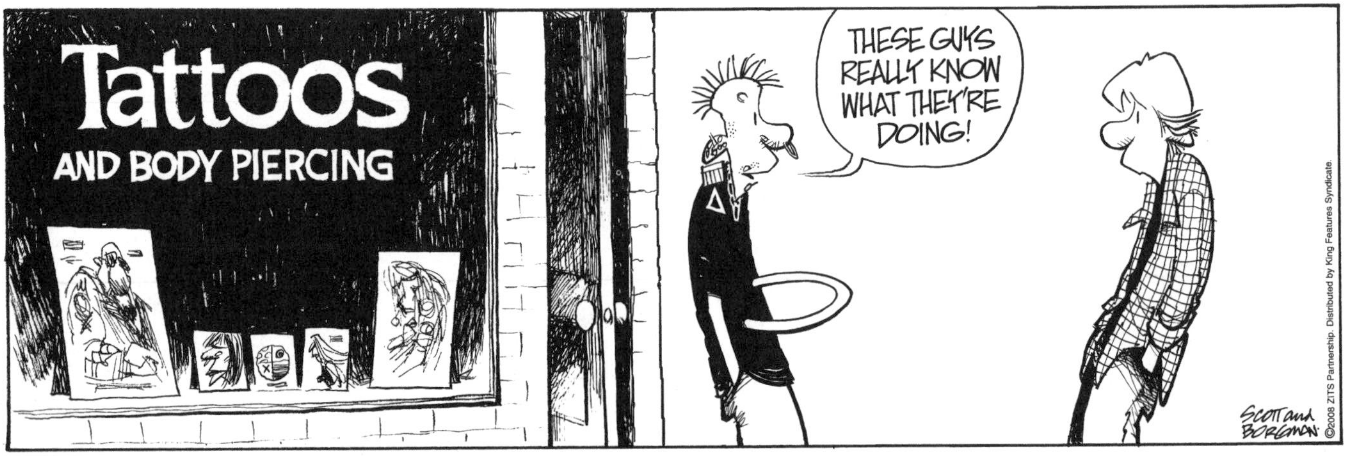
Tattoos
AND BODY PIERCING
THESE GUYS REALLY KNOW WHAT THEY'RE DOING!
©2008 ZITS Partnership. Distributed by King Features Syndicate.
SCOTT and BORGMAN

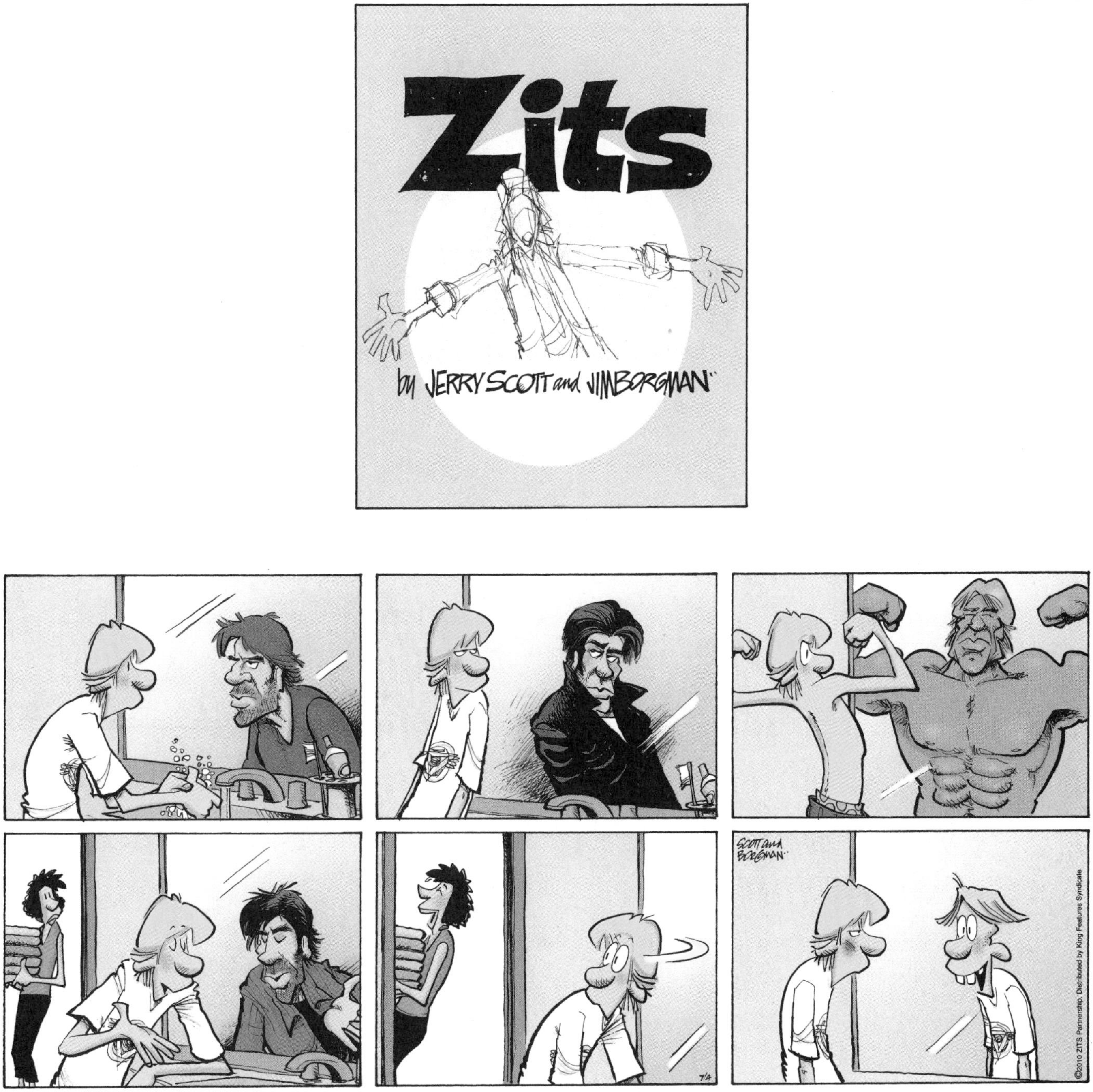
Zits
by JERRY SCOTT and JIM BORGMAN
SCOTT and BORGMAN
7/4
©2010 ZITS Partnership. Distributed by King Features Syndicate

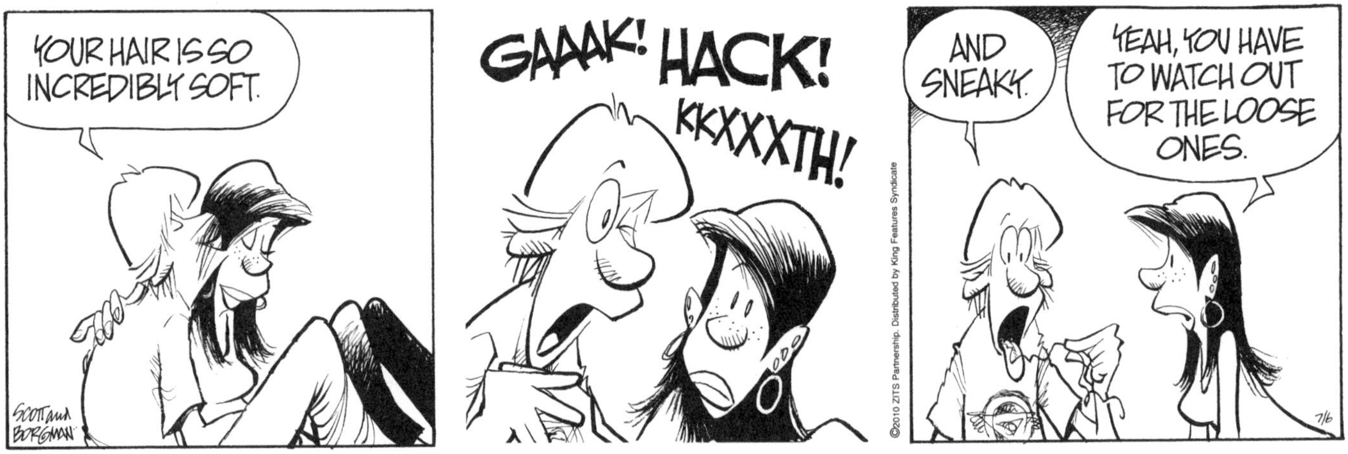
YOUR HAIR IS SO INCREDIBLY SOFT.
GAAAK! HACK! KKXXXTH!
AND SNEAKY.
YEAH, YOU HAVE TO WATCH OUT FOR THE LOOSE ONES.
SCOTT and BORGMAN
©2010 ZITS Partnership. Distributed by King Features Syndicate
7/6

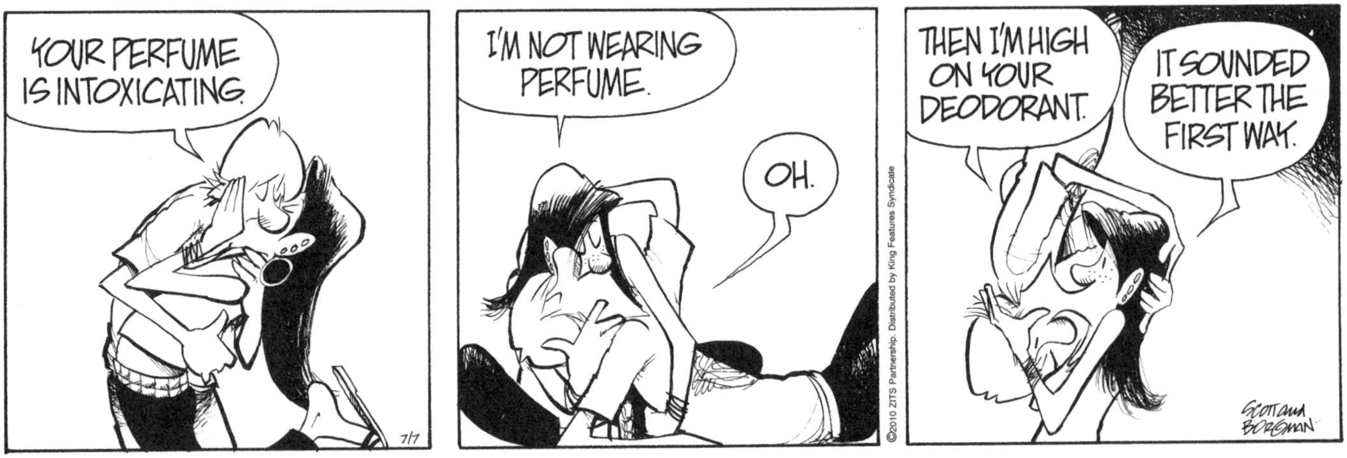
YOUR PERFUME IS INTOXICATING.
I'M NOT WEARING PERFUME.
OH.
THEN I'M HIGH ON YOUR DEODORANT.
IT SOUNDED BETTER THE FIRST WAY.
7/7
©2010 ZITS Partnership. Distributed by King Features Syndicate
SCOTT and BORGMAN

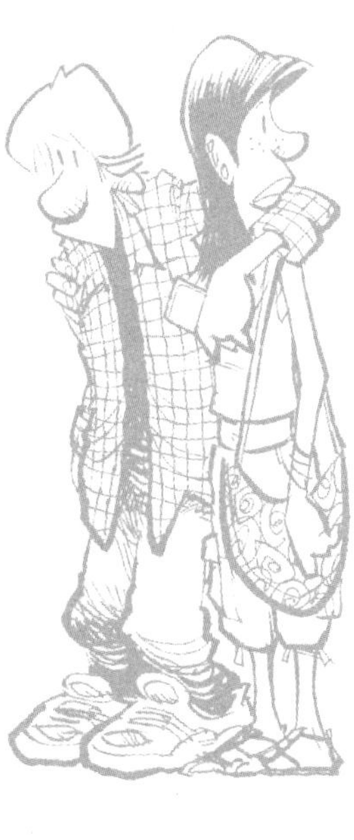

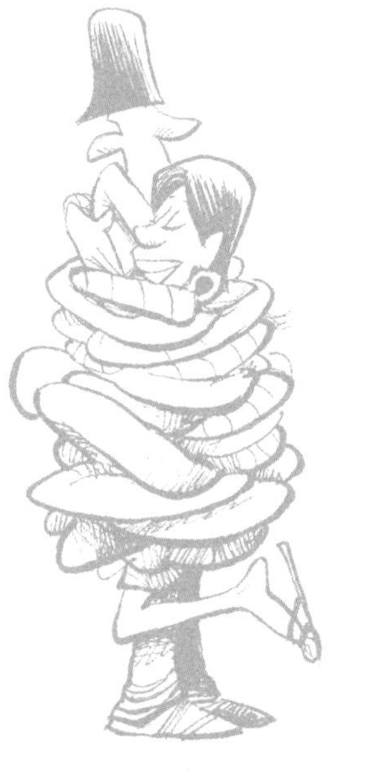

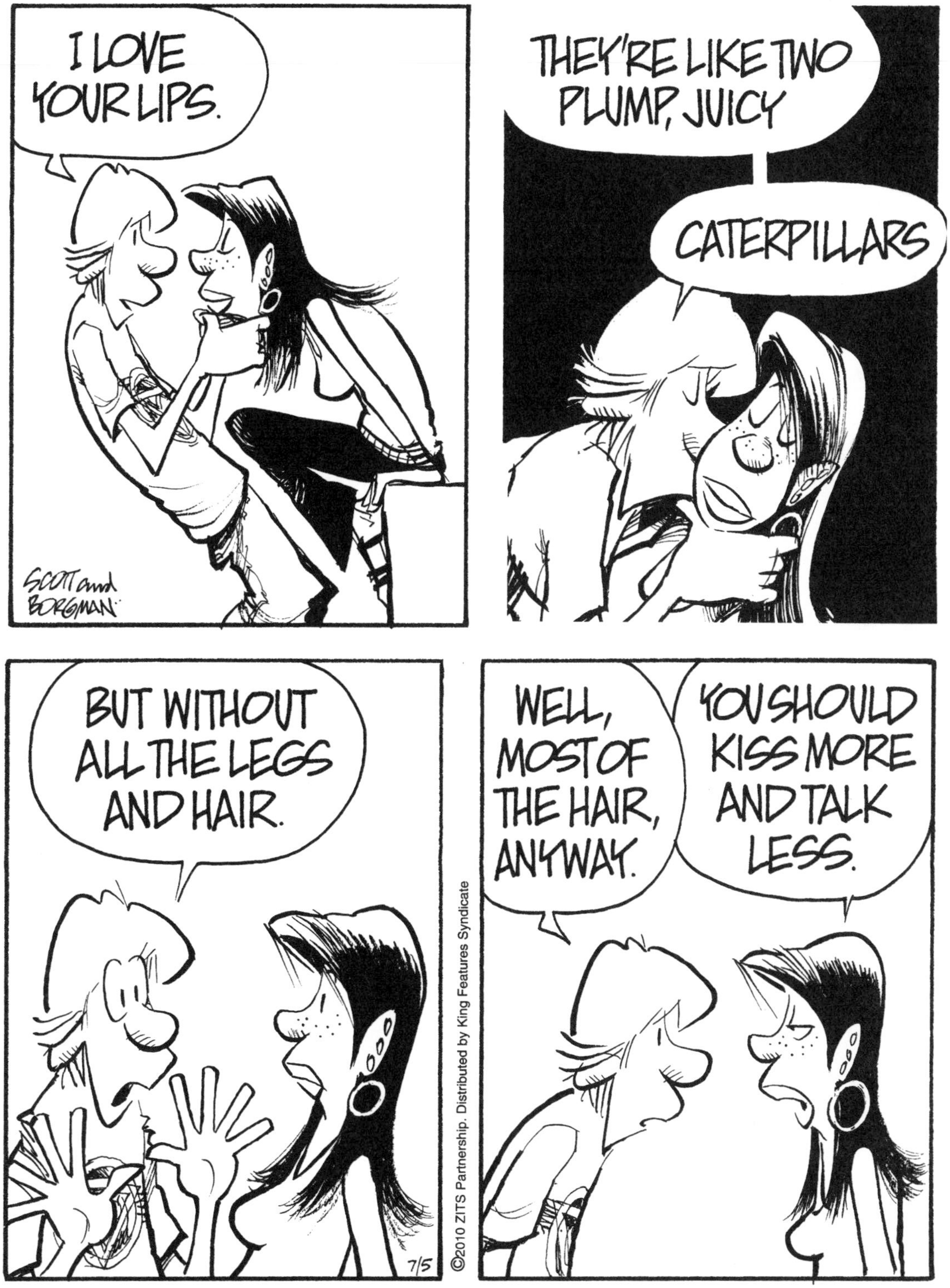
I LOVE YOUR LIPS.
THEY'RE LIKE TWO PLUMP, JUICY
CATERPILLARS
SCOTT and BORGMAN
BUT WITHOUT ALL THE LEGS AND HAIR.
7/5
©2010 ZITS Partnership. Distributed by King Features Syndicate
WELL, MOST OF THE HAIR, ANYWAY.
YOU SHOULD KISS MORE AND TALK LESS.

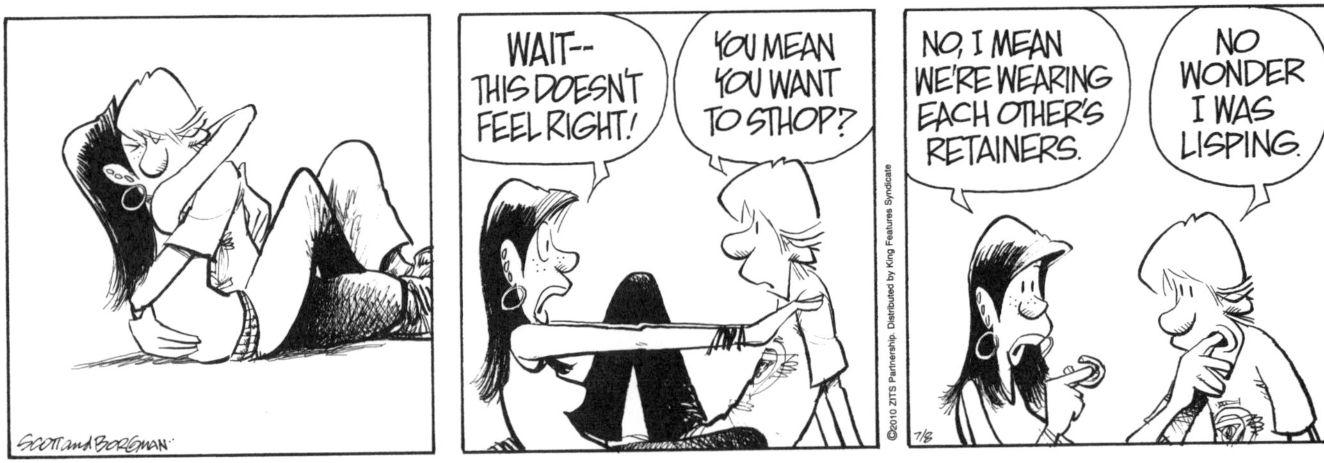
SCOTT and BORGMAN
WAIT-- THIS DOESN'T FEEL RIGHT!
YOU MEAN YOU WANT TO STHOP?
NO, I MEAN WE'RE WEARING EACH OTHER'S RETAINERS.
NO WONDER I WAS LISPING.
©2010 ZITS Partnership. Distributed by King Features Syndicate
7/8

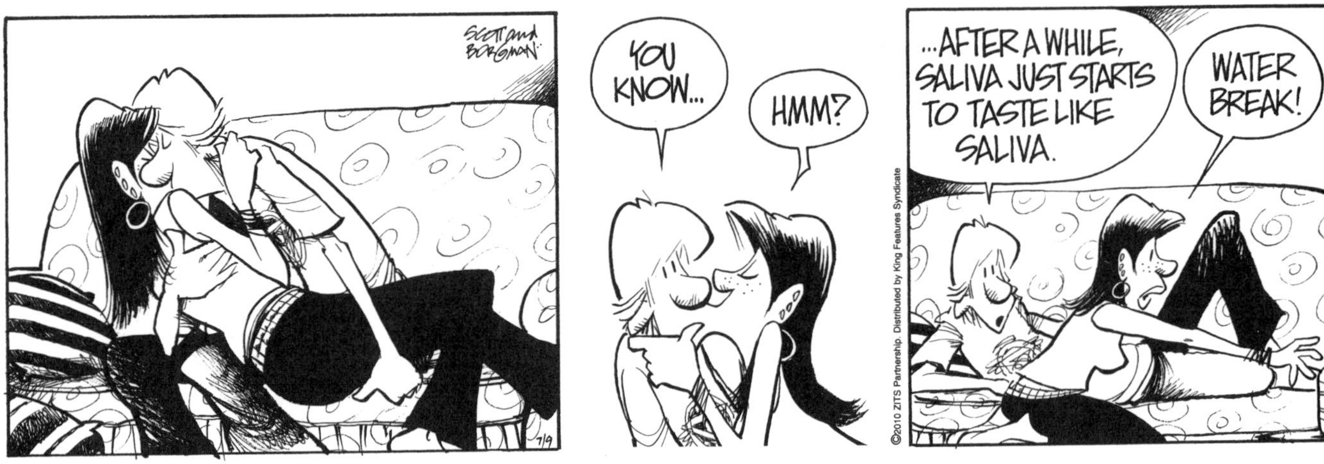
SCOTT and BORGMAN
7/9
YOU KNOW...
HMM?
...AFTER A WHILE, SALIVA JUST STARTS TO TASTE LIKE SALIVA.
WATER BREAK!
©2010 ZITS Partnership. Distributed by King Features Syndicate

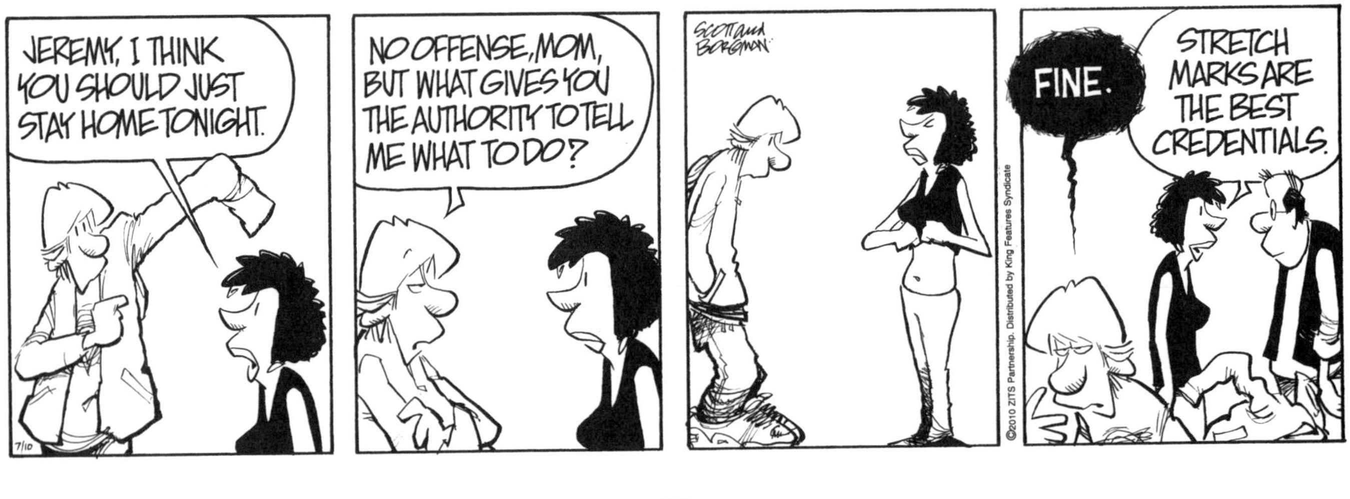
JEREMY, I THINK YOU SHOULD JUST STAY HOME TONIGHT.
7/10
NO OFFENSE, MOM, BUT WHAT GIVES YOU THE AUTHORITY TO TELL ME WHAT TO DO?
SCOTT and BORGMAN
STRETCH MARKS ARE THE BEST CREDENTIALS.
FINE.
©2010 ZITS Partnership. Distributed by King Features Syndicate

Zits
by JERRY SCOTT and JIM BORGMAN

WALT, CAN YOU TIGHTEN THIS SCREW SO I DON'T HAVE TO DO IT WITH THE BUTTER-KNIFE?
SURE...
BUT I'LL HAVE TO GET A SCREW-DRIVER.
WHICH MEANS I'LL HAVE TO GET TO MY WORKBENCH...
...WHICH MEANS I'LL HAVE TO LOG ONTO CRAIGSLIST AND SELL ALL THE JUNK THAT'S PILED IN FRONT OF THE WORKBENCH SO I CAN FIND A SCREWDRIVER TO TIGHTEN THE SCREW.
I'LL GET THE BUTTERKNIFE.
7/11
SCOTT and BORGMAN
©2010 ZITS Partnership. Distributed by King Features Syndicate

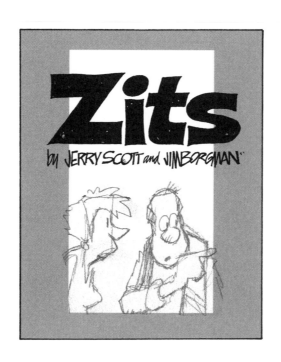

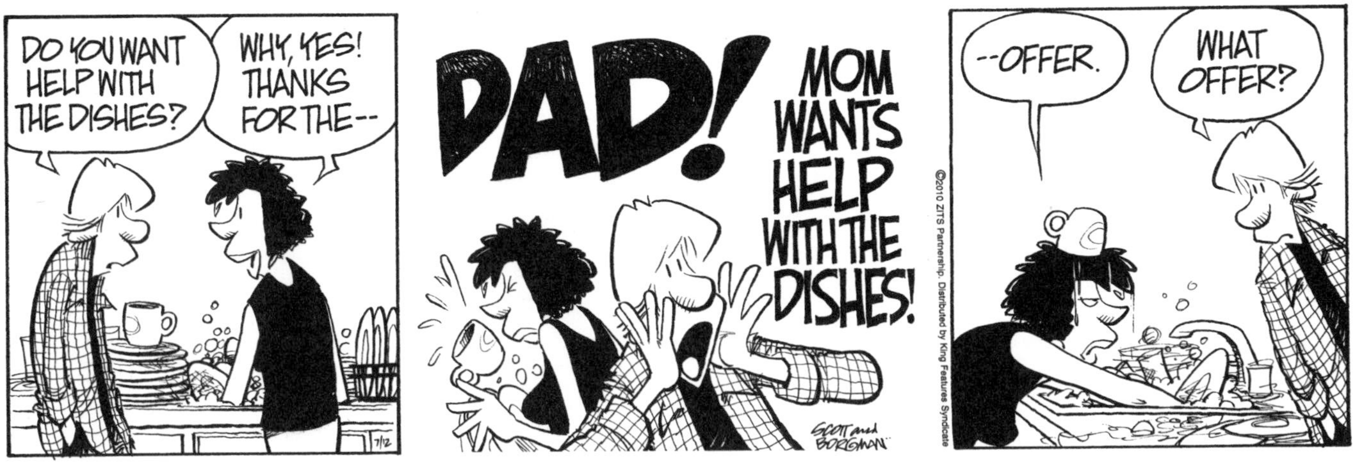
DO YOU WANT HELP WITH THE DISHES?
WHY, YES! THANKS FOR THE--
DAD!
MOM WANTS HELP WITH THE DISHES!
SCOTT and BORGMAN
©2010 ZITS Partnership. Distributed by King Features Syndicate
--OFFER.
WHAT OFFER?

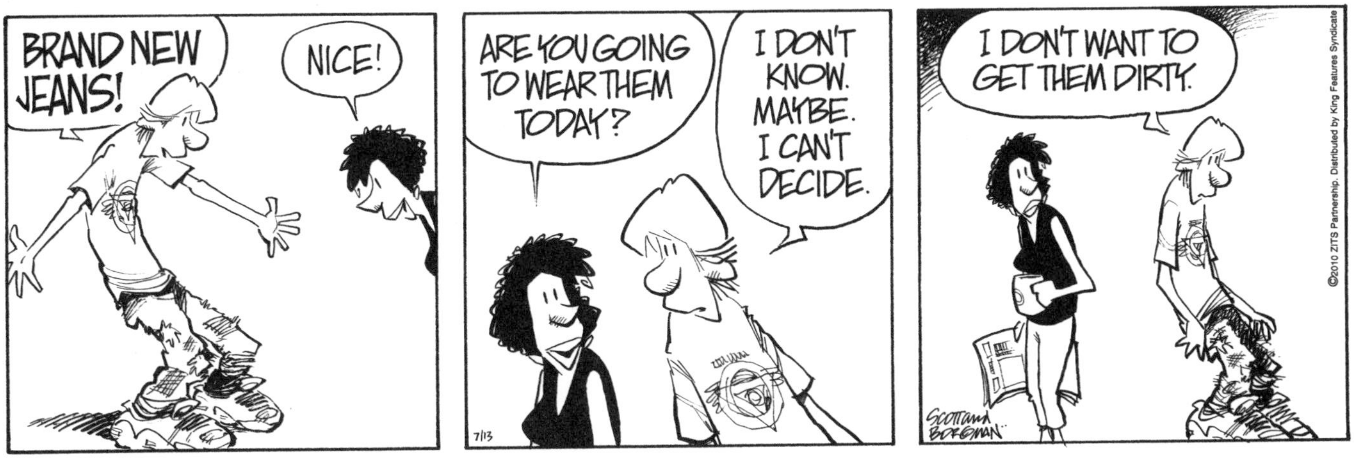
BRAND NEW JEANS!
NICE!
ARE YOU GOING TO WEAR THEM TODAY?
I DON'T KNOW. MAYBE. I CAN'T DECIDE.
I DON'T WANT TO GET THEM DIRTY.
SCOTT and BORGMAN
©2010 ZITS Partnership. Distributed by King Features Syndicate

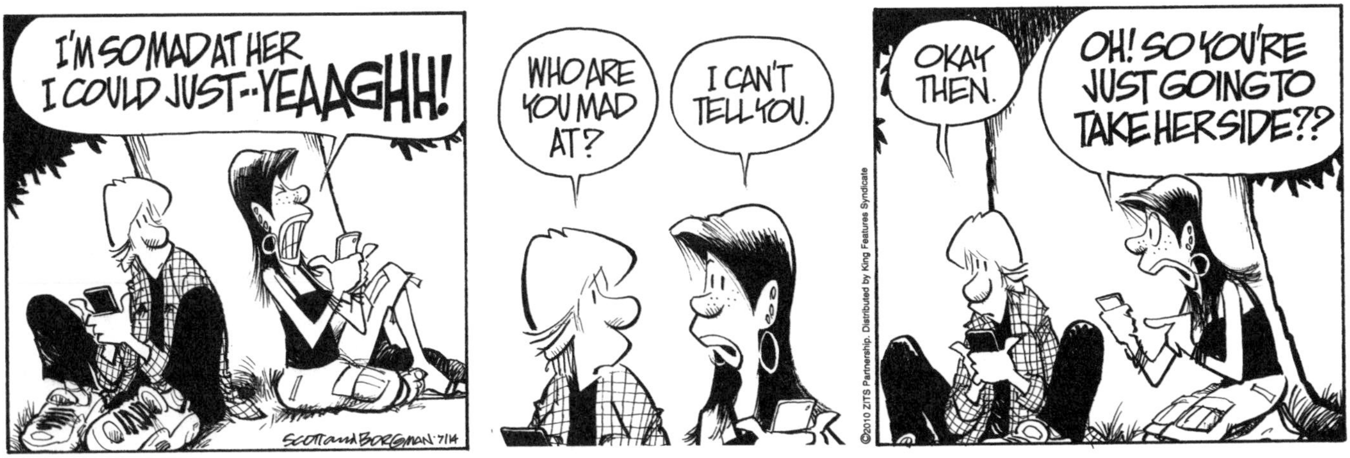
I'M SO MAD AT HER I COULD JUST--YEAAGHH!
SCOTT and BORGMAN 7/14
WHO ARE YOU MAD AT?
I CAN'T TELL YOU.
©2010 ZITS Partnership. Distributed by King Features Syndicate
OKAY THEN.
OH! SO YOU'RE JUST GOING TO TAKE HER SIDE??

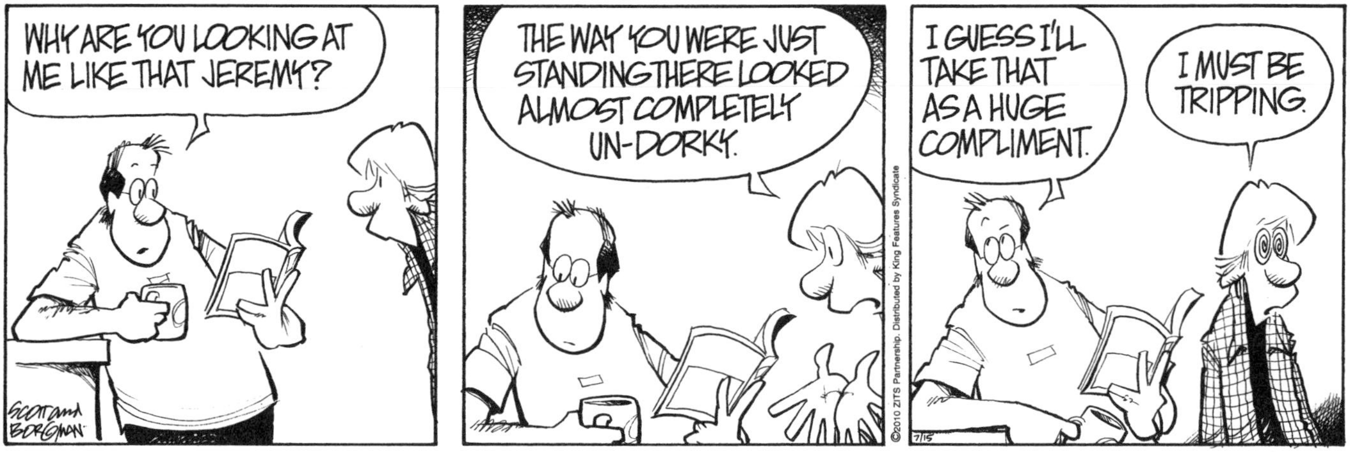
WHY ARE YOU LOOKING AT ME LIKE THAT JEREMY?
THE WAY YOU WERE JUST STANDING THERE LOOKED ALMOST COMPLETELY UN-DORKY.
I GUESS I'LL TAKE THAT AS A HUGE COMPLIMENT.
I MUST BE TRIPPING.
SCOTT and BORGMAN
©2010 ZITS Partnership. Distributed by King Features Syndicate
7/15

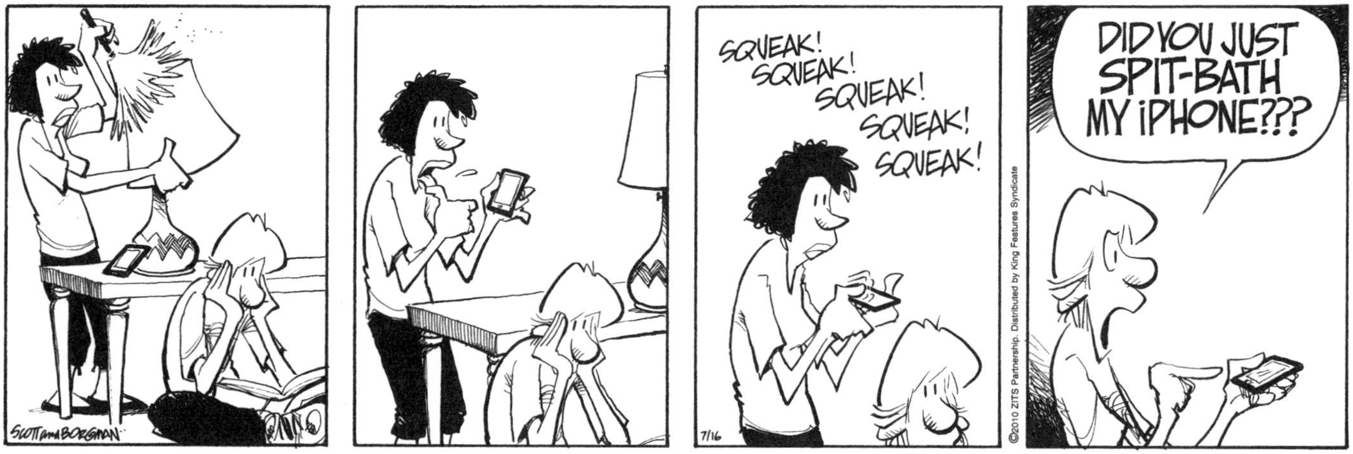
SCOTT and BORGMAN
SQUEAK! SQUEAK! SQUEAK! SQUEAK! SQUEAK!
7/16
©2010 ZITS Partnership. Distributed by King Features Syndicate
DID YOU JUST SPIT-BATH MY iPHONE???

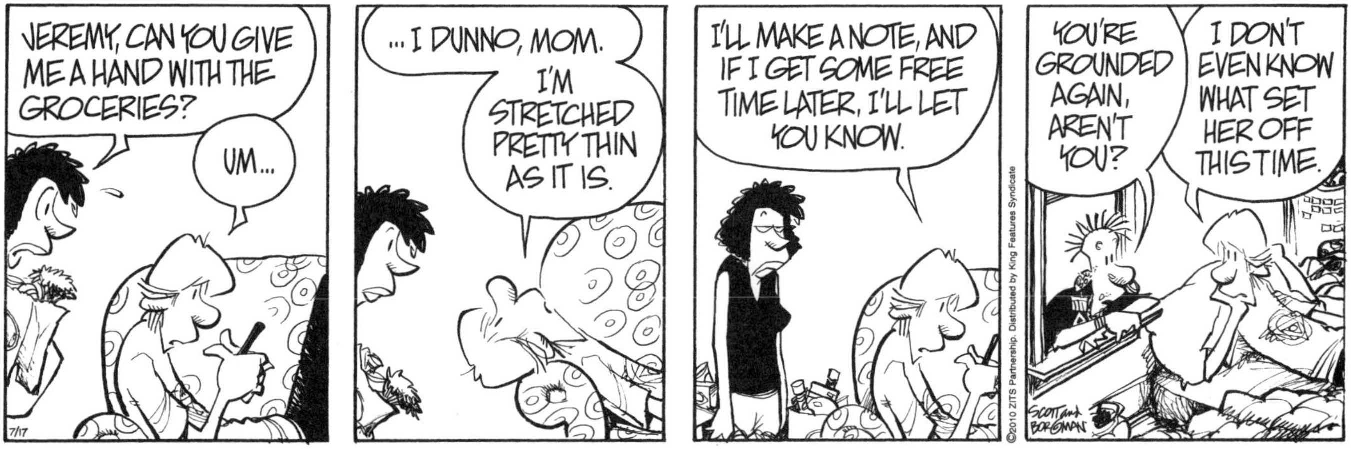
JEREMY, CAN YOU GIVE ME A HAND WITH THE GROCERIES?
UM...
7/17
...I DUNNO, MOM.
I'M STRETCHED PRETTY THIN AS IT IS.
I'LL MAKE A NOTE, AND IF I GET SOME FREE TIME LATER, I'LL LET YOU KNOW.
©2010 ZITS Partnership. Distributed by King Features Syndicate
YOU'RE GROUNDED AGAIN, AREN'T YOU?
I DON'T EVEN KNOW WHAT SET HER OFF THIS TIME.
SCOTT and BORGMAN

Zits
by JERRY SCOTT and JIM BORGMAN

BRUSH! BRUSH!
HOW'S THIS?
MUCH BETTER!
WHAT DID YOU USE TO WASH THAT SPOT OFF YOUR T-SHIRT?
NOTHING.
I JUST COLORED OVER IT WITH A MAGIC MARKER, LIKE USUAL.
7/18
©2010 ZITS Partnership. Distributed by King Features Syndicate.
GAAAA!
SCOTT and BORGMAN
IT'S A WONDER SHE ISN'T BALD FROM PULLING OUT HER HAIR LIKE THAT.
DO YOU STILL HAVE THAT MARKER ON YOU BY ANY CHANCE?

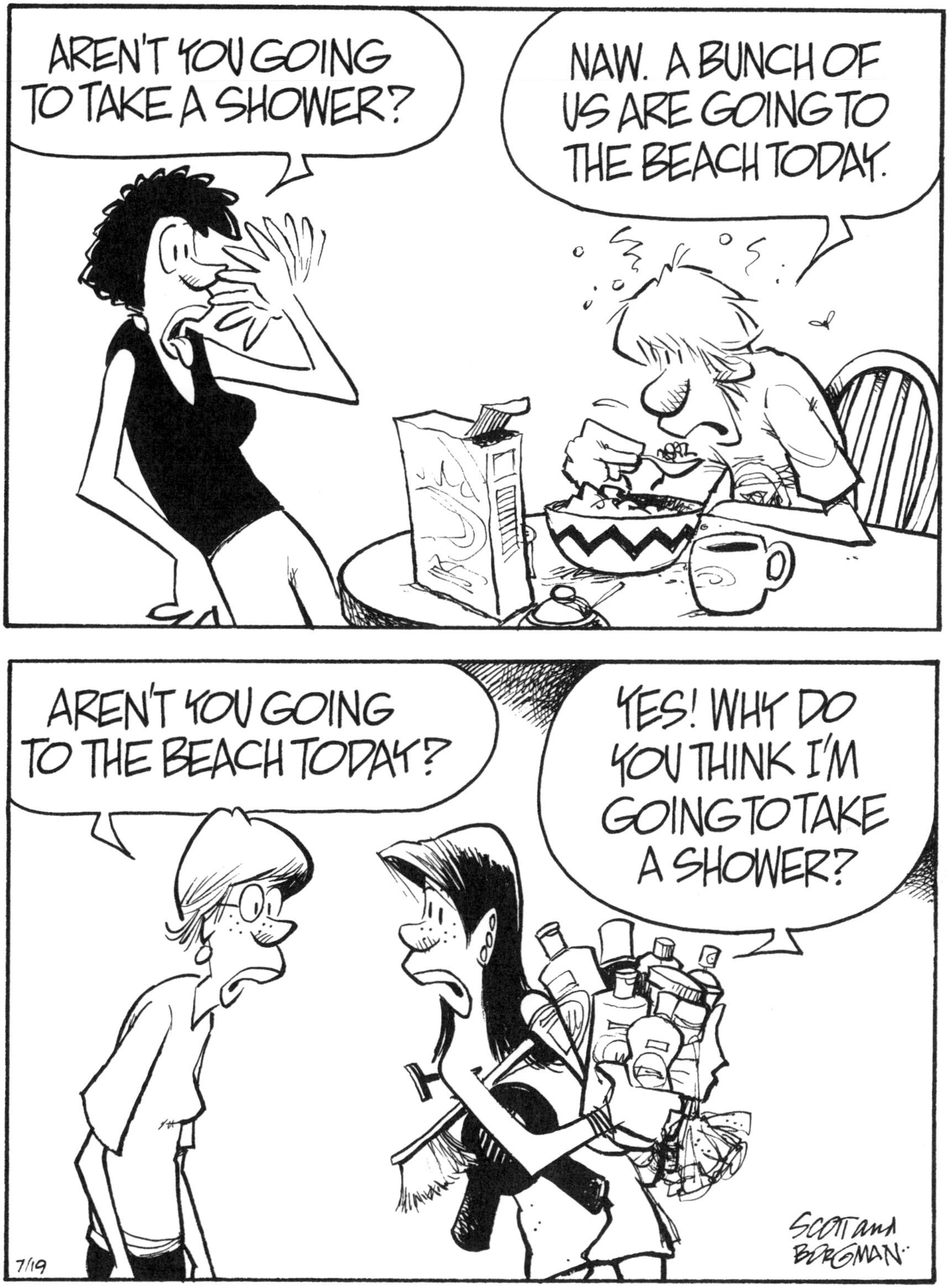
AREN'T YOU GOING TO TAKE A SHOWER?
NAW. A BUNCH OF US ARE GOING TO THE BEACH TODAY.
AREN'T YOU GOING TO THE BEACH TODAY?
YES! WHY DO YOU THINK I'M GOING TO TAKE A SHOWER?
7/19
SCOTT AND BORGMAN

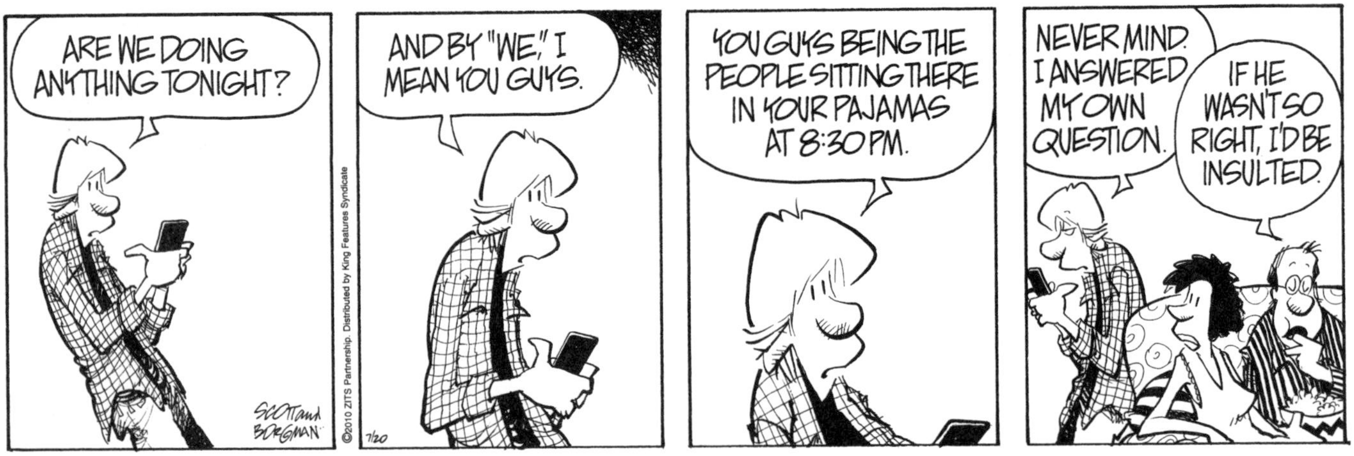
ARE WE DOING ANYTHING TONIGHT?
SCOTT and BORGMAN
AND BY "WE," I MEAN YOU GUYS.
©2010 ZITS Partnership. Distributed by King Features Syndicate
7/20
YOU GUYS BEING THE PEOPLE SITTING THERE IN YOUR PAJAMAS AT 8:30 PM.
NEVER MIND. I ANSWERED MY OWN QUESTION.
IF HE WASN'T SO RIGHT, I'D BE INSULTED.

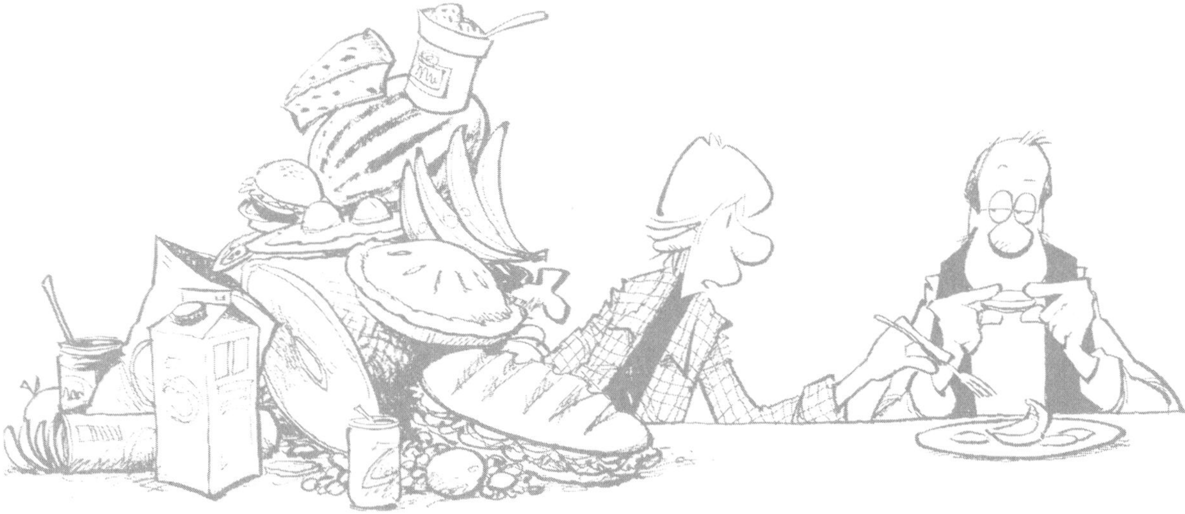

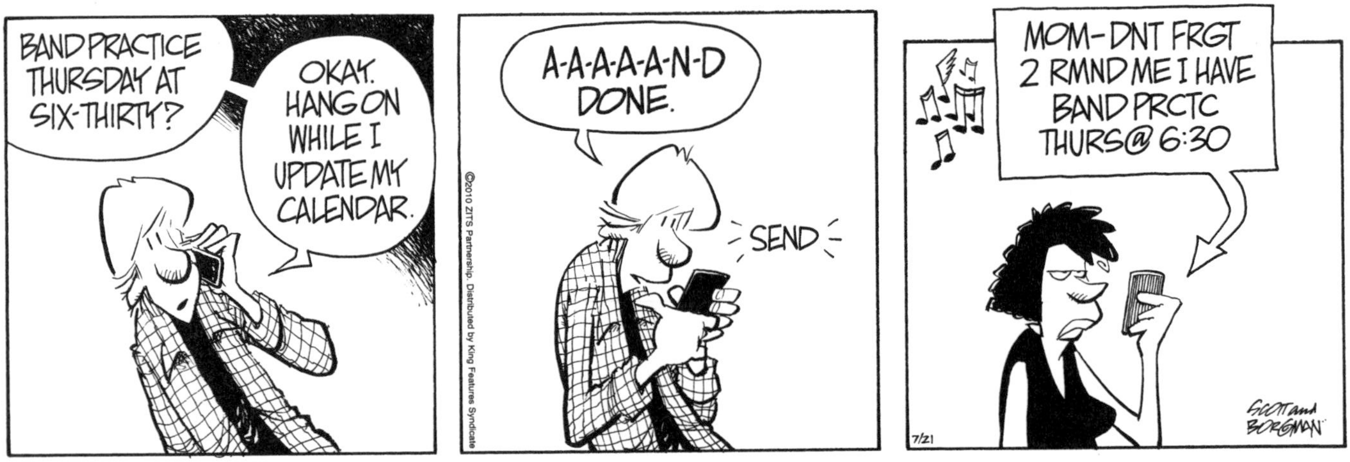
BAND PRACTICE THURSDAY AT SIX-THIRTY?
OKAY. HANG ON WHILE I UPDATE MY CALENDAR.
©2010 ZITS Partnership. Distributed by King Features Syndicate
A-A-A-A-A-N-D DONE.
SEND
MOM- DNT FRGT 2 RMND ME I HAVE BAND PRCTC THURS@ 6:30
7/21
SCOTT and BORGMAN

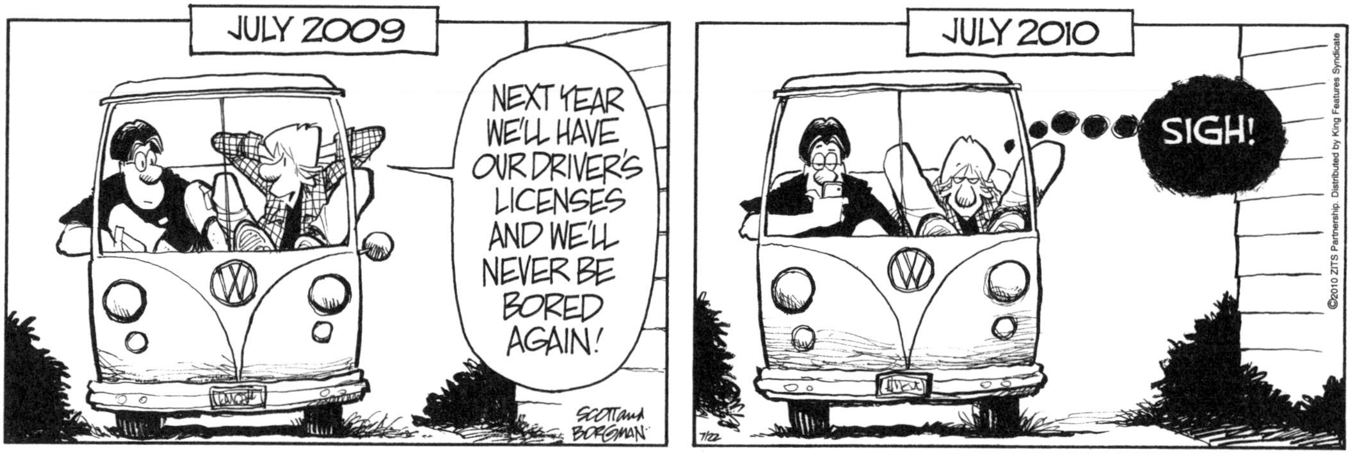
JULY 2009
NEXT YEAR WE'LL HAVE OUR DRIVER'S LICENSES AND WE'LL NEVER BE BORED AGAIN!
JULY 2010
SIGH!
©2010 ZITS Partnership. Distributed by King Features Syndicate

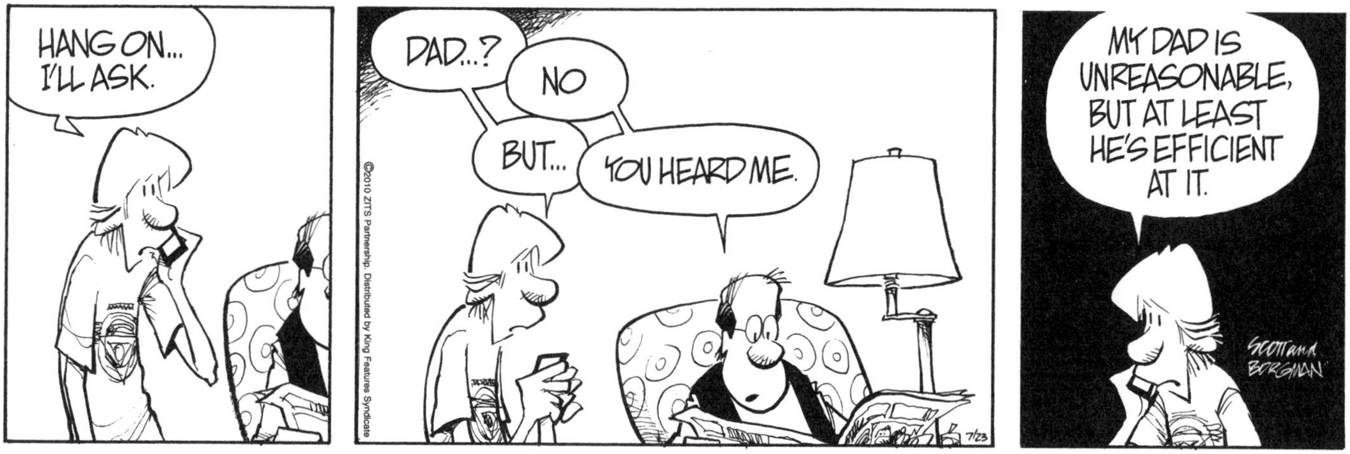
HANG ON... I'LL ASK.
DAD...?
NO
BUT...
YOU HEARD ME.
MY DAD IS UNREASONABLE, BUT AT LEAST HE'S EFFICIENT AT IT.
©2010 ZITS Partnership. Distributed by King Features Syndicate

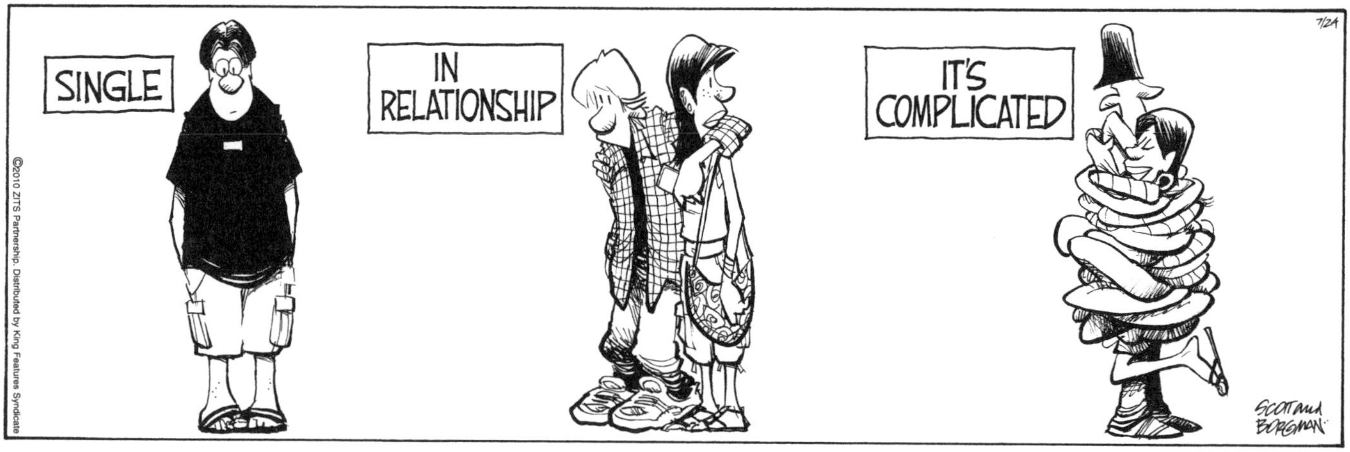
SINGLE
IN RELATIONSHIP
IT'S COMPLICATED
©2010 ZITS Partnership. Distributed by King Features Syndicate

Zits
by
JERRY SCOTT and
JIM BORGMAN

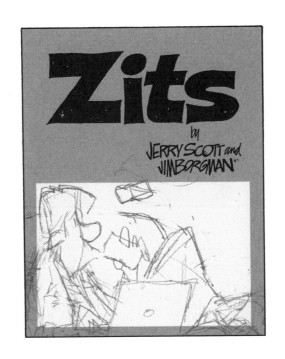

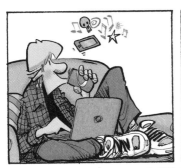

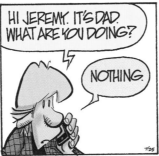

HI JEREMY. IT'S DAD. WHAT ARE YOU DOING?
NOTHING.
7/25
WANT TO GO OUT TO LUNCH?
SURE.
SLAM!
©2010 ZITS Partnership. Distributed by King Features Syndicate
SCOTT and BORGMAN
Menu
I MEANT WITH ME.
OH.

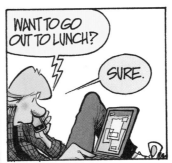

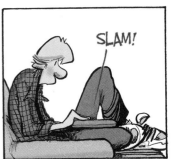

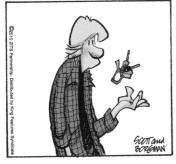

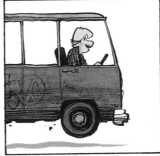

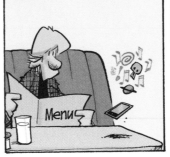

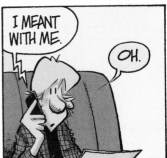

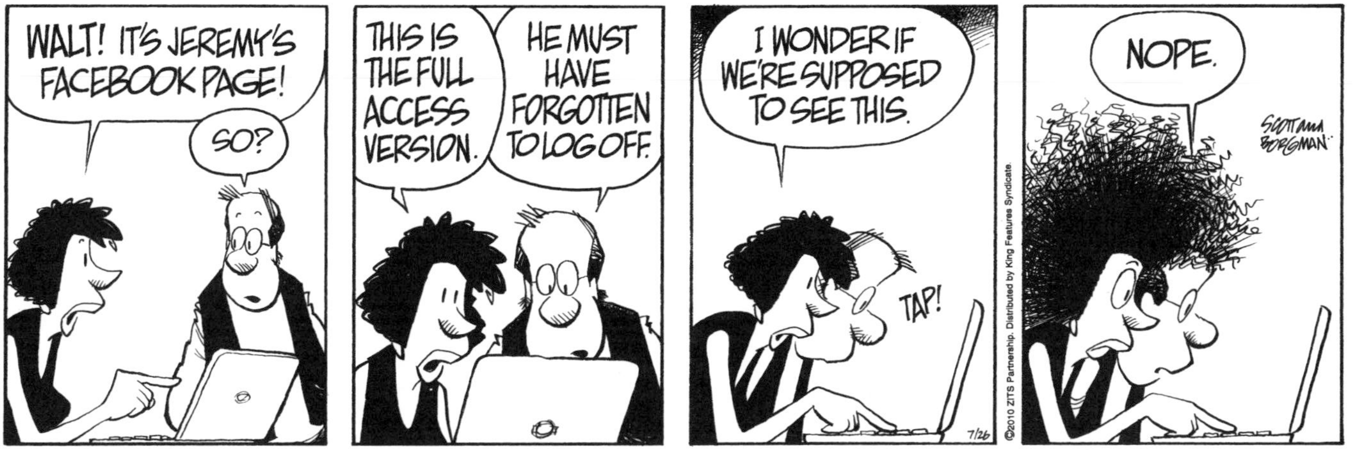
WALT! IT'S JEREMY'S FACEBOOK PAGE!
SO?
THIS IS THE FULL ACCESS VERSION.
HE MUST HAVE FORGOTTEN TO LOG OFF.
I WONDER IF WE'RE SUPPOSED TO SEE THIS.
TAP!
7/26
©2010 ZITS Partnership. Distributed by King Features Syndicate.
NOPE.
SCOTT AND BORGMAN

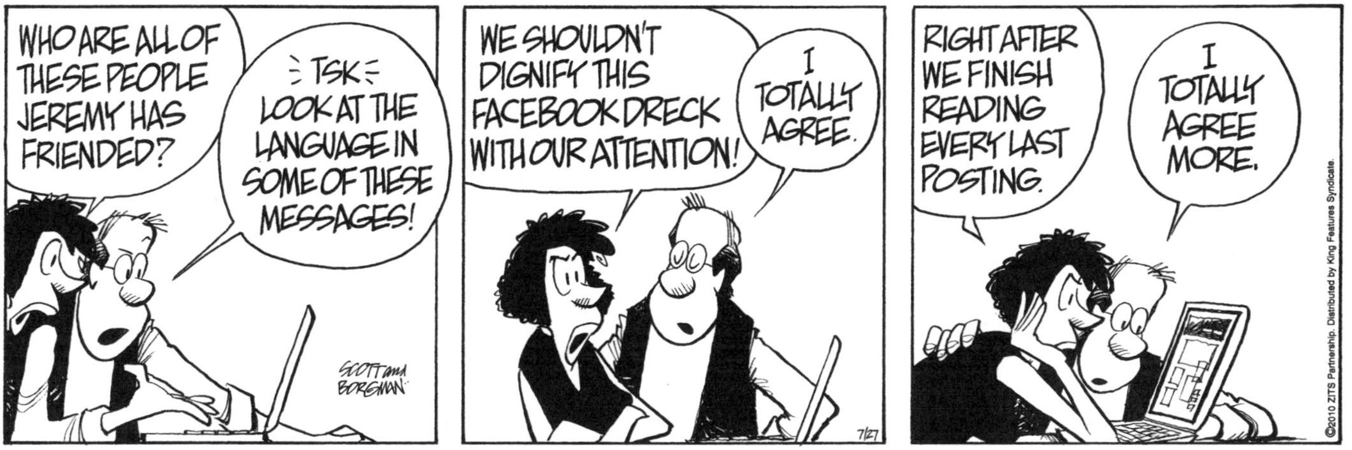
WHO ARE ALL OF THESE PEOPLE JEREMY HAS FRIENDED?
TSK
LOOK AT THE LANGUAGE IN SOME OF THESE MESSAGES!
SCOTT AND BORGMAN
WE SHOULDN'T DIGNIFY THIS FACEBOOK DRECK WITH OUR ATTENTION!
I TOTALLY AGREE.
7/27
RIGHT AFTER WE FINISH READING EVERY LAST POSTING.
I TOTALLY AGREE MORE.
©2010 ZITS Partnership. Distributed by King Features Syndicate.

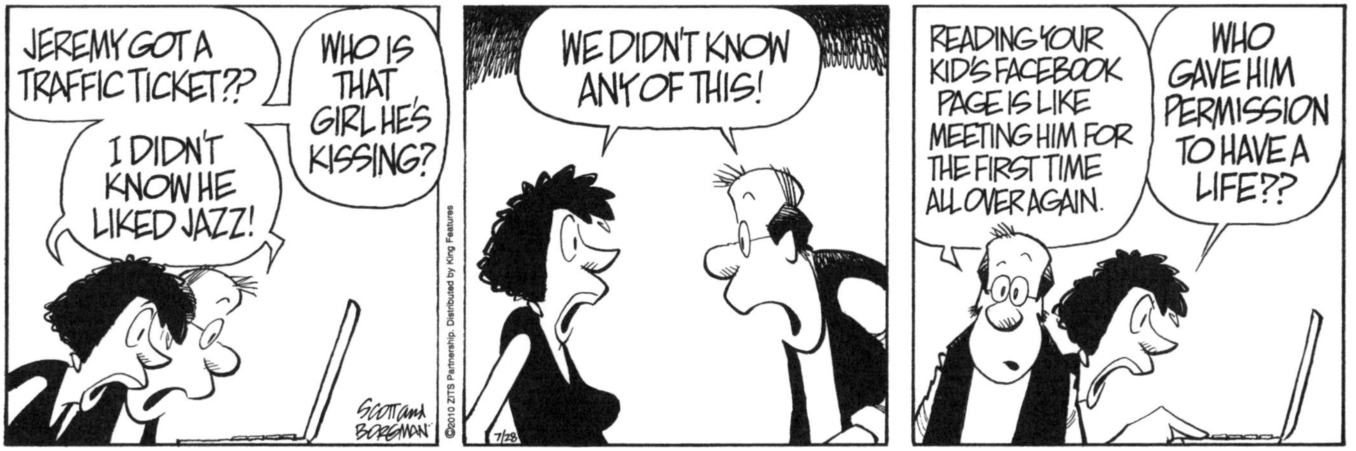
JEREMY GOT A TRAFFIC TICKET??
WHO IS THAT GIRL HE'S KISSING?
I DIDN'T KNOW HE LIKED JAZZ!
SCOTT AND BORGMAN
©2010 ZITS Partnership. Distributed by King Features
WE DIDN'T KNOW ANY OF THIS!
7/28
READING YOUR KID'S FACEBOOK PAGE IS LIKE MEETING HIM FOR THE FIRST TIME ALL OVER AGAIN.
WHO GAVE HIM PERMISSION TO HAVE A LIFE??

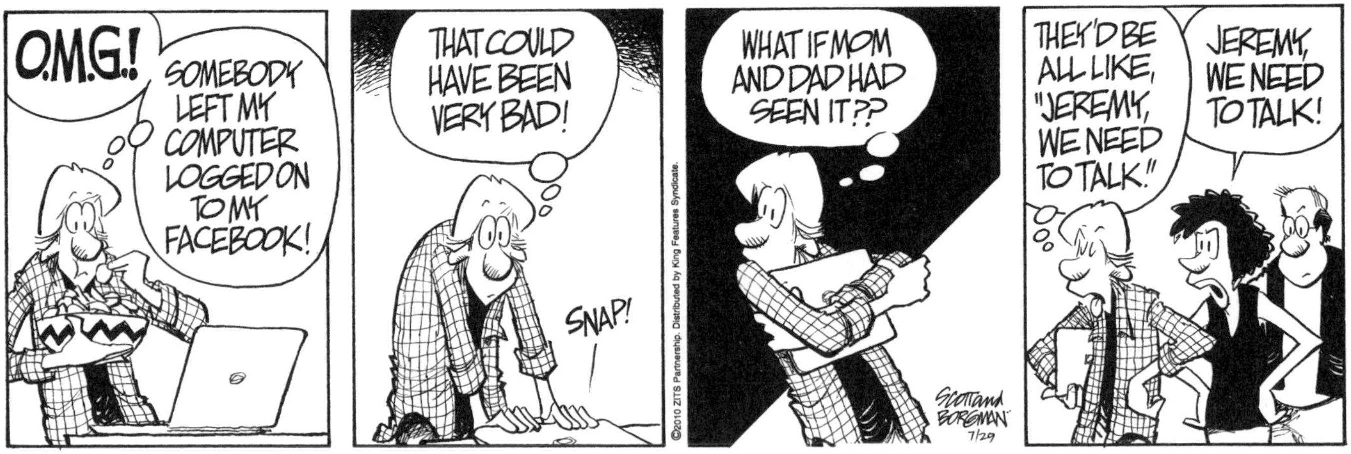
O.M.G.!
SOMEBODY LEFT MY COMPUTER LOGGED ON TO MY FACEBOOK!
THAT COULD HAVE BEEN VERY BAD!
SNAP!
WHAT IF MOM AND DAD HAD SEEN IT??
THEY'D BE ALL LIKE, "JEREMY, WE NEED TO TALK."
JEREMY, WE NEED TO TALK!
©2010 ZITS Partnership. Distributed by King Features Syndicate.
SCOTT and BORGMAN
7/29

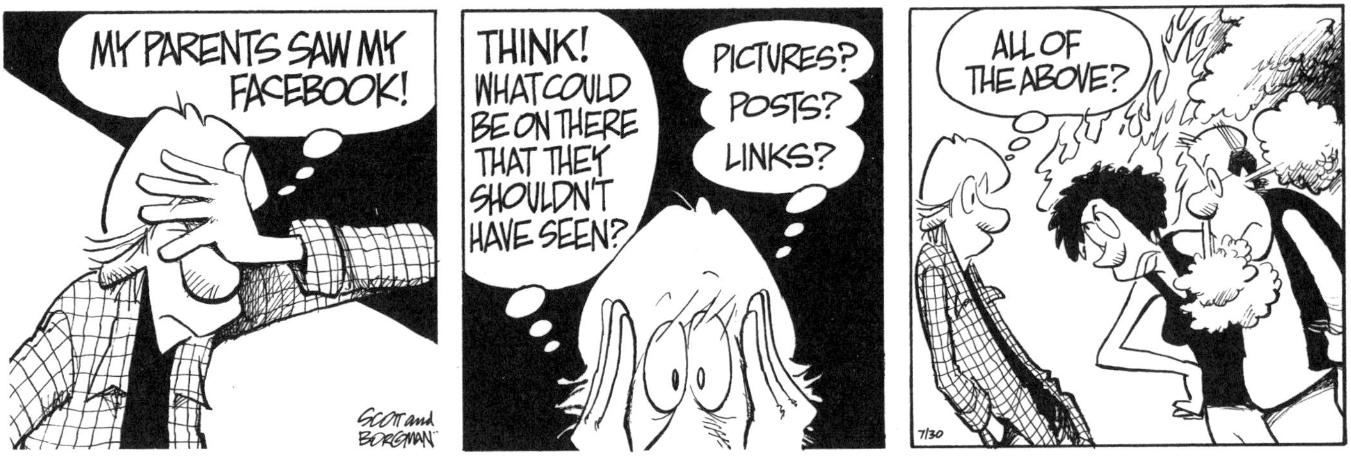
MY PARENTS SAW MY FACEBOOK!
SCOTT and BORGMAN
THINK! WHAT COULD BE ON THERE THAT THEY SHOULDN'T HAVE SEEN?
PICTURES?
POSTS?
LINKS?
ALL OF THE ABOVE?
7/30

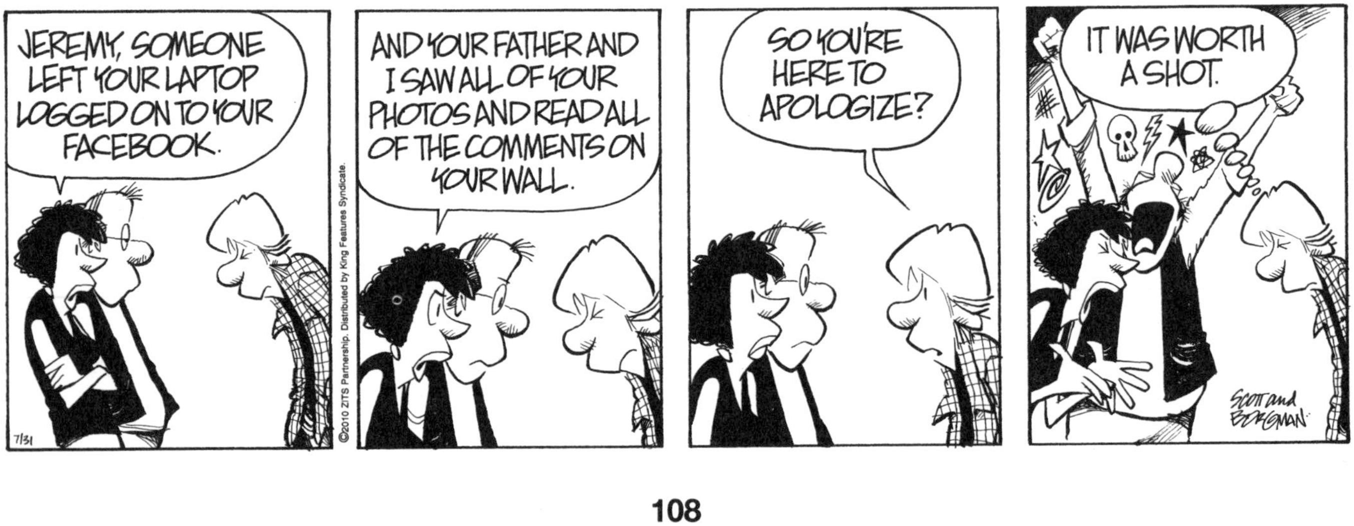
JEREMY, SOMEONE LEFT YOUR LAPTOP LOGGED ON TO YOUR FACEBOOK.
7/31
©2010 ZITS Partnership. Distributed by King Features Syndicate.
AND YOUR FATHER AND I SAW ALL OF YOUR PHOTOS AND READ ALL OF THE COMMENTS ON YOUR WALL.
SO YOU'RE HERE TO APOLOGIZE?
IT WAS WORTH A SHOT.
SCOTT and BORGMAN

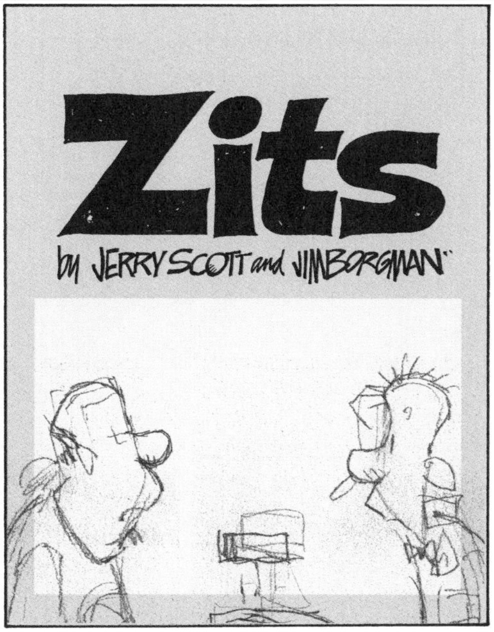
Zits
by JERRY SCOTT and JIM BORGMAN

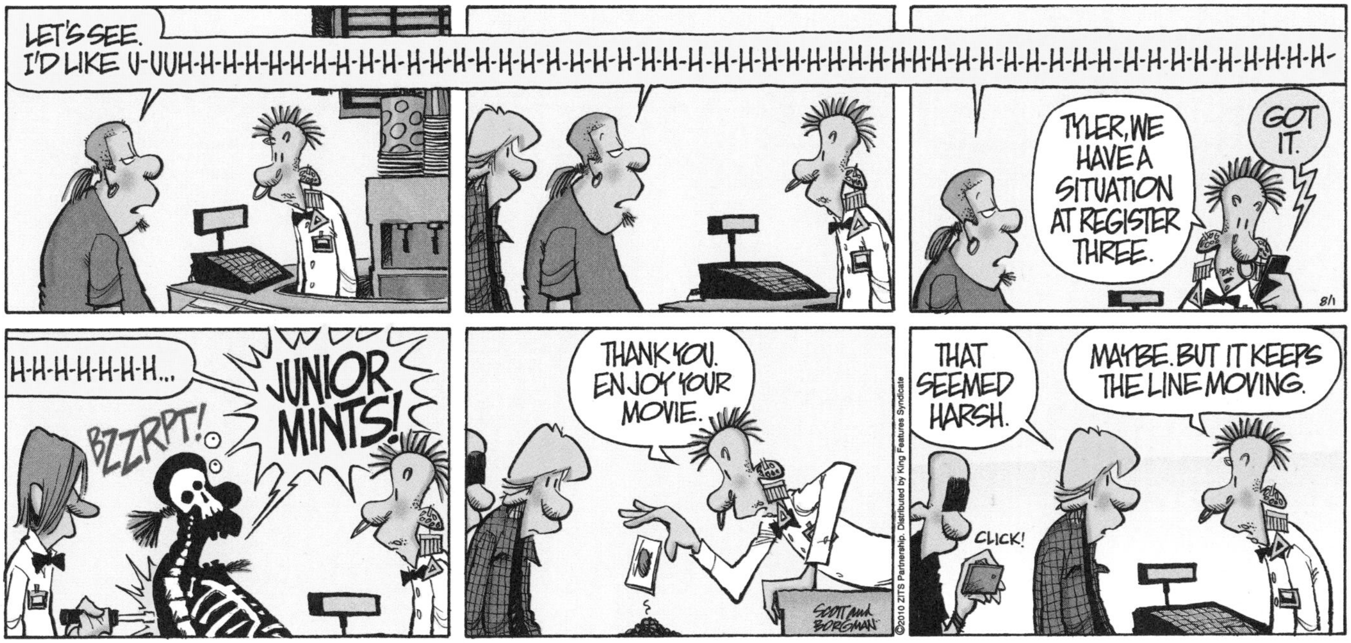
LET'S SEE. I'D LIKE U-UUH-H-H-H-H-H-H-H-H-H-H-H-H-H-H-H-H-H-H-H-H-H-H-H-H-H-H-H-H-H-H-H-H-H-H-H-H-H-H-H-H-H-H-H-H-H-H-H-H-H-H-
TYLER, WE HAVE A SITUATION AT REGISTER THREE.
GOT IT.
8/1
H-H-H-H-H-H-H...
BZZRPT!
JUNIOR MINTS!
THANK YOU. ENJOY YOUR MOVIE.
SCOTT and BORGMAN
©2010 ZITS Partnership. Distributed by King Features Syndicate
THAT SEEMED HARSH.
MAYBE. BUT IT KEEPS THE LINE MOVING.
CLICK!

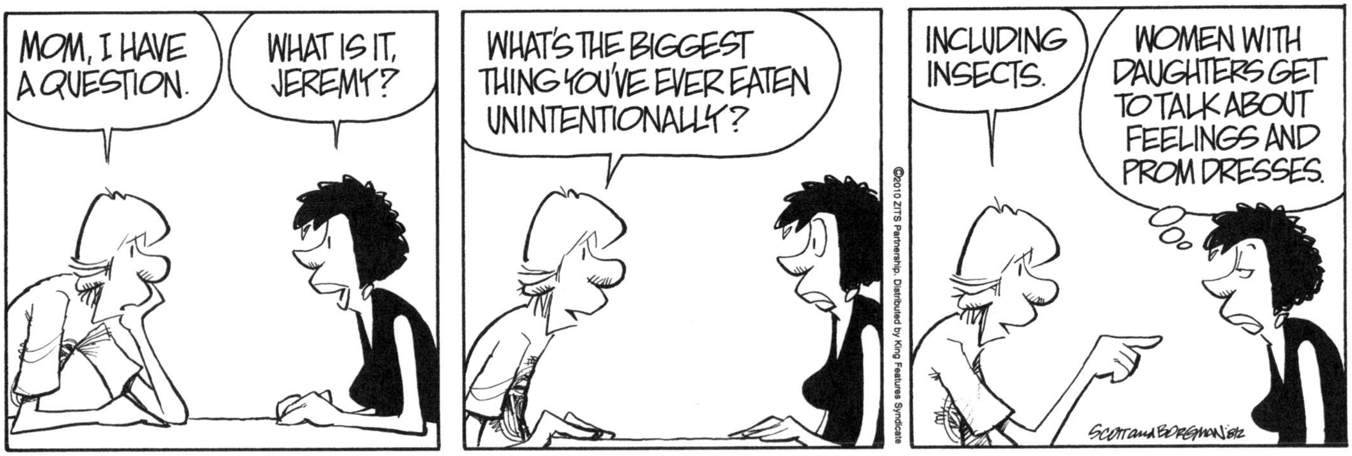
MOM, I HAVE A QUESTION.
WHAT IS IT, JEREMY?
WHAT'S THE BIGGEST THING YOU'VE EVER EATEN UNINTENTIONALLY?
INCLUDING INSECTS.
WOMEN WITH DAUGHTERS GET TO TALK ABOUT FEELINGS AND PROM DRESSES.
©2010 ZITS Partnership. Distributed by King Features Syndicate
SCOTT and BORGMAN 8/12

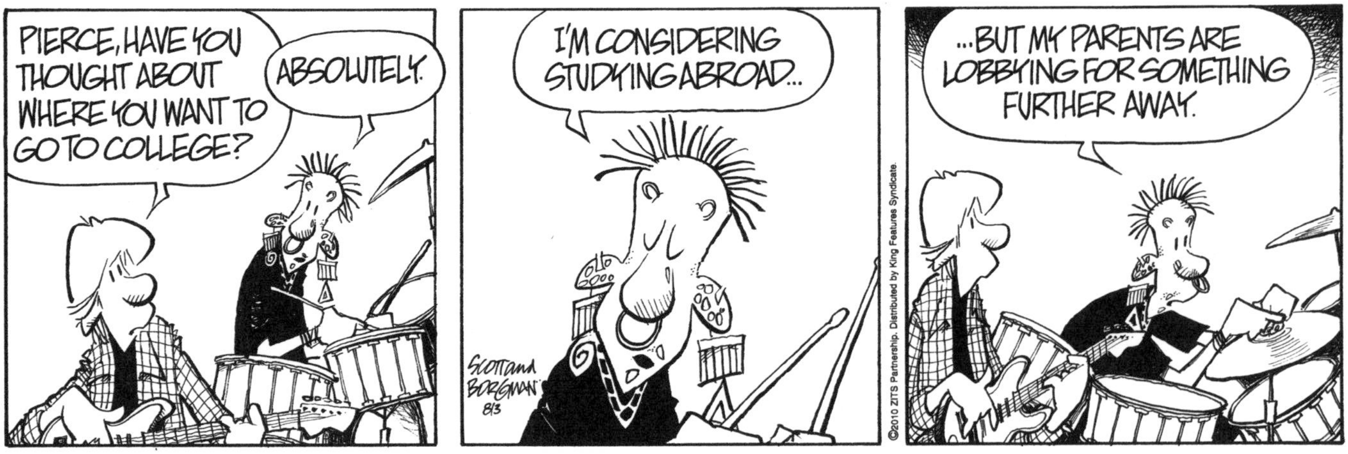
PIERCE, HAVE YOU THOUGHT ABOUT WHERE YOU WANT TO GO TO COLLEGE?
ABSOLUTELY.
I'M CONSIDERING STUDYING ABROAD...
...BUT MY PARENTS ARE LOBBYING FOR SOMETHING FURTHER AWAY.
SCOTT and BORGMAN 8/13
©2010 ZITS Partnership. Distributed by King Features Syndicate.

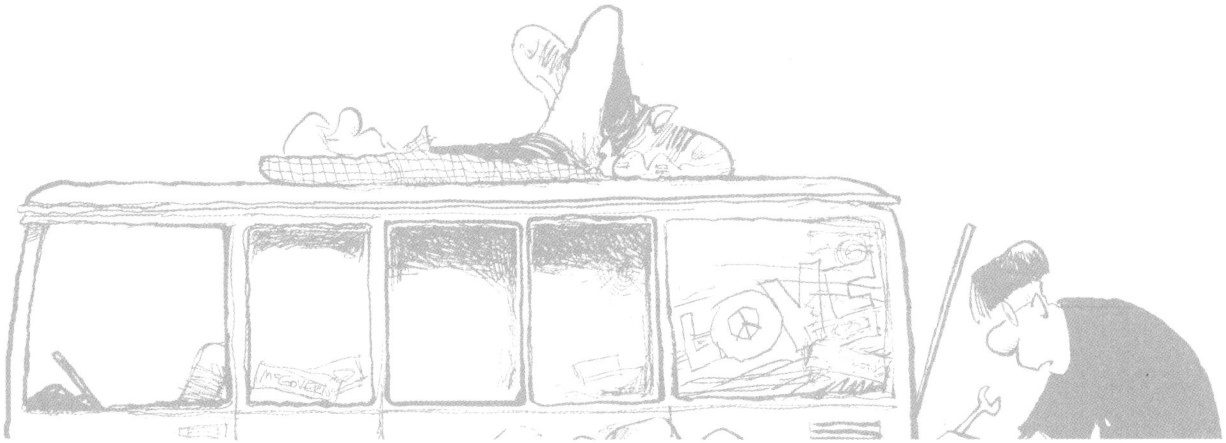
LOVE

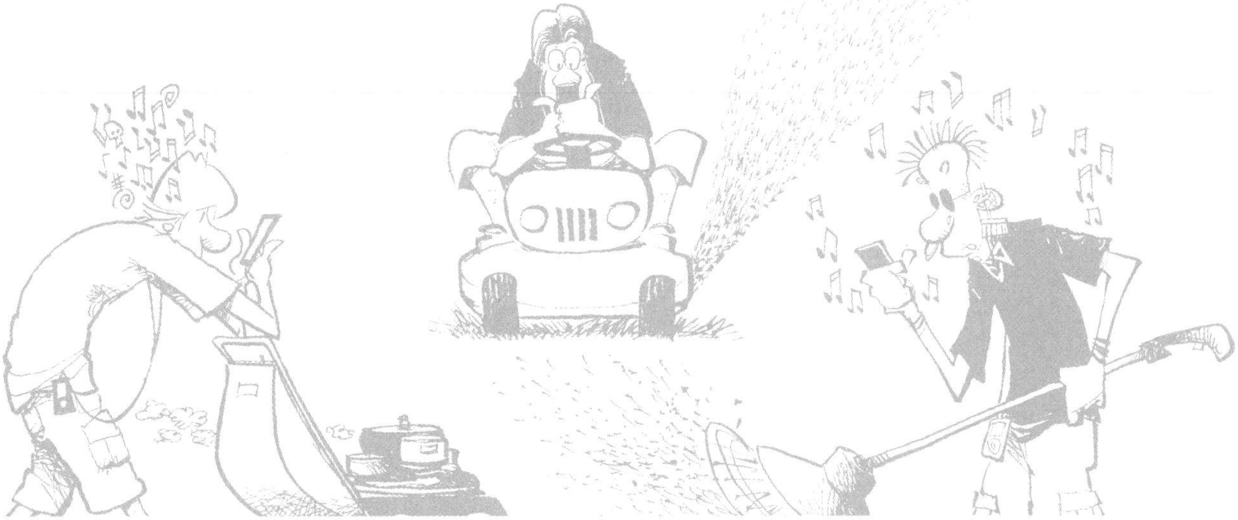

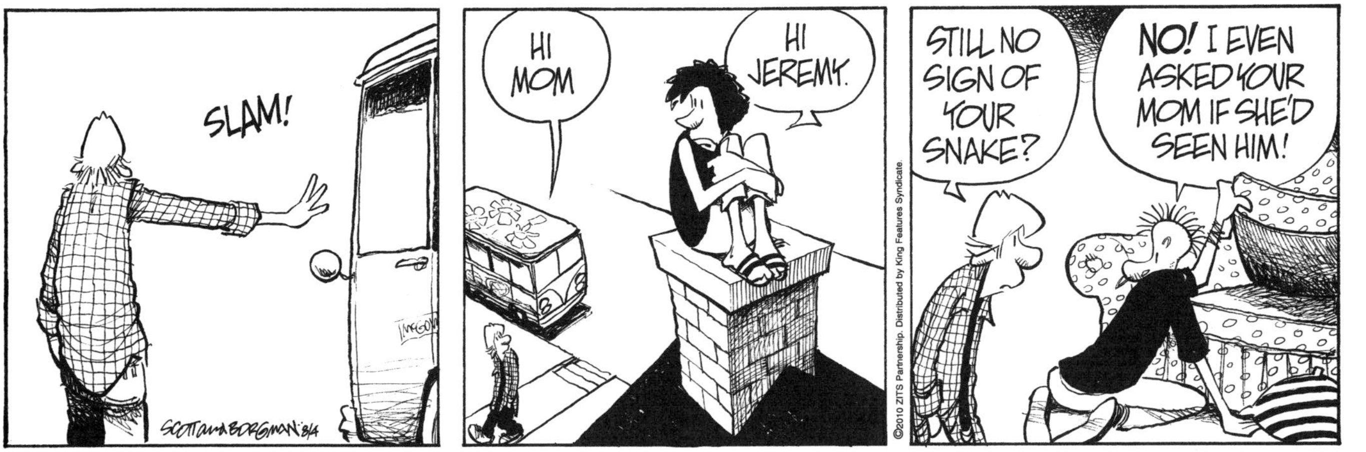
SLAM!
SCOTT and BORGMAN 8/4
HI MOM
HI JEREMY.
STILL NO SIGN OF YOUR SNAKE?
NO! I EVEN ASKED YOUR MOM IF SHE'D SEEN HIM!
©2010 ZITS Partnership. Distributed by King Features Syndicate.

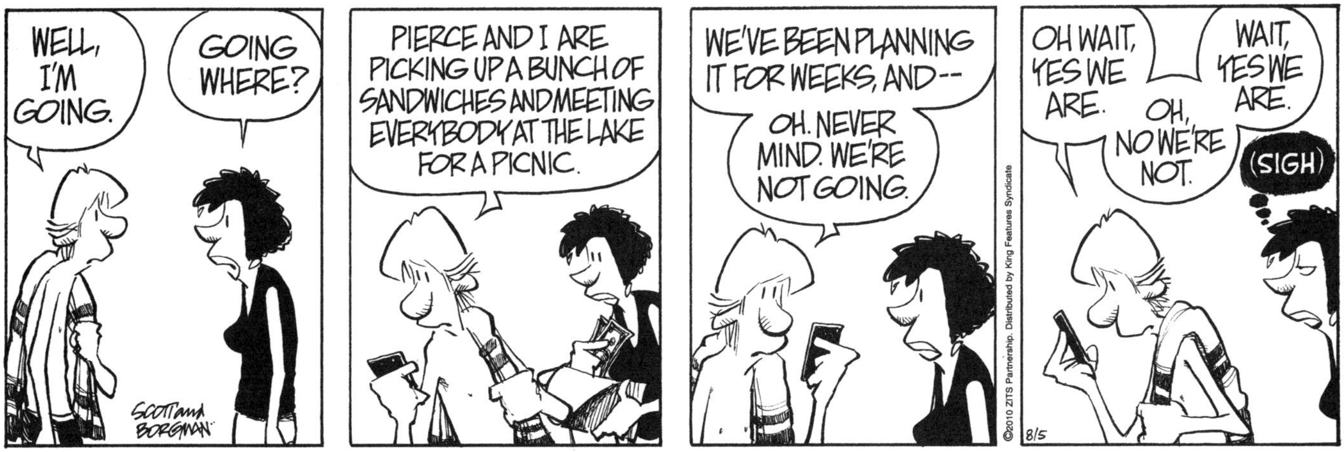
WELL, I'M GOING.
GOING WHERE?
SCOTT and BORGMAN
PIERCE AND I ARE PICKING UP A BUNCH OF SANDWICHES AND MEETING EVERYBODY AT THE LAKE FOR A PICNIC.
WE'VE BEEN PLANNING IT FOR WEEKS, AND--
OH. NEVER MIND. WE'RE NOT GOING.
OH WAIT, YES WE ARE.
OH, NO WE'RE NOT.
WAIT, YES WE ARE.
(SIGH)
8/5
©2010 ZITS Partnership. Distributed by King Features Syndicate

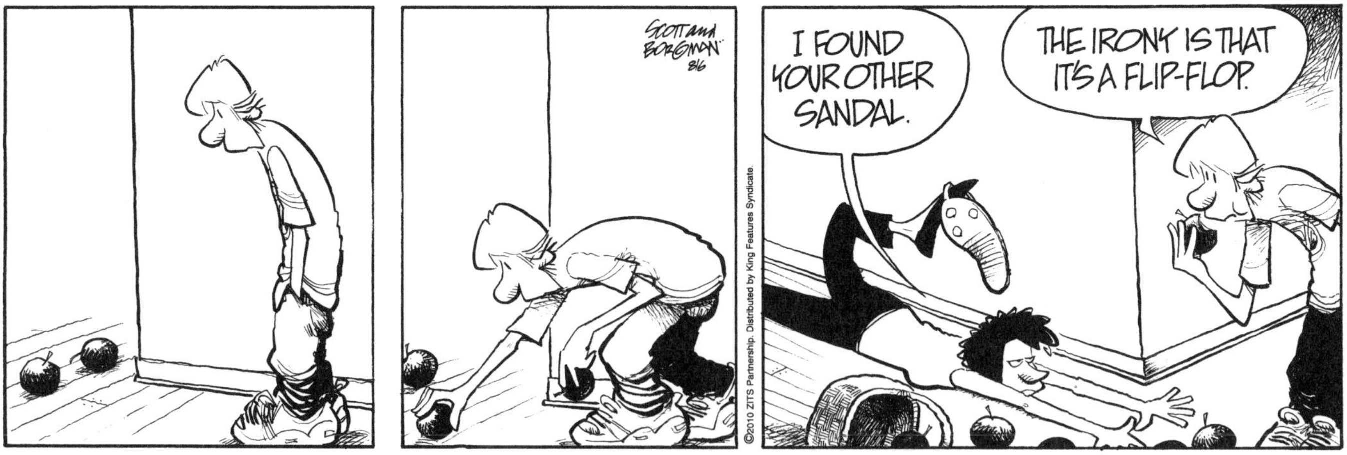
SCOTT and BORGMAN 8/6
©2010 ZITS Partnership. Distributed by King Features Syndicate.
I FOUND YOUR OTHER SANDAL.
THE IRONY IS THAT IT'S A FLIP-FLOP.

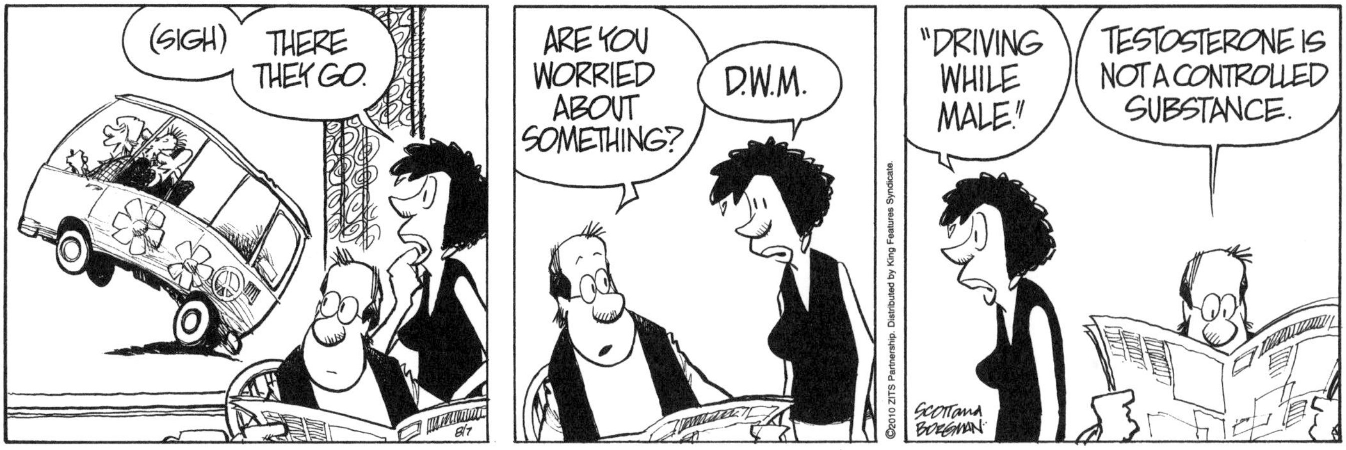
(SIGH)
THERE THEY GO.
8/7
ARE YOU WORRIED ABOUT SOMETHING?
D.W.M.
©2010 ZITS Partnership. Distributed by King Features Syndicate.
"DRIVING WHILE MALE."
TESTOSTERONE IS NOT A CONTROLLED SUBSTANCE.
SCOTT and BORGMAN

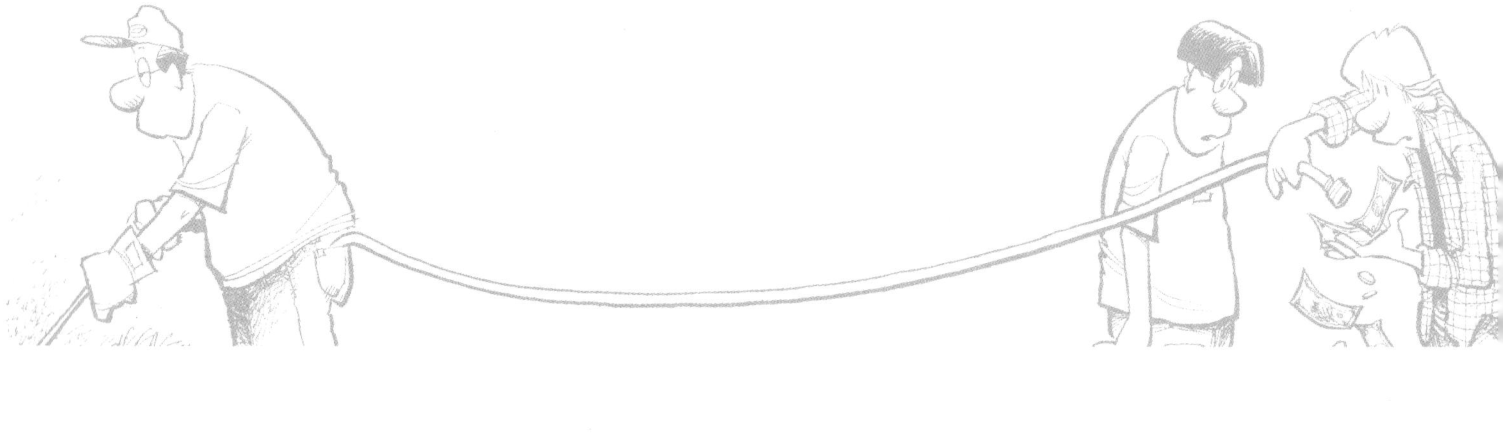

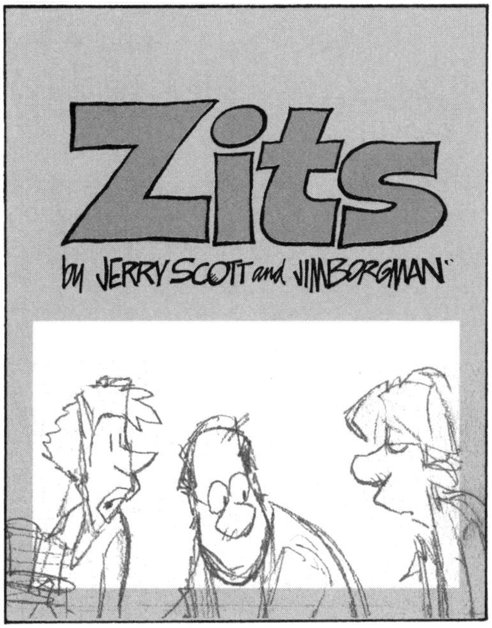
Zits
by JERRY SCOTT and JIM BORGMAN

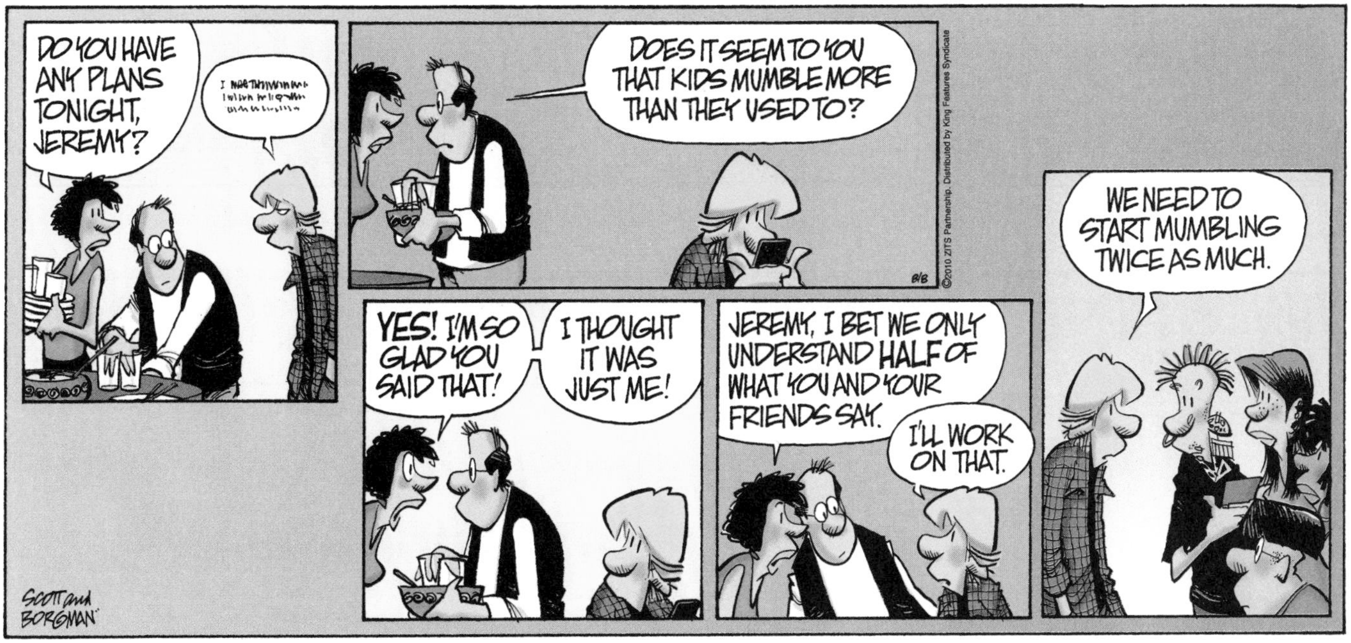
DO YOU HAVE ANY PLANS TONIGHT, JEREMY?
DOES IT SEEM TO YOU THAT KIDS MUMBLE MORE THAN THEY USED TO?
©2010 ZITS Partnership. Distributed by King Features Syndicate
8/8
YES! I'M SO GLAD YOU SAID THAT!
I THOUGHT IT WAS JUST ME!
JEREMY, I BET WE ONLY UNDERSTAND HALF OF WHAT YOU AND YOUR FRIENDS SAY.
I'LL WORK ON THAT.
WE NEED TO START MUMBLING TWICE AS MUCH.
SCOTT and BORGMAN

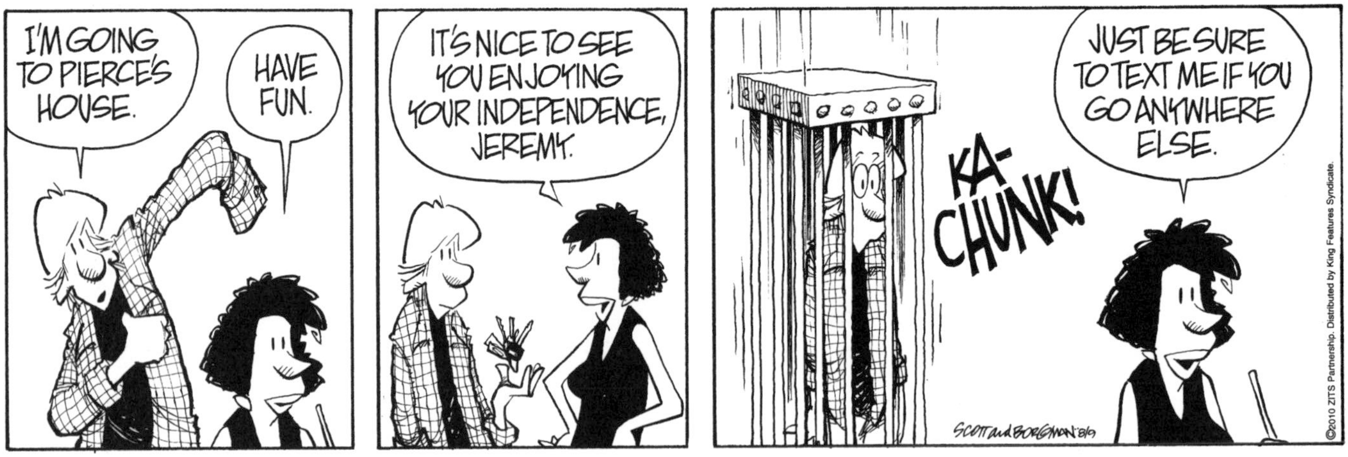
I'M GOING TO PIERCE'S HOUSE.
HAVE FUN.
IT'S NICE TO SEE YOU ENJOYING YOUR INDEPENDENCE, JEREMY.
KA-CHUNK!
JUST BE SURE TO TEXT ME IF YOU GO ANYWHERE ELSE.
©2010 ZITS Partnership. Distributed by King Features Syndicate.

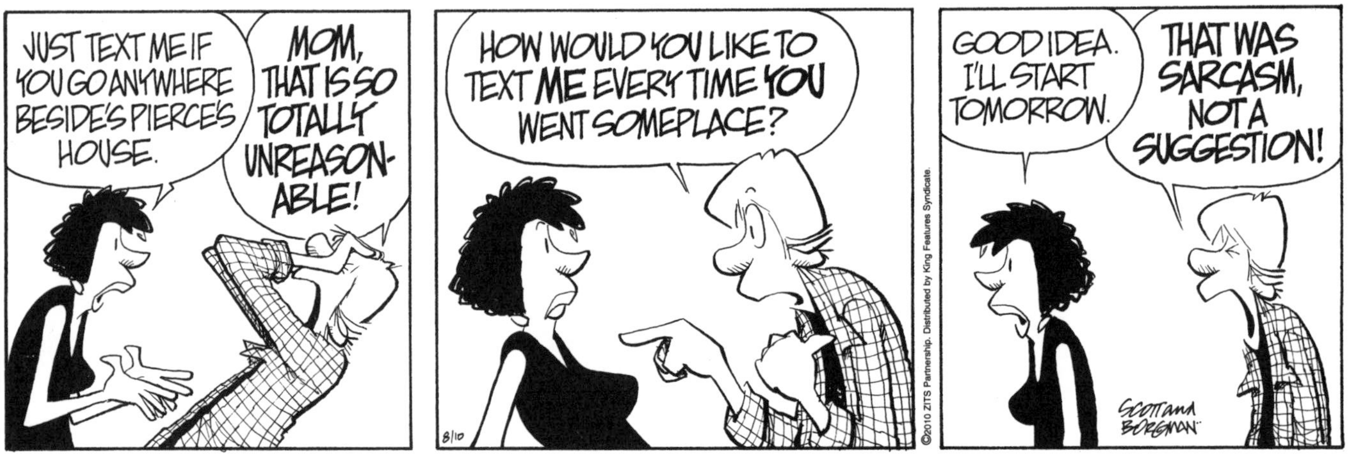
JUST TEXT ME IF YOU GO ANYWHERE BESIDE'S PIERCE'S HOUSE.
MOM, THAT IS SO TOTALLY UNREASON-ABLE!
HOW WOULD YOU LIKE TO TEXT ME EVERY TIME YOU WENT SOMEPLACE?
©2010 ZITS Partnership. Distributed by King Features Syndicate.
GOOD IDEA. I'LL START TOMORROW.
THAT WAS SARCASM, NOT A SUGGESTION!

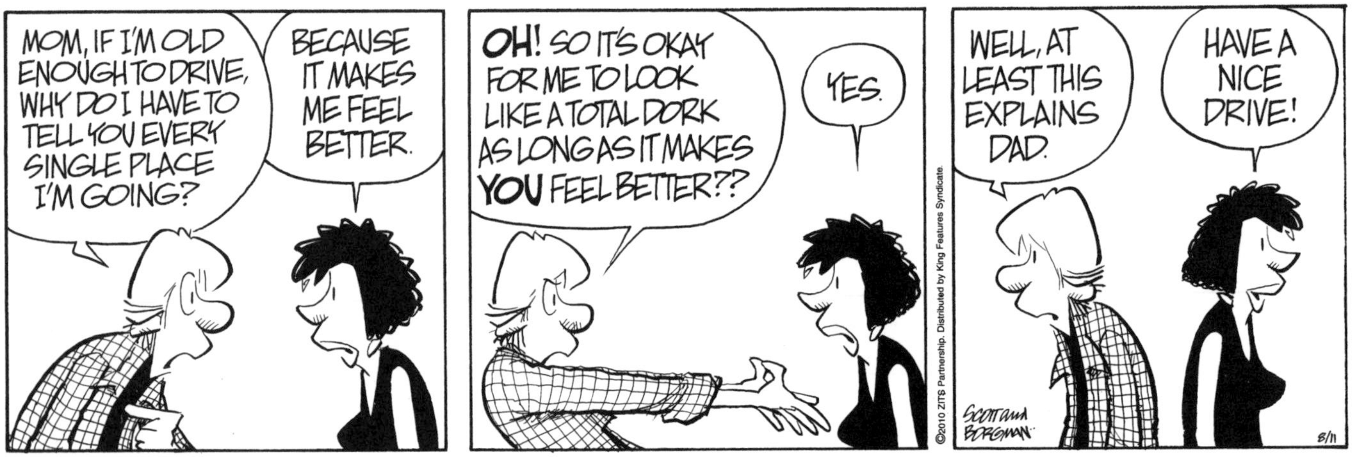
MOM, IF I'M OLD ENOUGH TO DRIVE, WHY DO I HAVE TO TELL YOU EVERY SINGLE PLACE I'M GOING?
BECAUSE IT MAKES ME FEEL BETTER.
OH! SO IT'S OKAY FOR ME TO LOOK LIKE A TOTAL DORK AS LONG AS IT MAKES YOU FEEL BETTER??
YES.
©2010 ZITS Partnership. Distributed by King Features Syndicate.
WELL, AT LEAST THIS EXPLAINS DAD.
HAVE A NICE DRIVE!

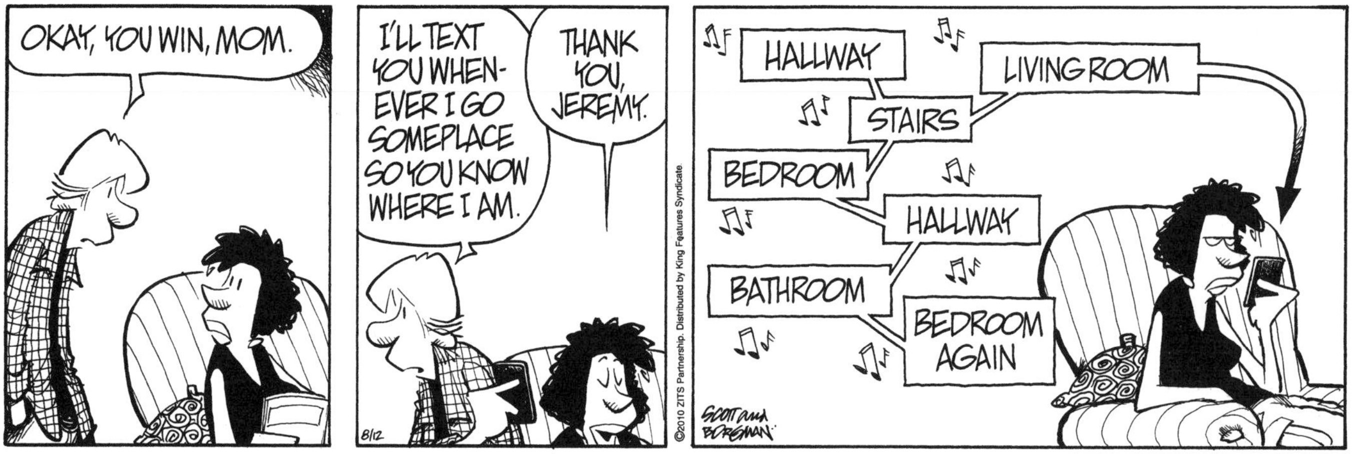
OKAY, YOU WIN, MOM.
I'LL TEXT YOU WHENEVER I GO SOMEPLACE SO YOU KNOW WHERE I AM.
THANK YOU, JEREMY.
HALLWAY
STAIRS
LIVING ROOM
BEDROOM
HALLWAY
BATHROOM
BEDROOM AGAIN
©2010 ZITS Partnership. Distributed by King Features Syndicate.
SCOTT and BORGMAN

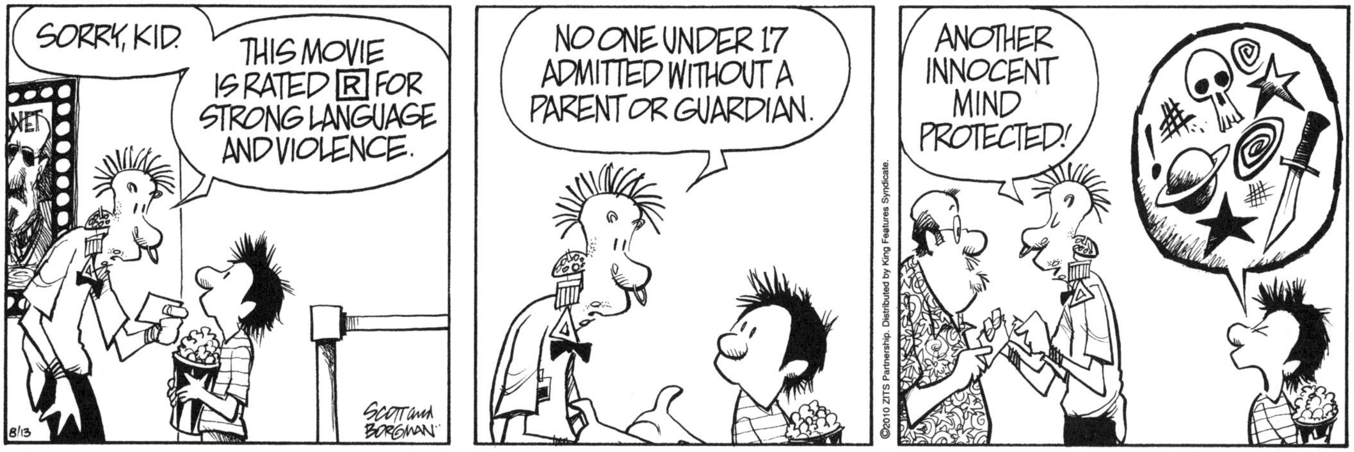
SORRY, KID.
THIS MOVIE IS RATED R FOR STRONG LANGUAGE AND VIOLENCE.
NO ONE UNDER 17 ADMITTED WITHOUT A PARENT OR GUARDIAN.
ANOTHER INNOCENT MIND PROTECTED!
©2010 ZITS Partnership. Distributed by King Features Syndicate.
SCOTT and BORGMAN

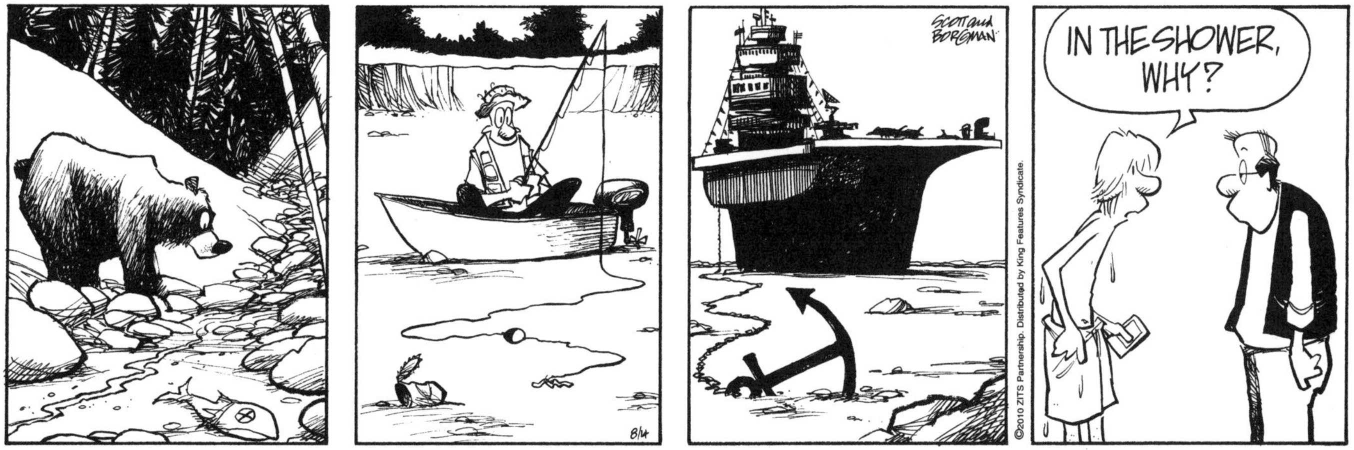
IN THE SHOWER, WHY?
©2010 ZITS Partnership. Distributed by King Features Syndicate.
SCOTT and BORGMAN

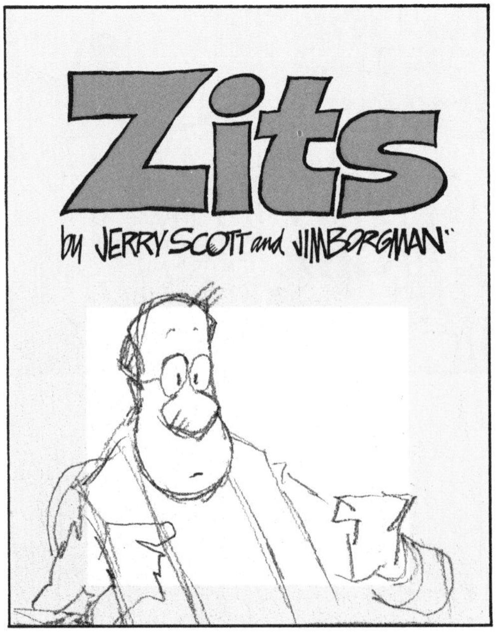
Zits
by JERRY SCOTT and JIM BORGMAN

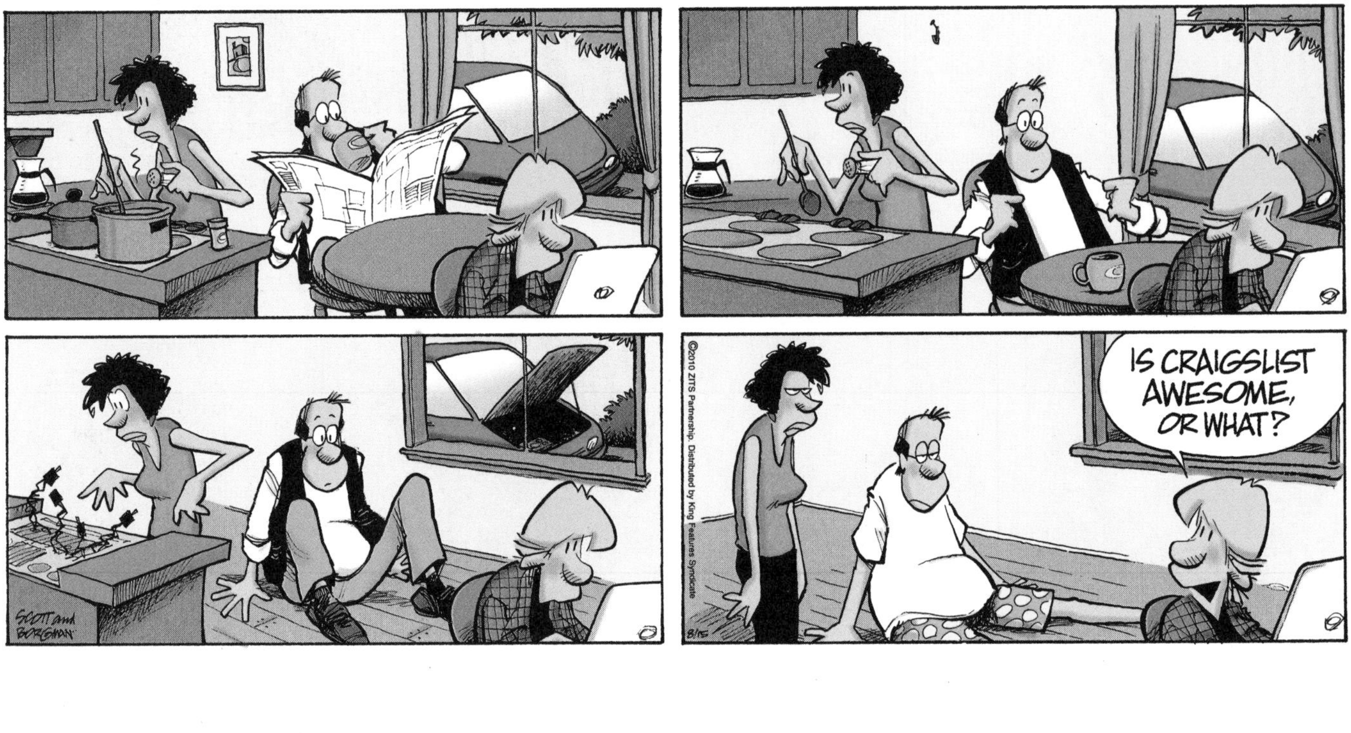
IS CRAIGSLIST AWESOME, OR WHAT?
©2010 ZITS Partnership. Distributed by King Features Syndicate
SCOTT and BORGMAN
8/15

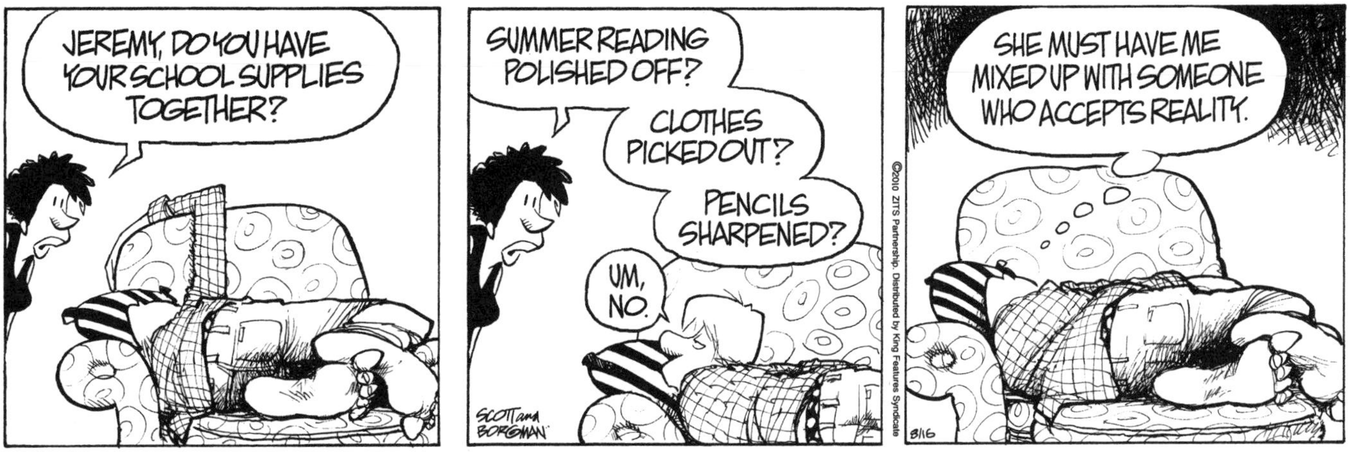

JEREMY, DO YOU HAVE YOUR SCHOOL SUPPLIES TOGETHER?
SUMMER READING POLISHED OFF?
CLOTHES PICKED OUT?
PENCILS SHARPENED?
UM, NO.
SCOTT and BORGMAN
©2010 ZITS Partnership. Distributed by King Features Syndicate
8/16
SHE MUST HAVE ME MIXED UP WITH SOMEONE WHO ACCEPTS REALITY.

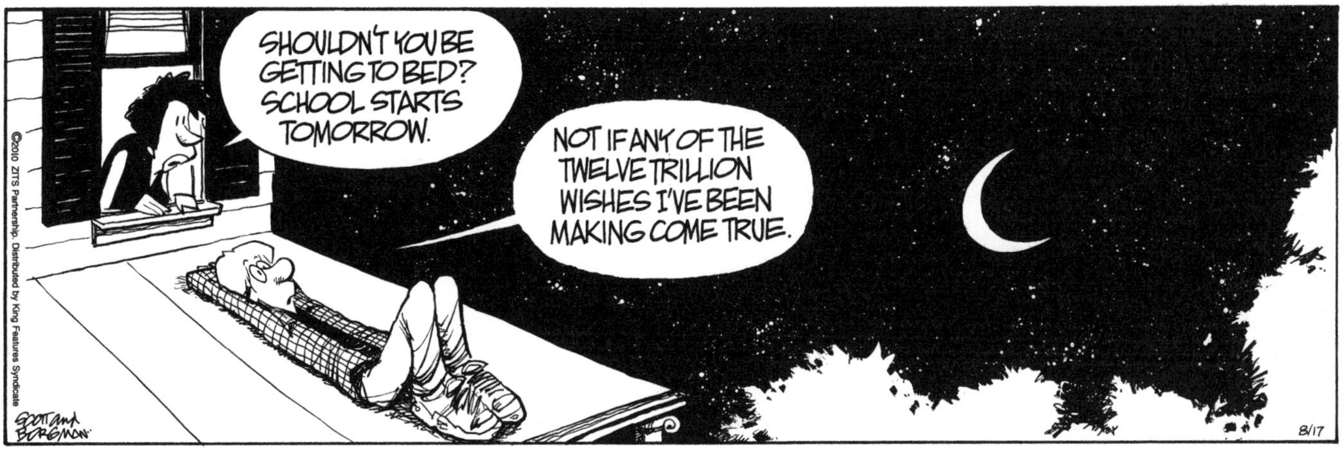

©2010 ZITS Partnership. Distributed by King Features Syndicate
SHOULDN'T YOU BE GETTING TO BED? SCHOOL STARTS TOMORROW.
NOT IF ANY OF THE TWELVE TRILLION WISHES I'VE BEEN MAKING COME TRUE.
SCOTT and BORGMAN
8/17

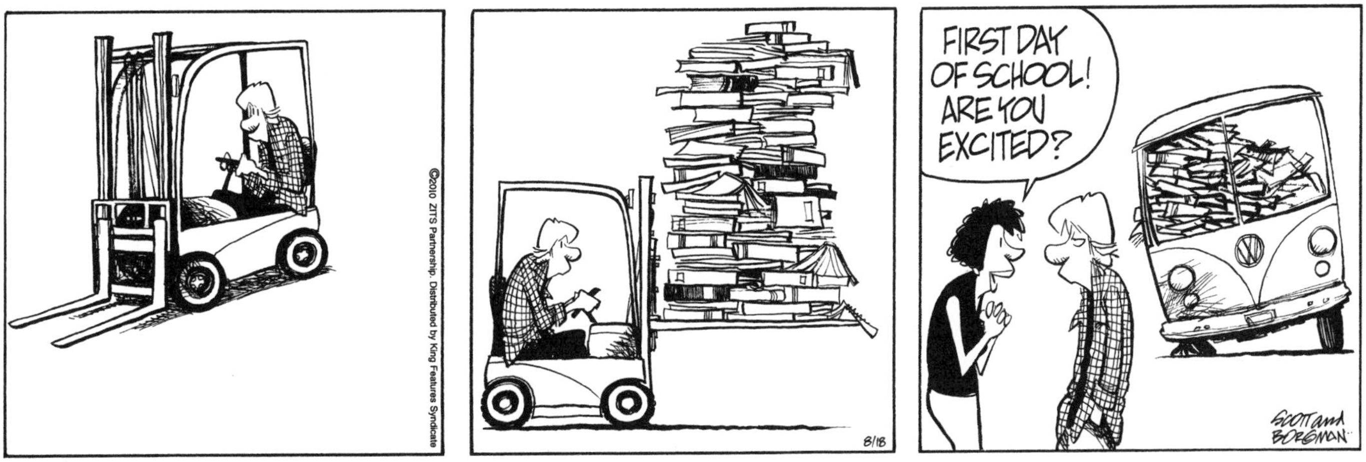

©2010 ZITS Partnership. Distributed by King Features Syndicate
8/18
FIRST DAY OF SCHOOL! ARE YOU EXCITED?
SCOTT and BORGMAN

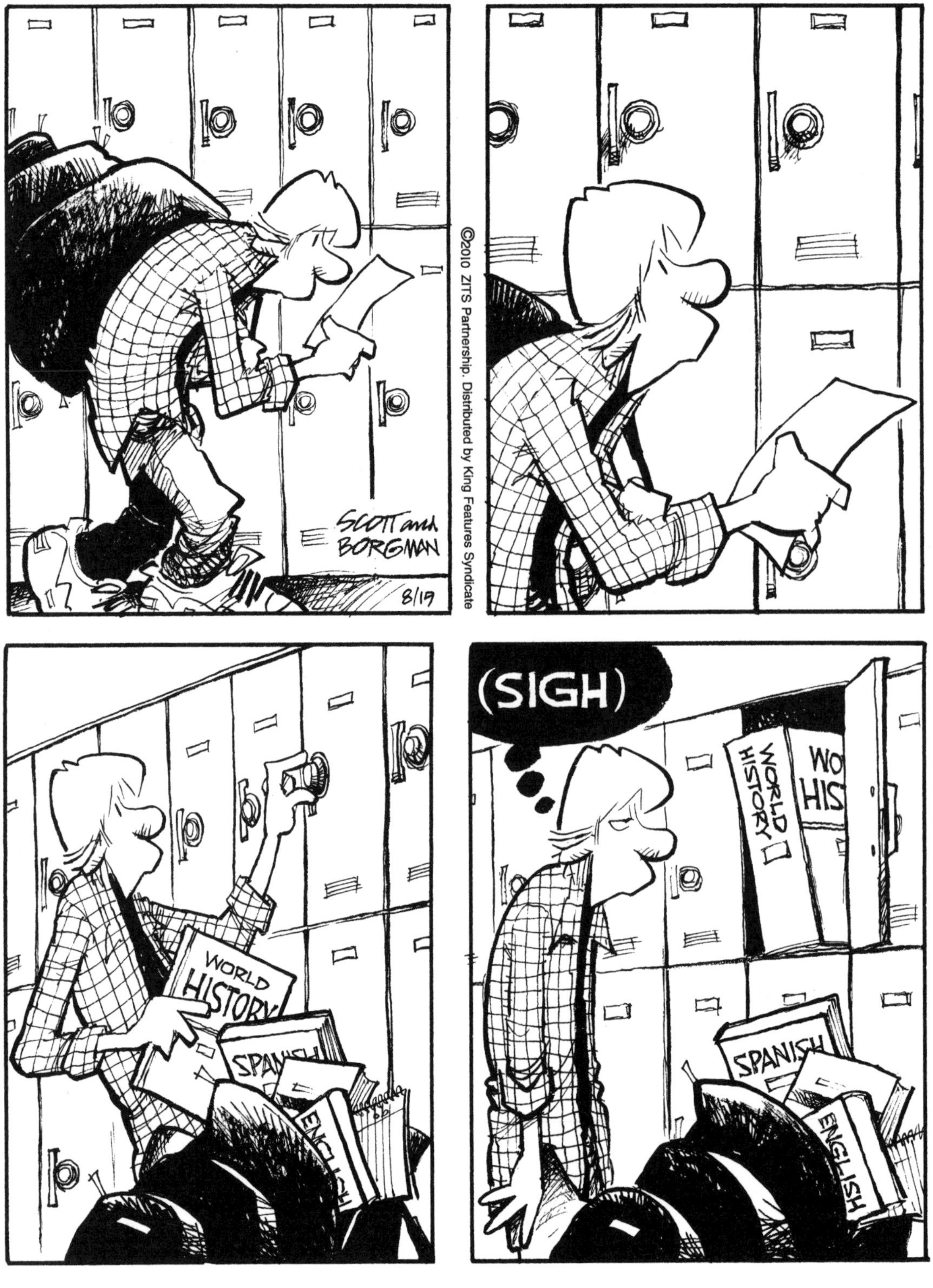
SCOTT and BORGMAN
8/17
©2010 ZITS Partnership. Distributed by King Features Syndicate
WORLD HISTORY
SPANISH
ENGLISH
(SIGH)
WORLD HISTORY
SPANISH
ENGLISH

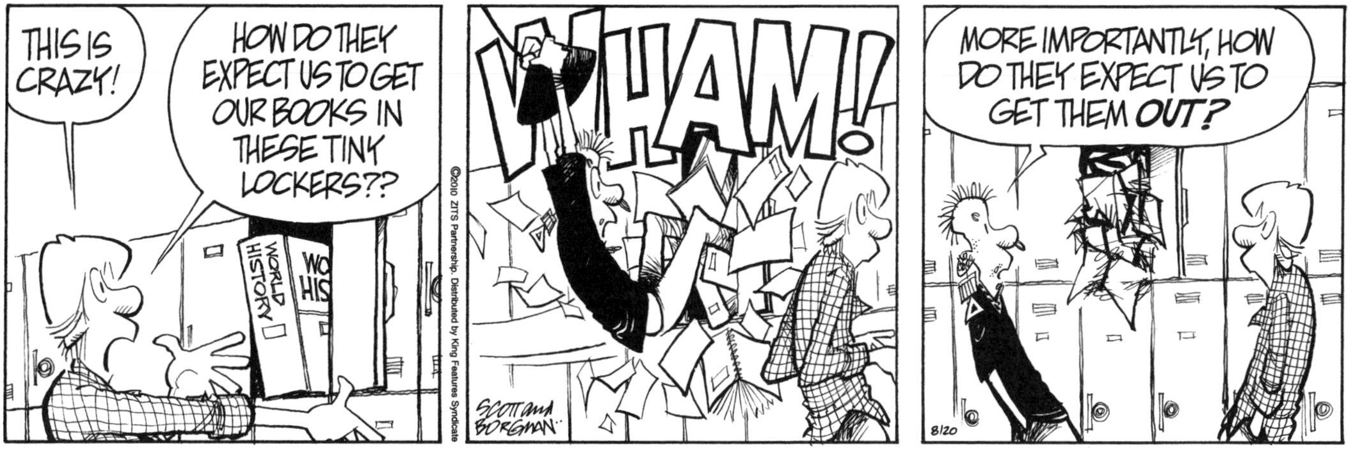
THIS IS CRAZY!
HOW DO THEY EXPECT US TO GET OUR BOOKS IN THESE TINY LOCKERS??
WORLD HISTORY
©2010 ZITS Partnership. Distributed by King Features Syndicate
WHAM!
SCOTT AND BORGMAN
MORE IMPORTANTLY, HOW DO THEY EXPECT US TO GET THEM *OUT?*
8/20

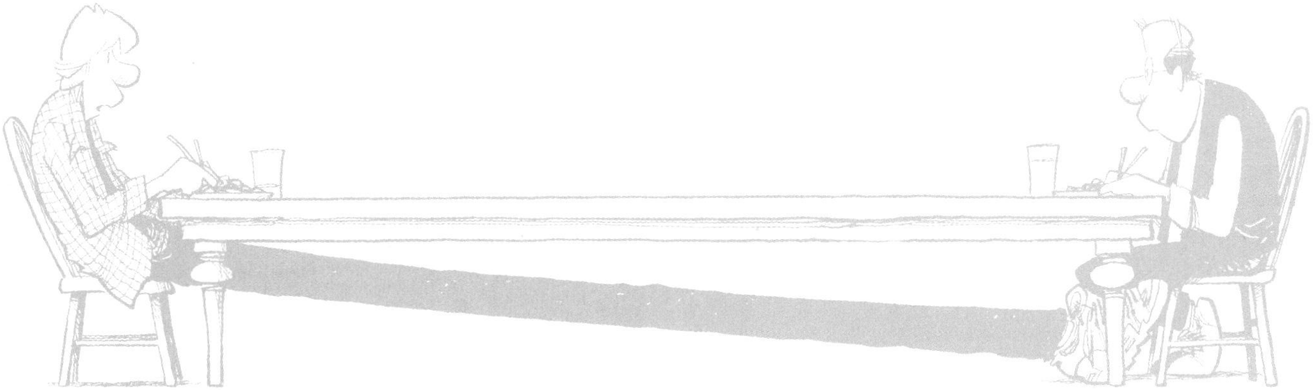

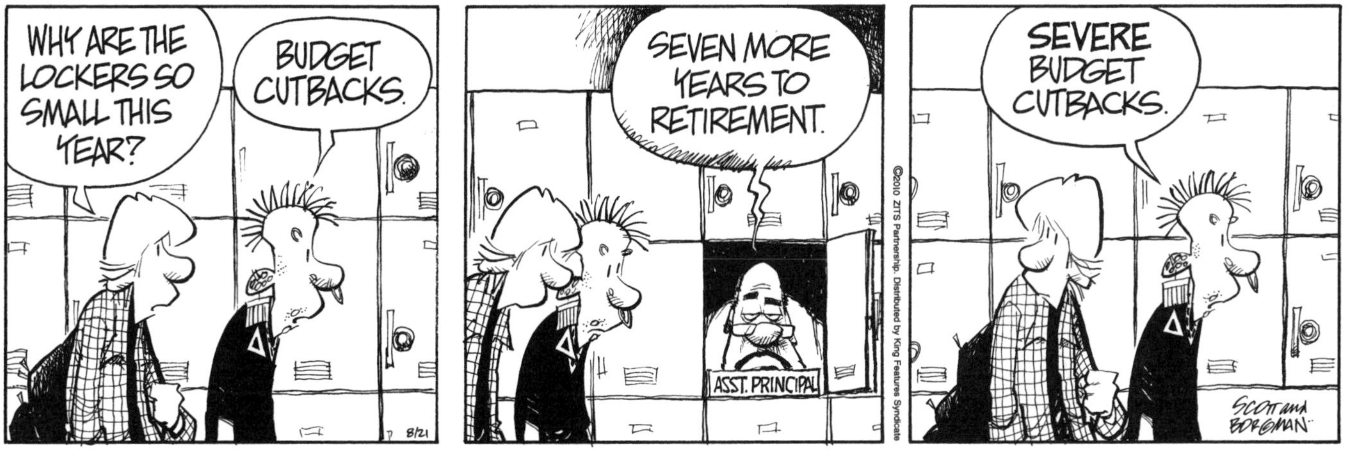
WHY ARE THE LOCKERS SO SMALL THIS YEAR?
BUDGET CUTBACKS.
8/21
SEVEN MORE YEARS TO RETIREMENT.
ASST. PRINCIPAL
©2010 ZITS Partnership. Distributed by King Features Syndicate
SEVERE BUDGET CUTBACKS.
SCOTT AND BORGMAN

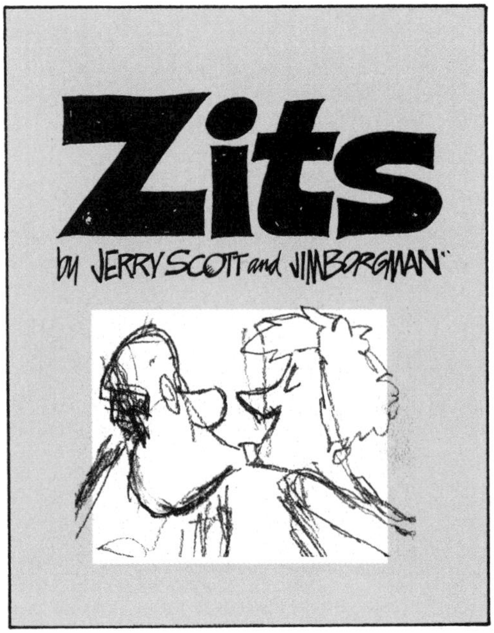
Zits
by JERRY SCOTT and JIM BORGMAN

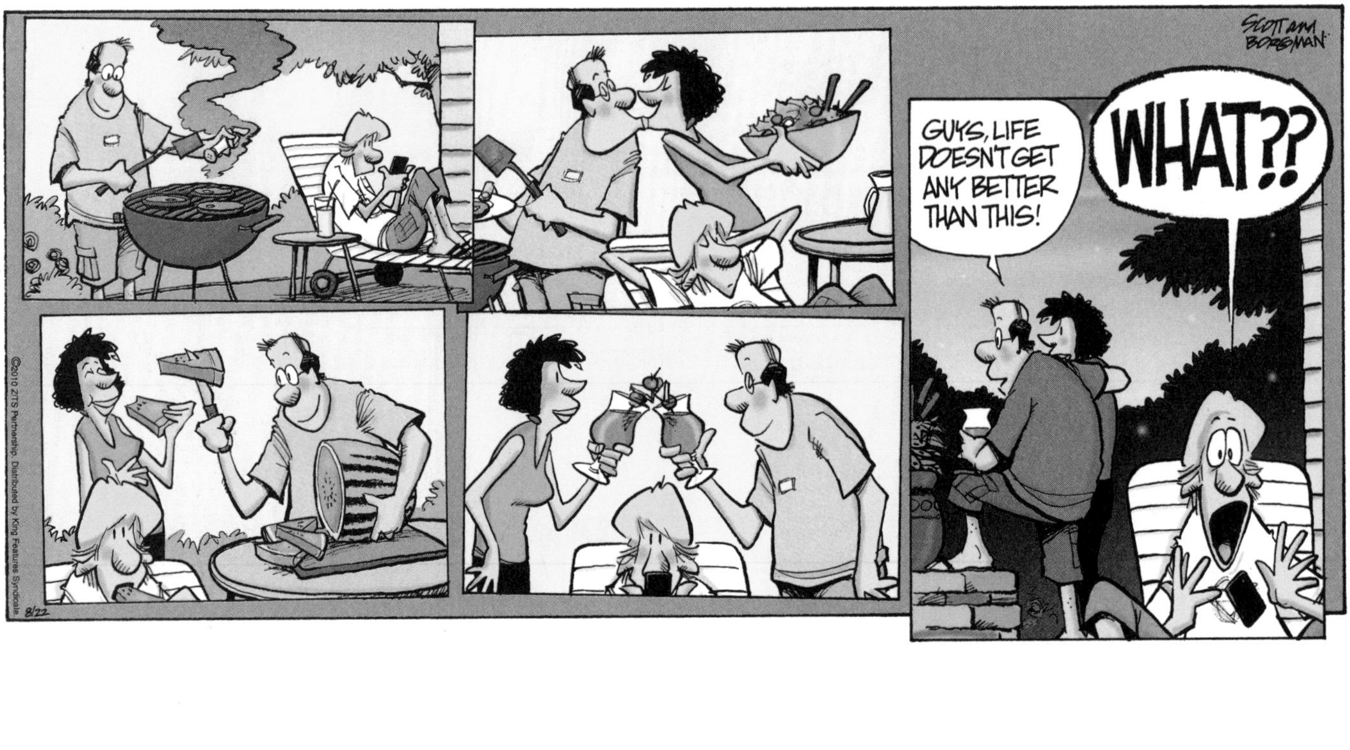
SCOTT AND BORGMAN
GUYS, LIFE DOESN'T GET ANY BETTER THAN THIS!
WHAT??
©2010 ZITS Partnership. Distributed by King Features Syndicate
8/22

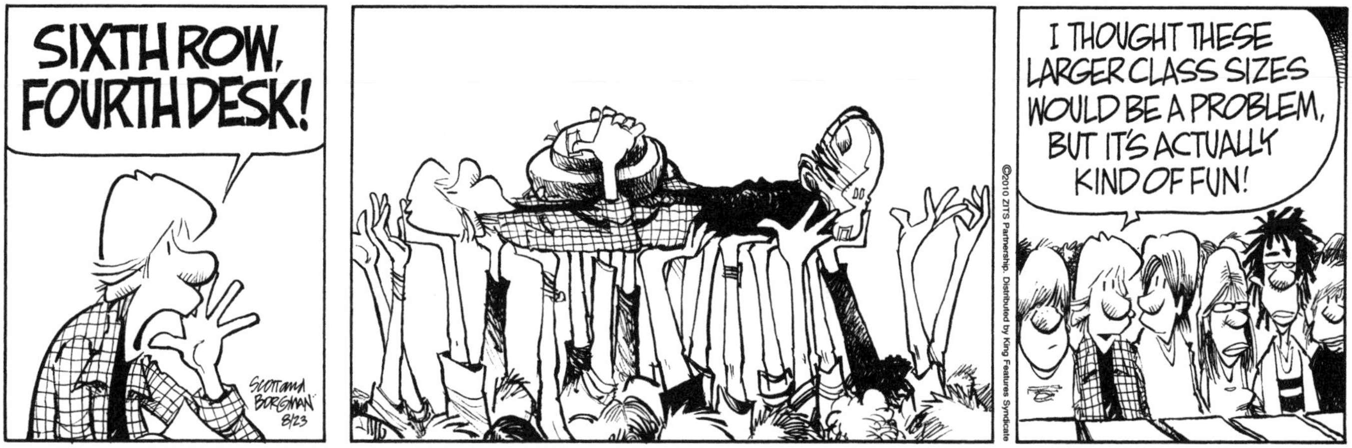
SIXTH ROW, FOURTH DESK!
SCOTT and BORGMAN 8/23
©2010 ZITS Partnership. Distributed by King Features Syndicate
I THOUGHT THESE LARGER CLASS SIZES WOULD BE A PROBLEM, BUT IT'S ACTUALLY KIND OF FUN!

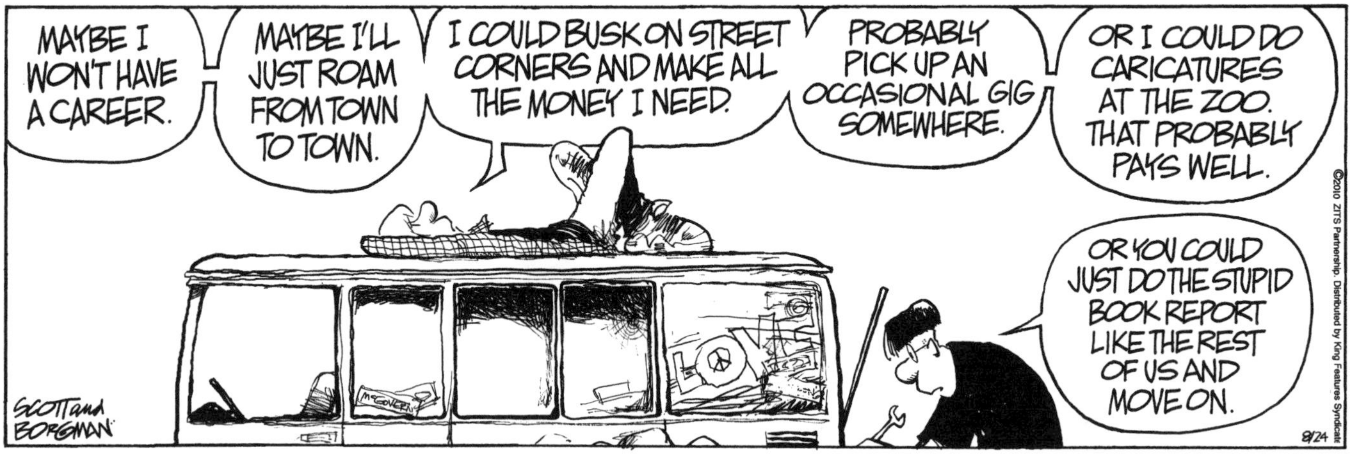
MAYBE I WON'T HAVE A CAREER.
MAYBE I'LL JUST ROAM FROM TOWN TO TOWN.
I COULD BUSK ON STREET CORNERS AND MAKE ALL THE MONEY I NEED.
PROBABLY PICK UP AN OCCASIONAL GIG SOMEWHERE.
OR I COULD DO CARICATURES AT THE ZOO. THAT PROBABLY PAYS WELL.
OR YOU COULD JUST DO THE STUPID BOOK REPORT LIKE THE REST OF US AND MOVE ON.
SCOTT and BORGMAN
8/24
©2010 ZITS Partnership. Distributed by King Features Syndicate

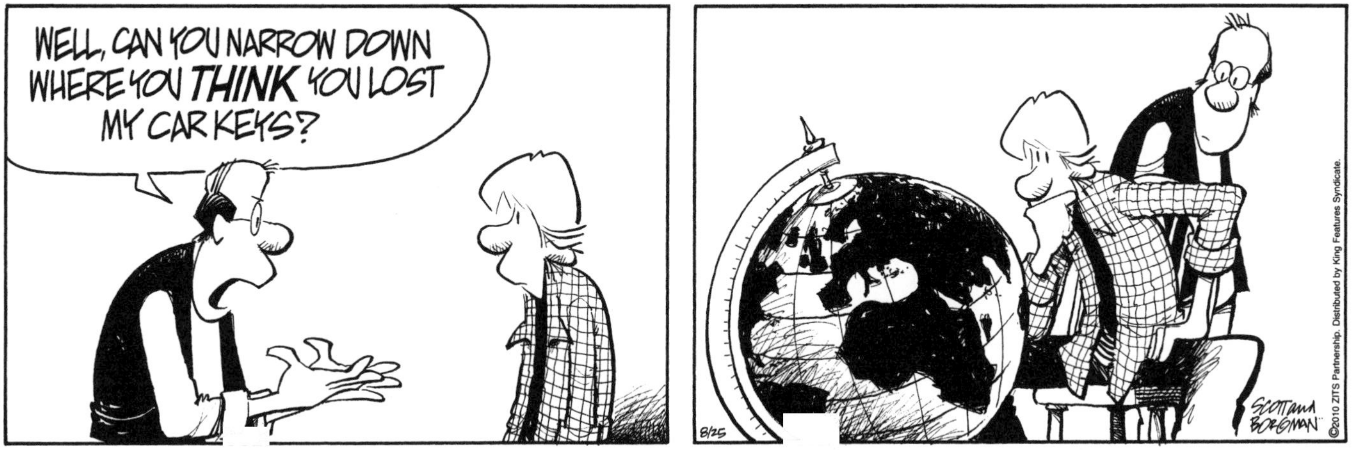
WELL, CAN YOU NARROW DOWN WHERE YOU *THINK* YOU LOST MY CAR KEYS?
8/25
SCOTT and BORGMAN
©2010 ZITS Partnership. Distributed by King Features Syndicate.

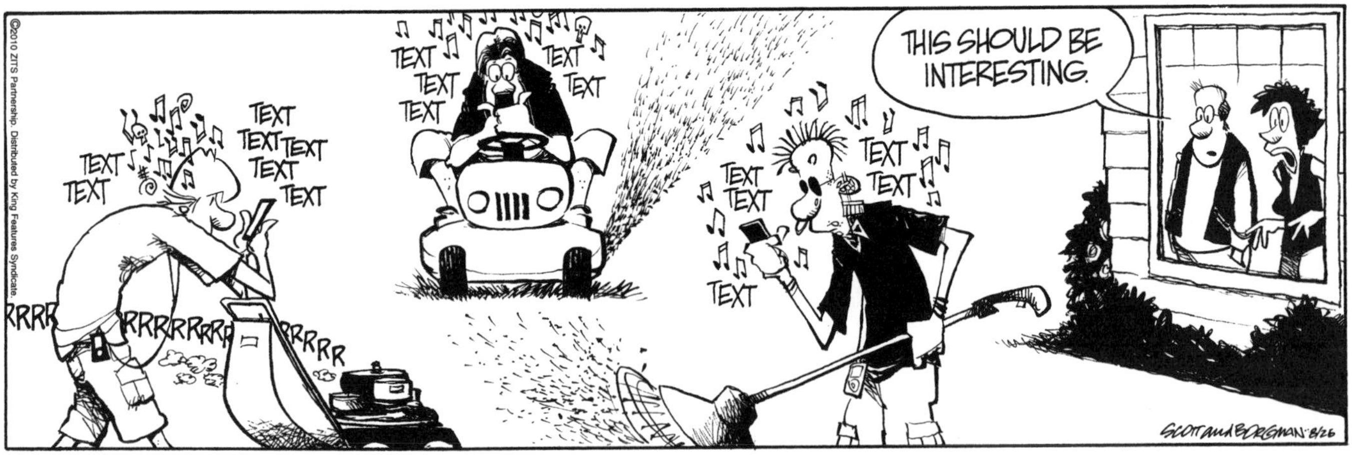
©2010 ZITS Partnership. Distributed by King Features Syndicate.
TEXT TEXT
TEXT TEXT TEXT TEXT TEXT
TEXT TEXT TEXT TEXT TEXT
TEXT TEXT TEXT TEXT TEXT
RRRR RRRRRRRRR RRRRR
THIS SHOULD BE INTERESTING.
SCOTT AND BORGMAN 8/26

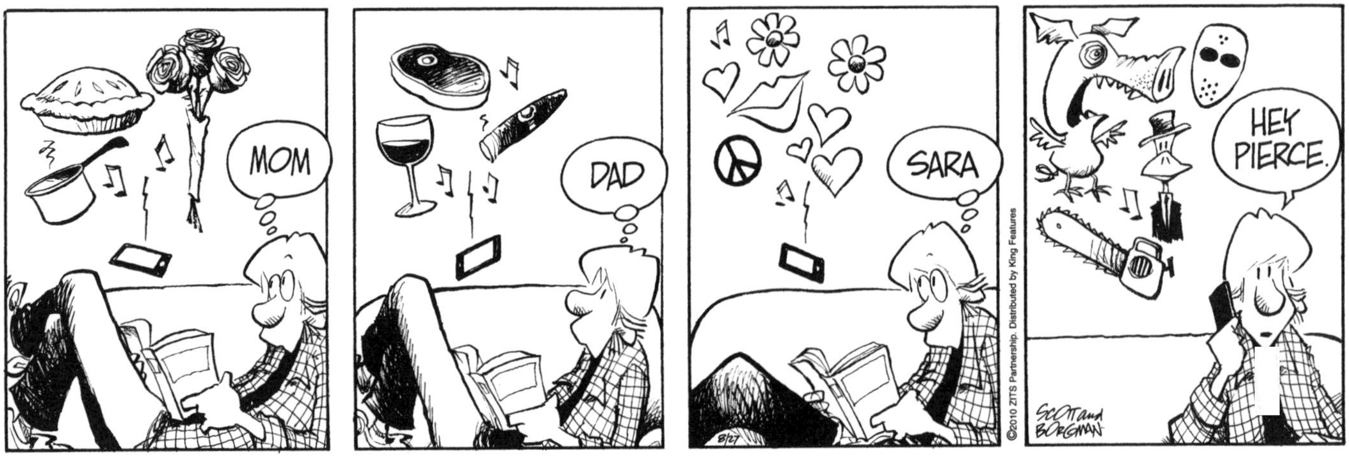
MOM
DAD
SARA
©2010 ZITS Partnership. Distributed by King Features
HEY PIERCE.
SCOTT AND BORGMAN
8/27

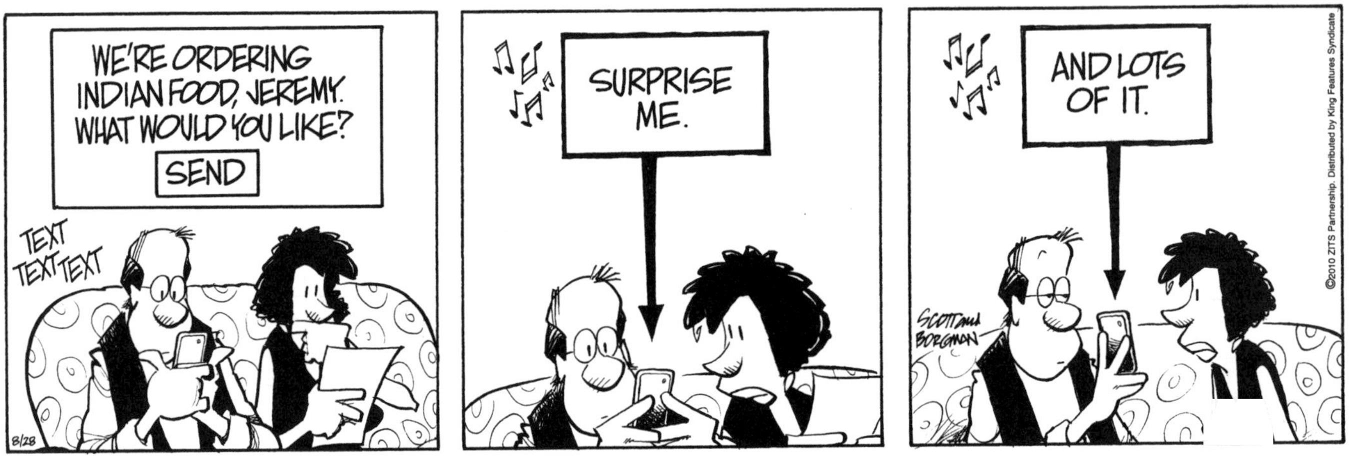
WE'RE ORDERING INDIAN FOOD, JEREMY. WHAT WOULD YOU LIKE?
SEND
TEXT TEXT TEXT
8/28
SURPRISE ME.
AND LOTS OF IT.
SCOTT AND BORGMAN
©2010 ZITS Partnership. Distributed by King Features Syndicate

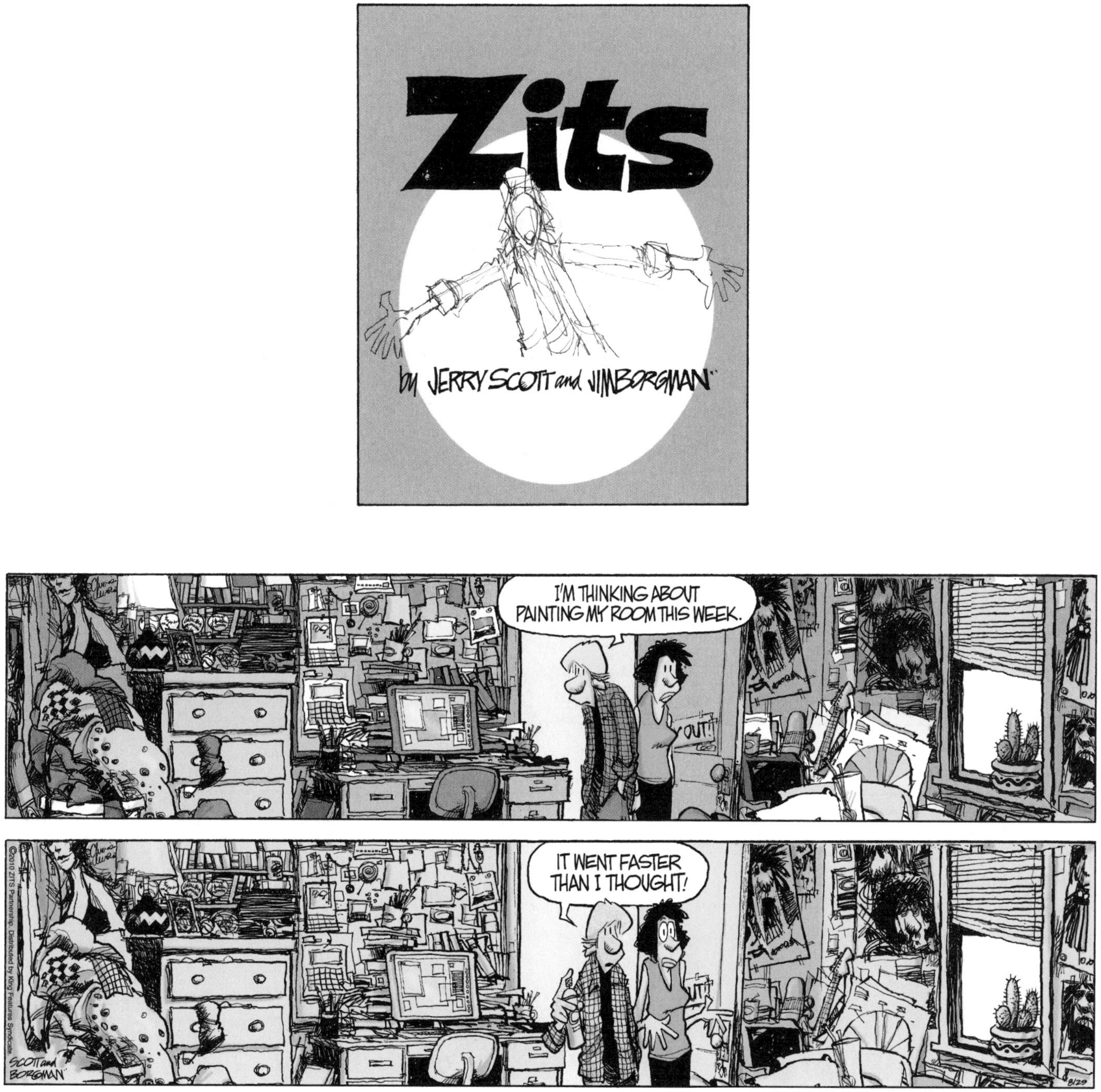
Zits
by JERRY SCOTT and JIM BORGMAN
I'M THINKING ABOUT PAINTING MY ROOM THIS WEEK.
OUT!
IT WENT FASTER THAN I THOUGHT!
©2010 ZITS Partnership. Distributed by King Features Syndicate
SCOTT and BORGMAN

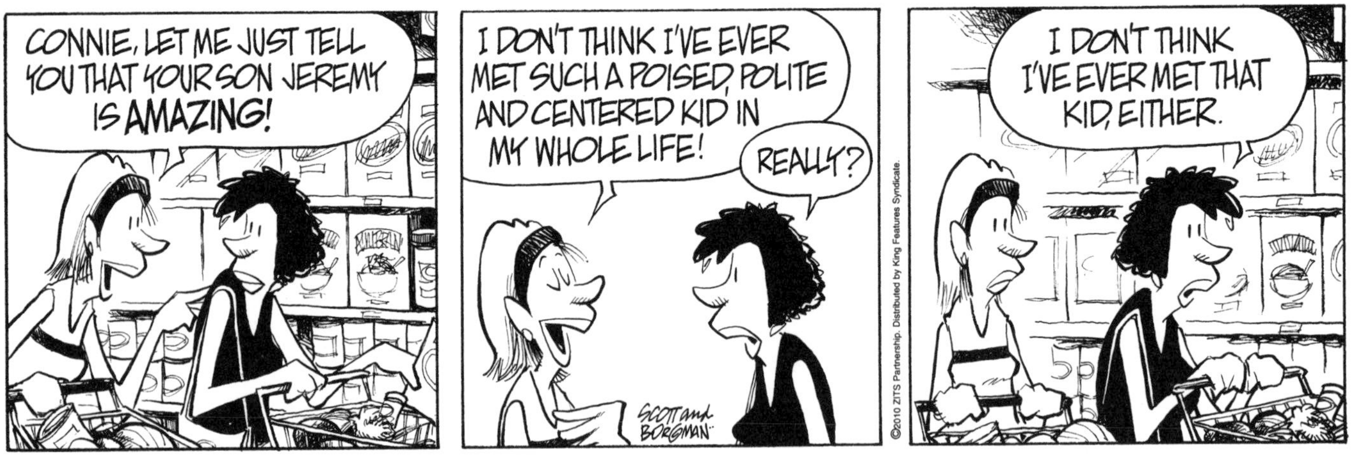
CONNIE, LET ME JUST TELL YOU THAT YOUR SON JEREMY IS AMAZING!
I DON'T THINK I'VE EVER MET SUCH A POISED, POLITE AND CENTERED KID IN MY WHOLE LIFE!
REALLY?
SCOTT and BORGMAN
©2010 ZITS Partnership. Distributed by King Features Syndicate.
I DON'T THINK I'VE EVER MET THAT KID, EITHER.

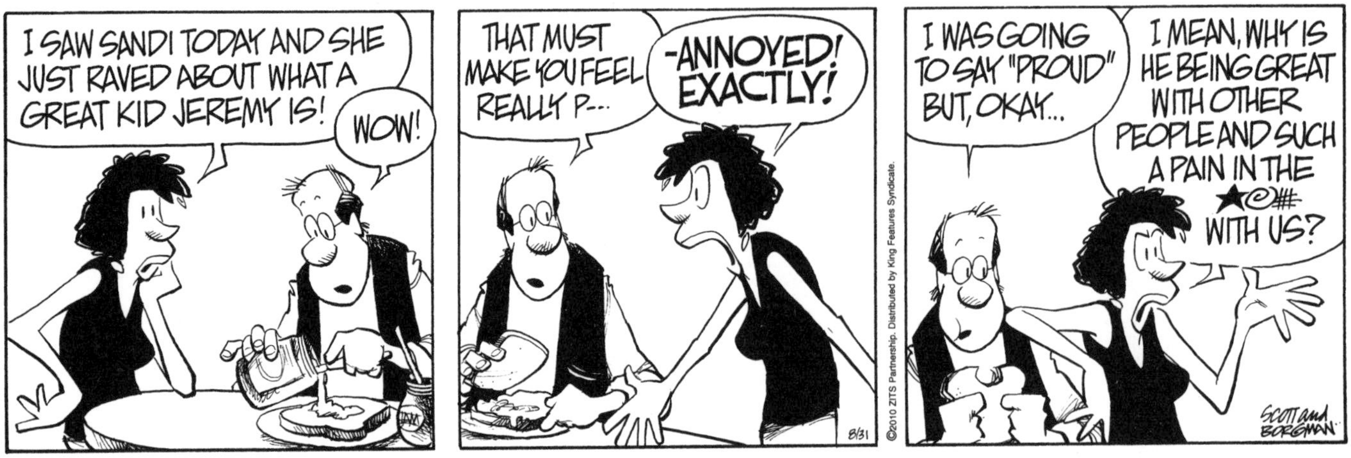
I SAW SANDI TODAY AND SHE JUST RAVED ABOUT WHAT A GREAT KID JEREMY IS!
WOW!
THAT MUST MAKE YOU FEEL REALLY P–..
-ANNOYED! EXACTLY!
8/31
©2010 ZITS Partnership. Distributed by King Features Syndicate.
I WAS GOING TO SAY "PROUD" BUT, OKAY...
I MEAN, WHY IS HE BEING GREAT WITH OTHER PEOPLE AND SUCH A PAIN IN THE ★@# WITH US?
SCOTT and BORGMAN

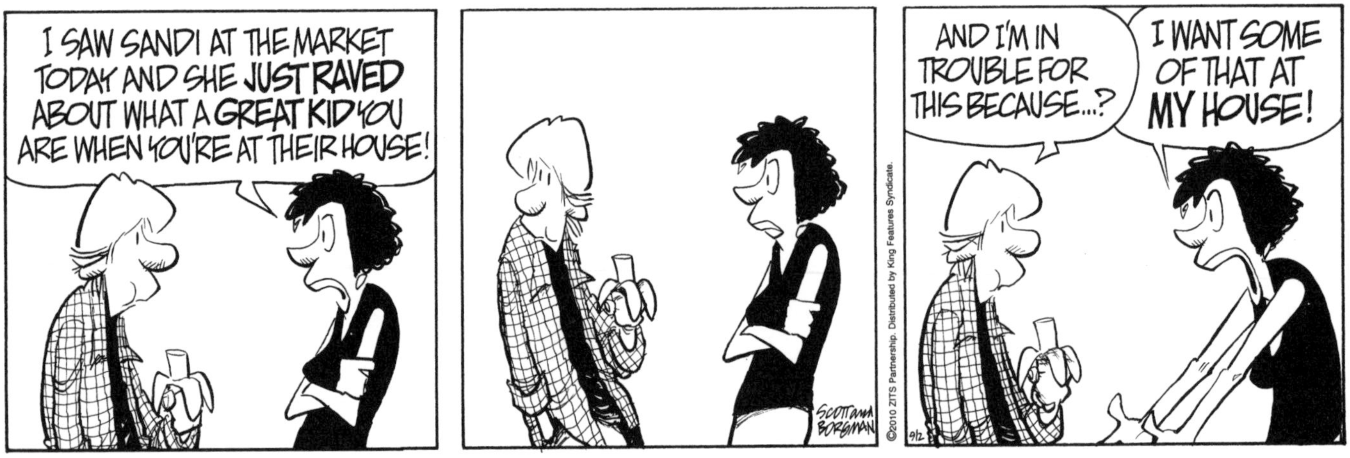
I SAW SANDI AT THE MARKET TODAY AND SHE JUST RAVED ABOUT WHAT A GREAT KID YOU ARE WHEN YOU'RE AT THEIR HOUSE!
SCOTT and BORGMAN
©2010 ZITS Partnership. Distributed by King Features Syndicate.
AND I'M IN TROUBLE FOR THIS BECAUSE...?
I WANT SOME OF THAT AT MY HOUSE!
9/2

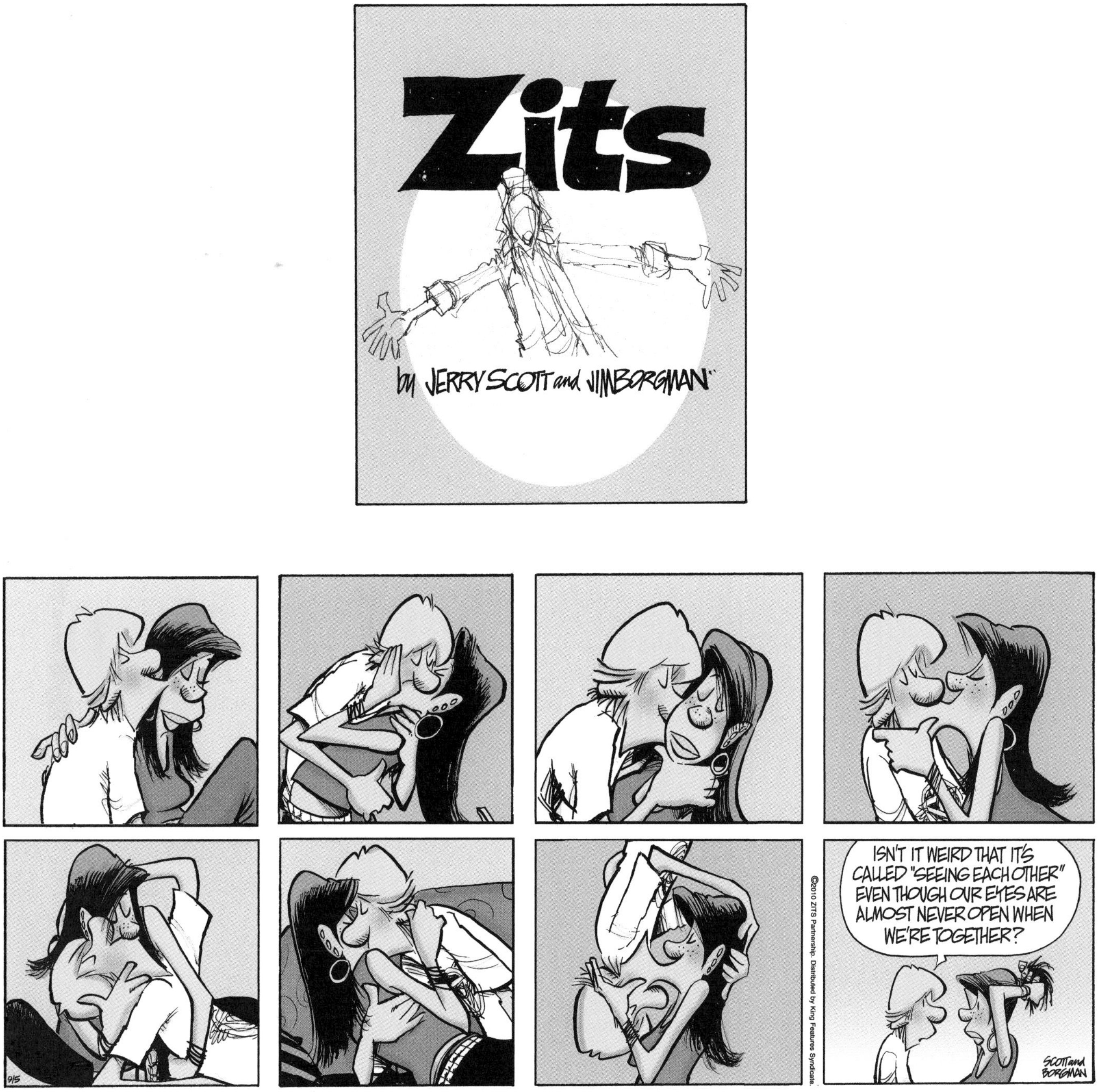
Zits
by JERRY SCOTT and JIM BORGMAN
9/15
©2010 ZITS Partnership. Distributed by King Features Syndicate.
ISN'T IT WEIRD THAT IT'S CALLED "SEEING EACH OTHER" EVEN THOUGH OUR EYES ARE ALMOST NEVER OPEN WHEN WE'RE TOGETHER?
SCOTT and BORGMAN